The LOIS WILSON *Story*

The LOIS WILSON *Story*

When Love Is Not Enough

William G. Borchert

HAZELDEN

Hazelden
Center City, Minnesota 55012-0176

1-800-328-0094
1-651-213-4590 (Fax)
www.hazelden.org

Library of Congress Cataloging-in-Publication Data

Borchert, William G.
    The Lois Wilson story: when love is not enough /
William G. Borchert.
        p. cm.
Includes bibliographical references and index.
978-1-59285-328-1 (hardcover)
978-1-59285-598-8 (paperback)
    1. Lois, 1894–1988. 2. W., Bill. 3. Al-Anon Family Group
Headquarters, Inc. 4. Alcoholics Anonymous. 5. Alcoholics'
spouses—United States—Biography. 6. Alcoholics—Family
relationships. I. Title.

HV5032.L28B67 2005
362.292'4'092—dc22
[B]   2005046021

Cover design by David Spohn
Interior design by Lightbourne
Typesetting by Lightbourne

To my loving wife, Bernadette,
without whom this book—nor me—would be.

Contents

Author's Note

FOR MORE THAN FOURTEEN YEARS PRIOR TO LOIS WILSON'S passing, my wife and I had the privilege of knowing her as a close and dear friend. I was also honored when Lois gave me permission to write a screenplay based on her and her husband Bill's life together and the founding of Alcoholics Anonymous. Titled *My Name Is Bill W.*, the movie starred James Garner as Dr. Robert Smith, James Woods as Bill Wilson, and JoBeth Williams as Lois.

Before I wrote this film, Lois generously allowed me to tape many of her remembrances of years past and her struggles before, during, and after Bill's drinking years. I used some of these poignant and intimate recollections to create a true-to-life movie that garnered a number of awards including a Best Actor award for James Woods.

But the film focused to a large extent on the accomplishments of Bill and Dr. Bob and the founding of Alcoholics Anonymous, barely addressing Lois's own personal inner conflicts that led to the founding of Al-Anon. That's why this book is long overdue.

In accepting Lois's confidence, I promised her one important thing— that I would always tell the truth of her story. She was comfortable with that, knowing that I would share the warts as well as the beauty marks, the pain as well as the joy, the intimate as well as the obvious.

For Lois, it was always Bill. I remember the Saturday afternoon I sat with her on the back porch of Stepping Stones, their home in Bedford Hills, New York, and read the movie script for her approval. When I finished, she simply smiled and said: "Bill would have loved it." And I recall the evening we were chatting in her living room about their early days together and she remarked: "I used to think my life really began the day I met Bill. He was handsome and exciting and I just knew he was capable of great things. I guess I was as addicted to him as he was to alcohol. Then he got sober—and I got well."

But that deep love between them remained. As Lois Wilson lay dying in Mount Kisco Hospital with a breathing tube down her throat so that she couldn't speak, I was told she scribbled a note to her nurse, "I want to see my Bill." A family member gave permission for the tube to be removed. Lois was able to breathe on her own long enough to say good-bye to the friends and loved ones gathered at her bedside. She died later that day at the age of ninety-seven.

In writing this biography, I hope that many of the poignant and intimate remembrances Lois shared with me will help the reader come to know the lady I knew and to understand the enduring gifts she left us and the entire world. For Lois Wilson was also capable of great things. Perhaps that's why her greatest dream was that some day the whole world would live by the Twelve Steps of AA and Al-Anon and there would be true peace upon the earth.

Indeed, the famous writer Aldous Huxley once said that when the history of the twentieth century is finally written, the greatest achievements America will be known for is giving the world Alcoholics Anonymous and Al-Anon.

$\mathcal{F}oreword$

$\maltese$

$\mathcal{A}$LCOHOLICS DAMAGE OTHERS AS WELL AS THEMSELVES. On average they dramatically affect at least four other people, usually close family members, who are caught up in the vortex created by the alcoholic's destructive behavior. Spouses, parents, children, and even co-workers can find their lives being taken over by an alcoholic; they begin to lose control of their own actions.

The story of Bill Wilson, Lois's husband of fifty-three years and the co-founder of AA, is well known. However, in spite of the importance of Lois Wilson's contribution in bringing relief to the multitudes affected by alcoholics, little has been written about her. Bill Borchert's *The Lois Wilson Story*, the first comprehensive biography of Lois Wilson, fills this void.

The author of *My Name Is Bill W.*, the acclaimed and Emmy Award-winning 1989 film biography of Bill Wilson, Bill Borchert was a frequent visitor in Lois's home during the last fourteen years of her life. He is one of the few left who knew her well. His personal experiences of her are buttressed by almost eight hours of exclusive interviews with Lois in addition to materials from numerous other sources, including the Stepping Stones Foundation Archives.

The result is a book that tells it all. *The Lois Wilson Story* describes in compelling detail Lois's comfortable beginnings, her attraction to a clever and persistent young man, her years of despair as drinking claimed an ever-increasing part of Bill, her joy when he sobered up, and her frustration as AA came to dominate Bill's life.

Charmed by Bill's vibrant personality and promise in their early life together, Lois spent years making excuses for him and covering up his behavior when he was drinking. She never stopped loving him and believing in him even as his disease progressed, but she felt shame, anger, humiliation, anxiety, and fear as his actions became increasingly unreliable and boorish. She shared Bill's elation along with his sense of discovery and mission when he sobered up, only to find herself irritated with Bill over his subsequent preoccupation with AA and lack of attention to her.

The climactic moment of this roller-coaster ride came one evening in 1937 when she threw a shoe at him for abruptly putting her off in order to hurry away to a meeting with other recovering alcoholics. With her action came an epiphany—the realization that she, too, needed to change. Her next inspiration was to seek out and talk to the wives of other alcoholics. Their honest and intimate sharing of experiences led to the discovery that she was not alone in her plight. Al-Anon was born from that common understanding, from the realization that continuing to share their "experience, strength, and hope" could help family members and others affected by an alcoholic to recover, just as sharing common experiences can help alcoholics recover in AA. For over fifty years now, Al-Anon has provided hope and help to millions of those close to alcoholics.

Lois Wilson, who survived Bill by seventeen years, continued to work until the end of her life to reduce the stigma of alcoholism and to raise public awareness of its effects on family and society. In 1979 she created the Stepping Stones Foundation to preserve and welcome visitors to Stepping Stones, the home in Westchester County, New York, that she and Bill moved into in 1941, and to carry on her work. The Foundation's purpose remains to share the story of hope for recovery from alcoholism.

The Lois Wilson Story offers something for anyone interested in or affected by alcoholism. For the general reader, it offers insight into the impact the alcoholic can have on the lives and health of those near to him or her. For those who may be close to an alcoholic, whether active or in recovery, it offers an intimate story with which they may identify. And for those in Al-Anon, the program that offers hope and help to the families and friends of alcoholics, it offers a detailed history of Lois's struggle and the birth of Al-Anon—a history that may enhance their experience of recovery.

ROBERT L. HOGUET
President, Stepping Stones Foundation

Preface

*I*T'S THE FIRST SATURDAY OF JUNE, 1983. THE THIRTIETH ANNUAL Al-Anon Family Picnic at Stepping Stones, the home of Lois Burnham Wilson in Bedford Hills, New York, is coming to an end. The large crowd in attendance is beginning to pack up for the long journeys back to homes throughout the Northeast, and for some, as far away as Texas, California, Hawaii, Alaska, and London, England.

Dads lift their sleepy children lovingly into their arms while their wives close picnic baskets and gather blankets from the sprawling green lawn that slopes gently from the old brown-shingled house on the hill above.

Most people have spent the morning and early afternoon touring the grounds and visiting or revisiting the house that, as many comment, is almost a historical museum. Lois has filled it with pictures and memorabilia of the programs she and her late husband, Bill, started—programs that are still flourishing around the world, helping millions to find a wonderful new way of life.

On the upstairs walls in particular hang photos and keepsakes of Alcoholics Anonymous and Al-Anon members and supporters. The most sought out photos are those of Bill Wilson and Dr. Robert Smith, the two men who started AA in 1935. Others want to see pictures of Dr. Bob's wife, Annie Smith, who Lois called one of her dearest friends and greatest inspirations, and, of course, Anne Bingham, who helped Lois organize Al-Anon in 1951. Anne Bingham, Annie Smith, Dr. Bob, and Bill have long since passed on.

The visitors gaze in awe and talk in hushed tones of respect for those who built the pathway along which they now walk to sobriety. The scene resembles a Hall of Fame, in a way, except these fading photos of men and women have nothing to do with a mere game of sport. Here are people who truly won at the challenging game of life.

It's now time to go back outside, where Lois introduces the AA, Al-Anon, and Alateen speakers for the day.

The recovered alcoholic speaker describes himself as a successful advertising executive in his early forties. His bouts with booze had led to loss of family, friends, good jobs, and good health, but after a stint on park benches, several rehabs, and nine years of sobriety in AA, his gains now far exceed his losses.

His wife, the Al-Anon speaker, attests to all the pain, despair, and humiliation. Only today, their three children sit before her on the lawn trying to hold back tears as they smile at a mother who now yells far less and loves them so much more.

The Alateen speaker is a very nervous and very attractive high school sophomore with long red hair and braces. Her mother is still drinking alcoholically, but she and her father are coping better through their programs . . . for now anyway.

The talks are moving to say the least. They are honest reflections of lives shared to help others identify and recover from the very same illness.

The speakers are finished, and it's time to pull up stakes. One senses a touch of sadness mixed in with the warm good-bye hugs and kisses among the hundreds of men, women, and children here for the day. It seems most don't really want to leave.

These visitors to Stepping Stones come from all walks of life, all backgrounds, all nationalities. They are young and old, healthy and ailing, well off and not so well off. And they talk openly and willingly about their experiences and about alcoholism as a family disease that can touch anyone—butcher, baker; lawyer, policeman; hairdresser, housewife; rich man, poor man; pilot, priest. But now they are sober in AA, recovered in Al-Anon and Alateen, and each one seems to emanate an indescribable sense of joy. And even on close inspection, that joy is not feigned. It is very real.

A few begin to straggle off toward their cars parked in the nearby field. Most line the porch of Lois's home to bid farewell to a woman they worship, a woman more than a few feel may not be here next year. For Lois Wilson is now ninety-two and quite frail. She walks with a cane and was forced to give up her driver's license last year. Still, she doesn't seem to have lost one iota of her mental alertness and wit, which she uses mainly to poke fun at herself.

Yes, *worship* is a very strong word. I know. Yet, as I stand here next to the old stone fireplace in her living room on this uplifting June afternoon, I am actually witnessing it for myself.

I first met Lois several years ago. By then my wife, Bernadette, had come to know her quite well. We visited often and Lois spent a number of Thanksgiving and Christmas holidays at our home, where she enjoyed our nine children and they thoroughly enjoyed her. In fact, one Thanksgiving holiday, our kids gave her a beautiful, purring, white-and-rust-colored kitten. Lois loved her and promptly named her Borchey in their honor.

I always knew this gentle and humble lady was greatly admired, but not until this moment did I realize the depth of that admiration. This was my first Al-Anon Family Picnic, the result of my wife's constant nagging at a guy who always thought himself too busy for such all-day affairs. This was also my first chance to observe people kneel before Lois, kiss her hands, present her with tokens of their love, and hug her with tears streaming down their faces.

As I watch, I wonder what effect this kind of adoration, this kind of worship, can have on someone, even someone as humble and self-deprecating as Lois Wilson.

It's now late in the afternoon. The last visitor has said good-bye. Even the volunteer cleanup committee has dispersed. I'm seated on the couch with Lois. Harriet Sevarino, her longtime housekeeper and caring friend, has brought us both some tea and cookies, remarking that Lois always overdoes things and that "people don't have the sense they're born with not to see that you're wore out, and if they really cared they'd leave sooner than later."

Lois smiles up at her. "Thank you for the tea and cookies, Harriet," she says. Harriet shrugs, then looks at me. "I don't mean you, Mr. Bill.

You know that. But maybe you can talk some sense into her. She don't listen to me no more." Then she shrugs again and heads for the kitchen.

As Lois and I talk, I'm dying to ask the question that's been bugging me for almost two hours. So, finally, here it comes.

"Lois," I begin somewhat falteringly. "All these people kneeling down before you, kissing your hands and feet, telling you how you saved their lives, restored their families. Even God Himself would be flattered by such adulation. How must it make you feel?"

She turns and looks up at me with that cute but patient smile that says, "You're probably not going to understand, but I'll tell you anyway." Then she reaches out and touches my hand.

"It's not me," she answers softly. "I'm only a symbol. It's what Al-Anon has done for them, and I simply represent Al-Anon."

I want to ask more, but she has answered it all. Here is a woman who truly knows herself and her own significance—and insignificance. If humility really is truth, then I was witnessing true humility. My mouth hangs open, but no more words come out. Then she gently pats my hand and says: "Now drink your tea and eat your cookies before Harriet comes back and gives us both the what-fors all over again."

Lois Wilson may not have been a "liberated woman" according to today's definition. "Renaissance woman" might suit her better. Indeed, if style, grace, intellect, and capacity for rebirth are the hallmarks of such a woman, then Lois Wilson qualified in every sense.

She believed deeply in commitment. That belief, and her undying love for her husband, are what kept her with Bill. That belief succored him through his raging torment with alcoholism and supported him in his struggle to recover. And then, after he and Dr. Bob founded AA, she came to understand how she herself was affected by the disease and reached out to help others in order to help herself.

While Lois went on to build Al-Anon into a worldwide fellowship for spouses and families suffering from the effects of alcoholism, there are many recovered alcoholics today who would quickly tell you that without Lois there would be no Bill Wilson, and without Bill Wilson there would be no worldwide fellowship of Alcoholics Anonymous and the many millions it continues to save.

To that enormous compliment Lois would respond in the very same way: "I am only a symbol."

Lois Wilson died on October 5, 1988. My wife and I and our whole family, together with millions of other families around the world, miss her dearly. But while she is gone, her "symbol"—her spirit—will always live on through Al-Anon and the many other Twelve Step programs she and Bill inspired.

Acknowledgments

THERE ARE NO WORDS TO EXPRESS MY HEARTFELT THANKS TO Lois Wilson for the trust and confidence she placed in me and for the openness in which she shared her life and her experiences with me and my family.

The same holds true for my wife, Bernadette, to whom I owe an enormous debt of gratitude together with my three wonderful daughters and six great sons who have always given me their unconditional love and support even during those sometimes difficult growing-up years.

In acknowledging the important contributions of others to his book, it must be said that such a sensitive and truly historical biography such as this requires the care and guidance of a dedicated and experienced editor. I was indeed blessed to have such a wonderful editor in the person of Karen Chernyaev of Hazelden Publishing. Immense plaudits are due her and her great staff.

I also wish to thank Robert Hoguet, the president of Stepping Stones Foundation, Eileen Giuliani, our longtime executive director, Annah Perch, our new executive director, as well as the entire board of trustees for their generous support and for opening the Stepping Stones Foundation Archives for my research.

And, finally, many thanks to all my friends and fellow travelers who encouraged me to tell Lois's story so that all those in need of hearing it can hear it. For that, I have been both privileged and blessed.

Reprint acknowledgments:

Photography is courtesy of the Stepping Stones Foundation, Katonah, New York.

Quoted material from *Lois Remembers*, © 1979, by Al-Anon Family Group Headquarters, Inc., is reprinted by permission of Al-Anon Family Group Headquarters, Inc.

Quoted material from *First Steps*, © 1986, by Al-Anon Family Group Headquarters, Inc., is reprinted by permission of Al-Anon Family Group Headquarters, Inc.

Al-Anon's Twelve Traditions, © Al-Anon Family Group Headquarters, Inc., are reprinted with permission.

Permission to reprint Al-Anon excerpts does not mean that Al-Anon Family Group Headquarters, Inc., has reviewed or approved the contents of this publication, or that Al-Anon Family Group Headquarters Inc., necessarily agrees with the views expressed herein. Al-Anon is a program of recovery for families and friends of alcoholics—use of these excerpts in any non-Al-Anon context does not imply endorsement or affiliation by Al-Anon.

The Twelve Steps and brief excerpts from the book *Pass It On* are reprinted with permission of Alcoholics Anonymous World Services, Inc. (AAWS). Permission to reprint brief excerpts from the book *Pass It On* and the Twelve Steps does not mean that AAWS has reviewed or approved the contents of this publication, or that AAWS necessarily agrees with the views expressed herein. AA is a program of recovery from alcoholism *only*—use of the Twelve Steps in connection with programs and activities which are patterned after AA, but which address other problems, or in any other non-AA context, does not imply otherwise.

The LOIS WILSON *Story*

I

When Will It End?

*I*T WAS JUST PAST FIVE-THIRTY WHEN LOIS WILSON SQUEEZED OUT of the jammed subway car at the Fulton Street station and elbowed her way through the rush hour crowd up the stairs and into the clamor of downtown Brooklyn under a steady downpour. It was almost dark by now, and the street lamps and colorful store lights glistened in the puddles.

She slid her purse up her arm to open her bumbershoot, the colorful term she liked to call her umbrella, perhaps because it brought back warm memories of her mother and the many "old-fashioned" words she refused to discard right up to the day she died. That was Christmas night, 1930, just two short years ago. Tonight it seemed like yesterday.

Lois's lovely face looked pale and drawn as she paused for a moment to take a deep breath. She had hoped to leave her job at Macy's department store earlier that afternoon, but the onset of the holiday season coupled with staff cuts due to the Depression had every sales clerk doing double duty. After a moment, she turned and headed down Atlantic Avenue toward the quiet residential section of Brooklyn Heights not far away.

Before she had gone two blocks, the heavy rain running off the umbrella and onto her shoulders and back made her coat feel like two tons of wet cotton. That, and the pounding headache she'd had since early this morning, brought tears to her soft brown eyes.

"When will it end?" she thought to herself. "When will life get just a little bit easier?"[1]

The din of the downtown area lessened perceptibly as Lois turned into Smith Street and quickened her pace toward Clinton Street and her home six blocks away. But the headache was getting even worse. She glanced across the road and noticed that Slavin's Drugstore was still open. She hesitated, squeezed her fingers against her nose, then reluctantly crossed and made her way through deep puddles to the neighborhood pharmacy— reluctantly because Slavin's was one of her husband Bill's hush-hush bootleg establishments in this era of Prohibition. And while Barry Slavin, the rather handsome bachelor who owned the pharmacy, feigned ambivalence to Bill's "drinking problem" and never said a word about it, Lois felt rather uncomfortable that he knew so much about the personal problems it created in their marriage. She knew he heard stories—both from Bill and the neighborhood gossipers. In spite of all this, she liked him.

Barry was just pulling down the shade on the front door and placing the "Closed" sign in the window when he spied Lois approaching. He smiled and opened the door halfway. She could see that most of the store lights were already out.

"I was sneaking off early, what with the rain and all," he confessed. "But if you need something, Lois . . ."

"Thanks," she replied. "I . . . I have a splitting headache. I could use some aspirin."

"Sure." He pulled the door all the way open. Lois entered. Then he locked the door behind her but left the lights out. It was a rather large store with the pharmacy to the rear, a long soda fountain counter on one side, replete with black leather stools, and cosmetics and other sundries across the way. Barry directed Lois to a seat at the soda fountain, then headed for the pharmacy to get the headache pills.

What happened next was something Lois Wilson never shared with anyone for many years, and only then with her husband and her closest friends. It remained one of her deep, dark secrets, perhaps because she couldn't honestly say whether she had unconsciously invited the incident or was so dispirited at the moment that she simply let it happen. Either way, it filled her with guilt, anger, and shame.

Lois was a product of her time, born near the turn of the century. She was raised by a loving but spartan disciplinarian father and deeply religious mother to be a lady of purity and grace. Certainly the Roaring Twenties had a bit of an influence on her, but now it was the difficult thirties and social morality had come roaring back, tightening behavioral standards for troubled, poor, and struggling Americans. Prohibition was just one example. "Loose women" were few and far between these days, at least in Lois's small and shrinking world. It wasn't that she was naive. She simply believed that when a man made "a pass," particularly at a married woman, it should lead the lady to question her own actions and sense of values rather than respond to such false flattery, which could only exacerbate the situation.

But here at the soda fountain in Slavin's drugstore on this wet and chilly December evening sat a tense, fretful, lonely, and attractive forty-year-old woman beaten down by recent disappointments, including a husband whose love she questioned and whose out-of-control drinking she could no longer understand or deal with. So when Barry exited the pharmacy and walked toward her with a remedy for her headache, she was not only vulnerable, she had few defenses against any remedies he had in mind for the other problems in her life.

His warm, innocuous smile put her off guard. He went behind the soda fountain, filled a glass with water, then came back around and stood next to her. He opened his hand. She took the two tablets, then the water, and swallowed them. He smiled again, said she could pay next time, and handed her the full bottle of aspirin tablets. She put them in her purse.

"It's all the stress and tension, isn't it, Lois?" she recalled him commenting as he moved behind her and began to gently massage her neck and shoulders. It felt wonderful, so tingly and relaxing. No one had done this for her in a long, long time—maybe not since the night after their motorcycle accident when Bill realized her neck was so sore she couldn't sleep. He began to rub it softly and seductively and, despite all their aches and pains, they made love in that old dilapidated hotel room in Dayton, Tennessee.

She closed her eyes and moved her head and shoulders slowly back and forth with the motions of Barry's strong hands, hoping he wouldn't stop right away. She could smell the fragrance of his expensive cologne, not the harsh, nosebiting stench of Bill's bootleg liquor. She could feel her muscles loosen as the tension seemed to ooze down her arms and out through her fingertips.

His left hand continued to massage her neck as his right hand began to move slowly down her back. He said something like, "I don't understand. A beautiful woman like you letting yourself get into a situation like this."

Lois didn't reply, but suddenly she felt the tension returning. She heard Barry continue: "We both know Bill's problem. And you working all the time to support him. Never going out having any fun. It's admirable, I guess, to sacrifice like that, but . . ."

She could feel his breath close to her ear. She opened her eyes. His face was next to hers. Then he kissed her gently on the cheek.

Lois's first reaction was panic, but only for a brief moment. Then she suddenly, almost involuntarily exploded into rage. She shoved him away and leapt from the stool. The pharmacist appeared stunned, wondering how what he thought was an unspoken yes could turn in the flash of a second to a resounding no. "How dare you!" she recalled screaming at him. "How dare you!"

Her hand came up to slap him. Perhaps it was that shocked, I-got-caught-in-the-cookie-jar look on his face that stopped her. Or perhaps it was her own sense of guilt. Either way, she just glared at him for a moment, then turned and charged toward the door. It was locked. She pulled and yanked at it until Barry, now shaken and embarrassed, finally came over and flicked the bolt. Lois flung the door open and stormed out into the still-pouring rain, her unopened bumbershoot clutched tightly in her clenched fist.

Lois half-ran, half-stumbled along those next few tree-lined blocks to Clinton Street, sloshing through deep puddles, almost bumping into people who looked askance from under their umbrellas, probably wondering what emergency might have befallen this poor lady on this terribly dank night. The tension had now given way to sheer anger and was rapidly turning into shame and self-reprisal for allowing such a thing to happen. Her mind was spinning. She couldn't collect her thoughts. Maybe she didn't want to collect her thoughts, not just yet anyway.

Her low-heeled black leather shoes were filled with rainwater by the time she reached the long cement steps that led up to the front door of 182 Clinton Street, the large, impressive brownstone that was her birth-place and childhood home, and where she now felt like a sponging guest who had overstayed her welcome, even though she knew this not to be true. But feelings often have nothing to do with truth. The simple fact was that she and Bill had lost everything over the past four years because of his drinking, and they had no place else to go. So, at her widowed father's behest, she swallowed her pride and moved back into this stately old house. Bill had little choice. Besides, it seemed that he was seldom there anyway once he was able to gin up enough money to get started on another toot.

She grabbed the newel on the stoop railing and stood there for a long moment trying to catch her breath. The rain mixed with her tears as she stared up at the house and its dark, curtained windows. She was soaked inside and out, and her hair hung like a wet mop under the drenched pillbox hat that now lay almost flat on her head. But she gave no thought to her appearance. It was her insides that were churning, her heart that wouldn't stop pounding, and her stomach that was on the verge of nausea. A chill ran through her, so she turned and pulled herself slowly up the steps to the double glass door entrance still decorated with her mother's hand-sewn lace curtains. Fumbling in her purse, she found the key, then dropped it from her trembling fingers. After several tries, she finally opened the door and entered the large dark foyer as if in a trance.

As much as she resisted them, her thoughts began to come together, and she started to weep once more. Then she yanked the wet pillbox hat from her head and flung it against the wall. It took a few more moments for her to turn on the foyer light and move slowly down the hall and into the kitchen, her clothes dripping water behind her.

Her mind was racing now. She yanked the string on the overhead globe light, grabbed the teakettle, and filled it at the sink. Then she moved to the stove. The water running down her hand from her soaked clothing fizzled the flame on the first matchstick. It took two more to light the gas. All the while she kept thinking, "It can't go on like this. It can't."

She knew instinctively that Bill wasn't home. She would have either tripped over him in the doorway, or he would be lying unconscious on the hall stairs, unable to make it up to their bedroom on the second floor. That's the way it was. That's the way it had been since . . . she tried to remember, but too many thoughts were coming all at the same time.

The chills started again, this time running deep into her bones. She had to get out of these soggy things before she caught pneumonia. First the coat. She hung it on a hook above the large washbasin to let it drip dry. Next the shoes. They needed to be stuffed with newspaper so they wouldn't shrink too much. The newspapers were piled next to the old vegetable bin in the corner. It took only a few moments to do the job, but it distracted her mind from the things she didn't want to think about. Now, upstairs and out of the rest of these wet clothes.[2]

Her bedroom flashed memories almost every time she entered it, particularly since moving back into this old house . . . God, what was it . . . almost three years ago now? She couldn't believe it. This had been her room growing up on Clinton Street. She shared it for a while with her little sister Barbara, because, well, after that horrible accident, somebody had to watch over her every night. Being the oldest and most dependable, Lois was assigned that task. She didn't mind. She loved Barbara and felt so deeply sorry for her.

Lois was eight years old when it happened. She was playing near the lake at the family's summer place in Vermont when she heard screams coming from the cottage. They were so terrifying she was afraid to go inside. Barbara, who was two, had found a vase filled with long, decorative stick matches and was playing with them under the kitchen table. She managed to strike one on the table leg, and the beautiful colored flame that flickered from the match immediately set her white lace dress on fire. Fortunately, Annie the cook heard the child's agonized screams, pulled her out, and covered her with towels to douse the flames. Annie was burned herself, but she saved Barbara's life.

It would take some years of treatment and skin grafts to fix the deep burns on her sister's face and hands, but she eventually recovered surprisingly well. Meanwhile, Lois would lie here in her bedroom every night watching her baby sister toss and turn and often wake up crying. She'd bring her a glass of water, stroke her soft brown hair, and perhaps read her a story until she went back to sleep.

As Lois slipped out of her dripping dress and undergarments, she thought how ironic it was to be back in the same room, taking care of a drunken husband in the very same way.

She put on her warm cotton bathrobe over a flannel nightgown and was brushing her hair in the dresser mirror when she heard the teakettle whistling through the empty house. Hurrying downstairs, she stepped around the puddles in the hallway, making a mental note to wipe them up as soon as she had something to eat. The nausea had gone, and she knew she needed something in her stomach to keep that pounding headache from coming back.

Suddenly she spied her pillbox hat. It was leaning against the far wall where she had flung it. As she picked it up to hang it on the nearby coatrack, the face of Barry Slavin flashed before her. She stood there frozen, her jaws clenched. Then, telling herself she didn't have to deal with this anymore tonight, she turned and headed down the hall.

The wind was whipping the rain against the kitchen windows. Lois sat at the white cast-iron table bobbing the tea bag in her cup and staring down at the vegetable sandwich she had thrown together on whole wheat bread. If only Mother were here now, she thought. How much time there would be just to talk, to get things out, to listen to her pearls of wisdom cultured from years of experience and a deep faith in her God. Matilda Burnham was a kind, loving soul who had great and usually very practical insight. It was she who told her daughter that Bill was sick, that his craving for drink was the devil's curse, and that God Himself must find a way to shake it from him. But in the meantime, if Lois truly loved her husband, she must do everything in her power to help him, to pray for him, to encourage him to seek the Lord.

Lois believed Bill truly loved her mother. At least he always said so and showed her great respect and consideration when he was sober. But then why wasn't he there when she died? Why wasn't he there for her funeral? Why didn't he express much deeper regret and remorse four days later when Lois bailed him out of the drunk tank once again? She knew what her mother would have said. A man who does this kind of terrible thing to a wife and family he loves has to be a very sick man who needs a great deal of love and help himself.

But how far must one go? How far do you let a man drag you down, force you to wallow in the muck he brings home? Did her mother really understand what she had gone through? What she was still going through?[3] Her father, on the other hand, would just as soon have Lois leave Bill. "You can't help this man anymore," he would half-shout at her each time Bill roared off on another spree. And now here they were, living with Dr. Burnham in his home, Lois witnessing the pain and confusion in her father's eyes each time she returned from work, fearful of what the night would bring. And here was Dr. Burnham, with no idea how to comfort his own dear daughter.

Their only conversation topic now was his forthcoming wedding to a lady he had known and was seeing on occasion even while Matilda lay dying. This had upset Lois greatly, but how does the pot call the kettle black when the pot has no answers for herself and is currently sponging off the kettle? Soon, however, Dr. Burnham and his wife-to-be would be moving into their own place, and at least that source of household tension would come to an end. But then who would help her, she thought, when Bill made another of his feeble attempts to stop drinking on his own and began to shake and sweat? Who would inject him, as her father frequently did, with a strong sedative or give him a dose of that horrible smelling paraldehyde to calm his tremors?[4]

Then again, maybe she was worried for absolutely no reason. The way things were going, Lois felt almost certain she would get a call one night and learn that Bill had been found dead in the streets, hit by a car, beaten to death, or dead from an overdose of liquor. Such tragedies were in the newspapers every day. Every single day. She grabbed her forehead and wished her mind would stop racing like this.[5] Lois glanced at the kitchen clock. It was almost quarter to eight. Perhaps she'd take a hot bath and then start that new Somerset Maugham novel that had been on her night table for weeks. Her bones actually ached when she cleaned the few dishes at the sink and put them back in the cupboard. She turned off the kitchen light, left the one on in the foyer, and went back upstairs to fill the tub.

It was well past midnight when Lois came to with a start. A loud noise from downstairs had awakened her. The bedside lamp was still on, and the novel she had been reading lay across her chest. She sat up and listened. Then she heard another noise, like something being pushed across a carpet, followed by those familiar grunts and groans and loud curse words. She didn't have to hear anything more to know that her husband had finally arrived home, and in his usual condition.

Lois slipped out of bed, put her bathrobe back on, and walked slowly down the stairs to the entrance hall. Bill was lying halfway into the parlor. He had knocked over a lamp table, broken the shade and bulb, and was reaching for a nearby chair to pull himself erect. The trouble was, each time he clutched at it, he pushed the chair further away. His "goddams" and "Jesus Christs" were getting louder as his frustration grew. Lois switched on the hallway light to see better. What she saw was nothing worse than usual, but the brighter light stunned her husband momentarily and made him fall back down on his side.

He looked up at her. Bill, too, was soaking wet. There was a cut and several scrapes on his face, his nose was running, and saliva drooled from his mouth, across his chin. That terrible stench of cheap booze filled her nostrils. Suddenly she watched as her husband reached his arm up toward her, smiled that stupid drunken smile, and mumbled in a hoarse whisper: "There's my lady. She's always there. Come on, Pal. Give your boy a big kiss."

The shame and revulsion from the incident at the pharmacy, the pounding headache she had suffered all day long, the ever-present pain of losing her mother, and now looking down and seeing the Bowery being dragged into her home once again—it all seemed to strike her at once. She couldn't hold back. Lois later recalled slumping to her knees, leaning over her husband, and pounding him on the chest and arms, lightly at first, then harder and harder. She grew hysterical, saying, "I lie for you. I cover up for you. I can't even look my own father in the face because of you. Every time you get drunk, I'm the one who feels guilty. Like it's my fault. Because I couldn't have children. That I'm not a good enough wife. But it's not my fault! It's not my fault! You can go to your bootleggers, your speakeasies. Where can I go? Tell me! Where can I go?"

The next thing she recalled saying haunted her for some time after that. In fact, Lois said, it haunted her right up until the day Bill finally found sobriety in Towns Hospital and began to get well.

"I thought tonight," she recalled shouting through her tears, "that maybe I would never see you again. But you don't even have the decency to die."[6]

2

How It All Began

❧

*I*T WAS A LITTLE PAST EIGHT O'CLOCK THAT CRISP OCTOBER MORNING in 1897 when the black brougham, an enclosed horse-drawn carriage from Pratt Institute's new kindergarten school, pulled up in front of Dr. Clark Burnham's spacious brownstone on Clinton Street in the well-to-do section of Brooklyn Heights, New York. The home's impressive scalloped-glass front door opened, and out onto the porch stepped the good doctor's housekeeper, Maggie Fay. She had a prettily dressed little girl in hand. As Maggie started to help her down the wide cement steps, the girl shook her tiny hand loose and climbed down the rest of the way by herself. The carriage driver assisted her into the coach already filled with a half dozen other boys and girls her age, all from "special" families like the Burnhams.

Watching the brougham drive off, the housekeeper smiled and shook her head, for she knew that even at "almost six," the charming, tawny-haired Lois Burnham loved to feel older and somewhat independent, perhaps the result of already becoming "Mommy's little helper." For when Maggie was busy or off somewhere else, Lois was both pleased and proud to help her mother care for her younger brother, Rogers, and her newborn baby sister, Barbara.

Not only that, here she was one of the first children in her neighborhood to attend kindergarten, a new type of preschool education recently imported from Germany by the forward-thinking faculty at New York's well-known Pratt Institute.

As the carriage bounced slowly down the bumpy street, one of the young boys stuck his head out the window. His hand accidentally leaned against the door handle. Suddenly the door flew open and the boy fell out into the road, injuring his arm and cutting his head open. The driver leapt down, tied his handkerchief around the youngster's head, put him back inside next to Lois, and raced off for medical assistance. Lois never forgot that incident mainly because, as she shared it with others later on, "I remember feeling very grown-up mothering him as we drove to the hospital."[1] Perhaps that's why the boy recovered so quickly, she would laughingly add.

While it remained a vivid childhood memory, it certainly was a sign that Lois Wilson's loving and caring instincts and even perhaps her "need to nurture" began at a very early age. For as she grew in beauty and grace, and as the eldest of what were soon to be six siblings, it was simply understood that she was to mete out an extra measure of caretaking and responsibility. This further instilled in her, as she often said, the belief that her will and loving influence could change most things in her life for the better, including people themselves.

This strong will and self-confidence was quite obviously inherited from her father. Practically everyone who came to know Clark Burnham well described him as one of the most determined, disciplined, and courageous persons they had ever encountered. He stood only five feet eight, but his strong, chiseled countenance, his forceful personality, and his almost strut-like bearing gave the impression of a man of much larger stature.

Born in Lancaster, Pennsylvania, Clark was in the middle of ten children. His father, Nathan Clark Burnham, practiced both law and medicine and was also a minister of the Swedenborgian Church, which had only recently planted its roots in America. It preached finding a wise balance between the spiritual and the natural life, and some of its more famous members would be Helen Keller and Robert Frost.

Perhaps Clark's initial interest in medicine, aside from his father's strong example, came when he tried to save his younger brother Charley's life one day. Unbeknownst to Clark, the always-fractious sibling had found two sticks of phosphorus on their way home from school and put them in his pants pocket. When his older brother challenged him to their usual race across the neighbor's meadow, Charley apparently had it in mind to win this time. He ran so hard that the friction ignited the phosphorus and set the boy's clothes on fire. Shouting for his father, Clark rolled his brother over and over in the grass, trying at the same time to pull off his burning pants and heavy jacket. Their father did all he could, but Charley died of his burns a few days later.

Not in his wildest imagination could Clark Burnham ever conceive that some day he'd find himself in the very same situation—only this time with one of his own little daughters.

After recovering from his loss and the guilty sense that if he hadn't raced Charley that day it never would have happened, the young man soon regained his "zest for life," as Lois always called it.[2] It began to take him down many paths, prodding him to explore many aspects of life, until once again he found himself considering a career in medicine. He soon came to realize the field of medicine offered him the opportunity to accomplish the three primary goals he had set for himself: to be challenged mentally and physically, to be of meaningful help to the world, and to achieve significant material success. In the ensuing years, Clark Burnham managed to accomplish all of these goals.[3]

Is it any wonder, then, why he later could not fathom a child of his—especially his oldest and dearest—allowing herself to be dragged down into such squalor and degradation after growing up in a house and in a world of such splendor? It was simply the antithesis of every virtue, of every desire, of every decent human emotion he had tried to instill in Lois. And, as in many families affected by the disease of alcoholism, his failure to change her way of life—he had long since given up on his drunken son-in-law—drove him to confusion, anger, and despair.

Upon graduating with honors from Franklin and Marshall College, Clark entered the Hahnemann School of Medicine in Philadelphia. During his last year of study, he visited an uncle and "benefactor" who owned a dry goods store in the Prospect Park section of Brooklyn, a bustling blue-collar neighborhood. Because of his dealings, the uncle knew and was close to many people in the area. He casually suggested this could be an excellent place for a young doctor to start a practice.

At that time, the sparsely settled region of Brooklyn was composed of a series of small towns and communities that were rapidly being annexed and merged into the already established and growing "City of Brooklyn," where Prospect Park was located.

Originally settled in 1636 by Dutch farmers who found the burgh of New Amsterdam across the river—later New York City—unsuited to their rural way of life, the area soon began to sprout farmlands along Gowanus Bay, Jamaica Bay, and in the rich soil of the Flatlands. By 1645, the settlements were joined together into a township called Breuckelen, meaning "marshlands" and echoing the name of the low-lying district the settlers had emigrated from back in Breuckelen, Holland.

As more settlers came and the region began to grow, more towns sprang up—New Utrecht, Midwood, Flatbush, Bushwick, Gowanus, New Lots, Williamsburg, Prospect Park, Gravesend, and the Heights. By 1646, ferry systems were established across the East River, which spurred development and trade throughout Breuckelen. Over the years, the name of the region evolved into a number of forms, from Breuckelen to Breuckeleen to Brookline to Brucklyn. By the close of the eighteenth century, the commonly accepted name was Brooklyn.

By 1884, when Clark Burnham was ready to begin his medical practice as a specialist in gynecology, the population of Brooklyn, which had now become a city, was about 130,000. Fifteen years later, on January 1, 1898, when the city of Brooklyn officially became a borough of New York City, the population had grown to over 200,000 and was a vibrant and flourishing community.

After passing his medical boards in surgery and gynecology, Clark took his uncle's suggestion and headed back to Brooklyn. With some additional help from his benefactor, he rented a furnished room, bought an old saddle horse for house calls, and was in business.

While word spread that a fine young doctor had moved into the neighborhood, many in the area couldn't afford professional medical care, and those who could were not able to pay very much. So it wasn't long before Clark realized he had settled in the wrong part of Brooklyn. He should be in "the Heights," as people called the upscale section of Brooklyn Heights that bordered on the East River and overlooked the growing financial district of lower Manhattan.

It wasn't that he had no empathy for the hoi polloi, but they had their charity clinics and their midwives. Besides, paying patients required his services just as much—and of course he would always make himself available to anyone who needed him. That was his oath, one the record shows he kept.

So, much to the dismay of his uncle, the goal-oriented physician packed up his few things and moved a few miles away to charm a wealthier clientele. Clark Burnham soon found he fit in quite well with the movers and shakers and the elite of Brooklyn Heights society.

Before long he was able to trade in his old saddle horse for a brand-new fringe-topped horse and carriage. As his practice grew, so did his social life. The gentlemen invited him to their clubs, and the ladies invited him to their parties. In fact, that's how he met his bride-to-be, one Matilda Hoyt Spelman, when he was invited to her coming-out party.

He happened to be tending a sick patient in the neighborhood that evening, so he had his medical case with him when he arrived at the Spelmans'. He thought he'd just leave it with his hat and coat, as Lois would later tell the story, always laughing heartily at her father's embarrassing predicament. Upon entering the house with his bag in hand, Dr. Burnham was mistaken for one of the musicians. He was immediately directed upstairs to wait with the rest of the small orchestra until it was time for dancing. Matilda happened to be leaving her room nearby when she spied the young physician trying to catch the attention of one of the servants. She recognized him because she had once accompanied her mother to his office, and he apparently had made a strong impression on her. She rescued Clark from the confusion, and they were formally introduced by her father when they arrived downstairs for the party. A week later they were courting.

The oldest of four children and some seven years younger than her handsome escort, Matilda Spelman was both attractive and adventurous. She, like her also-adventurous beau, had watched the completion and dedication of the famous Brooklyn Bridge in 1883, just three years before they met. The bridge was a mighty and impressive span of 1,595 feet that crossed the river from the Heights to downtown Manhattan. Its huge cables and support towers were designed by the renowned bridge architect John A. Roebling and built by his son Washington Roebling over a fifteen-year period.

During their courtship, Clark loved to take Matilda hiking across the bridge whenever he had the time. There was no heavy vehicular traffic back then, although it was soon to come. One day as they were walking, Matilda stopped in the middle of the bridge and confessed that she had done a very foolish thing just before the structure was finished. She pointed to the sixteen-inch-wide walkway atop the steel encasements containing giant support cables that ran all the way up to the huge stone towers above—and back down the other side. According to Lois, her mother admitted to accepting a challenge from some friends and climbed up the cable walk to the towers and down the other side. She said with tongue in cheek that it was a very precarious way to get to Manhattan, even though quite exhilarating. Clark made her promise never to do such a dangerous thing again. She promised. Then he hugged her and admitted how much he admired her spunk.

The Spelmans were all New Englanders at the root and quite religious. Born in Granville, Massachusetts, Matilda's father, William Chapman Spelman was, as were his father and grandfather, a Congregationalist. The Hoyts, her mother's family, were a well-known Lutheran clan from Manchester, Vermont. The money was on the Spelman side. In fact, Laura Spelman, a close cousin, was married to John D. Rockefeller, Sr.

Lois recalled her aunt Eliza Spelman taking her for a visit one day to Laura's home in Pocantico Hills, New York, a sprawling estate of lawns and gardens that surrounded their enormous mansion. Though very young at the time, Lois remembered John D. standing near the huge fireplace in his living room of green and gold, smiling at her.

Also a financier, William Spelman moved to New York City to advance his career. He and his wife, Sarah, bought a large home on Willow Street in Brooklyn, where Matilda was born.

Matilda loved the arts, studying drama and literature at school. She was also a member of the school's choral group and had a very lovely voice. Later on, as a mother herself, Matilda would gather her children together just before bedtime and read stories, recite poetry, or sing them lullabies. Such times were among Lois's favorite memories.

Clark and Matilda married in 1888. They leased the house at 182 Clinton Street and turned one of the back rooms into a medical office. He worked diligently, and she handled all the business affairs including billing patients. They were a well-matched pair. While Clark was extremely self-disciplined and expected others to be the same, especially his children, Matilda was softer, kinder, and more loving and forgiving— traits Lois would inherit.

Lois was their first child, born on March 4, 1891, pink, bright-eyed, and healthy. Then came Rogers, Barbara, Katherine, Lyman, and Matilda. There was great heartbreak in the Burnham household, however, when young Matilda, always sickly since her difficult birth, died before her first birthday. Lois couldn't understand why an innocent little baby had to die, and was forced to accept her mother's explanation that it was simply "God's will."

But the young girl would have difficulty for many years accepting God's will whenever it didn't agree with hers, always feeling that somehow, some way, she could change things with her own will. As she often shared later on, this brought her much pain and confusion until she was finally able to see she was actually powerless over many things in her life and that acceptance was the true key to serenity.

After attending kindergarten, Lois was placed in a Quaker school called Friends School. Her father had checked out a whole list of private schools and found this to be one of the finest.

There was a quiet and lovely little girl sitting next to Lois that first day in class named Elise Valentine. They would sit next to each other for the next twelve years, right through Friends School and Packer Collegiate Institute.

Lois and Elise shared much of their lives with each other growing up and had quite a bit in common. They both played on the basketball team at Packer Collegiate. They both wore middy blouses and bloomers in the gym and ribbon bows at the end of their long braids, although Lois alternated between blue and yellow and Elise always wore white.

Many afternoons on the way home from school, they walked together to the foot of Montague Street on the Heights above New York Harbor. It was and still is a spectacular sight. There, Lois often recalled, they would share their dreams as they watched the large ships steam past the Statue of Liberty and the setting sun cast its beautiful streaks of color across the shimmering water.

And there was something else they both had very much in common. At Packer, an all-girls school, they frequently looked down their noses and laughed whenever one of their classmates ogled the boys from neighboring Polytechnic Institute as they passed by. You see, Lois and Elise had already attended school with boys at Friends, a coeducational facility. They thought they knew a great deal about the opposite sex. Parading around with a rather superior attitude, they'd smugly tell the other girls, "Most boys are clumsy and stupid and nothing to get excited about." But that came from their experience with "little boys."

Later Lois chuckled when she recalled how quickly that superior attitude vanished when they had their first real encounter with "bigger boys." She and Elise were crossing the Packer campus one day when out of nowhere, two high school seniors from Polytechnic approached and began making "passes." The two sophomores giggled at first—that is, until the boys stopped and stood directly in front of them, blocking their path. They insisted they wouldn't move until the girls agreed to join them for a soda at the local ice cream parlor.

Lois and Elise clasped hands, glanced nervously at each other, then turned and dashed back inside the school building, leaving the young men standing there nonplussed. They waited inside the school until they were certain their admirers had gone.

As Lois often explained to the more liberated young women she came to know later on in life, the customs and mores regarding the opposite sex were a whole lot different in 1910 than today, regardless of one's superior attitude. And there was always that fear of being branded "a scarlet woman" if one succumbed to a young man's charms too soon—certainly not upon their first encounter.[4]

While Lois thought she knew her close friend quite well, there was always something just a bit mysterious, a bit strange. Elise spent much time at the Burnham house, but Lois spent little time at the Valentine house. It wasn't that she didn't want to. She was seldom invited.

Elise seemed comfortable and at ease with Mrs. Burnham, although somewhat shy and timid in the presence of the more forceful Dr. Burnham. But Lois barely knew Mrs. Valentine and had never met Elise's father at all. She had no idea until years later that her dear friend's father was an "inebriate," the kindest term they used back then for a boozer, and that Elise tried not to let on how it affected her.

They remained close friends over the years, through thick and thin as Lois would say, until that awful day in the summer of 1929 when they found themselves deeply split by the disease of alcoholism. It affected each of them in her own way. It would wash away all understanding and keep them apart for many years after that.[5]

Sundays were always special at the Burnham household. After proudly showing off his family at the church service, Dr. Burnham would invite the minister and other guests back to their home on Clinton Street to dine and discuss religion and world affairs. As the guests gathered, the two subjects never seemed to clash until the good doctor began serving the fine wines and alcoholic beverages given to him by his grateful patients, who Lois referred to as "GP's." But before the verbal exchanges got too hot and heavy, Matilda always knew when to call everyone into her large formal dining room for a sumptuous meal.

Before eating, it was the Burnhams' custom to stand around the table holding hands while the minister or sometimes the doctor himself offered a blessing to the Lord for His generosity. Some of the less religious guests were not used to holding hands—particularly one man with another. They might self-consciously fidget and squirm. Young Lois always found it hard to keep from laughing out loud watching the faces of those guests turn red. But then moments later she would feel guilty, remembering that her mother always told her to be especially kind to people on Sundays because that's the Lord's day.

On those Sundays when the minister couldn't attend, the family took long walks together or drove around the burgeoning community of Brooklyn in their large, new, yellow-wheeled horse-drawn carriage.

Often they stopped off and visited some relatives, such as Lois's great-aunt Emma who lived on Fort Greene Place with her sister, Anne, a spinster. Now an aging widow, Aunt Emma had long white curls dangling down from under a baggy lace cap, Lois remembered. She thought they looked a bit funny. All the aunts ever seemed to talk about whenever they visited was how seasick they had been as they traveled from England on a great sailing vessel, and how difficult it was to start a new life in a new and completely different land.

It all sounded very exciting to Lois at the time, and she often wondered why her aunts seemed so sorrowful. Many times she left their house with a sense of deep sadness, believing that her aunts felt useless and alone. But one day she would understand better, because she would feel the same way.

A few years after Lois was born, her father reluctantly acceded to his wife's wishes that he take some time off to vacation with her elderly father in Manchester, Vermont. William Spelman's wife had passed away a few years earlier, and he was living in their large home all by himself. The trip that summer turned into an instant love affair between Clark and the Green Mountain State.

A great believer that most infirmities can be overcome by fresh air, a good diet, spartan discipline, and a strenuous outdoor life, he found Vermont the perfect place to enforce this regimen on himself and his growing family. Returning to Brooklyn, he preached Vermont to all his patients, his neighbors, and his friends. Lois remembered his soliloquy well: "The air is cleaner, the sky bluer, the flowers prettier, the mountains taller, the birds happier and the maple trees produce the finest and purest syrup in the whole wide world."[6]

Before long, the family was spending the entire summer in Manchester. Soon some of Dr. Burnham's patients were making the trek north to check things out for themselves, and in no time they became "summer people"— the term the natives politely applied to their temporary visitors. Before long even the "locals"—the year-round residents—began coming to him with their ailments, impressed by his knowledge of homeopathic medicine.

Matilda's father especially loved having the children around. Since he was now older and more feeble, he offered to sell his house and all its beautiful antique furnishings to his son-in-law at a very attractive price. Clark wasted no time in accepting the offer. He took out a large mortgage in order to buy the Clinton Street house at the same time, eliminating the costly rental there.

With his interest and involvement in the Green Mountain State growing along with his roster of patients, the doctor and his family started living from May to November at their "summer home." Since Lois and Rogers were now in school back in Brooklyn, Matilda had their teachers give her their spring and fall lessons so she could tutor them herself. Lois remembered how attentive her mother was to make sure they studied and understood everything she taught them.

The young girl was gifted at an early age with the ability to read and comprehend a growing vocabulary. Before too many years, she was reading Charles Dickens, William Thackeray, Sir Walter Scott, Jane Austen, Louisa May Alcott, Bret Harte, and Rudyard Kipling. She was experiencing flights of fancy and derring-do one day and human tragedy coupled with world events the next. It was quite a challenging, liberal education, and she enjoyed every moment of it.

That was something Dr. Burnham insisted upon: that each of his children receive a demanding education in order to develop not only a strong inner character but also the knowledge, intellect, and judgment to meet the world head on. And, being a gynecologist, he made sure all of them—his daughters in particular—were well educated on the subject of sex and where it fit into the overall context of their moral upbringing.

Moreover, unlike many parents in the Victorian era, Clark and Matilda Burnham were openly affectionate with each other in front of their children. This not only attested to the deep love they had for each other, but enabled their children to see that love between a man and a woman was natural and virtuous.

To round out her education, Lois took dancing and music lessons when she was back home in Brooklyn Heights and, upon returning to Vermont, she was frequently called upon to entertain summer guests, both dancing for them and playing the piano.

The doctor and his wife quickly became enmeshed in Manchester society, hosting and attending parties, serving on club committees, having prominent guests to their home. And the Burnham children were part of it. Clark made sure his flock was a shining example of what the best children should be like, and his wife went along with his wishes. In fact, they both took great pride in their children's appearance—robust, polite, and well-groomed. There was that distinctive style in dress and manner that never failed to produce flattering comments from the Burnhams' wealthy neighbors and the elite summer crowd from Brooklyn Heights.

But now with four children and another on the way, Matilda's never-ending social activities were beginning to wear on her. She never complained, but her husband could see it. That's when he found the perfect solution.

Clark had become enamored with a charming, roomy cottage on Emerald Lake in East Dorset, Vermont, about twenty miles away. It would put enough distance between them and Manchester so they could politely ease out of many of their social commitments while still maintaining contact with his patients and their many friends. Matilda loved the idea, so Clark rented out the Manchester house and purchased not only the charming cottage but also two nearby bungalows. And the trip between East Dorset and Manchester would be much easier now, since he had traded in his old buckboard for a brand-new Pierce Arrow with running boards, a rear trunk, and teak-spoked wheels.

Lois absolutely loved the move to Emerald Lake. She was "almost nine" at the time and recalled later how it was like "getting out of a tight-fitting girdle and into a loose pair of bloomers."[7] She became a tomboy, fishing and swimming, climbing trees, catching frogs, and picking beautiful ripe berries along the lake for her mother's pies.

She enjoyed waking early in the morning, sitting on the dock, and staring into the mist rising from the clear, deep green water. Emerald Lake was only about a mile wide and a mile long, but for young Lois it went on forever. It lay between two mountain ranges, the Taconic and the Green Mountains. The Taconic was known for its exquisite marble deposits. It was the chemical dust from the old quarries running down the mountain streams and into the lake that gave it its deep green color and eventually its name. But the mines had long since been shut and the lake was now pristine.

It was on one of those quiet, peaceful mornings as young Lois sat on the dock that the silence was suddenly shattered by agonizing screams coming from the cottage. Afraid to go in, she stood frozen, simply staring and listening.

Finally, when she made her way to the kitchen door, she saw her baby sister, Barbara, who had just turned two, lying on the floor surrounded by her parents and Annie, the cook, whose hands were wrapped in a wet towel. Annie was weeping hysterically while Dr. Burnham and his wife kept laying more wet towels across Barbara's face and arms as the child twisted and screeched unmercifully. Lois soon learned that unbeknownst to Annie, her sister had been playing with stick matches under the kitchen table. She had set fire to her lace dress and it scorched her terribly. Had the poor Irish cook not been there to douse the flames with kitchen towels, burning herself in the process, little Barbara would have died.

Lois remembered her mother describing to her one day the shocking number of skin grafts that were required to cover the burns on her little sister's face and body, grafts that enabled her to recover from the ordeal remarkably well. But the story that impressed Lois the most concerned her father who, at one critical moment and without any anesthetic, sliced skin from his own leg to graft onto his daughter's face. It was difficult to believe, Lois would explain, unless you knew Clark Burnham and the feelings he still had deep inside about not being able to help his younger brother Charley.

After that, Lois said, her father always called Barbara "his special little girl" because part of her had literally once been part of him. That gave Lois and her sister Katherine a twinge of jealousy now and then.

Matilda's father, just before he died, gave the family a beautiful white skiff with mast and sail. Being the oldest child, Lois quickly learned to master the craft and often was out on the lake from sunup until sundown. She loved being challenged by the wind as it whipped the waters into white-crested waves. Lois had inherited her father's courage, his sense of adventure, and his passion to enjoy nature and the beauty of life to the fullest.

And when the waters were calm, she set her sail and glided serenely over the lake, leaning back to watch the clouds move slowly across the sun and to wonder what might lie above and beyond them. As she grew older, she yearned to know more about the universe and its Creator. She would "talk to Him" rather than recite those formal prayers she learned in church. But somehow she could never quite reach "Him" in a personal way, no matter how hard she tried. It would take time and a great deal of inner struggle, but it did happen one day.[8]

In the meantime, Lois immersed herself in the shimmering green waters of Emerald Lake, totally unaware that in a few short years on this very lake she would collide with a young man who would change her life in more ways than she could have possibly imagined.

3

Love Almost at First Sight

*B*ACK IN THE EARLY 1900S, THE SOCIAL CONVENTIONS FOR young ladies were quite restrictive, nothing like today's rather liberated standards. "Spooning," for example, which later became "necking," "petting," and even "foreplay" to some, was considered most improper and was frowned upon before couples became formally engaged. And sex itself—even the mere discussion of it, in many cases— was left for after the wedding vows and for the highly anticipated, often tense, climactic honeymoon night.

While young men knew how they were expected to comport themselves when wooing a young lady, testosterone was just as potent then as now. Many, therefore, challenged convention whenever the opportunity presented itself. That's one reason why even in the best of families, daughters were chaperoned on dates and vigilantly watched when entertaining a young gentleman caller at home.

World War I and the free-wheeling Roaring Twenties that followed began to change things just a bit, but the "sexual revolution," as we know it today, was nowhere in sight when Lois became a young lady.

Even so, by the time she was twenty-one, the charming and alluring Miss Burnham was having difficulty herself with some of these social conventions. She had graduated from Packer Collegiate Institute and was studying drawing and painting at the New York School of Fine and Applied Art—and working with live models. There were several young men in her life now to whom she felt physically attracted, and despite her strict moral upbringing, Lois's interests were admittedly neither "platonic" nor "old-maidenish," nor did she fit into any of those other similar categories. As she herself shared later in her memoirs, "Sometimes it was hard for me to keep to all those strict rules. I knew other girls who didn't and in some cases saw how much trouble they brought upon themselves. I didn't want that to happen to me. Still, when I sat with a young man all evening in our front parlor at Clinton Street, I was often tempted when he wanted to spoon. Both of us frequently found it difficult to create enough interesting conversation to distract us from what we may have had in mind. But I did my best to hold faithfully to our conventions. Fortunately, just when it would become the most difficult to do so, mother would call down from the top of the stairs that it was time for the young gentleman to go home."[1]

There was one other thing that made Lois's physical desires a little bit easier to contain. She hadn't fallen in love yet.

It was around the middle of May 1914, early on a Saturday morning, Lois recalled, when she heard someone yanking incessantly on the bell chain outside the front door of the Burnham cottage on Emerald Lake. She was making a cup of tea for herself at the time. Annie the cook was busy feeding the younger children in the kitchen, her father was reading some papers in his study, and her mother was in her bedroom still recuperating from a virus she had picked up only a few days before the family left the city for Vermont.

There was a momentary pause, then the bells rang again . . . and again. By the time Lois reached the front door she was quite peeved. She glanced through the sunroom window to see a tall, lanky young man standing outside with a half dozen or so kerosene lamps tied to a pole that was slung across his broad shoulder. When Lois shoved open the outer door, she hit the young peddler on his leg, almost knocking him and his wares off the small front porch.

After regaining his balance and spotting the rather unfriendly look on Lois's face, his own countenance turned beet red. He stared at the ground and uttered:

"Need any kerosene lamps, ma'am?"

Lois now recognized the young man as one of her brother Rogers's summer friends, and she slowly pulled in her horns. While she had never actually met him before, she had seen him a number of times over the years and knew him as one of the "natives," the term the elite summer crowd applied to the local folks of East Dorset and its environs, some of whom worked in the small shops and restaurants and handled all sorts of handyman chores for a fee.

With an apologetic tone in her voice, Lois replied: "I'm very sorry. I didn't mean to hit you with the door like that."

The young man forced a shy smile on his handsome face as he wiggled uncomfortably back and forth, making his kerosene lamps clang together.

"You're Rogers's friend. But I . . . I don't recall your name."

"It's Bill, ma'am. Bill Wilson."

"How much are the lamps?"

"Seventy-five cents."

"Seventy-five cents? But they're only fifty cents at the store."

"Not with delivery, ma'am."

"But . . . twenty-five cents more!"

Now the young man was getting peeved. Suddenly Dr. Burnham was at the door.

"We could use two of those. And if you could bring some extra kerosene by, I would appreciate it."

Lois recalled feeling slightly embarrassed by her father's quick dismissal of her attempt to negotiate a lower price.[2] However, later he would tell her how he was impressed by young Wilson's ambition and grit. Rogers said he was working two jobs plus peddling lamps on weekends to pay for his expenses at Norwich University, a military college in Northfield, Vermont, just outside Montpelier, the state capital. She could tell from her father's expression that Bill reminded him of himself at that age.

Still, Lois wasn't all that impressed. At least that's what she told herself. This Bill Wilson fellow wasn't even that good-looking in spite of those bright, expressive eyes and that thick sandy-colored hair. And he seemed clumsy and slow and not at all personable. But most of all, her father said Bill was almost nineteen. She was already twenty-two, and that made him much too young for her. What would people think?

Then why did his brief visit to her front door remain on her mind all that day, that night, and even the following few days?

Bill Wilson, on the other hand, was very impressed. First, he appreciated Dr. Burnham's friendly, businesslike manner and his payment up front in cold hard cash. Second, Lois's challenging, almost intimidating attitude impressed him to the point where he swore he'd get even before the summer was over. One thing he couldn't stand was a patronizing attitude. He'd get even, all right, and the opportunity would present itself sooner than he anticipated.

Here was a determined, generally amiable, sometimes confused and distant young man whose roots ran deep into the Vermont soil. Bill Wilson came from a lineage of tall, raw-boned quarrymen who loved to spin great yarns in the local taverns while matching their peers drink for drink. And his father, Gilman Wilson—known as "Gilly" to his drinking buddies—was one of the best at both storytelling and drinking.

Gilly was born in the town of East Dorset in 1870, in the very same year and in the very same township as Emily Griffith, the first daughter of Gardener Fayette Griffith, a serious man who tilled the soil and loved it and his country deeply. His eldest daughter inherited his serious side: she grew into a tall, handsome woman with fixed notions that no one could alter no matter how hard or how long they tried. She was an avid reader, and when she discovered on a page an idea or provocative thought that she agreed with, it would become an unshakable part of her worldview. And she remained that way her entire life.[3]

Although Gilly was completely different—a man who could make up his mind one minute and change it the next—there was something about him that attracted Emily from the first day they met. Perhaps it was his ruggedly handsome looks, his thick, wavy hair, or the easy way he laughed. They both attended the same school, attended the same church, played in the same park, and went to the same parties. Before long they fell in love and were married. Many townsfolk whispered they were a completely unmatched pair, Emily a college graduate and Gilly a humble quarry worker. But Emily seemed happy at first, and Gilly—well, he always seemed happy.

Gilly's father, William C. Wilson, a Civil War veteran, had worked in the quarries himself until he met and married Helen Barrows, who had inherited the largest house in East Dorset. It was a great rambling structure that for some years now had been a local inn called the Barrows House. Willie Wilson decided he'd enjoy running an inn more than running a quarry gang, so he renamed the place the Wilson House and settled down to wine and dine a constant stream of guests.

When his son decided to marry Emily Griffith, Willie not only threw a big wedding banquet but also set the young couple up in their first apartment—two rooms in the rear of the Wilson House. And it was there about a year later, almost as an omen of things to come, that their first child, William G. Wilson, was born on November 26, 1895—in one of those small rooms right behind the bar.

No one could conceive what great things William G. Wilson would accomplish, nor could anyone conceive the great difficulties, disappointments, and tragedies that would buffet him along the way. It was only when he shared all of this with Lois in his sober years that she would finally come to understand just how powerless she had been to help him all along. Yet she would have to endure all his pain and degradation with him before achieving such awareness.

Young Billy was only nine when the first tragedy struck. His father and mother separated and eventually divorced. The townsfolk weren't surprised. Bill once shared with Lois that he should have seen it coming but closed his eyes and pretended when he opened them again things would be different. But they weren't. The bickering, the quarreling, the outright screaming matches were still there and had been ever since his sister Dorothy was born. His mother kept saying she felt "stuck in a rut" and needed to find her way out.

Gilly was now managing a large granite quarry in the nearby Taconic Mountains and they had moved into a home of their own, a small but attractive green-shingled cottage a few blocks from the inn. But Emily wanted more and Gilly knew he couldn't get it for her, not on a quarry manager's paycheck. His drinking increased along with Emily's aloofness. Billy loved his father, and the night he left was a night he never forgot. In a way, he blamed himself even though his father swore it had nothing to do with him. But Billy just couldn't accept what his father said, especially when his insides kept telling him he had done something wrong—that his father no longer loved him.

Gilly headed for western Canada to manage another quarry. Emily sat down to plot her future. She was thirty-five now and had a son and a daughter to look after. She also had her own life to live, a life up until now of unfulfilled dreams. Conjuring up one particular dream, Emily soon developed another "fixed notion," one that not even her kind and loving father could dissuade her from and one that led to Billy's second deep disappointment and still deeper self-recrimination.

It was 1905. Emily would file for divorce, leave the children with her father and mother, head for Boston, enroll in medical school, and become an osteopath. The children would see her only occasionally for some years after that.

And so it happened. And while Billy loved his grandparents, he had great difficulty ignoring those confusing emotions deep inside that made him feel unlovable, that he must surely be to blame for his mother leaving. He never discussed any of this with his mother or anyone. He just kept it all inside.

Growing up in the rolling green pastures and rugged mountains of Vermont with a loving grandfather who shared his patriotism for America and taught him how to make and fly a boomerang, how to repair and play an old violin, how to fish, hunt, and read *Huckleberry Finn* and *Tom Sawyer* took much of Billy's pain and sadness away, but not all of it.

He and his sister Dorothy attended the two-room schoolhouse in East Dorset, and their teachers were both dedicated and strict. And their grandparents made sure every bit of their homework was done before bedtime. Outside of class, the young boy's agility and strength made him an excellent athlete. He eagerly looked forward to entering the local high school and playing organized sports with his friends. But Emily had a different idea—another "fixed notion." Although living and studying in Boston, she stayed in touch with her father and kept track of her children's progress, especially their education. She was determined they would make something of themselves. She'd die before her son ever wound up in the quarries like her husband.

By the time Bill was ready for high school, Emily was now part of an osteopathic medical group in Boston and could afford to send him and his sister to a private school. Without consulting anyone, including her son, she had her father enroll him in Burr and Burton Academy, a well-respected coeducational boarding school in nearby Manchester, Vermont. The young man was devastated when he received the news. But there was nothing he could do about it, so again he just buried his feelings inside.

Late that summer, before he left for school, his longtime friend Mark Whalon, a man eight years Bill's senior, whom he looked upon as a "kind and caring uncle," decided to throw his young sidekick a going-away party.[4] Mark was a rather heavy-drinking local handyman who loved to share his great dreams and aspirations with Bill who, in turn, often wondered why Mark wasn't trying to achieve them. He gathered some of Bill's companions together one evening on the shore of Emerald Lake—strangely enough, only a stone's throw from the Burnham cottage—and pulled out a jug of home brew for everyone to have a swig from. When Bill's turn came, he passed. Perhaps it was those memories of his father and how drinking affected him. While his friends laughed and ribbed him, Mark Whalon didn't. He already knew how the damn stuff could grow on you and was happy about his young friend's decision.

Those first few days and weeks at Burr and Burton were black and lonely. Competing in sports against local farm boys was one thing. Competing here against skilled young men from throughout the country was something else. At first Bill felt dumb and awkward. Some of the boys laughed at him at tryouts. Others called him "the Stilt" because of his leanness and lankiness. But the determination his grandfather had planted deep in his belly when trying to make and fly that boomerang was still there. So he didn't give up.

Bill Wilson made the football team that first year but spent most of the time on the bench. By his sophomore year he was the starting fullback and recognized as the best punter on the team. He also pitched baseball, and by his junior year he was captain of the varsity baseball team. While he gained the respect and admiration of his classmates, that gap was still inside him, the feeling that he didn't quite measure up. One day he would come to know why that feeling of low self-esteem was there and, as with most alcoholics, always would be.

Perhaps that's why girls played little or no part in his life up until now. He still considered himself not very good-looking: his ears were too big; he was clumsy and much too skinny. At least that's how he felt until the spring of his junior year—until that day when he was leaving the baseball field and accidentally stumbled into Bertha Banford, the prettiest, the brightest, and surely the most alluring girl in school. She had been in the stands watching the team practice. Unbeknownst to Bill, she had actually come to watch him. She had been doing so for the past few months, ever since this charming young lady, whose father was a minister in New York City, had developed a crush on the team captain.

But now as they both stood there on the path leading back to the gymnasium, Bill couldn't believe that Bertha Banford, the girl every guy in school wanted to date, was actually smiling up at him with a loving look in those sensuous brown eyes. He fell in love instantly. He fell in love deeply. And when he learned that Bertha loved him too, he discovered something that turned his life completely around. He found that for a man like him, when someone else thinks you're handsome, you're handsome. When someone else thinks you're bright and intelligent, you're bright and intelligent. And when someone like Bertha Banford says she loves you, that makes you lovable once again.

He saw her in chapel every morning, glanced across his book at her in class as she did the same. They walked together around the campus almost every evening, watching the sun set and the moon rise. It was difficult to part that summer, but they knew they'd be together again in the fall.

Bill met Bertha's parents that September, the start of his senior year. He was invited to spend the Thanksgiving holidays with them in the city. A few weeks before, Bertha told him she had to leave school for some medical tests. She didn't appear concerned, so neither was he, although he knew she hadn't been feeling well since returning to school. She promised to write and keep him informed. But no letters came. He phoned her once in the city, but there was no answer.

Bill Wilson was in chapel that chilly November morning four days before Thanksgiving. They had just finished singing a hymn when the headmaster entered, whispered something to the chaplain, and then moved slowly to the pulpit. Everyone could see he was quite nervous and upset. He reached into his jacket pocket and pulled out a telegram. He began, "I received this telegram only an hour ago. It informs me that someone very near and dear to our hearts, Bertha Banford, died last night following surgery at the First Avenue Hospital in New York City." Then he asked everyone to kneel and say a prayer for this special young lady.[5]

Bill remained standing while everyone else in the chapel fell to their knees, murmuring sadly to each other. His legs wouldn't bend. His mind wouldn't function. All he felt was his heart thumping madly in his chest as if trying to burst through his ribs and reach out to the girl he loved so dearly . . . the girl he knew he couldn't live without. Tragedy had struck once again in the life of young Bill Wilson, only this time he had no idea how to face it, how to handle it, how to survive it even if he wanted to. The only thing he remembered thinking before he left chapel that morning was, "If there is a God, He can go to hell!"[6]

A week later there was a memorial service for Bertha in that same chapel at Burr and Burton Academy. It was packed with students and teachers and many of her friends and relatives. The Reverend and Mrs. Banford also attended. Bill's classmates understood as they watched him weep in Mrs. Banford's arms. Before Bertha's mother left, she took Bill's hand and pressed into it her favorite picture of her daughter. Perhaps she knew that this young man would need something more than just a memory to hang on to.

The rest of the school year was almost a total blackout. Bill remembered attending classes and spending most of the time staring out the window. He barely squeaked by. He tried to go on with his activities in the glee club and school orchestra, where he now played the violin. But he walked around in a fog, as he had once seen Mark Whalon stumble around town. But unlike Mark, Bill had nothing to support him, nothing inside to dull the pain. He fell into a depression. It would plague him on and off over the next several years. Even when he managed to pass the entrance exam for his first choice, Norwich University, which his grandfather battled with his mother so that he could attend, the painful memories were still there.

And they would stay until that day two years hence when, in the middle of Emerald Lake, he tried to get even with Lois Burnham—and something magical happened instead.

Meanwhile, as 1914 rolled around, Lois was busy working with the Central Branch of the Young Women's Christian Association in Brooklyn and helping Elise Valentine prepare for her marriage to Frank Shaw, an energetic and dapper Wall Street stockbroker. They had been courting for some time because Elise wanted to wait until Frank got "a little more settled." Now he was and could afford to spring for a rather swank and showy wedding. Lois felt it was just what Elise needed at the time, given all the problems still going on at her home. Besides, Lois liked Frank and thought he was kind and generous. Little did she know the important role he would play in Bill Wilson's life in the not-too-distant future.

While Elise and Frank were courting, Lois and one of her several beaux often double-dated. Or they arranged group outings, finding blind dates for other close friends such as Edith Roberts, who had been their class president at Packer Collegiate Institute, and Helen Cruden, a quiet, bashful young lady.

"We were just a bunch of social butterflies back then," Lois recalled of those days.[7] She loved music—everything from jazz to classical concerts, from vaudeville to the opera. She played the piano well and later accompanied Bill on his violin. Lois would glow when she'd talk about seeing the great Enrico Caruso perform in *Aida* and *Samson and Delilah* at the Metropolitan Opera House or Sarah Bernhardt, John Barrymore, and his sister, Ethel Barrymore, in plays on Broadway.

It was also around this time she met Norman Schneider, a pleasant, stocky young man about her own age who lived in Kitchener, Ontario. They were introduced by a mutual friend when he came to New York City for a Swedenborgian church convention. She knew right from the start that Norman was taken with her. She didn't feel the same right off, but she enjoyed his company. Norman was nice looking, well mannered, well read, and easy to talk to. While he was more on the serious side, he did manage to laugh at her silly jokes, which revealed how much he cared about her.

Clark and Matilda also liked Norman. In fact, after a short time Lois sensed they were encouraging the relationship more than she wished. Clark in particular considered the young man a fine catch since his family owned a large meatpacking company in Canada. Then, before Lois could interject, the Burnhams invited Norman to spend a week with the family on Emerald Lake. He accepted before Lois could say a word. She had to spend one of her vacation weeks on the lake entertaining him.

Norman Schneider arrived at the Burnham cottage only a few weeks after Bill Wilson had shown up with his "expensive" kerosene lamps. The visit would at least afford Lois the opportunity to get him off her mind . . . for a while anyway.

She and the young Canadian toured the antique shops in Manchester, picnicked in the mountains, swam in the lake, and chatted late into the night about everything from religion to the growing problems in Europe that were beginning to threaten the world with war. She recalled that it was a pleasant enough time, but there was one thing Lois was forced to admit. Norman Schneider was no sailor. The day she took him out in the skiff he was a bit squeamish—and turned ashen, in fact, each time the sail filled and the craft ran swiftly with the wind, its railing dipping nearly flush with the foaming green waters. When Norman gripped the mast and closed his eyes, Lois thought it best to tack to port, bring the rudder around to slow the skiff, and gently maneuver back to the dock. When they got out of the boat, she could see the gratitude mixed with embarrassment on his face.

The day before Norman left Emerald Lake, he wanted to have "a serious talk." Lois knew what was coming and decided simply to postpone the conversation for now. She said that since they had only known each other a short while, they should correspond and visit from time to time and see how things went. Then, perhaps by next summer, she might be in a position to hear what he had to say. Not only was Norman disappointed by her decision, so were Clark and Matilda. But something deep inside Lois told her she was doing the right thing. She needed time to think things through.

But Bill Wilson didn't need any time to think things through. He knew exactly what his next move would be regarding this haughty Lois Burnham and her dainty little sailing skiff. Her attitude toward him and his kerosene lamps only weeks before was still fresh on his mind.

Having made a boomerang that flew, repaired a violin so that it played sweet music, and put together a crystal radio that picked up stations from as far away as Pittsburgh, what would it take to make a sailboat that could outrun some fancy store-bought skiff? he thought. So the determined young man, prodded by resentment and an "I'll show you" attitude, went to work on his grandfather's old rowboat. He painted her up, streamlined the bow, fastened a handmade rudder and tiller, and carefully drove a heavy pole through the center seat to use as a mast. He "borrowed" one of his grandparents' old bedsheets for a sail and fastened it deftly and tightly to the mast. He even tied a red, white, and blue pennant to the top. He worked on the boat every hour he could spare between his jobs and selling those lamps. By the end of June he was ready. And it didn't make any difference to him that he had never sailed before. He'd find a way to cut her off and give her the biggest dunking of her life.

Bill knew from his friend Rogers that his sister worked in the city but came up to the lake practically every weekend. She also had the whole month of August off for vacation. He knew from watching that she loved to sail her skiff almost every Saturday morning. Lois was certain it was the first Saturday of July when it all came to pass without the slightest warning.

The morning began clear and calm. Not a leaf on the trees was stirring. The lake was like glass. But by eleven the wind came up, soft and gentle at first, but you could tell the gusts would be getting stronger. Lois untied the skiff at the dock and set sail. Bill Wilson was waiting in a cove on the far shore.

It started off as a pretty fair race. Bill was handicapped only by his complete lack of sailing acumen, a leaky old boat that was meant to be rowed, and Lois's superior skill, experience, and equipment. But he'd be damned if he didn't give it one helluva try.

The wind caught the bedsheet as the rowboat came out of the cove, thrusting it ahead like a dog coughing out a chicken bone. Bill hung on for dear life. He aimed the tiller toward Lois's skiff as best he could. Suddenly he realized he was closing in on her. His face became one huge, excited grin, and his long sandy hair blew wildly in the breeze.

Lois happened to glance back. Then she did a quick double take. She had never seen such a contraption on the lake before. Then a third look back—and she caught the grinning countenance of its skipper. She couldn't believe it. After a moment of shock, she broke out into laughter. Almost simultaneously she had a warm, tingling feeling inside, a feeling new and strange to her and one she couldn't explain.

But this was no time for self-diagnosis. This was a time for action. She let the sail out a bit. She felt the boat grab the wind and pull ahead. As she turned again, Bill spotted her and saluted as if to say: "I've got you exactly where I want you." But those old Clark Burnham genes were rattling inside her, those genes that relished a challenge. They came out shouting: "Not today, my friend. Not today."

Lois tacked to starboard, right into the path of Bill's old rowboat. He was close behind her now and didn't know which way to turn—or how. He swung the tiller to port. A heavy gust of wind hit the bedsheet like a sledgehammer. Lacking a deep keel, the rowboat came up, out, and then down into the water like a paper kite caught in a downdraft. Bill smashed into the homemade mast and was flung into the air. He hit the lake all tangled up in the bedsheet.

Lois saw it all. She was horrified and frightened at first. Her mouth was agape. She quickly came about and headed for Bill, who was still struggling to tear himself loose of the sail. Finally he was free. Once Lois saw he was all right, she began to chuckle. After all, it was a very funny sight. The chuckle turned into laughter. She was now alongside him—and still laughing.

She reached down and helped pull him into her boat. He slumped dripping wet into the seat across from her, rubbing his head.

"Are you all right?" she asked, trying unsuccessfully to stop laughing. He still had that big, silly grin on his face. Lois recalled he said something like, "I would've had you if my head didn't break the broomstick and my bedsheet didn't wrap me up like some Egyptian mummy."[8]

Then they both burst out again into raucous laughter for several more moments. Then it stopped. They could hear the water lapping against the bow. They looked at each other. That's when it happened . . . that special something only people who fall in love can feel but can't quite explain. They both knew it, but neither could nor would put it into words. Not just yet, anyway. That would take some time. But for Bill, those sad, painful memories of Bertha Banford would soon disappear. And Lois, although uncomfortable for a while about "what people might say," would soon forget about the disparity in their ages. For what is three-and-a-half years when there's a whole lifetime ahead?

When asked later on in life how she felt at the time, Lois replied with a twinkle in her eye: "Right from the beginning, there was that special something about Bill—something so refreshing, so impressive, so determined that I simply fell totally in love with him. Yes, for a short while I was nervous and unsure of myself, but I soon came to find Bill to be the most interesting, the most knowledgeable, the finest man I ever met. I saw things in him he didn't see in himself. Was I ever disappointed later on? You bet. Did I ever have any regrets for marrying him? Never, never, never, never. I never ever dreamed about anyone but Bill Wilson."[9]

Still, there was another omen of things to come on that beautiful and exciting morning on Emerald Lake. When Lois went to Bill's rescue, little did she know how often she would be doing the same thing over and over again in the future.

It was several weeks before they saw each other again. One night Rogers and Barbara were meeting some friends at a dance in Manchester. They tried to coax Lois into joining them. Rogers was particularly insistent for some reason, but Lois recalled it was her mother who finally convinced her to stop moping and go out and have some fun. Actually, Matilda and Clark thought their daughter was missing Norman Schneider. Little did they know. So Lois drove those twenty miles to Manchester with her siblings, quiet and unsmiling most of the way. She had no idea what Rogers had been instigating.

The dance hall was jammed with summer visitors. Rogers pulled his reluctant older sister onto the dance floor, and while they were waltzing, Bill Wilson suddenly appeared in the large open doorway leading to a wide veranda, watching and grinning at her. Lois closed her eyes tight, hoping with all her heart he would walk over, cut in, and ask her to dance. But when she opened her eyes, Bill was still standing in the doorway, watching and grinning.

As soon as the music stopped, Rogers ran over, grabbed his friend by the arm, and half-dragged him to their table. Since everyone was already acquainted, no introductions were necessary. The music started again. Rogers grabbed a different partner and joined the others back out on the dance floor. Bill slid slowly into a chair across from Lois. After a moment, she later recalled, he said quietly with that silly disarming grin on his face, "I love to sail but I hate to dance. Everybody staring at my two wooden legs. But if I could . . . I would ask you."

"Then, let's go where no one is staring," she said, smiling.[10]

They walked out onto the veranda and found a quiet spot away from the crowd. That's where she taught Bill how to dance. Few words were spoken except for her necessary explanation of the dance steps. And when the music ended, they went back inside for a soda. They made small talk while watching their friends dance. Bill still wasn't quite ready to test out his two wooden legs.

When it was time to leave, they shook hands, not knowing exactly when they'd see each other again but knowing for sure they would. Lois and the gang piled into Rogers's car, and she continued to stare back until Bill was out of sight. When she turned back around, she noticed a small, knowing smile on her brother's face and then a loving wink that said: "Don't worry, sis. It's just between us."

And it was, for no one else really knew the rest of that summer of 1914 what was growing between Lois and Bill. Even her parents didn't question why this young Bill Wilson fellow was visiting Rogers more frequently than usual. And besides, Dr. Burnham still liked and admired the lad.

Their relationship grew slowly and easily until Bill had to return to Norwich University that fall. But they were rarely alone, usually going picnicking, dancing, or on hayrides with "the gang"—Rogers and one of his two or three girlfriends, Barbara and her new beaux, or Ebby Thacher, Bill's longtime pal whom he often tried to "fix up" with a date, usually one of the local girls. Sometimes he was successful, most times not. And when he was not, he often talked his sister Dorothy into joining them.

In her later years, Lois would sometimes reluctantly admit how she honestly felt about Ebby Thacher when she first met him.

"I always tried to be polite in the beginning," she would say. "But at first all I saw was a rather homely young man who was always bragging about something, and as far as I could see, he had nothing to brag about. But he was Bill's closest and dearest friend so I made him mine too. Later on he would play a crucial role in helping Bill find sobriety, so in the end, I came to truly love Ebby Thacher."[11]

Edwin "Ebby" Thacher came from a wealthy Albany, New York, family that had made their money in manufacturing cast-iron stoves. They had been summering in Vermont for many years and had developed a reputation as part of the "heavy drinking crowd." Bill first met Ebby through Mark Whalon, and they became fast friends when they both attended Burr and Burton Academy. During those terrible days following Bertha Banford's death, Ebby didn't want to leave Bill's side. He was deeply concerned about the way his friend was acting. Even though Bill always found a way to go off and mourn by himself and think those crazy thoughts that frightened even himself sometimes, he was very grateful for Ebby's concern and support. That made them practically blood brothers. And now Bill and Ebby were even closer since they were both attending Norwich University, wearing military uniforms on campus, and talking at home about how they would save the world should war ever come. At the time, Lois knew nothing about the depth of the relationship.

Lois and Bill's parting in late August that year was quite abrupt. Lois couldn't get away from her job the weekend Bill returned to school. Bill wanted to write but he was fearful of rejection, for by now he was aware of Norman Schneider and how Dr. Burnham and his wife were disposed to Lois marrying him. Lois, on the other hand, didn't write because she didn't want to put any stress on Bill. She knew he had some problems with school in the past—although she only learned about Bertha much later—and was concerned about distracting him.

So the fall and winter months dragged on interminably for both of them. Bill wanted to do well to earn Lois's respect and to prepare for his future, so he did. Lois simply had to figure out her life at this juncture, facing pressure at her job, pressure from her parents to "make the right decisions," and pressure from two relationships she had to sort out. The one thing Lois did decide that winter was to quit her job and try her hand at a small venture she had always wanted to pursue: a snack bar some-where near their summer home in Vermont. Perhaps unconsciously—or consciously—the venture's close proximity to East Dorset and Bill had something to do with her timing.

The days passed much faster as she made her plans, designing the structure, its decor, its colors, its menu. She was filled with both excite-ment and trepidation by the time she was ready to open for business in the middle of May 1915. Lois created a simple but lovely stopping-off place for hungry and thirsty travelers, appropriately named "Lois's Tea Arbor." Located at the north end of Emerald Lake, it was a charming, open-sided grotto offering tea, sandwiches, and cakes. It sat atop a green knoll, its roof supported by vine-covered birch poles. The rustic chairs and tables were handmade of maple, the floor was painted green, and pretty flowers and native plants hung in pots from the ceiling.

Less than ten miles from Manchester on a well-traveled thoroughfare, the tea arbor could be seen from the other side of the road. But Lois hadn't realized how difficult it would be for cars and even carriages to cross the brook at the foot of the knoll. And she failed to put up any signs or advertise. She thought just the sight of the delightful grotto and word of mouth would do the trick. It didn't.

Business started off very slowly and never picked up—except, that is, for one particular customer who stopped by practically every afternoon after peddling his kerosene lamps. Bill always insisted on paying cash for his tea and cakes even though he wasn't selling many lamps. But then Lois wasn't selling much tea, either. Still, they had wonderful visits together. Sometimes she simply left the grotto with her Prince Charming to pick wild strawberries or the delicious mushrooms that grew out of the hillside.

Bill tried to keep her spirits up as the business wound down, but he soon realized he was in love with a lady who hated to fail, a lady who had inherited her father's determination to stay the course no matter what. Here again, Lois was certain her strong will would make things turn out all right—and, oh yes, that new sign Bill suggested, along with a small ad in the local paper, might also help. But they didn't. She closed the tea arbor for good at summer's end.

Then, much to Lois's further dismay, Bill told her he had to visit his mother in Boston for several weeks in August. It just happened to be the same time Norman Schneider was due to spend a week with the Burnhams on Emerald Lake. Bill knew nothing about Norman's visit. Lois felt her emotions being pulled in a number of different directions and, coupled with her business venture going downhill, she was in a real tizzy by the time the young Canadian arrived on her doorstep.

He had been corresponding regularly, as she had suggested, even though her brief notes were far less frequent. But she knew from his letters what he still had in mind and prepared herself as best she could for that pivotal moment. This time, Clark and Matilda did most of the entertaining since, despite their frowns, Lois was not always "up to going out." Norman sensed her interest in him was nowhere as deep as his interest in her, but he didn't give up.

Lois offered Norman little chance to "speak his mind" during his stay. Then came the day he was leaving for Montreal. He asked her to walk with him to the train station. There was simply no way she could refuse. She chatted aimlessly about everything from her business venture to the weather until they finally reached the depot and watched the train pull in.

Lois didn't know Bill was returning from Boston that very same day, so she didn't notice him hop off the rear car and freeze at the sight of her and Norman standing close together. She didn't see the expression on Bill's face when Norman, determined to the last, kissed Lois on the cheek and asked her to marry him. While Bill never heard the words nor Lois's reply, he could feel the anger and jealousy rising inside him even when Norman boarded the train and waved good-bye as it left the station.

It was only when Lois turned to leave that she saw Bill standing there staring at her, this time without that disarming grin. She was startled at first, but then smiled at him very warmly. She could tell by the deep frown on his forehead that something was wrong. Something was bothering him. He came close to her and stopped.

"You'll miss him, won't you?" he said quietly.

"Yes," she replied. "He is a very nice person. But . . . I'm not in love with him."

"You're not?" Bill gulped.

"No. I'm in love with you."

The glow she saw spread across Bill's face at that very moment was something she would remember for years to come—something that would help carry her through some of those difficult times ahead. It was not only the glow, but the words that followed:

"I . . . I love you too, Lois. I . . . I have now for a long, long time."

Only moments before, Bill Wilson was on the verge of feeling unlovable once again as he stood and watched his precious Lois being kissed by another man. What Bertha Banford had given him and was taken away by her death had been replaced by the warm smiles, the gentle touches, and the caring looks of Lois Burnham. She had made him feel whole again. And now her declaration of love healed every past wound and turned his fears and anxieties into indescribable joy.

He took Lois into his arms. He pulled her close to him. They kissed, warmly and gently. Then they smiled again at each other, clasped hands, and walked slowly from the train station, their eyes never leaving each other's face.

They sat together on the dock outside the Burnham cottage that evening talking about the future, their hopes, their dreams. Lois squeezed Bill's hand and told him what great things she saw ahead for him—that he could be anything he aspired to be—that he held as much promise inside him as this great country itself. Bill almost exploded with pride. He agreed with every word she said, only adding that he could not do it without her—that he needed her beside him every step of the way—that he was the sail but she was the rudder. They laughed and hugged and kissed, saying over and over how much they loved each other.[12]

Before the moon rose over Emerald Lake, they were betrothed.

4

War Changes Many Things

*B*Y THE SUMMER OF 1916, THE WAR CLOUDS THAT FILLED THE
skies over Europe were beginning to drift slowly and inexorably
toward America . . . but toward an America still not ready to go to war.

Overseas, however, on the war's Eastern Front, the Russian and
Serbian armies were on the verge of collapse under the intense bombardment of the better-equipped and better-trained German and Austrian
forces. But on the Western Front, these same forces were locked in almost
intractable trench warfare with the defending French and British troops.

On the high seas, Germany's effective submarine campaign was sinking large numbers of Allied supply ships, gradually depleting the cache of
weapons and ammunition necessary for France and England to break
through the German lines. But the U-boat siege had become "unrestrict-
ed"; the German navy was sinking British and French passenger ships
without warning, claiming they carried war supplies.

At this juncture, U.S. President Woodrow Wilson, who held
staunchly to a neutrality policy, demanded that this type of indiscrimi-
nate warfare be abandoned. The German government responded by
sinking the British liner *Lusitania* on May 7, 1915, killing more than
a thousand passengers, among them 128 Americans. Still, President
Wilson continued to cling to his neutral stance despite the growing
number of leading political and social figures demanding that America
enter the fray.

Against this background, Lois Burnham and William G. Wilson were contemplating their future together.

Since Bill still had almost a year and a half remaining at Norwich before graduation and then a two-year stint with the army after that, the idea of marrying before then was out of the question. Well, not completely. But they decided to keep their engagement a secret for a while nevertheless.

Lois corresponded regularly with Bill from her home in Brooklyn—in fact, much more than regularly. She once said she wrote her fiancé so many letters from the fall of 1915 to the summer of 1916 that she could have used them to wallpaper an entire room at Clinton Street. His letters were not nearly as frequent but were equally effusive in their expressions of love and commitment.[1]

After a while Lois's mother became rather curious about all these missives, but it wasn't until she and Clark received a Christmas card from Norman Schneider that the cat finally crawled out of the sack. Norman simply wanted to thank Dr. and Mrs. Burnham for all their warm hospitality during his several stays with them, adding that he wished Lois and Bill much happiness together.

Dr. Burnham waited several days before broaching the subject with his daughter. Lois was never one to hem and haw. She was always truthful and direct once things were out in the open. She told her father that she and Bill were deeply in love, were unofficially engaged, and would like to make their betrothal formal when the time was appropriate.

Clark Burnham was also very truthful and direct, especially with his children. He said a young man of twenty, still in college and with no career goals except the army, was hardly a brilliant prospect for a son-in-law, particularly when compared to the wealthy young gentleman from Kitchener, Ontario, whom she had recently discarded. But since his daughter wasn't prone to flights of fancy, he said, he knew she must have given all of this and its possible pitfalls serious consideration. He concluded that if she was so deeply in love with Bill Wilson, he would not stand in her way. He said he and her mother were genuinely fond of the young man and would be pleased to make the formal announcement of their engagement whenever she wished.

Lois burst into tears. She hugged her father, then ran into the kitchen to hug her mother while Clark called her brothers and sisters into the parlor and broke the news. Everyone in the Burnham clan—with the exception of Rogers—was stunned by Lois's decision, but since they were also truly fond of Bill, they were very happy for both of them.[2] The Burnhams decided that since Bill was in school and the family would be summering as usual at Emerald Lake, any formal announcement of the engagement should be put off until the fall, when they would have a large gathering at their home in Brooklyn. Because there were no immediate plans to marry, the young couple thought that was fine. This decision also gave Lois the opportunity to spend some time with Bill's mother, Emily, that summer. Emily had now remarried and was living in a comfortable home on the outskirts of Boston.

"She was very polite but rather aloof at first," Lois recalled of their initial visit. "But after a while, with the help of her charming husband who was also a doctor, she warmed up and told some very funny stories about Bill as a baby. He seemed to get embarrassed, but she continued right on regardless. All he said when we left was, 'Well, that's my mother. I guess you'll just have to get used to her.' That was easy since she moved to San Diego, California, shortly after that and we seldom saw her."[3]

Lois simply adored Bill's grandparents, particularly Grandpa Griffith. "He would just rave on and on about his grandson's exploits as a child. He claimed there was practically nothing Bill couldn't do if he put his mind to it. This also embarrassed Bill but in a much different way. There was always that touch of pride in his eyes when we left Grandpa Griffith's house."[4]

While Lois had now taken a position with a private school, and Bill worked for the local phone company in East Dorset and chopped down trees in the mountains to earn extra money, they did manage to find time together. Sometimes it was a Saturday sail on the lake, or breaking a new trail in the Taconic Range, or simply sitting on the dock outside the Burnham cottage sharing their dreams about the future.

"We had so many wonderful times during those two-and-a-half years of our engagement," Lois recalled, "both the unofficial then the formal part. We yearned to be married since our love for each other was so intense, but we fought to remain practical and use our common sense. Then the war changed everything."⁵ The formal announcement of their engagement was finally set for the Thanksgiving of 1916. While Lois crossed off the days on her calendar, Bill kept chopping down trees and looking forward to his first excursion to an exciting place he had only heard about from the "summer people."

He took the early train from Manchester that Wednesday. Lois met him at Grand Central Station. It was as if they had been apart forever. Even before he could loosen his backpack, they were kissing and hugging as though the hundreds of commuters rushing by were invisible.

Lois had the whole day planned. First they would shop for her engagement ring, as Bill had insisted. Lois led him around to the less expensive jewelers even though Bill kept telling her there was only one place he wanted to go—Tiffany's. He had heard the "summer people" say it was the finest jewelry store in the world, and for his girl, only the finest would do. So finally that's where they went, and to Lois's amazement, she found a ring there she absolutely loved. And it accommodated Bill's budget exactly—a small amethyst for twenty-five dollars. Tears welled up in her eyes as she tried the ring on for size. It fit perfectly. The sales clerk wrapped the silver ring box in shining pink paper with white ribbon. Bill stuffed it into his coat pocket and they walked out of Tiffany's arm in arm.

The next stop was the wilds of Staten Island for a picnic by the bay. Back then the borough was quite unsettled, with large open lands and marshy areas. This was Lois's idea—to show Bill the "outdoors" of New York. Fortunately the day was sunny and mild for November, although a little breezy. It took a subway ride, a ferry crossing, a bus, and a trolley to get there, but it was exciting, especially for Bill who had never seen a subway, a ferry, or a trolley before. Lois knew the area from some outings she had taken with the Brooklyn YWCA. They bought a steak and some potatoes at a small market, then meandered down toward New York Bay, where they found a grassy spot surrounded by marsh reeds.

They threw the potatoes in the hole Bill dug for the fire, and Lois sat on his overcoat while he cooked the steak on a large stick he used as a spit. They had done this often back in Vermont. They treasured those days when they would hike together in the lush Green Mountains, swim in the lake, and work up a ravaging appetite. Things were a bit different here among the reeds on Staten Island, of course, but they had worked up a pretty fair appetite.

It happened before they had a chance to eat. While the steak was still sizzling and the potatoes baking, the breeze from the bay suddenly kicked up into stiff gusts. The wind blew the burning embers across the grass and into the reeds. The dry marsh plants burst into flames. Fearing the worst, Bill took off his jacket and began beating out the fire. Lois grabbed his overcoat off the ground and did the same.

When the immediate crisis was over and the fire completely out, the steak lay blackened in the pit next to the potatoes, and, worst of all, Bill's jacket and overcoat were scorched and covered with soot. Lois blamed herself. Bill could see it in her face. Bill touched her cheek, then suddenly dug into his coat pocket and fumbled around as though he had lost something. After a moment, he grinned, and slowly pulled out the shining pink-papered package that contained Lois's engagement ring. The paper was smudged but the ring was fine. He held it up for her. She started to laugh. So did he. They both took a deep breath, kissed and hugged, and then headed for Brooklyn—smoky clothes and all.[6]

Nothing could have prepared Bill Wilson for Clinton Street, not from the moment he crossed the large entrance foyer to the moment he entered the elegant living room where he was greeted by Dr. and Mrs. Burnham. While Lois apologized for their sooty appearance and slightly charred clothing, Bill gazed around, his eyes and mouth wide open.

The oak-paneled walls above the doctor's massive bookcases were lined with paintings and engravings. The floor was covered with thick carpeting colored in rich, soft tones. The furniture spoke of wealth and authority. He glanced across into the spacious dining room with its brilliant chandelier and mahogany buffet filled with sterling silver and the finest china. It was only then that it struck him. This was Lois Burnham's world, not his. This was where and how she had grown up, in a style and fashion far removed from anything he had ever known. That's when he began to feel small and insignificant, like an alien in some strange universe. He felt he didn't fit in a place like this. Perhaps he never would. That familiar gap inside his gut opened wide once more. It had never really closed, but now it was making him twist and turn uncomfortably like that morning on the porch of the Burnham cottage on Emerald Lake when he felt stupid and clumsy peddling his kerosene lamps.[7]

Suddenly he sensed Lois squeezing his hand. Her arm snuggled into his as she moved closer. The look on her face told him everything was going to be all right. He wanted to believe her. He had to believe her. He needed her love and assurance to feel whole.

Lois, on the other hand, was elated and at ease with herself. After all, the man she loved, the man who was on her mind and in her heart every waking moment, was being accepted by her parents and her entire family. But if she had known what was going on inside Bill at this very moment, she would have caressed him, nestled him in her arms, and told him not to fear, that she would take care of everything.

In fact, she did. The first thing was to have the housekeeper arrange to have Bill's jacket and coat cleaned and repaired. Then she had the sleeves taken down in one of Rogers's jackets to fit Bill's long, lanky arms so he wouldn't miss the next event she had planned—lunch the very next day with Elise and Frank Shaw.

They met at the Tavern on the Green in Central Park. It was jammed with Thanksgiving holiday visitors. Elise and Frank still acted like newlyweds even after more than a year of marriage. Lois was very happy for both of them. After lunch they toured the city and enjoyed the excited look on Bill's face every time he stopped and stared at the huge crowds. Traffic was heavy in midtown Manhattan, even back in 1916. Bill was impressed by Frank Shaw's sophistication and his high-powered Wall Street connections. It stirred something inside him—the magnet of wealth and position. Shaw, on the other hand, seemed quite taken with Bill's unabashed patriotism and his eagerness to defend his country. While Shaw was several years older, he treated Bill as a peer, which pleased Lois immensely.[8]

The Shaws came to the formal dinner party at the Burnhams' that evening, where the engagement was announced and Lois accepted Bill's ring. As they joined the other guests and the family around the dining room table, Bill faced still another awkward moment. There weren't just one spoon and one fork beside his dinner plate but several forks and several spoons. Which one was he supposed to use and for what? But as they all sat down, Lois rode to his rescue once again. She nudged him very gently, smiled, then reached down and picked up the outside spoon. It was for the soup now being served. He followed her lead and almost immediately felt himself relaxing.

While Lois probably would have denied it, most would agree that it took a very special lady to do such a thing without drawing attention and making her fiancé feel like a fool. As a result of her loving actions, the rest of the evening, and the next four days in fact, went splendidly. Bill found himself telling stories of his sometimes near-disastrous hunting and fishing escapades back home, the hilarious practical jokes he and Ebby cooked up at school, the mysterious and funny characters he grew up with in East Dorset. Before long he had everyone roaring with laughter, including the good doctor and his wife. The family loved him. Lois simply sat back, smiling with pride.[9] By the time Bill said good-bye to Lois and her family and left Brooklyn Heights, the gap inside had almost vanished, and he was walking with both feet planted firmly in midair. However, by the time he returned to Norwich, war clouds were drifting even closer to U.S. shores, and he would soon be faced with some momentous decisions.

Despite incessant provocation for two years since the sinking of the *Lusitania*, President Wilson held to his neutrality policy. While his patience angered many, it did help to solidify American public opinion that peace could not be made with such ruthless enemies and that the time had come to support and defend the nation's allies. Finally, when German U-boats began sinking American supply ships, President Wilson hesitated no longer. The United States entered the war against Germany and Austria on April 6, 1917.

Lois and Bill happened to be having lunch together that weekend in Manchester. They passed a newsstand on their way down the street and saw the headline. Bill bought a paper and read part of President Wilson's statement to Lois while deep concern and apprehension swirled through her. "It is a fearful thing to lead this great, peaceful people into the most terrible and disastrous of all wars, civilization itself seeming to be in the balance. But the right is more precious than peace and we shall fight for the things we have always carried nearest our hearts."[10]

Lois put her arms around Bill and held him tightly for many moments. He looked toward the mountains and remembered the stories of glory, honor, and patriotism his grandfather had etched in his mind and heart as a youngster. Now it was all about to become a reality.

The U.S. Congress quickly passed a defense bill sanctioning an expeditionary force of 175,000 men and authorizing an Officers Training Corps. Norwich cadets, like their West Point counterparts, were immediately called up for military duty. As a result, Bill became a soldier before he could graduate from the university. He went instead directly to the officers training camp in Plattsburgh, New York, and then for final training at Fort Monroe, Virginia, where he was commissioned a second lieutenant in the U.S. Army.

As an officer, Bill was given a choice of duties. Despite the great and heroic tradition of military service in the Wilson clan and his deep belief in patriotism, he chose to serve in the Coastal Artillery rather than the Army Infantry, as his friend Ebby and other classmates did. He feared being thrown into trench warfare. He had pangs of guilt over that decision for many years and admitted later on to some close friends, "The great upwellings of patriotism would overtake me one day—and the next day I would just be funked and scared to death. And I think that the thing that scared me most was that I might never live my life out with Lois, with whom I was in love."[11]

Bill kept that guilt locked inside, never sharing it with Lois until much later in life, always hoping she would never find out what a real coward he thought he was. It was one more blow to his already low self-esteem.

Less than a week after he was commissioned, he was transferred to Fort Rodman just outside New Bedford, Massachusetts, a camp filled with seasoned officers and noncoms along with gung-ho volunteers. There was a lot of drinking. Almost immediately, Bill's life changed. Little did he know it had changed forever. For this was where he discovered alcohol—

and the convincing voice inside his head that told him it was really not his enemy and, in fact, it could be his very, very good friend. That's what the "magic elixir" did for this young second lieutenant right from the start. With a few drinks, he no longer felt inferior.

Until now Bill had feared drinking, and for very good reasons. There was a long family history: booze had wrought terrible damage and havoc on some of the Wilsons including Bill's own father, Gilman. But now it was wartime. Despite being in the Coastal Artillery, there was every likelihood he would be sent to France to command an artillery unit there. Would he have the courage to face the enemy, or would he be shamed in front of his own men?

As a youngster, he had seen how drinking used to fortify Mark Whalon. Now here at Fort Rodman, all the men around him seemed to enjoy a few drinks now and then. It seemed to boost their morale and fill them with camaraderie. Maybe it was just a matter of being careful, very careful.

There was a wealthy family in New Bedford called the Grinnells. Practically every weekend they threw a party at their estate for the young officers like Bill who were away from their families, friends, and loved ones. His fellow "second looies" dragged him there with them one Saturday evening. At first he was the only wallflower in the whole Grinnell mansion. Then a very pretty young lady approached him with a "Bronx cocktail" in hand—a delightful mixture of gin, dry and sweet vermouth, and orange juice. She stood there holding the glass to his lips. In spite of all the warning signs, all his previous knowledge, all the factual evidence, and his deepest fears about drinking, he drank it. Then he had another—and another.

Before nine o'clock that evening, Bill Wilson was playing a hoedown on a borrowed violin for a wildly stomping crowd and patting every saucy young lady on the fanny as she passed by. His fellow officers had to carry him back to camp.

Since Fort Rodman was not too far from New York, Lois visited every few weeks or so—without a chaperone. As she once explained, "My mother and father's understanding and their trust in Bill and me were very unusual for that conventional era. I would sometimes get

strange looks from other parents accompanying their daughters when
they realized I was alone. Perhaps they thought I was a 'camp follower.'
Certainly Bill and I were sometimes tempted to go off alone, but then
we would remind each other we had our whole lives ahead of us even
in the face of this war."[12]

Lois was totally shocked one night when they went to dinner with his
fellow officers—she thought it might have been her second or third
visit—and Bill ordered a cocktail. He ordered one for her too. When Bill
noticed the dumbfounded look on his fiancée's face, he grinned that silly
grin and said: "This is what soldiers do during wartime I guess. Besides,
I only have a few once in awhile."[13]

She wanted to believe him. She almost did until the very next visit
when she happened to overhear some of his army buddies talking about
how they had to carry Bill home a few nights before and put him to bed.
Lois later admitted she didn't get very upset at the time because she
believed in her heart that if it ever got any worse, she would surely be
able to persuade him to return to his former abstinence. While Lois had
a glass of wine on social occasions at home, it was something she could
easily do without.

"Living with me," she later shared, partly with tongue in cheek,
"would be such an inspiration, I thought, such fun and so exciting that
I was sure he would not need alcohol. Talk about being smug and
self-centered."[14]

The year 1918 was fast approaching. America was fully engaged on
Europe's Western Front. Bill could be shipped out at almost any time
now. Before Christmas, he and Lois went to Clinton Street and sat down
with her parents. Bill said there were strong rumors he could be headed
for France by the end of February. They wanted to get married before
then—so they could at least have a short time together as husband and
wife. Clark and Matilda gave them their blessing. The wedding was set
for January 24.

All the young couple really wanted was a small, private affair. Dr.
Burnham would not hear of it—certainly not for his first and dearest daughter. Matilda agreed and even had Jewelson's Printery design special invitations
and rush them out to the guest list only two weeks before the wedding.

"My sister Barbara arranged for the church service, the flowers, and the music," Lois happily recalled. "Father hired the limousine and the caterer. The most difficult part was getting my wedding gown finished in time. My mother insisted on using the lace from my grandmother's old wedding dress she still kept in a trunk in the attic. It needed to be cleaned and caused the dressmaker fits. But somehow everything was ready in time."[15]

Elise was her maid of honor and Rogers, who had already joined the army himself at this point and later served in France, was Bill's best man. Apparently because the Burnhams had organized the entire affair without asking any advice from Emily Griffith, Bill's mother decided not to come. She called at the last minute saying she and her daughter Dorothy both had very bad colds and would not be able to attend.

Bill knew it was a lie. So did Lois. When she had first met "Mother Griffith" that day outside of Boston, Lois sensed that this stern, very controlling woman felt her son was too young to be considering marriage, especially to a lady almost four years his senior.

Lois recalled that when she received word Bill's mother wasn't coming, she asked Bill how he felt since he didn't appear to be very disappointed. He said he'd miss Dorothy but that's the way his mother was and Lois would just have to live with it. "I must admit I was grateful she moved to San Diego," Lois added.[16]

The only hitch at the wedding came during the reception, when Dr. Burnham saw his new son-in-law guzzling down a full glass of Scotch. The good doctor almost dropped his bifocals in the punch bowl. He said nothing about it then, but the incident remained embedded in his mind. It would one day return to haunt him.

"Not only was the reception crowded with family, friends, and special guests," Lois recalled, "but many of the soldiers from Fort Rodman came all the way down from Massachusetts to congratulate Bill and I. My mother remarked that Bill must have been the most popular Second Lieutenant on the post. It was really a wonderful wedding and a wonderful two-day honeymoon afterwards in Manhattan." Lois later discovered, however, that Bill always tried to "keep a lid on it" when they were together—that is, control his drinking. But that soon changed too.[17]

Rogers shipped out in February. Bill did not. It wasn't until early summer that he was sent to Fort Adams near Newport, Rhode Island, to await embarkation. Lois took a small apartment nearby.

It was a balmy evening in the beginning of August, just a matter of hours before Bill was to leave for England. They climbed to the top of a cliff overlooking the Atlantic Ocean and stood with their arms wrapped around each other. Lois would vividly remember that moonlit night. "We gazed out over the ocean. I was filled with so much pride in my husband. Yes, I was fearful too but somehow I just knew Bill was coming back to me and we would have a glorious future together."[18]

Bill boarded a troop train at eight o'clock that morning. As Lois waved farewell, she felt a sudden twinge near her midriff. She touched her stomach and thought she could sense a baby stirring in her womb.

Marching through the French countryside, Bill saw the devastation of war in stark reality as they passed the empty trenches where thousands of young men like himself had been blown to shreds by German shells or gassed to death by chemical warfare. As he stared at scarred helmets and damaged weapons strewn across the landscape, those pangs of guilt returned. But he hid his feelings well and his men came to respect him.

His artillery unit was assigned to a small mountain town miles from the front. Still, the constant fierce bombardment in the distance could be heard echoing through the hills and across the open countryside. But the young Vermont doughboy soon discovered that French wine could calm his nerves as well as New Bedford whiskey. The grateful townsfolk supplied him and his men with as much as they desired. So the young second lieutenant would sit at his gun emplacement, drink wine, and wash away his guilt. Before the bottle was empty, he was a heroic soldier once more defending his country against the enemy horde.

Back home, Lois approached her old friends at the Brooklyn YWCA about their program that sent women overseas to help care for the wounded. She was willing to do almost anything to feel close to Bill during this time of war. But then she had her first miscarriage. She was devastated. She had been planning to write Bill about her pregnancy, but now she would have to keep this terrible news all to herself until he came home. She wouldn't think of burdening him with it when he was already in such a dire situation and had always told her how much he wanted to have children. It took all of her mental stamina to sound cheerful in her letters to her husband, for inside she kept asking herself the question that many women dread—*What if I can never have children?*

When Lois recovered physically, she went directly to the national YWCA board with her request to go overseas, but they turned her down. Lois was deeply upset that Swedenborgians (her religious sect) and Unitarians were not considered Christians by the YWCA according to the letter they sent rejecting her services. She couldn't understand why a so-called "non-Christian" was allowed to instruct children at the YW yet not allowed to care for wounded soldiers as she wanted to do.[19]

So instead of going overseas Lois headed to New York Presbyterian Hospital for training in a new method of helping the seriously war-wounded recover. It was called occupational therapy. Upon graduation from the program, she was assigned to the "shell-shock ward" at Walter Reed Army Hospital in Washington, D.C. During her stay in Washington, Lois was reunited with some of her old friends from Packer Collegiate Institute who made her stay there more bearable. Talking later about her work at Walter Reed, she said, "The experience there was often heartbreaking, for I saw at close hand what war does to young men, and I kept wondering what it was doing to Bill."[20] Lois worried constantly even though she knew Bill was safe and far removed from the front. Before he shipped out, Lois had worked out a private code with him that was designed to get past the censors and let her know how he was and how close he was to the fighting. If he signed his letter "Billy" with the Y's tail going straight down, that meant he was safe and not involved in the action. If it had a curve, he was at the front. The Y's in his letters always had straight tails.

While Bill saw no action in France, he did keep his artillery unit constantly prepared with frequent practice firing sessions. His senior officers were very impressed with his attitude and readiness. The truth is, drinking was not interfering with his military career or his personal life at that time. Alcoholism is a progressive disease. The downward spiral leading almost inexorably to an ultimate disaster may take time. But it does lead there eventually and too often, much too soon.

Bill, in fact, was recommended for promotion and received a special commendation from his own unit just as the war was coming to a close.

The armistice was signed in November of 1918. Rogers came home before Christmas, but Bill didn't return from France until March of 1919. When the S.S. *Powhatan* steamed into New York Harbor that day and the troops disembarked amid a roaring throng there to welcome home their heroes, Bill ran straight into Lois's arms. They kissed and embraced until their lips and bodies ached from their love. Inside their spirits soared. Bill had returned home safely. The country was alive with promise. A whole new world awaited them.

Much to her chagrin, the first stop for Bill and his army buddies was a Manhattan saloon to celebrate. Lois wanted him all to herself at that moment, but, after all, they did have the whole rest of their lives ahead of them.

For Lois, the next few weeks Bill was home was like a second honeymoon. Although now working as a physical therapist at the Brooklyn Naval Hospital, she was given two weeks off with pay to be with her returning hero. Bill didn't want to talk about the war, so she didn't force him. In fact, they didn't talk very much at all. She only wanted to be with him. That was what made her happy—with one exception, the new habit he had picked up while overseas: smoking cigarettes. It was something she never got used to.

Bill, on the other hand, while glad to be back, was rather uncomfortable living with Lois at Clinton Street. He was eager to find some kind of job so they could have their own place. He was treated well by the family but felt rubbed the wrong way whenever his father-in-law made what Bill took as patronizing remarks such as: "You've got to get on with your life" or "It's about time to start thinking about a career."

Lois had been waiting for the right moment to tell Bill about her miscarriage. She was filled with anxiety. But it was difficult for them to find time alone at the house except in their bedroom where, of course, they had other things in mind. She finally drummed up the courage to tell him one evening as they walked together along a pathway near the Brooklyn Bridge.

"When you were overseas, I never wanted to write you about any bad news," she recalled saying as her heart beat so fast she had to stop walking in order to continue speaking. Bill just looked at her knowing she had something serious to tell him.

"I had a miscarriage while you were gone. Oh, Bill, I'm so sorry."

He took her into his arms as she began to weep very softly. She remembered him saying with that disarming smile: "Don't worry, Lo. We'll keep trying. That's the fun part. We'll have a dozen kids, you'll see."

Then, not wanting to say it, she let the words out. "But what if I can never have a baby?" she murmured.

Bill looked into her eyes. His voice was filled with emotion. "Lois, all I need is you. You're all I ever wanted. All I'll ever need."[21]

They embraced for a long time. Then they continued walking arm in arm along the pathway by the river. Lois remembered how relieved she was after telling him and how deeply loved she felt at that special moment. If only it could have lasted longer.

Only a few days after Lois had resumed her job at the naval hospital, she came home early one afternoon to find her mother beside herself. Barbara was there in the kitchen trying to calm her down.

"They're in the basement and I can't get them out," Matilda kept saying. "Someone has to get them out. They're smashing everything to pieces."[22] Lois rushed down into the dusty cellar where her father stored all the wine and liquor he was given by his "GP's"—grateful patients. Bill and her brother Rogers, now also home from the war, had raided the stash. They were both uproariously drunk and were making a shambles of the place. Broken bottles were scattered everywhere. Lois had never seen her brother so intoxicated before and never saw him that way afterward. With Bill, it was no longer a surprise.

She managed somehow to coax her husband upstairs and into a cold shower. It took both Barbara and Katherine to get their brother into the bathroom and into a tub of cold water—fully clothed. The conquering heroes became so deathly sick from mixing bourbon with wine, and Scotch with gin, that Lois and her siblings worked for more than an hour to clean up the mess. Matilda blamed it on their war experiences and quickly forgave them, as did the rest of the family.

Fortunately, Clark was busy at the hospital at the time. While no

one told him of the incident, Lois suspected her father knew something
had gone on the next time he checked his liquor supply. But he never
said a word.

Lois was fearful Bill's spree had something to do with her losing their
baby. He swore it didn't—he and Rog had simply started swapping war
stories over a few drinks, got steamed at the "Krauts," and began throwing the empties against the basement walls as if they were hand grenades.
He appeared so humbled that she simply let it pass.

The incident did accomplish one thing, however. It got Bill looking
much harder for a job so they could move out of the house on Clinton
Street. He found one a few weeks later as a bookkeeper for the New York
Central Railroad at $105 a month. It wasn't much, but between that and
Lois's monthly salary of $150, they were able to rent a small furnished
apartment on State Street, only a few blocks from Clinton. They were
finally on their own.

It wasn't long before Lois realized how much Bill hated that job. There
was nothing creative, nothing challenging, nothing rewarding about it. It
gave him an excuse to stop at the corner saloon almost every night before
coming home. But soon that would end, she thought, because Prohibition
was on its way. It was something she now eagerly awaited.

The temperance movement that had been growing in this country
since the late 1800s, driven by social and religious activists well organized
by the Woman's Christian Temperance Union, finally led to the passage
of the Eighteenth Amendment to the Constitution on January 16,
1919—only two months before Bill arrived home from Europe.
However, it wouldn't take effect until February of 1920. It was now
almost Christmas. Lois had only two more months to wait.

Prohibition would last fourteen long years, but it stopped almost
no one from getting a drink. Instead, it led to speakeasies in every
neighborhood, bathtub gin and bad whiskey, and the likes of Al
Capone creating an era of crime, murder, and mayhem. And it never
once kept Bill Wilson from finding booze whenever he wanted it—and
soon, whenever he needed it.

Lois remained encouraging no matter how depressed Bill became at
times. He quit his job at the New York Central Railroad and began

bouncing from one dead-end job to another, growing more and more discouraged. It was those depressions that concerned Lois the most; they would be with her husband on and off for years. She would try to lift his spirits by reminding him of the dreams they shared at Emerald Lake and how Grandpa Griffith always said he could do anything he set his mind to. She would nestle him in her arms and tell him she was behind him and always would be, no matter what.

Then, much to her surprise and delight, Bill came home one evening with that big, silly grin back on his face. He had finally found a terrific new job, one that offered him a great future. He had been hired as an investigator for the U.S. Fidelity and Guaranty Bank to look into defaults of stock exchange firms on Wall Street. And, he proudly boasted, his experience as an army officer clinched the position for him.

Bill had been enamored with the promise of Wall Street ever since he first met Frank Shaw. Suddenly, here was the chance to get his start in the investment community even though it would be through what he considered the rather boring banking industry. The opportunity began to spark those dreams of wealth and position once again and put that old fire back in his belly. Then, almost as an afterthought, Lois recalled, he said, "Since this new job pays a lot more, I decided to enroll in some night courses at Brooklyn Law School . . . if that's okay with you."[23]

Not only could Bill afford law school, they could now afford that larger apartment they had been eyeing on Amity Street and furnish it the way Lois wanted.

She was thrilled. They went out to dinner that night and celebrated. Bill didn't drink. She felt in her heart that this was the turning point in their life together. Now all they needed was a baby to make it complete.

The pressure Lois felt to have children didn't necessarily come from Bill—at least not at this point. It came more from watching those around her raise growing families. Bill's sister, Dorothy, for example, had married a doctor, Leonard Strong, and was now living in Tarrytown, New York. She already had one child and another on the way. And Elise and Frank Shaw were constantly inviting them to visit their lovely home on Long Island and see their growing brood of two girls and a boy. Even with Bill's prodding, Lois was finding excuses not to go.

Things only got worse when Lois found herself pregnant again—and less than a month later, having another miscarriage. This time it had been an ectopic pregnancy: the fetus was growing in one of her fallopian tubes. She required hospitalization for a few days before going home.

"We stayed again with my family at Clinton Street for some days since Bill was working and going to school and I needed someone looking after me," she recalled. "I remember lying in bed staring at the ceiling. For some silly reason I was afraid to look into Bill's eyes for fear of seeing his reproach. How foolish. He was nothing but loving and supportive. I was my own worst enemy. I never realized then that it was my pride that was causing me so much pain."[24]

Bill and the specialist Dr. Burnham had recommended kept assuring Lois that everything would be fine, that nature could sometimes be cruel for a while but then could reward one beyond measure. So after a few months, she and Bill started working on forgetting the past and facing the future with hope and optimism.

Lois began to thrive on the newfound energy and excitement flowing through her husband. He loved his investigative position with the Wall Street bank and was doing very well in his law courses. One weekend while reading the newspapers together, they both noticed a *New York Times* article concerning a competition Edison Laboratories had initiated to find a few "outstanding young men of all around abilities" to assist and support the activities of Thomas Alva Edison.

What an opportunity, Lois thought, to work with the famous inventor himself. She challenged Bill to take the test. She teased him so much that "as a lark" he accepted her challenge. He admitted later how awestruck he was that day in New Jersey when, after finishing the exam at the company's lab, he met the famous man himself and shook his hand.

A few weeks went by. Then a month or so. They heard nothing. Then late one night, only a short time after Bill had arrived home from law school, their doorbell rang and a reporter and a photographer from the *New York Times* came charging up the stairs. The results of the competition were to be announced in the morning. William G. Wilson was one of the winners.[25]

They snapped his picture with his half-asleep yet glowing wife nestled in his arms. They asked him a million questions about his background, his family, and his plans. He was a hot news story: another young genius inventor in the making.

Bill enjoyed the inner satisfaction of accomplishing such a feat, the resulting notoriety, and especially the pride in his wife's eyes. But before he left for work that morning, he had already made up his mind about his future direction. He had talked it over with Lois, and she was behind him all the way.

It was 1923. A stock market boom was just beginning. Right or wrong, he would build a career for himself on Wall Street—and maybe invest someday in Thomas Alva Edison's next great invention.

Bill was twenty-eight now and establishing a reputation for himself as one of the most energetic and innovative investigators at U.S. Fidelity. He was not only uncovering fraud behind some stock defaults but discovering how it began and what it was costing naive investors.

One morning while working on a case in his office, he received a phone call from his old and dear friend Ebby Thacher. He hadn't seen his close pal in more than two years, not since the last reunion they attended together at Norwich University shortly after returning from Europe. Ebby had been working for the family's cast-iron stove business in Albany and said he almost died of boredom. A wealthy cousin hooked him up with Baylis and Company, a small New York stock brokerage firm, and he was now plying his wares on Wall Street. They had lunch the following day and for several days after.

As they chatted about old times and new times, Bill shared with his boyhood chum the facts he was uncovering while working at the bank and his rationale for all the defaults and fraud in the marketplace. He said his law courses were a great help. People just didn't know enough about the companies they were investing in, he told Ebby. It was a crapshoot. People conducting business ventures could get away with murder because nobody was looking over their shoulders and demanding the factual information behind the financial reports they issued on occasion. There should be regular and specific analytical reports, and perhaps Bill was the one to start the ball rolling.

The truth is, back in 1923, there was no such animal on Wall Street as a financial research analyst to meet with companies, discuss their operations in detail, walk the production line, "kick the tires," and then write factual reports for prospective investors to review. Nor was there a Securities and Exchange Commission to oversee corporate financial reporting, auditing methods, and public stock offerings. Bill Wilson was far ahead of his time in recognizing the need for such valuable tools to protect the investing community.

Ebby was impressed, really impressed. He suggested his friend try out his thoughts on some of the bigwigs at the leading investment firms. He felt confident Bill was onto something. But months went by and Bill still hesitated.

Strolling together one weekend, Lois became very excited when Bill told her about his ideas and his conversations with Ebby. She immediately suggested he see Frank Shaw, who was now one of the senior partners at J.K. Rice & Company, a substantial Wall Street stockbroker. She even offered to call Elise, but Bill thought it better to keep it strictly business and do it on his own.

He tried to reach Frank for an appointment the following week, but he was out of town and wouldn't return until Friday. That's the day Bill found himself in Shaw's large, ostentatious office overlooking New York Harbor and the Statue of Liberty. The young investigator was more than impressed. Frank sat behind his huge oak desk and watched Bill gather moxie as he prattled on in a rather self-serving manner. He talked about the need to clean up the "Street" and open up the corporate information spigot so investors could find out exactly how well companies were doing in terms of current growth and earnings and future prospects.

The face of the bigwig at Rice & Company began turning slightly pink as the blood moved slowly from his neck to his clenched jaw. When Frank finally spoke, he spoke in a defensive if not belligerent manner.

He wanted to know how, after only three years at U.S. Fidelity and Guaranty Bank, Bill already had all the answers. He suggested that he first understand the questions. Bill quickly realized that Frank Shaw had taken everything he said as a personal affront and an indictment of the way his company ran its business. As Shaw walked toward his office door and opened it, he suggested Bill think more about his ideas, get more experience under his belt, put more information in his portfolio, and then come back for another chat.[26]

It goes without saying that Bill Wilson left Rice & Company with his tail between his legs. He didn't believe he was wrong, but he knew he had approached Shaw the wrong way. That made him very angry—not so much at Shaw as at himself. He called Ebby. They met at a nearby speakeasy that afternoon to talk things over.

That same week, Lois had seen her doctor. She thought she might be pregnant again. The tests confirmed it.

"I was scared to death about telling Bill," she recalled. "What if it should happen again, was all I could think about. This was my third pregnancy."[27]

She decided to wait until the weekend. She reasoned that Bill worked hard all day and came home too late and too tired from Brooklyn Law School for any serious conversation—except for Friday when he had no school. She would make a nice dinner, tell him the news, and they would have the whole weekend together to assure each other that everything was going to be all right.

It was around six o'clock when Bill arrived home for dinner. He had Ebby Thacher with him. They were both very drunk.

5

The Open Road to Success

❧

*B*ILL CHOSE THE MOST ELEGANT AND EXPENSIVE RESTAURANT IN midtown Manhattan for the occasion. The salad was crisp, the steak tender, the service excellent, and the baked Alaska a delightful treat. While the evening was to celebrate their expectant parenthood, Lois knew her husband was trying at the same time to make up for his boorish behavior over the past several days.

He had told her all about his disastrous meeting with Frank Shaw, his resultant anger and depression, and his deep disappointment over royally screwing up a great opportunity. He feared he had lost a strong Wall Street ally and perhaps even Frank Shaw's friendship. Lois squeezed his hand and assured him that couldn't be the case, not with Frank. He wasn't like that.

Still, as her humbled husband confessed, even this disaster was no reason to come home drunk three nights in a row, spoil the whole weekend for Lois, and rain on the parade of her exciting news. He promised it would never happen again.

They kissed and toasted with their water glasses. "The third time's a charm," he kept saying. "You'll see, Lo. The third time's a charm."

They made love again that night and Bill fell asleep in her arms. She stroked his hair and touched his cheek, hoping and praying that he was right—that the third time nature, as the doctor had said, would reward them beyond measure. Two nights later, Bill came home unusually late from school. He tiptoed into the bedroom trying not to wake her. When he crawled under the covers, she pretended to be asleep. Her heart sank when she smelled the liquor on his breath.

A little over a month into her pregnancy, Lois's doctor strongly suggested she request a leave of absence from her job in order to take every precaution possible. Her father agreed and came by regularly to check on her. The leave may have been good for her physically but perhaps not so good emotionally. Every twinge, every sensation would raise her anxiety. Lois simply had too much time on her hands to sit around and think—not only about the baby but also about what Bill might be doing at the moment.[1]

Why was he continuing to drink? she would ask herself. He still loved his job. He told her so whenever she asked. And he was still attending law school although now he was missing some classes, saying he was stuck at the office or at a late business meeting. Bill was a terrible liar. Even he realized Lois knew he was at some speakeasy with Ebby or with another bunch of hard-drinking friends.

What was happening to him? What was happening to them? Lois would sit by the window and recall the promises they made when they were courting back in Vermont. They would never lose their love of nature, their love of the outdoors, they swore to each other. Those weekends before she became pregnant again, when they hiked in the Palisades or rented a boat and sailed along the Hudson River, filled them with such peace, joy, and contentment. It was so puzzling to her that on those treks, Bill never seemed to think about alcohol.

Perhaps the combination of the fresh air and strenuous exercise created some special inner potion that took away the need for booze. Because when he returned to the city, trudging those dim chasms of Wall Street, that potion seemed to disappear and he was looking for a drink. And it was no longer just one drink, or even a couple. A couple always led to a couple more. If only they could both be back in the countryside right now, she would sigh.

Maybe, just maybe, she would then say to herself, hoping and praying she was right, this time they would have a strong, healthy baby, and the excitement of fatherhood would prove to be the most effective potion of all to quench Bill's desire for alcohol.[2]

Little did Lois realize that her husband was struggling himself with the same questions at the very same time—mainly, why couldn't he simply stop drinking so much? He always started with such good intentions. He would only have a few. This time he meant it, he'd insist. But those few always seemed to turn into a few more and then one too many—and he was off to the races. Even that hurt look on Lois's face when he staggered in past midnight couldn't seem to slow him down.

He had to shake off this Frank Shaw mess, he kept telling himself. He'd sit down and put together a new and more positive spin on his company research idea. That's what he'd do. Then he would present it to some other heavy hitters on the Street. Once they backed him and things got rolling, those damn speakeasies could take all their damn booze and flush it down the damn toilet because he wouldn't need it anymore. He'd be on top of the world. But in the meantime, maybe he'd have just one more for the road.

It was now May of 1924. As the weeks passed, Lois grew tired of sitting around reading books or talking on the telephone. One afternoon she decided she had to stop this moping business. She was feeling a lot better, she told herself, and there hadn't been any twinges or strange sensations in quite a while. Standing in the parlor, she ran her finger across the nearby lamp table. It was covered with dust. So were the lamp shade, the coffee table, and the old rocking chair she inherited from Aunt Emma. Before long she was dusting and cleaning and feeling useful again.

The pains didn't start until she reached for some towels in a closet above the kitchen sink. Lois grabbed her side and sank into a chair at the kitchen table. Then she felt another pain, sharp and stabbing like the first. She tried to take a deep breath and couldn't. Beads of perspiration broke out on her forehead. When the next pain hit, she decided to call Bill. The phone was on the cabinet next to her.

Bill wasn't in his office. She was told he was out at a meeting. She called Ebby. He was gone for the day. She glanced at the clock above the stove. It was almost four thirty. She tried to stand. There was a slight twinge, and then nothing. She moved to the sink and filled a glass with water. It cooled her insides going down. The pains seemed to be subsiding.

Lois decided to wait until after six, when Bill was due at Brooklyn Law School. She switched on the radio, but even the music and occasional news report didn't help pass the time. It simply dragged on.

By six fifteen the pains had grown more intense. She called the school but Bill was not in class. As she hung up the phone, she suddenly realized she was bleeding. Trying to control her emotions, Lois immediately called her father. He had just arrived home.

A half hour later, Lois was in an ambulance on her way to Skene Sanitarium, a women's hospital in Brooklyn where Dr. Burnham was on the staff. The specialist he brought in quickly discovered that a second ectopic pregnancy had burst a fallopian tube. Lois was rushed into surgery. The surgical team also found an ovarian cyst and was forced to remove her ovaries and both fallopian tubes. While they left her uterus intact to help maintain Lois's normal sexual feelings and desires, her worst fears of never having children were now a reality.[3]

Bill staggered into their apartment well past midnight. He was confused when he discovered Lois wasn't home. *Perhaps she had gone to see her mother*, was the first thought that entered his clouded mind. But she'd never stay out so late, not in her condition. He put on some coffee and waited. He finally concluded something must be wrong. Despite the late hour, he called Clinton Street. Katherine gave him the news.

Dr. Burnham was still at Skene Sanitarium when his somewhat-disheveled son-in-law arrived, still slightly inebriated even after several cups of black coffee. Being a direct man, and now a very weary and worried one, Clark Burnham tore into Bill with all the anger and frustration a caring father can generate under such circumstances. He told him his wife could have bled to death waiting for the likes of him to come home from one of his damn speakeasies. He castigated him for his carousing and his total irresponsibility with regard to Lois, who deserved far better than she was getting.

Finally, when the good doctor gained control of himself, he explained frankly and fully the medical procedures that were required and then stormed out of the hospital leaving Bill to contemplate what to do next.

As he watched his father-in-law exit the dim, quiet lobby, the trembling young Wall Street want-to-be was shocked by the very next thought that jumped into his head. While he knew this was certainly neither the time nor the place, what he wanted right now more than anything was another drink. He fought off the insane impulse and went looking instead for a nurse.[4]

Upstairs, Lois was beginning to wake and was about to face her cruel reality. When asked later in life how she felt while lying in that hospital bed trying to accept such tragic news, Lois sadly replied, "When I was told about the surgery and that I could never have a baby, I cried for a long, long time. I didn't want to see Bill at first. Naturally he thought I was angry because he wasn't there when I needed him. But it wasn't that at all. My feelings were all mixed up and I didn't know what to say to him. I knew how disappointed he would be."[5]

Bill sat in the waiting room for hours, smoking and drinking glasses of cold water. Sometimes he paced up and down, filled with guilt over what he had done. But mostly he was torn by his love and concern for his beloved Lois, who didn't deserve all this pain and anguish. When he shared these feelings with her later, it helped lift her spirits. But now all Bill wanted to know was when he could see his wife. He was told she was still recovering from the ether; perhaps he should go home and come back later. He refused. He would wait. He would be here when she was able to see him.

It was around dawn when the nurse on duty, a motherly woman in her fifties, entered Lois's room, saw she was awake, and asked if she needed anything. Lois needed to talk.

"This kind and lovely nurse helped me to realize what I already knew in my heart," Lois recalled. "I had done nothing wrong to prevent our having children. She said I had to accept this burden as God's will even if I couldn't understand it or agree with it, and that none of this was my fault. Still, somehow I could not help feeling guilty. I came to realize later this was one reason why I didn't blame Bill so much when he continued to drink more and more."[6] Shortly afterward, Bill walked nervously into her room, his head down, tears welling in his eyes. They didn't speak about what had happened right away. He just sat there at her bedside holding her hand. After all, what words could adequately express what they both felt at that moment? A moment that seemed like the end of something for Lois and posed a bleak, bewildering fog for Bill. How could they pick up the pieces, find a new direction, and move on?

It was several months before Lois regained her strength. It was really her emotional lassitude, which she later described as "self-pity," that prevented her from recovering more quickly. Bill took two weeks off from work and they traveled to Vermont hoping, perhaps, to find something there that would rekindle their life, spark the kind of hope and joy they always found in the mountains and at the lake. Grandpa Griffith passed away while they were in East Dorset, which only added to their sadness.

The next six or seven months dragged by. Lois went back to work at the Brooklyn Naval Hospital, and Bill continued his sporadic drinking, somehow managing to hold on to his job at the bank. The evening he took his final exams at Brooklyn Law School he was so intoxicated he couldn't read most of the questions. He justified his failure by telling himself he never wanted to be a lawyer anyway.

One night in early March of 1925, Bill came home so drunk he fell asleep on the parlor couch with all his clothes on. Lois couldn't get him up and into bed so she simply threw a blanket over him and put a water bucket next to the couch just in case. Once too often he had thrown up on the floor and the furniture before he could reach the bathroom.

As Lois got up at about seven the next morning, she heard Bill in the kitchen making coffee. When she entered, he was at the window, smoking a cigarette and staring out into the street. He looked terrible—red-eyed, pale, and hungover. As she later recalled, he reached out his hand to her and, almost pleading, whispered in a hoarse voice, "Lo, let's get out of this. I've been thinking. This idea I have . . . it can change everything, I know it can. Nobody's ready to back me yet because they don't understand. They can't see it. But . . . would you take the chance with me, Lo? I finally realized . . . I just can't go on like this anymore."[7]

They sat at the kitchen table and, over coffee, Bill outlined his plan. He wanted to travel the country with her. He would visit companies, get on the inside, find out what was really going on, and write reports for Wall Street investors who could then put their money into sure winners, not crapshoots.

He felt certain that once some Wall Street big shots saw he could deliver cold, hard facts about a company's growth and earnings potential, they'd pay handsomely for such information. Even Frank Shaw would then understand what Bill had been trying to tell him all along.

First, Bill would buy a few shares of stock in the companies he wanted to investigate, just enough to give him an entrée as a stockholder. This way he would have access to top management. He would also go in the back door and talk to the workers who knew all about the quality of the things they were producing. Then he'd check on the firm's reputation in the community and within its industry. By the time he was finished, his investigative skills would have gleaned all the in-depth knowledge any investor would need to make an intelligent investment decision.

As he talked on and on, the pallor left his face. His enthusiasm and excitement became infectious. Lois could feel her insides coming back to life, her hope for the future rising, her belief in her man being restored. There was no doubt that Bill absolutely believed everything he was saying. What intrigued Lois the most, and what finally wiped away any hesitation, was that this wild excursion would take them out of the city and away from the speakeasies. They would be together in the country once more where the fresh air and exercise could work its magic, as it had before, and Bill wouldn't find it necessary to drink. Lois went to work late that morning and gave the hospital her two-week notice.

Next, the soon-to-be cross-country explorers sat down and added up their assets. They had a little less than a thousand dollars. That would get them started and, if need be, they could pick up odd jobs along the way to supplement the kitty. But first they would require transportation, something reliable but inexpensive.

That weekend found Lois and Bill at the army surplus depot in Fort Hamilton, Brooklyn. They spotted a used but sturdy Harley-Davidson motorcycle with a large sidecar attached. Bill laughed and guessed that by the size of the sidecar it probably served a general or at least a bird colonel. Anyway, he was sure he could whip the motorcycle into shape in no time. They also purchased two canteens, a kerosene stove, and a passel of army blankets. The tents were all too small or in disrepair, so that important piece of equipment was left up to Lois's ingenuity, as were many other things. Their preparations for the trip and her eagerness for the outdoor life were things she loved to talk about later on in life.

Lois purchased a tent from Sears Roebuck. It had a canvas floor and a net over the entrance to keep out mosquitoes, and it stood seven feet high and seven feet wide. She stitched in a window with netting for ventilation.

For sleeping, Lois's mother helped her sew together seven army blankets, which gave the couple a variety of "warmth" layers for whenever the weather turned cold or hot. They rolled the blankets together with a light kapok mattress into a small bundle for easy storage on the Harley.

When it came to packing food, toiletries, pajamas, towels, and other miscellaneous items, Lois's ingenuity paid off again. She made storage containers out of black oilcloth and lined them with rubber and tape to make them waterproof. She even made watertight coveralls for her and Bill and oil-silk liners to protect everything they took with them.

Then Lois added with a sparkle in her eye, "We felt well-prepared for anything. Crazy or not, it was fun to anticipate the open road and unknown adventures ahead."[8]

Bill managed to squeeze in four huge Moody's manuals on industrial companies. They contained general information about the firms he planned to investigate. For starters, he selected the General Electric plant in Schenectady, New York, and Giant Portland Cement in Egypt, Pennsylvania. He bought several shares in each company before leaving.

A week prior to their departure, Bill drove the motorcycle out to Prospect Park, Brooklyn, where there was still a great deal of open space. His partner was in the bumpy sidecar next to him. Did Lois remember that this was the neighborhood where a young doctor named Clark Burnham began his medical career some forty-one years earlier? She never said. The goal this day was to teach her how to handle the Harley-Davidson since traveling so many miles with only one experienced driver would be quite a chore. Lois had already driven an automobile, but the thought of sitting directly on top of the hot, noisy engine of a motorcycle gave her pause. But not for long.

Bill coaxed her into the driver's seat and, snuggling behind her, he carefully explained all the controls—the gas, the brake, the gear shift, and the speedometer. Then he revved it up and drove very slowly in wide circles, gradually letting her take control of the steering. When it was her turn to solo, those old Clark Burnham genes took over. Once Lois felt certain the engine below wouldn't burn her pants off, she was off and running. Her husband watched with pride and, of course, with that silly grin on his face, as Lois drove in wider and wider circles and at faster and faster speeds.[9]

On April 16, 1925, Lois and Bill Wilson headed for America's heartland, bound and determined to put all the pieces back together, find the joy and contentment they had lost, and finally realize the great dreams Lois always knew her Bill was capable of achieving. And as they left that day, Lois Wilson was in the driver's seat.

Roaring away from the crowded streets of Brooklyn into the open country before them, these bold "pioneers" could feel deep in their souls the great and exciting adventure that lay ahead.

It was the era of Bonnie and Clyde and Rudolph Valentino, a period that would see talking motion pictures and the phonograph record. They would find a vibrant land exploding with new energy and new industry, one that would produce vast cement highways and awesome power-producing dams.

Lois and Bill Wilson were entering a new world, part of a new generation. They could smell it in the air and sense its grand potential throughout every tingling nerve in their bodies.

That momentous day as Lois climbed into the driver's seat, pulled down her goggles, and revved up the engine, she felt the world belonged to her and Bill alone and that whatever lay ahead could only be magnificent.[10]

Riding a motorcycle without a windshield in early April in upstate New York can be very invigorating, if not bone-chilling. Perhaps that's why, when the trunk rack came loose less than fifty miles from home, neither of these "explorers" was too unhappy about stopping to fix it. They were somewhere outside of Poughkeepsie at the time, so they decided to camp for the night. Bill set up the tent, then belted the trunk rack to a post under the front seat. Meanwhile, Lois cooked them a nice supper. After a cup of coffee, they crawled under the army blankets and made love for the first time in months. They both had a very sound sleep.

Since Bill's first target was the General Electric Company, they head-ed straight for Schenectady the next day, arriving early in the afternoon. A dairy farmer by the name of Jake Morowski gave them permission to camp in his pasture. While Bill pitched the tent under a large oak tree, Lois found some old boards next to the barn and asked Morowski if she could have them. No problem, he said. She and Bill used them to build a small table and bench to cook and eat on. Lois said later she could have spent a lifetime living in that beautiful open field under that gorgeous oak tree. But soon Bill was about his business.

The very next day he put on his best suit (actually the only one he brought along), reviewed Moody's comments about GE, and then head-ed due east for the plant. His primary interest in the company, one of the early producers of electric generation equipment, was the new line of "futuristic" products rumored to be under development.

Identifying himself as a "significant investor," he was cordially received by a staffer in the personnel department. However, when Bill asked for a tour of the production facilities and research laboratory, he was given a company brochure and a stiff good-bye handshake.

Bill arrived back at the Morowski farm quite discouraged. Lois could tell. She tried to cheer him up with the fresh apple pie she helped Mrs. Morowski bake that day. She told him about all the fun she had watching the cows being milked and chasing some strays away from their tent—beautiful little calves she'd love to take home as pets. Her husband sensed she might enjoy the life of a dairy farmer but he knew instinctively this type of rugged existence was not for him. Lois contin-ued her chatter over dinner, telling Bill about her meeting that afternoon with a Mr. Goldfoot who owned the dairy farm right next to the Morowskis. It just so happened that Mr. Goldfoot's two sons worked for General Electric since, with wives and families, they were not able to sustain them all with the farm. The detail about "working for General Electric" raised Bill's eyebrows.

The next morning, the young investigator paid a call on Mr. Goldfoot. It was about a week later when he was invited to join the farmer and his boys at Dawson's Cafe, which happened to be one of the two speakeasies in Schenectady. Bill told Lois they'd be having a bite to eat so she needn't bother cooking him supper. He didn't want to worry her unnecessarily—about the speakeasy, that is.

That night turned into the kind of colossal event Bill Wilson would never forget. First he bought a few rounds of beers, having one himself, naturally. Then, after convincing the Goldfoots he once worked for Thomas Edison, he said he still was not permitted to reveal the fantastic inventions on the old man's drawing board. Feeling challenged, the farm boys drove Bill out to the GE research laboratory where they worked and showed him the "fantastic things" they were involved in.

Bill couldn't believe his eyes. There, stretched out before him was a display of equipment and prototype devices only hinted at in science magazines—experiments in sound motion pictures, console sets, electric phonographs, magnets, and all sorts of shortwave communications. In less than an hour, he had the inside track on what General Electric was soon to become.

It was after one in the morning when Bill returned to the campsite. His Harley backfired as he approached, startling Lois, who was still awake and very tense from hearing strange noises all night. Her husband was so excited that he accidentally stumbled into the tent. He could hardly begin to tell Lois all he had just seen. As he came close, she smelled the beer on his breath. She remembered shouting:

"You're drunk! After all your promises, you're drunk again!"

Bill was taken aback. He knew he wasn't. He tried hard to convince her that all he had was a few beers—that he wasn't staggering or slurring his words. He was just excited, that's all.

"Honest, Lo," he kept saying. "It was just to prime the pump. Just business. I bought the Goldfoots some drinks so they would take me into the plant. Sure I had a few myself but I know now that if it's just for business, I can handle it. Look at me."[11]

As she calmed down, she could see he really wasn't intoxicated by the booze, only by the excitement of what he had just discovered. After a few moments, she became excited along with him. *Maybe he's right*, she thought to herself. *If he can control his drinking like this, then maybe everything will be okay.* She had met other men on Wall Street who drank with business associates and then went home to their families. Her own father drank occasionally on weekends. Perhaps Bill had finally found a way to control it himself. Yet those nagging butterflies still remained in the pit of her stomach, spurred on by a few more "slips" he would have along the way.

The following day Bill sent a brief note to Frank Shaw about his look inside GE's research laboratory. Lois helped him with the letter. He requested a meeting to present a detailed report. Then he broke the news to Lois that they would be moving on, the next stop being Egypt, Pennsylvania, just outside Allentown. She was a bit disappointed. But they said their farewells to the Morowskis and Goldfoots, packed up, and went noisily on their way with Lois again at the wheel and Bill attempting to study his Moody's manual in the bumpy sidecar.

They were about twenty miles from Egypt when ominous black clouds began building in the skies ahead. They decided to stop and camp in a nearby field next to a running stream. Late that evening, the thunderstorms crashed and crackled overhead. It rained those proverbial cats and dogs for the next three days. Lois described the "Noah's Ark" event in her memoirs.

This was the first real test of their new tent, especially its guaranteed canvas floor, and it was a dandy test. When camping in Vermont, they had always dug a ditch around their army pup tent for drainage, but naively they imagined this to be unnecessary with their miraculous new one—that they could even pitch it in a puddle and remain dry. They soon learned the truth, however.

Feeling the dampness seeping through the floor, Lois awakened Bill. Donning their waterproof zippered coveralls, they bravely launched forth into the pouring rain and discovered that the tent was standing in a small lake, three inches deep, in a claylike hollow. But the canvas floor hadn't done too badly after all . . . that is, if they didn't mind sleeping in a little water.

Sponging up the puddles and pushing a mass of ferns underneath to raise the floor off the ground, they then dug a drainage ditch around the outside despite all that muddy clay and deep water. Inside finally, a bunch of old newspapers kept them fairly dry the rest of the night and the ensuing nights.

In spite of all the problems, Lois was delighted that the homemade window she had cut and sewn into the tent had not leaked one single drop during the entire storm.[12]

With the country's economy starting to boom and the automobile industry pouring out affordable cars, Bill knew what a great demand there would be for concrete roads, bridges, and other such infrastructure. He had studied every cement manufacturer listed in his manuals before finally zeroing in on Giant Portland Cement Company, which was listed on the small Philadelphia Stock Exchange. He felt its shares were exceedingly cheap when compared to its growth potential.

By now, Lois and Bill's assets were running low with all the initial expenses for the Harley-Davidson, the camping equipment, the special clothing, and the shares Bill had purchased in his targeted companies. They needed to replenish their kitty.

This fit right in with Bill's latest scheme. What better way to get inside information than by actually being on the inside? So they pitched their tent less than a mile from the cement company—this time on top of a lovely hill where the rain wasn't likely to gather—and Bill rode over to the plant and was hired on the spot.

"From our campsite," Lois recalled, "we could see in all four directions. This part of Pennsylvania has fascinating steep hills like green chocolate drops and little toy villages hidden in narrow valleys where pretty brooks run all the way down into green pastures. I must admit, however, that I did have a little difficulty with some of those long Dutch names painted on the signboards in town."[13] While Bill snooped around the plant during his work breaks, Lois found a job with a couple named Baer who had a large vegetable farm nearby. Mostly Lois cared for Mrs. Baer's three little girls, which she enjoyed immensely.

Working at Giant Portland, the undercover investigator was gathering a great deal of vital information: how much coal they were burning to produce a barrel of cement, what quantities they were shipping each day, and how the installation of some brand-new expensive equipment was about to greatly increase production, reducing the cost to less than a dollar per barrel. This would give the company a tremendous competitive edge.

Then one day, Bill Wilson showed up at the front entrance to Giant

Portland as a "significant investor" dressed in his best and only suit instead of driving up as usual to the employees' gate in his coveralls and cap. He confronted a stunned management trio with the facts he had uncovered and, before he was ushered out, he could tell by their faces and their off-the-cuff comments that his findings were absolutely correct. After visiting a few more companies in Pennsylvania, he and Lois headed back to New York.

A month later, Bill was at J.K. Rice & Company, standing in the boardroom before Frank Shaw and the firm's major partners. He made a brilliant presentation. Lois had helped him polish it. He talked about what he had discovered at General Electric and at Giant Portland. On the basis of his reports, the firm purchased five thousand shares each of GE and Portland for starters, and bought thousands more after that. They also purchased several hundred shares for Bill, put him on the payroll, and authorized him to draw additional funds to buy more shares as they rose in value.

Bill left the Rice & Company boardroom that afternoon with Frank Shaw's arm around his shoulder. He was suddenly a rising star on Wall Street. And before the year was over, the Giant Portland stock that had been purchased for $20 per share had risen to over $75 per share. General Electric did equally as well.

There were other companies the firm now wanted Bill to investigate—American Cyanamid and the Aluminum Company of America, for instance, as well as certain steel and coal mining interests. But first Lois and Bill had some important family matters to attend to, along with getting the shakes and rattles out of their mile-weary Harley-Davidson by putting on a new set of tires and getting it completely overhauled for the next leg of their excursion.

Lois's mother Matilda hadn't been feeling very well, and Matilda didn't want to write her for fear of cutting their journey short. Her daughter spent almost a month with her at Emerald Lake that summer, and by the time she left, Matilda convinced her she was feeling much better. If Dr. Burnham seemed pleased when he heard all about Bill's success, it was mainly because Lois convinced him that his son-in-law wasn't drinking nearly as much. In fact, Bill was still managing to control his alcohol intake at that time.

Dorothy Strong, Bill's sister, also hadn't been well since the birth of her last child. While Lois was at the lake, Bill spent ten days with his sister and his brother-in-law, Leonard, at their home in Tarrytown. He and Dr. Strong had formed a close friendship, one that would be a great help to Bill during his heavy drinking days.

Also, Bill's mother's husband, Dr. John Strobel, had called and asked for his assistance with a pending legal matter in New York, where he had once worked at Sloan-Kettering Cancer Hospital. Bill was quite flattered by the request. Even though he never graduated from Brooklyn Law School, the knowledge he gained there was enough to help settle Dr. Strobel's legal troubles and please his mother greatly.

By now it was late September of 1925, Lois's favorite time of year, the fall. Bill's career was apparently set so they decided to combine their next business junket with a long overdue vacation. With Frank Shaw's blessing, they planned a slow "investigative tour" of the southern states to check out their "business investment potential." Besides, Bill's next prime target was American Cyanamid in Brewster, Florida, so they could plan to arrive there during Lois's least favorite time of year—the dead of winter.

The warm autumn air scented with wildflowers and southern pines stirred the sexual juices of these motorcycle companions as they crossed the Mason-Dixon line. They frolicked in mountain streams, bathed and swam naked at sunset in tree-shrouded lakes, and made love under the stars as they listened to the crackling of their campfire and the hooting of owls in the forest's giant oaks. It was beyond Lois's fondest wishes, this fulfillment of her intense love for her husband and his love for her. She prayed it would never end, but those butterflies kept telling her one day it would.

Bill, with his long, lanky legs dangling out over the sidecar, often directed her to stop at small, unheard-of companies along the way. While he spent time chatting with the owners, she visited the town square to absorb the history of the place and its people, and also to replenish their food supply. After a few days, sometimes staying at a small hotel or country inn, they'd be off again, although never in a hurry.

Just before Christmas, they found themselves caught high in the

Appalachian Mountains of North Carolina while investigating several sizable logging companies near a small town called Pelham. Ensconced in their tent covered by a heavy snowfall from the night before, the young explorers were prepared to spend Christmas alone, warmed only by old newspapers, heated stones, and their faithful hot water bottle. Suddenly they heard a hoot and a holler outside. It was the voice of old Ed Brown, a logger Bill had met very briefly. He lived in a log cabin nearby with his wife and his son, daughter-in-law, and their six children. He was inviting Lois and Bill to spend Christmas with his family.

"Such generosity. Such warm hospitality," Lois wrote years after the trip. "In spite of being terribly hard up, there was not an ounce of self-pity in any of them. For Christmas dinner, we had salt pork, turnip greens, corn pone, sweet potato custard and for dessert, sweet potato pie."[14] After dinner, Bill happened to notice there were no presents around the sparsely decorated Christmas tree. He grabbed each of the children, sat the younger ones on his knee, and gave them all several dollars, saying Santa Claus had left the money for them in his tent. Mr. Brown and his son seemed embarrassed and tried to dissuade him but Bill would have none of it.

Lois recalled that Christmas night in Pelham, North Carolina, with mixed emotions.

"I must admit some of that old guilt came back as I watched Bill playing so happily with those children," she said. "But then some of the old fears came back too when Mr. Brown brought out a jug of white lightning—I think that's what he called it—and Bill got terribly drunk. We had to sleep on the cabin floor that night because we couldn't get Bill back to our campsite."[15]

The very next day they packed up and made a mad dash for the warm, sunny clime of Brewster, Florida, and Bill's primary target, American Cyanamid. They never once talked about that drinking incident.

Just before they reached Jacksonville, the front tire blew out. Lois almost swerved off the road. Bill patched the inner tube in fifteen minutes and they were on their way. But after a few more miles, the tire blew again. Lois was tired and now a bit nervous, so she let Bill take over the driving. Another patch, a few more miles, and it happened for a third time.

Bill had been relatively calm for most of the trip, but now he really lost his temper, cursing and kicking the side of the Harley. That's when he noticed that a broken spoke had been piercing the tube and causing the flats. He ate humble pie, patched the tire one more time, and drove slowly and carefully into Jacksonville, where they had the wheel repaired.

Back then the American Cyanamid Company owned and ran the town of Brewster in the north central part of Florida. Lois and Bill expected to find a ramshackle mining village. Instead, with a population of two thousand, it was laid out like a subdivision with vine-covered cottages for married couples, a central park, a golf course, tennis courts, a swimming pool, and separate dormitory housing for bachelor men and women.

For his report to Frank Shaw, Bill was mainly interested in the productivity of the company's phosphate mines and screening plant. He noted in his comments to Shaw, however, that the powerhouse that generated all the electricity for the mine, the plant, and the whole town contained nothing but General Electric equipment. He thought Frank would be pleased at that.

Lois recalled that they spent about a week there. She said that the town manager, a Mr. Curry, told her the area was once an anthropologist's paradise. There were still bone fragments scattered everywhere, mostly dug up by the mining excavations. Mr. Curry said the bones of the extinct three-toed horse and three-toed rhinoceros had been found there some years before.[16]

They traveled across the Florida Panhandle and then up into Montgomery, Alabama, where Bill checked out the Tennessee Coal and Iron Works owned by the United States Steel Company. This plant's major product was steel rails and, with the nation's railroads needing to upgrade to meet increased freight transportation, its growth potential appeared significant to Bill.

Lois was intrigued when they stopped outside of Birmingham, Alabama, so that Bill could investigate a large coal mine that supplied coke to the surrounding steel mills.

Camping that evening not far from the mine, Lois watched with great interest as the miners exited the pit wearing flickering lights on their helmets. Even though she found it a bit eerie, she had the urge to go down into the mine herself and explore the underground shafts. Bill and the foreman, however, put a quick end to her urge.[17]

By now Lois and Bill had received word that Lois's youngest sister, Katherine, had finalized her wedding date. It was scheduled for the middle of June. It was now nearing the end of April, 1926. They had been on the road for close to a year. They decided to head for home in order to have plenty of time to prepare for the grand occasion.

Lois said she could hardly wait to get there. Perhaps that's why she was a little careless driving through Tennessee. She said her head was back in Brooklyn, thinking about what she would wear, who she would see, and what a wonderful time she would have bragging about all of Bill's marvelous accomplishments.[18]

It happened as they were leaving the outskirts of Dayton, Tennessee, the town famous for the Scopes Evolution Trial the year before. Lois was driving the Harley over a sandy road that appeared to run straight ahead when suddenly, hidden by a large barn, a curve to the right appeared. The sand on the road ahead was quite deep. When Lois tried to jerk the wheel around the tight curve, the motorcycle spun out of control. Bill went flying out of the sidecar, breaking his collarbone as he landed. Lois cut her face and twisted her knee while their equipment scattered in every direction. Fortunately, a Good Samaritan happened along and took them to a doctor in town. Since there was no hospital, the doctor put them into a hotel room conveniently located above his office.[19]

They rested for a week. The man who rescued them collected their belongings from the road and brought them to the hotel. Not a single article was missing, which testified to the honesty of the people of Dayton and to the country in general back then. He also stored the damaged Harley in his barn.

Before they were ready to leave, Lois and Bill made arrangements to have the motorcycle and most of the gear shipped back to Brooklyn. As soon as the doctor said they could travel, they took the train home.

"Although we were in plenty of time for the wedding," Lois recounted later, "I made a sorry looking matron of honor when, with red gashes on my face, I limped up the aisle."[20]

She couldn't help but notice at the reception afterward how many people seem to treat a now spiffily dressed Bill Wilson differently than they had at their own wedding some seven years earlier. *What a little money and a little prestige can do*, she thought.

There was one person at the reception, however, who felt exactly the same way about Bill as he did seven years ago. That was Clark Burnham, as he watched his son-in-law once again guzzle down a full glass of his finest Scotch.

6

Social Drinking—Unsocial Behavior

$\mathcal{L}$OIS WAS BOTH HAPPY AND PROUD THAT PARTICULAR MONDAY morning, although strangely nervous as she straightened her husband's tie, patted down the lapels on his handsome dark gray suit, then sent him off to embark on his career as a Wall Street denizen. This was to be Bill's first official day in the offices of J.K. Rice & Company.

Soon these onetime eager "pioneers" would really be in the chips, making enough to greatly enlarge and handsomely redecorate their apartment in the heart of the most elite section of Brooklyn Heights.

Soon Lois would be out shopping with Elise Shaw and those other wealthy Wall Street wives, ogling the kind of furnishings only an interior decorator with a contempt for budgets can talk you into.

Lois felt suddenly overwhelmed. Before she could let all this happen, she thought to herself, she needed some time to slow down, if only for a few hours, preferably at least a few days. If it were possible, for a few weeks.

Yes, they had been on the road for almost a year—an excursion into the nation's heartland whose routes she would love to travel over and over again—but still, this success seemed to be coming much too fast. Heck, what did she really know about this Wall Street stuff anyway, people making so much money so easily and so quickly simply by buying and trading pieces of paper with impressive-looking pictures and stamps on them—like those stock certificates in the bottom of Bill's dresser drawer.

Lois was smart and sophisticated in many ways and about many things. She could draw, she could paint, she could design, and she could play the piano. She was well read, cultured, and knew a great deal about religion, medicine, and the history of this land and many other lands as well. And she was good at budgeting and conceptual planning, as she showed in her preparations for their research venture. But when it came to the stock market, she admittedly knew little about how it actually worked. She wanted to know more. She needed to know more, if only to hold an intelligent conversation on the subject with Bill's new associates.

Yes, she certainly knew a great deal about Bill's investigative work. She was right there with him when he explored America's industrial might. But what did investors actually do with the information? How did the mechanics of the financial marketplace really work? She went into the hall closet where Bill had stashed his Moody's manuals, dusted one off, and began to read. After digesting several pages, she decided to call the company to ask some simple questions. Identifying herself as Mr. Wilson's "research assistant," Lois found a gentleman who loved talking about the business he was in, particularly to such a charming voice on the other end of the line. Lois not only managed to get the thumbnail sketch she wanted but a historical overview as well.[1]

She learned from the Moody's man, for instance, that people in this country had been involved in trading government obligations and company interests ever since America was first colonized by Great Britain, which already had commercial involvements in practically every corner of the world. The buying and swapping was usually limited and informal and without charge, unless, of course, a barrister was necessary for the transaction.

The eighteenth century brought great expansion to world trade and to burgeoning business centers such as New York, creating even more interest in financial instruments. By the late 1700s, a number of merchants and brokers in the city began charging a commission to act as agents for other interested parties and for giving preference to each other in the purchase and sale of securities.

About two dozen of these merchants operated outdoors under a buttonwood tree on Wall Street, except during inclement weather when they gathered in a nearby coffeehouse. It was in May of 1792 that the group decided to informally organize to protect their mutual interests. This was the birth of the New York Stock Exchange.

From 1792 on, public interest in stocks and bonds rose largely as a result of the increase in government obligations and the growth of banks and insurance companies. As the number of actual brokers grew significantly, they got together and drew up a simple agreement, or constitution, and called themselves the New York Stock and Exchange Board. They rented a room at 40 Wall Street for $200 a year and began charging each member broker $25 for a "seat" in the room. That fledgling organization would grow into the booming financial trading arena called the New York Stock Exchange, now with its own large beehive of a building at the center of Wall Street's financial district.

After learning more about how the large investment firms had to own these now very expensive "seats" in order to trade on the exchange, and how such trading was conducted, Lois thanked the Moody's man and hung up. Her head was now filled with all sorts of minutiae she needed to know about the stock market, since she would soon be socializing with all those Wall Street wives.

If Lois thought things had been moving too quickly up until then, she had to fasten her seat belt for the roller-coaster ride that lay ahead. For right now, the stock market was booming, and she would soon find out how wrong she had been to believe that a year away from the New York bar scene would end her husband's drinking.

Caught up in the euphoria of the market, the wining and dining of big investors, an unlimited expense account, and a $20,000 line of credit from Rice & Company to buy stocks on margin for his own account, Bill Wilson was in seventh heaven. Still, for some inexplicable reason even most alcoholics themselves can't figure out, he always wanted to feel even better. So, before long, he was again drinking rather heavily while continuing to tell his wife it was "only for business."

As the months went by, things didn't go directly downhill, nor was every day bleak or unhappy. On the contrary. As Lois often shared in her

later years, they had a great deal of fun and excitement being back in the
city. They often met Frank and Elise and some wealthy clients and their
wives, usually at one of the most insanely expensive restaurants in
town—generally a Mob-controlled speakeasy with chorus girls out front
and gambling in the back room. These were the fruits of Prohibition.

The evening would begin with the finest wines or aperitifs, usually
accompanied by boastful stories of how well everyone did that day trading thousands of shares of this stock or that. Then would come the juici-
est steaks, the tenderest veal, the most succulent lamb chops. Many of
those nights Lois proudly watched Bill charm everyone with his wit and
Yankee humor. To her he was the most articulate, the most charming, the
most handsome man in the place, and on such nights the dreams he often
shared with her of achieving true greatness seemed possible, almost within reach.

But then, as Lois was learning, there were those other nights, which
soon became more and more frequent. Those were the nights when after
six or seven drinks or more—it was impossible to tell just when it would
happen—Bill would become less interested in what others had to say,
focusing only on what he was saying. And, if he was interrupted, he'd cast
a nasty look and continue, or worse yet, make a snide remark that often
offended everyone at the table. Many times people would excuse themselves and leave. As Lois recalled, "In the morning I would still be angry
about being so embarrassed the night before and Bill would be filled with
self-reproach. The problem was, his self-reproach would be gone long
before my anger."[2]

He would always sheepishly apologize to Lois but then try to justify
his actions, saying how he hated the patronizing and snobbish attitudes
of people who wouldn't know a Vermont maple from a Christmas tree.
Here he was making so much money for them, and they took it all for
granted.

The truth was, Bill's investigative genius was constantly pulling rabbits out of the hat and keeping Rice & Company clients quite pleased.
At the same time, while they maintained their business relationships with
the young broker, a number of customers began to lessen their social contact with him.

Almost every stock he recommended had a dramatic move up. In addition to investing for himself, he was building his own clientele, mainly from the recommendations among the customers in the speakeasies where he had become well known and respected. He also had Rogers and Dr. Leonard Strong investing with him now, as well as some of the wealthy summer people in Manchester he met during the sojourns he and Lois took together to Emerald Lake.

By August of 1927, he discovered that sitting in his office or in a gin mill wasn't producing enough new "targets of opportunity." And besides, with his drinking now increasing at home, Lois was talking more and more about getting him out into the country again. So he decided another research venture on the open road would help both situations.

Bill took out his Moody's manuals from the hall closet while Lois reviewed her old list of traveling supplies. Only now, their trusty old Harley-Davidson was in mothballs and a Dodge sedan was parked at their curbside instead.

Still, Lois hoped that somehow they could find a way of recapturing, at least in part, those warm and lovely moments of their trip the year before when they found as much time to make love as they did to investigate companies. Even though their world was different now, she could at least hope. And she would have her husband back out in the country where, perhaps, he would have one more chance to find sobriety.

After visiting companies in upstate New York and Connecticut, they headed for Holyoke, Massachusetts, and a firm by the name of the American Writing Paper Company. It was presently in receivership, but as Bill had explained to Frank and the other partners, with new management and an influx of cash, there was a good chance the company could be turned around and thus produce a substantial return on their investment. After a week of meetings, Bill telephoned Frank to say he was convinced this could be done.

One of American Writing Paper's board members—trying to polish the apple, no doubt—heard how much Lois and Bill loved to be surrounded by nature, so he loaned them his log cabin for the week. It was located in the nearby hills, only a few miles from the plant. Lois recalled the cozy place not only had heat and running water but also everything from clean sheets and towels to a radio and a telephone. But the thing she remembered the most was the lovely view of Mount Tom through the front picture window.[3]

Those few days together in Holyoke recaptured at least some of the feelings, some of the closeness, and some of the intimacy they had while touring the South. First of all, Bill did not have a single drink after leaving Brooklyn. *Maybe it was that old "fresh air and exercise" potion working again*, Lois thought. Second, their rugged surroundings and the crisp fall air reinvigorated them both. As Lois later wrote, "This morning, as there was not a soul around, we swam in the river 'au naturel.' Later, on a long walk, we picked a lot of hazelnuts which I haven't found for a long time. And for supper I stewed up the blueberries and elderberries which we had gathered earlier.

"That night when Bill and I went to town to the movies, clouds of white moths swarmed all around the street lights, whitening the ground with snow-like piles at the foot of every lamp post. Never having seen anything like it before, we inquired and learned they were gypsy moths and a great menace to the trees. Thank goodness I had never seen them in Vermont.

"Tomorrow we leave for Canada."[4]

That last comment said it all, for that's where Bill resumed his drinking despite still being "out in the country." They had been in Montreal for several weeks. Bill had been trying hard to get the goods on a major Canadian aluminum enterprise but without any luck. He was spurned by management as well as the workers, whom he said "didn't speak the same language even though it was English."[5] He hadn't received this much resistance since that very first call he made on General Electric, and this time there were no Goldfoots to soften up with a few beers. And, as for beer, Bill still hadn't had a drop, even though there was no Prohibition law in Canada. Finally, he gave up and headed for home. Lois could tell he was very down, almost depressed. Nothing she said cheered him up.

Just as they were about to cross the border back into the United States, Bill casually mentioned he had run out of cigarettes and needed to stop to pick up a few packs.

"I realized this was nonsense since cigarettes were a lot more expensive in Canada," Lois said. "But liquor was cheaper and more easily available than in the U.S. in those Prohibition days."[6]

Bill had parked the Dodge in the plaza near the International Bridge that marked the United States–Canadian border. He had gone off with both the car keys and all their money. Lois sat there and waited for several hours, trying to decide exactly what to do next. It was almost dark by the time she set out to look for him, passing by all the shops, restaurants, and tourist traps and surveying only the bars.

"In the very last saloon in the area, there he was hardly able to navigate," she recalled. "And he had spent practically all of our money except for a few dollars."[7]

Lois was exasperated, not so much by the fact that she now had to drive most of the way back to New York herself, but mainly because those ever-present butterflies in her stomach told her this was merely a precursor of things to come.

As the cold winds of late November blew in, so did another one of Bill's unusual investment ideas: Cuban sugar. With the economy booming and everyone he knew having a sweet tooth, he saw sugar as a growth industry and Cuba as the lowest-cost producer. So he talked Frank Shaw into an all-expense-paid trip: he and Lois would "investigate" the island just off the coast of Florida.

It was probably only a coincidence, of course, that Bill had received a letter at about that time from his father, Gilman, who had remarried. They hadn't seen each other in years. Gilly was working outside Miami, cutting rock to build the Overseas Highway that would connect the mainland with the Florida Keys. How convenient it would be to pay his father a visit on their way home.

In Cuba, Lois and Bill were given a warm reception and treated as important American investors in the island's economy. A car, a chauffeur, and even a motorboat were placed at their disposal. In Havana they stayed at the elaborate Hotel Sevila. Bill lived it up, especially when he took a fancy to two other island specialties: Cuban cigars and Cuban rum. It was the rum that turned the whole trip into a near disaster and almost a total waste of the firm's money. As Lois remembered quite vividly, "It was a frustrating time for me, though, because of Bill's drinking.

One day, to keep him from going down to the bar, I threw one of his shoes out the window, but this did no good. It landed on a nearby roof, and Bill simply called the porter to retrieve it. In no time, he was down at the bar wearing both shoes."[8]

Frank Shaw soon heard of Bill's escapades through one of his Cuban financial connections. He immediately called the hotel and read Bill the riot act. This so upset Bill that before leaving the island, he wrote Frank a letter of apology. It read, in part, "I have never said anything to you about the liquor question, but now that you mention it and also for the good reason that you are investing your perfectly good money in me, I am at last very happy to say that I have had a final showdown (with myself) on the matter . . . I am finally . . . rid of it . . . That is that so let us now forget it."[9]

With Bill making so much money for the firm, Shaw was happy to forget it—for a while anyway. On their way home, Lois and Bill did stop to see Gilly and his second wife, Christine. They also met Gilly and Christine's daughter, Helen, Bill's half sister who was only ten years old. The visit was pleasant enough, but Lois made sure to keep it short for fear her husband and father-in-law would start drinking together.

A few nights after they returned to Brooklyn, Bill came home drunker than usual. Lois helped him into the bedroom and undressed him. As she tried putting on his pajamas, he fell onto the bed and pulled her down on top of him. He wanted to make love. She could smell the whiskey coming out of every pore in his body as he rolled over on her. His hands were sweaty, his breath repulsive. She tried to move away but he wanted her. He kissed her and fondled her. She tried not to feel her feelings. This was her husband, but there must be times—there had to be times—when a wife had every right to say no to her husband.

His breath came hard and heavy as he struggled to perform. She gave him little help. Then she realized that the booze had made him impotent again. They had had problems before, but this night it was hopeless. After a few moments Bill, as drunk as he was, finally realized it himself. He crawled away from her and buried his head in a pillow. As he moaned like a poor, hurt little animal, Lois began to weep. Her feelings of disgust suddenly turned into deep empathy. "I love you, Bill," she murmured, running her fingers through his hair. "How can I help you to stop all of this? Dear God, please show me how I can help my husband."

The next morning, Bill had no recollection of the night before. He was now beginning to have "blackouts," a state where the brain becomes so dulled by alcohol that a person can continue to function but not remember what he did or when and where he did it. Bill only knew he had come home very drunk again, and judging by the look on his wife's face, he had probably hurt and embarrassed her one more time. So he apologized one more time and went off to work with a terrible hangover—almost certain to stop somewhere for "a hair of the dog."[10]

Despite lunching and attending the theater and such with Elise and the wives of other Wall Street executives and investors, Lois still had too much time just to sit around the house and think. Despite her disagreement with YWCA during the war years, she still had many friends there, and she returned now for some volunteer work. She not only enjoyed it, but it took her mind off the problems at hand.

A few weeks before Christmas, Lois planned to have her entire family and some guests over for a holiday dinner. She wanted everything to go well. She made Bill promise not to drink too much, at least not while everyone was there. He sarcastically tossed his glass of gin and tonic into the sink and promised to be "a good boy." By now, she was used to his sarcasm after he had had a few and wanted to continue drinking.

Lois decorated the Christmas tree and the entire apartment in the spirit of the season. Everything was beautiful. It made her feel better doing it. She even hung mistletoe over the front door. When the special evening arrived and the clock struck six, she put on a happy face and greeted everyone as though there wasn't one single problem in the entire Wilson household. Even Bill's sister, Dorothy, who had been expressing concern over his drinking to her doctor-husband, Leonard Strong, was fooled by Lois's performance. But two people there certainly were not— Elise Shaw and Clark Burnham.

During dinner, while Rogers and Leonard were complimenting their host for "buttering their bread" with such high-flying stocks, Bill turned to his father-in-law and graciously invited him to be his guest at the New York Stock Exchange one day soon "to see how your son-in-law works his magic," he winked. Then he toasted him with his glass of Chablis.

"Not on your life," Lois remembered her father replying rather abruptly. "I hear it's like watching a herd of wild buffalo stampede. Nothing but a parade of heart attacks all trying to get to the waterhole at the same time. No thanks."[11] Bill's face showed not only shock and dis- appointment but also deep hurt. Ever since he married Lois, he had been trying to earn Dr. Burnham's respect—not those measly, patronizing "Keep up the good work, son" platitudes, but his respect. Now here he was moving among the giants of Wall Street and showering the doctor's daughter with all the things the good life can bring, and getting no credit for it. "Well, he can go to hell," Bill said under his breath as he excused himself from the table and went into the parlor for a stiff belt.

There was a momentary pause in the conversation since everyone couldn't help but notice the incident. Lois quickly drew their attention by rising herself and inviting everyone to join her and Bill in the parlor for an after-dinner cordial and some dessert.

As the guests were leaving, Barbara, who had always liked and admired her brother-in-law, pulled Lois aside and naively told her she shouldn't get so upset just because her husband has a few social drinks once in a while, or even gets tight now and then. After all, wasn't it part of his doing business—entertaining people, being sociable, being a good host? And look at her lovely apartment. A phone in every room. Partying with the elite.

Lois wanted to grab her younger sister, look into her eyes, and tell her the man she admired so much insulted people in restaurants after "a few social drinks," that he bought so many rounds in a speakeasy he could have owned the place, that he often couldn't remember what had done last night or the night before, that he often came home so drunk she had to undress him and then, reeking of his stinking booze, he would try to make love to her—and couldn't.

Lois didn't say any of those things, nor did she admit she was now making up excuses for her husband with Frank Shaw and others when Bill was so hungover he couldn't keep his appointments. She didn't confess the "white lies" she would tell the family when they were invited for Sunday dinner and didn't show up. No, because she didn't want anyone to know she was slowly becoming the kind of person she herself couldn't stand—a person of low moral character. She had no idea then that alcoholism was a disease, not a moral issue.

Lois simply kissed Barbara goodnight and wished her a very merry Christmas.[12]

By the spring of 1928, Frank Shaw was growing much more concerned about Bill's drinking and how it was affecting the firm's important clients. He had been hearing some wild stories, but he also knew his highly successful research expert wasn't the only man on Wall Street nor the only one at Rice & Company for that matter to "tie one on" now and then. Still, he simply couldn't ignore the particularly embarrassing episodes his other partners were bringing to his attention.

Frank and Bill had another talk, this time eyeball to eyeball. Shaw said it had to stop—now. Bill agreed, admitting his drinking had gotten out of control at times and could lead to some serious problems if he didn't stop. He humbly assured his mentor that his heavy drinking days were over for good. From now on it would be just a few beers once in a while. Deep down in his gut, Bill really meant it.

Shaw was a man with a keen eye for the "long-haul situations" that his researcher was continuing to unearth. Their arrangement had already proven so profitable for both of them he really didn't want it to change. So once again he accepted Bill at his word. Back then, no one knew anything about the addiction of alcoholism and its downhill progression. Not only did he take Bill's word, but a few months later when Frank was made an offer he couldn't refuse and accepted the top spot at Tobey & Kirk, a major stockbrokerage firm on Broad Street, he talked Bill into coming along with him.

So on this particular day when they finished their tête-à-tête, Frank shook Bill's hand and invited him and Lois to a major fund-raiser that weekend at the palatial Long Island estate of Joseph Hirshhorn, the firm's biggest and most influential client. Bill swore he'd be on his best behavior.

Elise Shaw knew better. For months she had been listening to Frank complain about the pressure he was feeling from his partners to rein in the husband of his wife's closest friend. Now he told her the problem was solved. She merely smiled and shook her head.

A few days later, Elise met Lois in Manhattan on the pretense of viewing the latest exhibit at the Metropolitan Museum of Art. Lois was happy to be alone with her best friend for a change. Over a late lunch, Elise casually raised the subject of Frank's concern about Bill's drinking and that it seemed to be getting worse. These two women rarely kept secrets from one another or denied the obvious when it had import on their lives. But alcoholism is a disease of denial, and that denial also infects the spouses and families of alcoholics. Lois certainly knew none of this at the time. She only wanted to protect her husband's reputation and self-respect and, perhaps unconsciously or consciously, her own image and self-respect at the same time.

Lois admitted that Bill had gone off on a few sprees and done some very stupid things, generally when he was in bad company at those speakeasies—with men who had nothing else to do but drink. She had always suggested he stay away from that kind of crowd. However, after the fiasco in Cuba and his recent talk with Frank, all that was behind him now. Bill had finally turned over a new leaf.

When Elise tried to explain how it was with her growing up, how men with serious drinking problems were always promising to swear off but never could, she sensed Lois was turning a deaf ear. Bill wasn't like those men, her friend insisted. He had a strong will, and with her help and support she just knew he could stop drinking. Elise soon realized she was talking to the wall, and if she cherished their close friendship, she would back off. So she did.[13]

That Saturday evening Lois and Bill drove into the sprawling estate of Joe Hirshhorn and his wife on Great Neck, Long Island, for the gala garden party they were hosting to raise money for their synagogue. Lois, wearing a long red taffeta dress, was eager to see the well-known art collector's famous paintings and tapestries said to fill the lavish halls and rooms of their manor.

Joe was one of Bill Wilson's idols. He had been a poor boy from Brownsville, Brooklyn, who began his extraordinary financial career as a runner on Wall Street. He used every nickel he earned to trade stocks and he gradually amassed a large fortune. As the story goes, he found a calendar lying in the street one day with a picture on it so beautiful that he framed it for his mother. That's what sparked his interest in art. The financier went on to build one of the world's largest and finest art collections, which he later donated to the U.S. government. Today that collection is housed in the Hirshhorn Museum, Smithsonian Institution, on the National Mall in Washington, D.C.

Bill was already acquainted with Hirshhorn, having investigated several companies and a number of substantial real estate holdings at his request. Joe was so pleased with the results that he highly recommended the researcher to other big investors in the city. Bill felt very proud that night to introduce his wife, a painter herself, to one of the country's important art collectors, who then had an assistant give Lois a private tour of his many fine works. She was thrilled.

Bill was on his very best behavior—for about two-and-a-half hours. After Lois's tour of the house, they enjoyed the marvelous outdoor buffet with Elise and Frank and other business associates. Then they had several dances together. Spotting a few possible sales prospects in the elite crowd, Bill told Lois he'd be back shortly and began to circulate. That's when he bumped into Clint Harris, a fellow drinking buddy from Rice & Company, chatting with one of Great Neck's "gay divorcées" who knew the Hirshhorns quite well. They were both a bit tipsy.

Now, it's a matter of record that very few drunks consider having a small glass of champagne "drinking." So when the waiter passed by with a tray filled with champagne glasses and his fellow broker and his friend each took one, so did Bill. And then he took another, and another.

There are several versions of what happened next.[14] Bill remembered he and Clint following the charming divorcée down into Joe Hirshhorn's wine cellar to have their own private party. There were crates and crates of the finest French wine and champagne everywhere. His fellow broker—who wound up joining Bill in Alcoholics Anonymous seventeen years later—remembered unsealing the first crate and popping a cork.

"We sipped a little of the free bubbly in a dignified way," Clint recalled, "then sipped a little more, and then [got into it] for real."[15]

He said that the drunker they got, the more difficult it became to pop the corks. So they simply smashed the bottle necks against some piping and choked the stuff down like crazy. There was broken glass and sparkles all over the place and all over them. He didn't remember what happened after that.

Back out at the party, Lois became very uncomfortable and ill at ease waiting for Bill to return. More than an hour had passed and she had run out of small talk. She kept staring at the richly dressed couples on the dance floor, trying to avoid Elise's "I told you so" glances. Finally, she offered the "I have to powder my nose" excuse and set off to find her thoughtless husband. A guest who knew Bill said he had seen him and two companions headed for Joe Hirshhorn's wine cellar.

On this special night and in this elegant setting, this caring and sensitive lady couldn't believe the terrible drunken orgy she walked into. There were shards of glass all over the floor, puddles of champagne everywhere and the cellar smelled like soured wine. Bill was so drunk he could hardly stand. Clint had passed out on a bench. No one would say what had happened to the gay divorcée.

Certainly Lois had been angry before at her husband's shameful antics, but this was more humiliating and shocking than she could possibly stand. As she later shared, "I must admit I became a bit hysterical for a moment. I remember running at Bill and pummeling him on the arms and slapping him in the face. I kept crying 'Why? Why?' but it didn't make any difference. He was so intoxicated he simply staggered backwards and mumbled something I couldn't understand. I wanted to run and hide but there was nowhere I could go. I had never felt so low, so upset, so angry, so terribly humiliated in all my life. We had to sneak off from that lovely affair like thieves in the night."

Lois lingered until her husband was at least able to walk and until Elise and Frank Shaw had departed. A stranger at the party helped get Bill into the car. Lois didn't even remember driving home. She often said later how useless it was to yell at her husband when he was drunk. But she admitted she rarely raised her voice even the next morning because he looked so pitiful and hopeless. "He was always turning over a new leaf and I always wanted to believe him until finally he even gave up on himself."[16] What Lois never said about that night at the Hirshhorns—in fact, what she was never willing to talk about then or later—was how she felt about that gay divorcée. How many other women were there like the gay divorcée in those speakeasies her husband frequented? How alluring were their charms once he had had a few highballs? What could he possibly find in them when he had a wife at home who adored him, who was willing to give him all her love, all her understanding, all her support? Why wouldn't Lois ask herself these questions? Why would she be any different than the spouses of other alcoholics who asked the same questions and always feared the answers?[17]

Perhaps that's why when Bill woke from his drunken stupor the next morning, there was a note on his dresser. It merely said:

> *I am going away for awhile. I will let you know where I am.*
> *I will not return until you are sober. Lois.*

Lois had packed up and left for Washington, D.C., where she checked into a small hotel. Lois later admitted to a close friend that leaving Bill at that time was simply a ploy to get him to stop drinking. She wanted him to believe she wouldn't return until he did stop. She even had her mother drop by to check on Bill and reinforce her daughter's ultimatum. But the real truth was that Lois would rather be unhappy with Bill than unhappy without him and no matter what happened, she knew she would return to him.[18]

Even though Bill and Dr. Burnham were often at odds, mostly over his carousing, Matilda steadfastly defended her son-in-law, saying it was the devil's curse that had him in his grips and that prayer and patience were the only answers. She continued to love and pray for Bill and make excuses for him until the day she died.

Perhaps because he was never really close to his own mother or simply because of Matilda's obvious concern and affection for him, Bill truly loved his mother-in-law. He would try to do almost anything she asked—including not drinking. But at this point, that was impossible except in short, struggling spurts. Now, with Bill under great pressure both at home and on the Street, it was time for another of those spurts.

In Washington, Lois toured the Smithsonian, which always fascinated her, and then the monuments and some government buildings. She stopped by Walter Reed Army Hospital to visit with some old friends she had worked with during the war and lunched a few times with her college alumnae. She talked only about the good times, leaving out the bad—that she was on a brief holiday while her husband's business kept him tied to Wall Street. Just a few more white lies.

The days dragged on. Matilda reported Bill was staying sober, three days, four days, five days now.

It was while Lois was strolling through a small playground near her hotel that the thought struck her. The idea had always been somewhere deep in her heart but now suddenly it sprang out so clearly she smiled with delight. As she watched some mothers pushing their young children on the park swings and a father waiting at the foot of a slide to catch his excited toddler before she hit the ground, Lois found the answer to their problems. They would adopt a baby.

She called Bill immediately. He was at the office, sober. He seemed elated at the prospect.

The next train heading east from Washington, D.C., carried a lady whose face was now filled with a bright smile instead of sad tears. The guilt she had borne for so long for not being able to give her husband a family he always wanted would soon be assuaged, at least in part, by having a baby's cries, giggles, and laughter fill their apartment. Lois could hardly wait to get back to New York to begin the adoption process.

She went directly to the Spence-Chapin foundling hospital in Brooklyn. There, a very serious, matronly lady took down all the information and then showed Lois around. She even allowed the excited "mother-to-be" to hold several of the infants that had already been adopted and were simply waiting for the process to be completed so they could go home with their new mothers and fathers.[19]

Bill was still struggling to stay sober when he sat down with his wife each night to discuss all the intricate details they needed to supply the agency—information about his job, his salary, their family backgrounds, and the necessary recommendations from some close friends concerning their suitability as prospective parents. They also had to decide whether they preferred a boy or a girl, an infant, a toddler, or a young child. They both wanted an infant. It would be like having their very own baby right from the start.

The first person Lois went to see, of course, was Elise. From the moment Lois entered Elise's lovely home, she couldn't understand why her closest, dearest friend wasn't as excited about the adoption as she was.

Elise Valentine Shaw always knew Lois Burnham Wilson would make the greatest mother in the world. She was deeply saddened after her unfortunate surgery ruined all chances of that. But Lois's friend still carried the scars of her own childhood, growing up in an alcoholic home, being deprived of a father's love and attention, with a mother living in constant fear and anxiety, and all the shame and embarrassment this kind of life carried with it. That's why Elise firmly believed no innocent child should have to grow up in such torment.

Lois wondered at the time why her friend's eyes moistened when she handed her the papers from Spence-Chapin for her to fill out, recommending the Wilsons as suitable parents. She left that day feeling strangely tense and confused over what had just transpired between two women who had always been open and honest with each other. She didn't know then that the disease of alcoholism can affect even the closest relationships.[20]

Sadly recalling the adoption process, Lois said, "As weeks went by and we heard nothing, I inquired several times. The agency always replied that the suitable child had not yet been found."[21] She finally went back to Spence-Chapin. She sat down in the matronly woman's office and asked how much longer it would be before they could adopt their baby. There was a long, ominous pause. Bad news, particularly for a warm, caring, needy woman such as the one seated before her, was always difficult for the matronly lady to convey. It had been decided, she finally responded as tenderly as she could, that under the present circumstances the agency would not be able to approve any adoption by the Wilsons. That was all she had to say.

Lois was devastated. She could not believe what she was hearing. She stumbled past the cribs of smiling infants, out of the hospital, and into the street, not knowing where to go or what to do. It was one of the lowest points in her life. When she talked about it years later, one could still hear the pain in her voice: "Bill was always sure the real reason we were turned down was because of his drinking. It wasn't until later I learned this was so. I only had some doubts because Bill had been sober at the time."[22]

It would be almost two years—the fall of 1929—before Lois would learn that it was Elise who dissuaded the agency from allowing her and Bill to adopt a child. The shock and hurt would wash away all understanding between them, sever what had been a bond almost as strong as that of sisters, and keep them apart for a number of years after that—years when Lois could have used the kind of friendship they once had.[23] Bill stayed sober for two months. It was his longest dry period since their motorcycle trip through the South. When he started drinking again, it was worse than before. Lois didn't know if it was his disappointment again over not having a family, the continued pressure on him to find more and more investment opportunities for his clients, or—and this was always Lois's deepest fear—that she wasn't a good enough wife or a good enough lover. Whatever Bill offered as an excuse, Lois could always find some way to feel guilty about it. That's what makes the spouses of alcoholics such warm and wonderful "enablers."

Each night, while waiting for her husband to arrive home either for a late, cold dinner or a drunken midnight snack, Lois knelt in her bedroom and, remembering what her mother constantly told her, she would pray, "God help me to help him, my husband, my boy, who is more than life to me. God give me wisdom and strength and patience, for I love him, I love him, I love him."[24]

After her mother died only a few years later, these prayers became like ashes in her mouth and fodder for her anger at the Almighty.

7

The Crash

*T*HE RAMPAGING BULL OF THE 1929 STOCK MARKET RAN TOTALLY unabated not only through Wall Street but through the entire country as well.

Stockbrokers like Bill Wilson became revered seers since practically everything they recommended went up. Neighborhood barbershops hawked the latest stock tips, the corner shoeshine man owned at least a thousand shares of the riskiest penny stock available, and every overzealous political contender was promising a "chicken in every pot and a car in every garage."

Prohibition-born bootleggers were getting as rich as Wall Street tycoons and the female "flapper set" were setting the dress styles not only for Broadway but for B-girls and college coeds as well. As history now tells us, this period in America was aptly named the Roaring Twenties.

The country was feeling good about itself, and rightly so. After all, hadn't its doughboys brought to a successful conclusion "the war to end all wars?" Not only was the economy growing, but voters had seen the end of the scandal-ridden administration of Warren G. Harding, the nation's twenty-ninth president. While free from corruption himself, Harding had imprudently appointed at the behest of his unscrupulous political supporters an interior secretary who was close to "Big Oil." Accused of taking bribes for transferring large government mineral reserves to private interests, the interior secretary and his president found themselves in the spring of 1923 caught up in what was called the Teapot Dome scandal, named after the oil fields in question.

The betrayal of his cabinet officer and the never-ending scandal headlines broke President Harding's spirit. Already in poor health, this was said to have led to his untimely death only months later. His vice president, the taciturn John Calvin Coolidge, was sworn in as the thirtieth president of the United States in August of that year. Coolidge happened to be a Green Mountain man himself, born in Plymouth, Vermont, only a short distance from Bill Wilson's clan.

Plain in appearance and unimpressive in speech, Coolidge was an enigmatic man who slowly gained back the trust of the American people through his honesty, his openness, his quiet political skills, and his practical Yankee common sense. As a result, he was re-elected to his own four-year term in 1924 by a large plurality.

Calvin Coolidge believed that the backbone of America was its moral, hardworking men and women, not the get-rich-quick schemers and the loose-moral types. He told his cabinet officers: "Let men in public office enjoy the light that comes from burning the midnight oil, not the limelight."

While ridding the nation of scandal and demanding a lily-white administration, Coolidge oversaw a peaceful land and an expanding economy. But in the end, he made one gigantic blunder. He turned both a blind eye and a deaf ear to the inordinate speculative boom in the stock market which, less than a year after Coolidge left office in 1928, would have enormous repercussions on the nation.

One dramatic example of the stock market's extreme inflation was the fact that a seat on the New York Stock Exchange in 1929 sold for $625,000, while only ten years later that same seat sold for just $17,000.

In the midst of all this exuberance, Bill Wilson, in spite of his continued heavy drinking, was swept along with the tide and perhaps, like so many other wide-eyed optimists and fellow inebriates at the time, thought the financial orgy would never end.

But Lois Wilson, even with the little knowledge she had garnered about the workings of the stock market, grew more wary and more concerned by the day. Her Clark Burnham genes were telling her that life was not a free lunch, and those butterflies still in her stomach were whispering that one day soon, someone would have to pay the piper.[1]

Meanwhile, at Tobey & Kirk Investment Partners, one of the "Waspier" firms on the Street and quite protective of its impeccable reputation, Frank Shaw was trying to keep Bill on a tight leash. It wasn't long, however, before several partners began hearing stories about this Bill Wilson fellow and started warning Shaw not to let his escapades affect the firm or its prestigious clients.

Much to Lois's chagrin, her husband was also becoming an unwelcome guest in her own family. Once the lovable jokester and the life of the party, he was now often the pin that took all the air out of the balloon.

One particular evening, he showed up late and tipsy at a concert in which his mother-in-law was performing with the well-known Woodman Choral Club of New York. While squeezing into his seat, he stepped on Rogers's toes, apologized loudly and profusely, then sat down and proceeded to fall asleep and snore. Fortunately, Dr. Burnham was working late at the hospital. In the lobby, after the concert, while Bill was in the men's room, Rogers took Lois aside. He told her as kindly as he could that Bill's behavior had become embarrassing. He said she should think twice about bringing Bill to family affairs if he was drinking.[2]

When they arrived home that night, Lois lost her temper once again. She berated her husband for constantly causing her such humiliation, especially in front of her family and friends. She screamed and sobbed as he swayed before her, his eyes half-closed and his mind somewhere in oblivion. As Lois later shared so many times with the wives of other alcoholics, yelling at a drunk when he's drunk is like the sound of that proverbial tree falling in the forest. It's never heard.

While Lois and Bill continued to prosper financially, their relationship continued to deteriorate. There were more and more unhappy scenes in their luxurious apartment in Brooklyn Heights, more and more embarrassing moments with Lois's family, friends, and business associates, and more and more of Bill's empty promises to reform his ways.

So now Lois was beginning to isolate herself. She preferred staying home, reading, sewing, or on occasion visiting a museum by herself. But there were times she was forced to attend a luncheon or dinner with Bill and his clients or a gathering of their spouses.[3]

At one such reluctant luncheon of Wall Street wives, the waiter came by to take their drink order. One well-preened lady requested her usual Manhattan cocktail, another a very dry martini, and the other a pink lady. When Lois simply ordered tonic water, it immediately prompted comments from the others about whether they should be drinking so early in the day.

Lois recalled a flush-faced, rather heavyset woman questioning herself about her love for dry martinis and her husband's opinion that they made her talk too much and too loosely about their private affairs. Another lady prided herself on never drinking before noon and never having more than three cocktails in a single day—or perhaps four. "They make me too flirtatious," she giggled.

But the third lady grew quite serious when she told about her Irish neighbor who drank so much she finally had to take "a pledge."

"That's sort of an Irish thing," she remarked. "They do it with a priest."

"Does it work?" Lois asked very cautiously, always fearing to give away any possible hint that a drinking problem might exist in her own household. Later she learned that her husband's boozing was common gossip among most of these Wall Street matriarchs.

"I guess it does," the lady replied. "At least I haven't seen her staggering around her garden lately—or kicking the cat."

Despite the laughter from her luncheon companions, Lois latched on to this interesting bit of information and brought it home with her, trying to figure out how she could best use it with Bill.[4]

A few mornings later, as her husband sat on the edge of their bed with his head in his hands, trying to recover from another drinking bout, Lois came in and sat beside him. She was holding her family Bible. While Bill was not a churchgoer, Lois did attend services at the Swedenborgian church and had strong spiritual convictions at this time in her life. She told Bill she knew how badly he wanted to stop drinking, how hard he had been struggling, how ashamed he was for all the things he was doing. Perhaps, she said, simply promising himself and her that he would do it was not enough. Maybe he needed to promise Almighty God Himself. She gently placed the Bible into her husband's trembling hands and asked him to write a pledge in it.

Her remarks struck Bill's cobwebbed brain like an all-too-familiar headline from yesterday's newspaper. His wife had no idea how many times he had tried to reach out for help to the God she was talking about—to a God he really didn't believe had any personal concern for him anymore, if He ever had. She had no idea how many times he had tried to pray as she did, and when that didn't work, how he tried to beg, to plead, to grovel, all to no avail.

At this moment in his life, Bill Wilson had lost whatever connection he once may have had to God. And he knew exactly when it began—that day in the chapel at Burr and Burton Academy when the headmaster announced Bertha Banford had died. He remembered telling God to "go to hell." When he met Lois, he tried to grab on to her faith, her deep spiritual convictions. But when you start to lose faith in yourself, as he did each time he came off another binge, why, he thought, should a God, a Supreme Being, have any use for a drunken bum like him?

But this very morning, as he sat on the edge of the bed next to Lois and saw the love and faith in the eyes of his devoted and supportive wife, he was moved. He was touched. He could not refuse her request. It was October 20, 1928, and he wrote in that Bible—in what Lois always said was the most sacred place she knew—these words: "To my beloved wife that has endured so much, let this stand as evidence of my pledge to you that I have finished with drink forever."

He was drunk before the end of the week.

On Thanksgiving Day, only a month later, he wrote in her Bible again, "My strength is renewed a thousandfold in my love for you."[5]

Then he set off the next day on another toot. In January of 1929, he scrawled in the Bible for a third and final time. His handwriting was barely legible. "To tell you once more that I am finished with it!"

Deep in his heart, Bill knew even these sincerest of "pledges" were useless in the face of his intense craving for booze. His pain and despair were evident in the following note he wrote to Lois in the spring of 1929:

"I have failed again this day. That I should continue to even try to do right in the grand manner is perhaps a great foolishness. Righteousness simply does not seem to be in me. Nobody wishes it more than I. Yet no one flouts it more often." As he had told Lois earlier, "I'm halfway to hell now and going strong."[6]

Some years later, after founding Alcoholics Anonymous, Bill would describe such remarks as "a big fat bout of self-pity."[7]

Lois, however, could tell from notes like this that her husband desperately wanted to stop, and she continued to seek all kinds of ways to help him. Randolph, the night doorman at their luxury apartment building, was one of those many ways. He was a warm-hearted Rosicrucian from the West Indies. When Bill came staggering home in the wee hours, Randolph would always help him into the elevator and up to their apartment.

Lois grew comfortable with the doorman's quiet way of caring, and especially his way of keeping it all to himself. They became good friends and she soon found she was not the least embarrassed talking to this kind gentleman about her husband's problem since Randolph had told her: "I have the same problem with several in my own family. It's the Devil's curse." She would smile, since that's what her mother always used to say.

At Lois's request, Randolph kept tabs on Bill, discovering what speakeasies he frequented in the neighborhood and, when he was late coming home, he would actually leave his post, search the bars, find Bill, and drag him home to Lois.

Bill himself was also touched by Randolph's concern. When he and Lois learned his daughter was taking piano lessons, they gave the doorman a check for $2,500 to buy her a piano. Randolph remained a good friend of the Wilsons for many years.

In the Fellowship of Alcoholics Anonymous, one often hears mention of something called the "invisible line." This refers to the point at which a heavy drinker becomes an alcoholic, when his desire for a drink turns into a craving or an addiction. He or she then has a constant mental obsession for alcohol, which becomes a physical compulsion once the drink is taken. If there is such a line, Bill Wilson crossed it early in 1929.

The young Wall Street wizard began to imbibe as he never had before—straight shots with no chasers. Often the shots were doubles. He needed it now to "clear the vision," to fuel his fading dreams. With just enough in him, he could imagine himself the chairman of J.P. Morgan, a director of Standard Oil, an advisor to John D. Rockefeller himself. With a few more, he fell into oblivion—into a blackout from which he sometimes emerged in strange and unusual places—in doorways, on park benches, in grassy fields, or at the bar in another speakeasy far removed from the one in which he started out. At other times he'd come to in Randolph's arms, on his bathroom floor, or in his own bed with Lois placing an ice pack on his throbbing head.

He would often say to himself, *so what if I enjoy boozing? I'm healthy, wealthy, good at my job, and I have the support of a devoted wife.* This was the story he would tell himself the night before. It was always a different story the morning after.

By now, Lois clearly recognized her husband's drinking was completely out of control, yet she remained totally committed to helping him in any way she could. In her later years, she once shared some of her most intimate feelings with a very close friend: "I tried so hard to let him know how much I loved him and that I would always be there for him. I know now that was wrong. I did love him, but I was enabling him to drink because there were no consequences with me and he knew it.

"As Bill drank more and more, he was often impotent. We wouldn't make love for months at a time. Then I'd manage to coax him to take a few weeks off. I'd get him back out into the country, up to Emerald Lake, into the Green Mountains he so loved. We'd camp near a running brook and make love under the stars. These jaunts into the countryside became like a series of honeymoons—with hell in between. Then, after a while, these brief series of honeymoons stopped and there was nothing left but hell."[8]

It was while Lois was packing for another of those brief "honeymoons" in Vermont that Ebby Thacher phoned. He had been in Albany, New York, for almost a year trying to save the family business. While Lois never voiced it to Bill, Ebby's absence from the scene pleased her greatly since it meant one less drinking buddy to contend with.

Bill, on the other hand, missed his boyhood chum, so when he returned Ebby's call and learned his help was needed, there was no way he could turn him down. The Thacher family's cast-iron woodstove business was under heated competition from those new-fangled gas stoves. Ebby told Bill the company needed an influx of new capital to survive.

"There's been one too many boozers trying to run this damn place for too many years," Lois recalled Bill's friend saying.[9]

Bill had to chuckle, wondering if Ebby was including himself among the group. But he kept his thoughts to himself. Like most alcoholics, both Bill and Ebby could recognize a drinking problem in others long before they could see it in themselves.

Lois was disturbed when her husband told her the story and concluded that he had to try to help his good friend. She put her foot down. Lois insisted he come to Emerald Lake and let Ebby find some other way to solve his dilemma. It was the first real argument they had had in a long time when Bill was not in his cups.

In the end, they reached a compromise, which Lois reluctantly accepted—as if she had a choice. They would take the train together but Bill would get off in Albany and she would continue on to East Dorset. He swore he wouldn't take more than forty-eight hours to wrap things up and then would hop the next train and join her at the lake. It sounded very reasonable except, based on her past experiences, forty-eight hours could mean a week or two once he and his pal started drinking. Bill tried to convince her once again that it was all going to be strictly business. He put on that silly grin, crossed his heart and hoped to die, and she half-bought it as usual.

Bill and Ebby met at a speakeasy in downtown Albany. Where else? They tied one on but managed to sober up long enough to tour the cast-iron stove plant the next afternoon. Even before leaving New York, the experienced analyst knew in his heart this would be a hopeless venture. Once he saw the factory, he was convinced of it. Why would anyone keep making buggy whips, he thought, after Henry Ford created the auto assembly line? Why make woodstoves in the new age of natural gas?

But he put up a good front for his boyhood pal, saying he'd do whatever was possible. Ebby was no fool, however. He could tell from his best friend's demeanor there would be no influx of new capital for the failing family business.

That night they both got roaring drunk. They were joined in the speakeasy by several of Ebby's friends from the Albany airfield, barnstormers who called themselves Flyers Incorporated. When they heard

Bill had to hurry to East Dorset, Vermont, in order to stay out of his wife's doghouse, one of the heavy-drinking pilots—a Ted Burke by name—offered to fly him there the next morning for a small fee. Ebby said he'd like to come along to see Lois and some other old friends in Manchester.

So they partied all night and were flying higher than kites long before they took off from the Albany airfield the next morning.

It just so happened that the town of Manchester had recently completed its brand-new airport and was holding ceremonies to dedicate it the very day Bill, Ebby, and their pilot were due to arrive. Lois, having received a phone call from her husband the night before, was at the airport to pick him up. She was surprised by the crowd on hand, which included the mayor, the town band, and a delegation of excited citizens awaiting the arrival of the first official plane to touch down on the brand spanking new runway. To be sure, it was not the plane flown by a drunken barnstormer carrying two drunken passengers.

When Bill shared his experiences later on in Alcoholics Anonymous, he loved to tell the hilarious story of what happened next, although he always did it with some deference to Lois, who at the time saw no humor in it at all.

"We circled the field. But meantime, all three of us had been pulling at a bottle. Somehow, we lit on a pretty bumpy meadow. The delegation charged forward. It was up to Ebby and me to do something, but we could do absolutely nothing. We somehow slid out of the cockpit, fell on the ground, and there we lay, immobile. Such was the history-making episode of the first airplane to light at Manchester, Vermont."[10]

For Lois, it was simply another shameful and embarrassing episode. Several of her friends were part of the delegation, and others there were close to her parents. She ran off sobbing, hoping Bill wouldn't follow. But he did, and in spite of his apologies to the mayor and other leading citizens, Lois refused to accept his remorseful pleadings. They returned to New York the following week without a brief "honeymoon" and with only the expectancy of more hell to follow. And it did.

It was only a few weeks after they returned to Brooklyn Heights that Elise Shaw showed up unexpectedly at Lois's apartment. It was a hot

August afternoon. She apologized for not calling ahead but explained somewhat falteringly that she had to work up some courage to come. Lois didn't understand at first.

Politely refusing a cup of tea, Elise sat uncomfortably on the couch in the living room and began by telling her dear friend that Frank was under a great deal of pressure from his partners at Tobey & Kirk to fire Bill. This didn't come as any great surprise to Lois. In fact, she had considerable admiration for Frank Shaw for putting up with her husband's antics this long. She had often thought that losing his job might be just the jolt Bill needed to straighten out.

While these thoughts raced through her head, she vaguely heard Elise recite a series of incidents Frank had told her about—Bill's getting drunk on business trips, embarrassing some important clients, having nasty arguments with several executives at the firm. Lois heard nothing really new in her friend's litany except that Frank had given her husband his final warning.

Elise stopped for a moment and stared intently at this tender and kind lady she had known most of her life. Why was it so impossible to reach her, to get her to understand? She then said very simply that regardless of Lois's continued denial of the seriousness of her husband's problem, she should at least seek some professional help for him—for the sake of Bill's health and for the sake of their marriage.

Lois recognized the deep sincerity in her friend's eyes and trembling voice. She clumsily expressed her gratitude for Elise's concern, finally admitting she was absolutely right in everything she said. That the problem had grown much worse, although it was not completely hopeless.

Then suddenly Lois began talking at length about all she was still trying to do to help her husband, the pledges he was making in her Bible, the good times they had in Vermont, that he still wanted to stop so badly perhaps God would soon intervene.

Elise had all she could take. She rose from the couch and glared at Lois. "For God's sake," she said in a voice her childhood friend had never heard before, "you're dealing with something you have no control over. Why do you think I told the adoption agency all about Bill's drinking problem? Why?"

Then Elise Shaw burst into tears.

"I'm sorry, Lois . . . but . . . I had to do it. And . . . you still don't understand."

Then Lois Wilson's oldest and dearest companion turned and walked out of the apartment. Lois stood there in the middle of her well-furnished living room staring after her with those shocking and painful words still ringing in her ears: "I told the adoption agency all about Bill's drinking problem."[11]

That night when Randolph the doorman half-carried her husband through the front door and put him to bed, Lois was still seated in the darkened parlor staring out the window, her eyes red and glassy. Randolph simply whispered good night and left her there undisturbed. For the next several days, she walked around in a trance. She wouldn't answer the telephone or go out. She walked into another room whenever Bill wanted to talk. He knew something terrible had happened and as usual believed he had caused it. Since his wife refused to speak with him, he let her be and went to work with every intention of heeding Frank Shaw's final warning.

The emotional fog eventually lifted, and Lois came to terms with what happened between her and Elise. While it would take quite some time for their painful rift to heal, it did help her begin to understand the sheer hopelessness of the problem she faced. But for the moment and for some time to come, Lois put it all completely out of her mind. As she would share about it later on, "While it was all so terribly painful, it did eventually help me realize that Bill just couldn't stop with only my help. Neither of us knew at the time that he had a physical, mental, and spiritual illness. The traditional theory that drunkenness was a moral weakness kept us both from thinking clearly on the subject.

"I always considered my husband a morally strong person despite his alcoholism. His sense of right and wrong was vivid, and he also respected the rights of other people. When he was sober, for example, he would never walk across another person's lawn although I would at times. He had plenty of willpower but neither of us knew that willpower just wouldn't work against alcohol."[12]

Now in a deep quandary about why his wife wasn't speaking to him,

Bill found himself quite eager to comply with her very next request—that he have a complete physical examination and talk with someone knowledgeable about his inability to stop drinking on his own. When Bill suggested he seek the advice of his brother-in-law, Dr. Leonard Strong, Lois had no qualms. She had come to deeply respect Leonard and knew he was already concerned about her husband. So was her sister-in-law Dorothy, whom she had grown very fond of even though they rarely talked about personal matters.

Bill was actually surprised that Dr. Strong, a man he had come to greatly respect and admire, knew so much about the progressive nature of his problem—that he might stay on the wagon for several weeks but once he picked up another drink, the compulsion would set in and he would want more and more—that he drank to fortify himself for important occasions—that he drank to relax his nerves after a busy day on Wall Street—that he often lied, especially to Lois, about how many drinks he had actually had.

It seems more than coincidental that Leonard had learned much of this from his good friend and colleague Dr. William Duncan Silkworth, who ran Towns Hospital in New York City, an institution that specialized in the treatment of alcoholics—coincidental because Dr. Silkworth would play a prominent role in Bill's eventual sobriety and building the Fellowship of Alcoholics Anonymous.

Dr. Strong, however, was not yet convinced Bill was bad enough to be admitted to Towns, so he decided to send him to another colleague in Manhattan first for a complete physical examination. That would tell him what he needed to know medically.

Much to everyone's surprise, including Lois, the young New York internist found Leonard's patient to be in good physical health with only slightly elevated blood pressure, which—he agreed with Bill's assessment—could be due to the stress of a career in the stock market. Bill was only thirty-five at the time, so apparently his youth and stamina were still warding off any serious physical effects of alcoholism, although they were right around the corner. But on this particular day, he was told by this particular doctor there was no reason why with a little "willpower" he couldn't drink in "moderation."

Bill left that Manhattan medical office with little regard for the young physician except he now had the words "willpower" and "moderation" implanted firmly in his alcoholic brain. And when Dr. Strong received the results of his brother-in-law's physical examination, he had no reason to believe he needed to see a specialist such as Dr. Silkworth—at least not yet. But he kept the thought in the back of his mind.

As fall approached, the stock market began to gyrate a bit more than usual. Lois began reading predictions in the newspapers that the bubble was about to burst, that investors should take their profits and run. On those weekends when Bill was "drying out," she would ask him about these dire forecasts. He told her the best minds in the business said the market and their stocks in particular still had a long way to go, especially Penick & Ford.

Penick & Ford was a small molasses business that had merged with a large corn products company. After one of his inside inspections, Bill felt it was an "undiscovered jewel" and began buying it on margin. It was now the largest holding in his portfolio. He even persuaded Leonard and several close friends and associates to take positions in the stock although, like Leonard, most of them never bought anything on margin. They felt it was too risky, especially in such a speculative bull market.

But not Bill. He had started buying Penick & Ford on margin in the spring of 1929 at around $35 a share. By early October, it was close to $60. Even on October 23, when the market dropped significantly in the last hour of trading, and the next day, when over thirteen million shares were traded on the New York Stock Exchange, Bill hung on. And he was right—for two days, anyway. Penick & Ford dropped to $42 a share but had quickly risen back over $50. He sat in his favorite speakeasy and congratulated himself for being so smart and gutsy.

Like the bombing of Pearl Harbor, the assassination of President John F. Kennedy, and the Twin Towers tragedy in New York City on September 11, 2001, almost everyone remembered where they were on October 29, 1929, when the stock market crashed.

Lois had spent the morning with her mother at the hospital. Matilda was undergoing a series of tests for severe pains in her abdomen. Her daughter kissed her good-bye and returned home early that afternoon. It was some time around two o'clock, just an hour before the stock market closed. She turned on the radio and heard the news announcer shouting into his microphone, "The stock market is falling like an avalanche, like a plane crashing to earth. Even the wisest sages on Wall Street can't explain such a catastrophe or just where the bottom might be. There's not only complete pandemonium in the financial markets, it's sheer panic."[13]

Lois stood staring at the radio on the living-room table. Everything she feared could happen was happening. But it wasn't until the first report of someone leaping from a building in the Wall Street area that the impact of it all suddenly hit her. She ran to the telephone and called Bill. He wasn't in his office. Her suspicions were correct. He was in a Wall Street speakeasy with his drunken cronies trying to figure out what happened so quickly, so unexplainably, so disastrously.[14] Not only had the bubble burst, but the sudden and severe disruption in the financial markets would soon lead to America's Great Depression, which lasted through most of the 1930s.

This severe economic dislocation was caused not just by the stock market crash of 1929, but also by the failure of the nation's banks to meet the withdrawal demands of frightened depositors. Many had to close their doors due to the lack of liquidity. The Federal Reserve Board and the Securities and Exchange Commission were created a few years later to prevent just such financial catastrophes from occurring in the future.

That Monday morning when Bill Wilson walked into Tobey & Kirk, his prize investment, Penick & Ford, had risen to $55 a share. He was a happy man. But by noon, it was $45. By one o'clock, the company shares had made a sickening dive to $32. By the time the stock ticker stopped ticking, they were in the low $20s. He was on margin and he couldn't cover. The tremendous tumble in the market had also wiped out whatever equity he had in his other stocks. By three o'clock on October 29, 1929, Lois and Bill Wilson were broke.

Bill didn't come home that night. Lois paced the rooms of their apartment until she was so exhausted she sat on the couch and dozed. Every little noise awakened her with a start. By eight in the morning, she decided to phone the police. There was no William G. Wilson listed in the "accident reports." She waited until after ten before calling his office. When told he wasn't there, she nervously asked to speak with Frank Shaw.

Lois waited several minutes before Frank came to the phone. He was polite and discreet. He had no idea where her husband might be although his voice hinted she might scour the city's speakeasies. Before hanging up, the husband of her once dearest friend dealt her one more blow. It wasn't his intention to hurt her. He simply had to be honest. Frank said the partners at Tobey & Kirk had forced his hand. He had no other choice but to let Bill go.

She turned on the radio, then quickly shut it off as news announcers continued their gruesome reports of the many now-broke wealthy investors who had plummeted to their death from tall buildings.[15]

It was early that evening when Randolph dragged her husband into their apartment. His jacket and pants were torn, there was a cut on his face, and he was in the worst condition she had ever witnessed. Randolph suggested Lois watch him closely and if he began to sweat and shake very badly, she might want to call a doctor. She sat next to her husband on the bed all night, bathing his face with cold towels, wiping off the saliva drooling from his mouth, calming him each time he shuddered and shouted in his delirium. It was almost dawn before he fell into a deep sleep. Lois lay down next to him, and when her mind finally grew too weary to think anymore, she herself drifted off.[16]

Late that afternoon, Bill came quietly into the living room where Lois was again staring out the window. Trying to hide his trembling hands, Bill assured his wife he would pull himself together and start all over again. He forced himself as best he could to sound confident and determined. He said he wouldn't make any more empty promises about his drinking, but he wanted her to know this absolute disaster had finally taught him the lesson he needed to learn—that booze had ruined his life. He no longer had any doubts about that. Even one drink at this point was one drink too many. This time he'd climb on that water wagon and stay there.

All Lois could do was hug him and try to believe in him one more time. After all, she still loved her husband deeply, and in the face of such a calamity, wouldn't any reasonable, rational, intelligent person—and Bill was certainly all of these—finally make the same decision he just did?

Maybe in the face of doom, there was finally a little ray of hope.[17]

Bill began dropping by various Wall Street firms hoping to find a spot, but even former associates he had made a lot of money for in the past wouldn't give him the time of day. Not only were most of these companies quickly retrenching following the crash, but Bill's reputation always preceded him. Although he was known for his experienced analytical skills and ability to make money, no one was willing to take a chance on a "booze hound"—at least not in those trying times.

Over dinner one night, Lois said she had come across some letters from old friends they had met in Canada on their trip there a few years before. She wondered if things were as bad in Canada as they were here in the United States.

It was as if she had suddenly turned on a bright light. Bill's face lit up. Why hadn't he thought of that himself? No, things were still going great in Canada, especially in Toronto and Montreal and, as Lois said, he still had some good friends there. He gave his wife a big hug and kiss, then hurried into the den to shoot off a note to one of those good friends—Dick Johnson, who ran Greenshields and Company, a medium-sized brokerage firm in Montreal. He and Dick had done business in the past and several deals had proved quite lucrative for all concerned.

By the middle of November, he had received a wire from Dick Johnson telling him Greenshields would love to have him on board and to come to Montreal as soon as it was feasible. It appeared to be a golden opportunity, and Lois was overjoyed that she had played a small role in making it happen. So they sublet their apartment, put their furniture into storage, and set off for Canada where Bill was going to prove that he had weathered the storm and was on his way again. Lois's hopes began to soar and she simply refused this time to listen to those nagging butterflies in her stomach.

The day after they arrived in Montreal, Lois found a small but comfortable furnished apartment on Gerard Street. Bill immediately began networking with a number of old contacts he had around the city and its environs—brokers, analysts, corporate financial and investment officers. It started to pay dividends even sooner than he could have possibly imagined.

He met a charming young English playboy named Harry Bates

whose family had substantial mining interests in Canada. He and Bill hit it right off. Before long, Harry became a significant client and introduced Bill to a number of his wealthy friends. Dick Johnson and Greenshields were more than pleased to see the newest member of the firm fast becoming one of its biggest producers.

By the late spring of 1930, Lois and Bill had moved into an expensive apartment in Glen Eagle, high on a bluff overlooking the city of Montreal, and had their furniture shipped in from New York. They had also joined Harry Bates's elegant country club, where Bill fell in love with the game of golf.

"It was simply wonderful," Lois recalled, "but it was all happening much too fast like it did once before in our lives. The truth was, I wasn't overly concerned because Bill was staying sober. He seemed absolutely committed and determined to make a success out of this new God-given opportunity."[18]

But the disease of alcoholism is cunning, baffling, and powerful. It can lie dormant for a while and then suddenly erupt for no real reason and when least expected.

This time it began one lovely evening in June at their country club. Lois and Bill were having dinner with Harry Bates and his latest flame. The waiter handed the English playboy the wine list. He asked Lois if she had any particular preference. She smiled and said she always deferred to connoisseurs like himself. He enjoyed the flattery. When the expensive bottle of French wine Harry selected arrived at their table, he refused to accept Bill's flimsy excuse for not having at least one glass. Bill glanced at Lois. He was sure she would understand he couldn't possibly take the chance of offending his most important client. And after all, this time it really was only for business.

But Lois's worst fears were not realized that night. In fact, the couples consumed two bottles of wine, had an excellent dinner, danced until almost midnight, and then went home. As they entered their apartment, Lois kissed her husband and told him how proud she was of his determination to change the course of his life and finally achieve the kind of success they had always dreamed about.

Before the end of the week, the French wine had convinced Bill he could once again be a social drinker, so he began nipping on his way to work. Then he began buying bottles of whiskey to stash in his desk at the office. Soon he had one hidden behind the bookcase in their apartment. When Lois discovered what was happening again, she became so hurt and overwrought she simply did not know what to do.

By late summer, Dick Johnson began a series of meetings with Bill in an attempt to save their relationship and his job with Greenshields and Company. He told his friend that while it was true he was making money for the firm, his partners were hearing too many stories about his drinking, his fights at the country club and even on the golf course, and upsetting incidents involving potential customers. But despite these warnings and more chances to reform, Bill just couldn't stop his boozing.

It was late September when Lois received an ominous phone call from her sister Barbara. Their mother was back in the hospital for more tests, only this time the results were far from encouraging. Mrs. Burnham's condition had earlier been diagnosed as a low-grade infection in the abdomen. Now it was feared she might have cancer, and she had already begun radiation treatments.

Even though Lois knew her husband's job was in serious jeopardy, she felt she had to be with her mother, at least until she knew more about the seriousness of her condition. Bill said he understood and that she shouldn't worry about him. Greenshields wasn't the only firm in Canada that could use a good moneymaker like him. Lois could only shake her head. She left for Brooklyn Heights hoping and praying that he would somehow come to his senses before it was too late. The problem was, it already was too late.

While Canada had initially been spared the collapse that hit the U.S. stock market, it was only a matter of time before the ripple effect was to take its toll. It seemed that time coincided with Bill's downward plunge again into alcoholism. With Greenshields now cutting back on its staff and Bill unable to curb his lifestyle, Dick Johnson had no other choice but to let him go.

With Lois back in Brooklyn, her husband began drinking around the clock. It was several weeks before he finally came off his binge. It was only then that he realized after working for ten months in Montreal, and after being connected with so many substantial investors and important firms there and in the United States, he had absolutely nothing to show for it. All he could do now was put their furniture into storage again, sublet their Glen Eagles apartment, and head back to New York.

Bill Wilson was not only broke once again but, between his margin losses in both countries, his unpaid rents, and his drinking bills, he was $60,000 in debt. He had to humble himself at Greenshields to borrow $500 against his World War I life insurance policy to pay for his transportation home.

Lois had been trying to reach Bill during his drinking binge. She was ready to head for Montreal when he finally returned her calls. At first he said he planned to stay there and find another position but she knew just by listening to him that it was hopeless. A few days before leaving Canada, he received the following note from his heartsick wife:

> *Come home to me. My heart is breaking. How can we go on like this day after day! What's to become of us? I love you so, and yet my love doesn't seem to do you any good. Still I have faith that it must, someday. God grant that day be soon, for it doesn't seem as if I could go on like this, night after night, waiting for you hour after hour. Oh, that I had the wisdom to know what would help you, for I'm sure you could be helped if only I knew how. I'd do anything, dear, that would help you. I put faith in love, love, love—and patience. Oh, I hope I'll have the patience to go through with it, for it seems each night as though I couldn't stand another—and yet another comes, and still another, until my heart is like a stone. A great dullness spreads over me until all things, good and bad, seem to taste alike.*
> *. . . God give me wisdom and strength and patience.*[19]

It was snowing the day he arrived back in Brooklyn.

8

When Love Is Not Enough

*T*HE LATE NOVEMBER SNOW WAS BEGINNING TO STICK TO THE bare branches of the tall elm in the backyard of Clinton Street. Dr. Clark Burnham stood at the kitchen window staring out, his deeply lined face reflecting the white glow emanating from the heavy downfall. He had much on his mind.

Clark had just returned from the hospital, where his colleagues had given him the terrible news about his wife. The cancer was terminal. Matilda had but a few weeks to live. Now he must gather his family together and tell them in the most gentle and loving way possible in spite of all these mixed emotions stirring inside.

But first he must talk to his daughter Lois, who was standing at the stove only a few feet away making them both a cup of tea. Dr. Burnham rubbed the back of his neck, stiff and aching from the growing stress and tension suddenly filling his life. After another moment, he turned and sat at the kitchen table. Lois handed him a cup of tea, then sat down across from him. She fidgeted nervously with the wrinkled collar on her housedress, appearing too ashamed and embarrassed to look her father in the eye. Dr. Burnham sipped the steaming tea. Then after a moment he spoke. His first question was simple and direct, for he had no time or patience for sugarcoating, even with his oldest and dearest daughter.

"What do you plan to do now?" he asked.

Lois cast a quick glance toward the outside hall, then back at her teacup. Her father knew she was thinking about her husband, who was asleep in an upstairs bedroom having just arrived back from Montreal. Her whispered reply was also simple and direct, "I don't know, father. I just don't know."[1]

It was the sad and hopeless look in his daughter's eyes that finally took the sting out of his anger. After all, the damage had been done. There was nothing he could possibly do at this point about his drunken son-in-law. He wanted to throttle him, yes, but how would that help his Lois who, he knew for some inexplicable, insane reason, apparently still loved the lout?

Despite his deep resentment, it was quite obvious that Clark Burnham, in spite of being a doctor himself, understood little if anything about the disease of alcoholism. Few did in those days. He was simply one of the many who considered drunkenness immoral and a weakness of the will. It was perhaps the biggest bone of contention between himself and his wife, who for some strange reason always knew her son-in-law had a "sickness of the soul."

But now, filled with empathy for his daughter, Dr. Burnham reached out, took her hand, and said with as much warmth and understanding as he could muster under the circumstances, "You and Bill are welcome to stay here until he gets back on his feet. I'm sure that's what your mother would want, too." Then after a brief pause, he added: "We'll talk more later."[2] Lois squeezed her father's hand. No other words were necessary. Dr. Burnham got up, came around the table, kissed her cheek, then quickly left the kitchen. She watched him for a moment as he disappeared down the hall. Then she rose, walked to the window, and stared out.

Watching the snow continue to fall, Lois thought about her husband's humiliating return from Canada, the despair in his bloodshot eyes, the futility of the pledge he made to her again as he stumbled in the door. She wanted to ask him as her father had just asked her: "What do you plan to do now?" But she knew it wasn't the time and that the answer would simply involve another empty promise.

Her mind was racing again. Many times in the past when she wanted to capture her thoughts, she would write them down so she could look at them, consider them, glance back at them as her life continued to change from one day to the next. She found a pencil and some paper in a cabinet drawer. Sitting back down at the kitchen table, in the soft, gentle quietness a snowfall brings, Lois began taking an honest and painful inventory of her situation. She wrote the following:

> *What is one to think or do after so many failures? Is my theory of the importance of love and faith nothing but bunk? Is it best to recognize life as it seems—a series of failures—and that my husband is a weak, spineless creature who is never going to get over his drinking?*
>
> *If I should lose my love and faith, what then? As I see it now, there is nothing but emptiness, bickering, taunts and selfishness, each of us trying to get as much out of the other as possible in order to forget our lost ideals.*
>
> *I love my husband more than words can tell, and I know he loves me. He is a splendid, fine man—in fact an unusual man with qualities that could make him reach the top. His personality is endearing; everybody loves him; and he is a born leader . . .*
>
> *. . . The morning after he has been drunk, he is so penitent, self-derogatory and sweet that it takes the wind out of my sails, and I cannot upbraid him.*
>
> *He continually asks for my help, and we have been trying together almost daily for five years to find an answer to his drinking problem, but it is worse now than ever . . .*
>
> *. . . How can he ever accomplish anything with this frightful handicap? I worry more about the moral effect on him than I do the physical, although goodness knows the terrible stuff he drinks is enough to burn him up completely. Where can he ever go but down when he can't control this habit? And his aims have always been so high! . . .*
>
> *I believe that people are good if you give them half a chance and that good is more powerful than evil . . . Francis Bacon said that the human mind is easily fooled; that we*

*believe what we want to believe and recognize only those
facts which conform to that belief. Am I doing that identi-
cal thing? Are people bad, is love futile, and Bill doomed to
worse than mediocrity? Am I a fool not to recognize it and
grasp what pleasure and comfort I can?* [3]

Lois did not write an answer to that last question in so many words
that snowy morning at Clinton Street, but she did answer it by her
actions. Instead of leaving and seeking "pleasure and comfort" somewhere else, she stayed with her husband, not knowing how long it would
take or if ever such qualities would come into their lives. She could only
hope and pray they would.

Perhaps without realizing it, what this deeply committed and benevo-
lent lady decided to do at that moment in her life was to love her husband
"unconditionally." It wouldn't be "I'll love you if only . . . " or "I'll love you
once you . . . " No. With Lois Wilson, it was now: "I will love you no matter what." This principle of unconditional love was to become the corner-
stone of Alcoholics Anonymous and Al-Anon—the unconditional love of
one alcoholic for another, of one suffering spouse for another. [4]

But is love, no matter how strong and how unswerving, enough to
get an alcoholic sober and keep him or her sober? Lois was soon to find
the answer to this vital question in her own painful way.

After rereading her scribbled notes, she folded the paper and put it
into her pocket. Then she went upstairs, got dressed, and left for the hospital to see her mother. Bill continued to sleep it off.

Lois had been back in Brooklyn Heights since mid-October. She
had returned to help care for her mother, who wanted to be home with
her family, not "locked away in some lonely hospital all by myself." Dr.
Burnham had arranged to have his wife brought to the medical center
weekly for radium treatments until her condition suddenly worsened
and she required more frequent treatments and intensive pain medication. Matilda finally relented and just two days ago was readmitted to
the hospital.

While caring for her mother at Clinton Street, Lois rarely went out.
At the same time, she was so consumed by her husband's abject failure

and the humiliation of their move back into her father's house that she had given little thought to what was happening in the world around her. It wasn't until she boarded the crowded bus to the hospital that day and glanced around at her fellow passengers that a strange awareness came over her. The looks on their faces seemed to mirror how she felt inside— sad, bewildered, and frightened. And each time she caught someone's eye, they would look away—as did she.

Lois exited the bus at Flatbush Avenue, one of Brooklyn's main thoroughfares. The snow was still falling, but it didn't blind her from suddenly noticing the effects of last year's stock market crash on the ordinary hardworking men and women she began passing on the street . . . families in the long breadline in front of the First Presbyterian Church . . . clusters of men huddled in doorways, going nowhere . . . two elderly men across the way picking through trash barrels.

Having been in Canada for almost a year, Lois was essentially unaware of the shocking collapse of the U.S. economy. Certainly she heard stories from family members and friends, but she was so engrossed in trying to keep her husband sober and employed that she didn't entirely comprehend the catastrophic consequences of the crash.[5] Apparently neither did Herbert Clark Hoover, who succeeded Calvin Coolidge as the thirty-first president of the United States. Hoover and his cabinet had failed to recognize early enough that European countries had borrowed far too excessively from American banks. Now, with the collapsing stock market having worldwide impact, these countries were in no position to repay their enormous debts. Almost overnight, U.S. banks began to fail. Even the building and loan organizations, which had been established to help homeowners like Dr. Clark Burnham meet their mortgage commitments and the nation's farmers sustain their crop investments, were forced to close their doors.

The country quickly spun into a deep depression. Before the end of 1930, businesses were going bankrupt, family farms were being auctioned off, factories were firing thousands of workers, and once-wealthy investors were wallpapering their bathroom walls with worthless stock certificates. It was an economic nightmare of gigantic proportions that would take years to repair.

The wind was now blowing the snow into swirling gusts. As Lois turned into High Street and headed toward the hospital, she spotted a man standing in front of a boarded-up bakery shop selling apples from a cardboard box. He was in his thirties, about Bill's age. His clothes were shabby and he appeared ashamed that life had dealt him such a cruel blow. He stared at the ground as Lois passed. She hesitated for a moment, touched by his hopelessness, but then walked on. She wanted to help but had only enough change in her purse for bus fare back home. So she quickly continued on her way.[6]

Lois had always hated the smell of hospitals, and today for some reason the antiseptic odor seemed to fuel her anxieties even more. Her younger brother Lyman was at their mother's bedside when she arrived. They hadn't seen each other in over a year. He was now a doctor himself and had an active practice out of his home in New Jersey, where he lived with his lovely bride of less than two years.

They hugged warmly. Then after Lois hugged and kissed her mother, Lyman whispered that he would wait for her in the corridor outside. He knew his sister and mother needed to be alone together at this crucial juncture.

While Matilda had been back in the hospital only a few days, even she knew at this point the treatments were not working. She could no longer eat, and the pain medications were becoming less effective. No one had to tell this intelligent and compassionate woman that the end was drawing near. Still, she smiled through her suffering and fought to make her final days meaningful.

Lois sat at her mother's bedside holding her hand and chatting about the weather, the Christmas decorations already up in the stores, how quickly the holiday season was upon them. There were so many far more important things she wanted to say, so much she wanted to ask, so much she wanted to share—but for some inexplicable reason, only this stupid, meaningless small talk kept pouring out of her mouth. It had been the same way at home, too, never talking about dying. Then suddenly Matilda squeezed her daughter's hand and pulled her close. Lois never forgot what her mother said that afternoon, perhaps because of how she struggled to speak or because her words forced her to make some important decisions about the direction of her own life.

"Lyman told me Bill has finally come home," her mother began, speaking in a hoarse whisper. "I know how things still are and I have been wondering lately . . . can this really be enough for you? Yes, I know how much you say you still love him and want to take care of him and I admire you for that. He is a very sick man . . . and may get even sicker . . . and certainly he needs you. But Lois . . . you also have a life of your own to live . . . and you must live it. You must find what can truly fulfill you, otherwise . . . one day you will wake up and be consumed by anger and resentment for being cheated out of that life. Please don't let that happen to you, my child. Don't let that happen to you."[7]

Matilda touched a nerve. She verbalized frankly and honestly what her daughter had been refusing to face for several years now. For a long moment, they simply stared at each other, their eyes filled with tears. Finally Lois broke down and admitted her mother was right, that something must change and it had to be her. She promised then and there to heed her mother's advice: she would care for her husband but also take care of herself. She was a strong, well-educated woman with many talents and abilities, and there was no reason why she couldn't succeed in life and find some enjoyment for herself regardless of what happened to her husband. Yes, she would continue to try to help him but would also seek to help herself and improve her own life at the same time. As she shared these most intimate thoughts and feelings, she could tell by the wisp of a smile on her mother's face that she could be at peace now, knowing her daughter was ready to pull her life together and not be dragged down by her son-in-law's alcoholism. While she sensed her daughter's determination, even Matilda Burnham, who believed to the depths of her soul that alcoholism was a spiritual malady, had no idea what a powerful influence it could have over someone . . . even someone as strong and determined as Lois Burnham Wilson. But for now at least, having shared her deepest concerns with her daughter, Matilda could rest more comfortably as she waited for her God to take her.[8]

They continued to talk for a short while before Lois noticed her mother becoming totally fatigued. She urged her to rest, but the pain was returning. Just then the nurse entered with a timely dose of morphine. Lois waited as her mother dropped into a deep sleep. Then she kissed her

on the forehead and walked quietly from the room. Lyman was still waiting in the corridor. He invited his sister to join him for some coffee in
the hospital cafeteria. He said there were some things they needed to talk
about.

While never one to point fingers, Lois's younger brother had grown
up to be the most serious sibling in the family and, though tactful, always
said what was on his mind. Over coffee and a sandwich, he told his older
sister something she was completely unaware of—that their father had
suffered heavy financial losses as a result of the 1929 crash and that he
was also carrying most of his patients on credit since so many of them
had lost their jobs or businesses. Lyman also revealed that a very close
friend in Vermont had told him the good doctor was quietly inquiring
about the possibility of selling the cottage on Emerald Lake and that he
had already remortgaged Clinton Street.

They both knew their father was too proud to discuss any of this with
his family, but Lyman thought Lois should know the entirety of the situation. Then he tactfully remarked that with her and Bill now living at
Clinton Street and with Bill possibly finding a job, perhaps they could
help lessen the financial burden on their father, who was carrying the
mortgage on the large brownstone all by himself.

While her younger sibling's revelation of their father's financial mis-
fortunes came as a shock, the more Lois thought about it, the more she
sensed that her father's plight could be the reason for Dr. Burnham's quiet
demeanor ever since she had returned home from Montreal—followed
by Bill's sudden arrival in his somewhat inebriated condition. Then, the
more she considered all her brother had said, the more embarrassed and
ashamed she began to feel.

After all, if Lyman knew all about their father's situation, then so did
the rest of the family by now. And as much as she had tried to hide the
seriousness of her husband's drinking problem and his inability to hold a
job, she felt certain that they, like Lyman, had their suspicions and probably shared the same attitude—that her and Bill's presence at Clinton
Street was simply another burden their father shouldn't have to shoulder,
especially in the midst of his current emotional and financial travails.

Lois sensed her younger brother was a bit uncomfortable as they said their good-byes. He offered a halfhearted apology in case he had said anything that might have offended her and then quickly dashed off. This was a conversation she wished they hadn't had, but then, she told herself, she had to stop running away from reality if she was sincere about finding and living her own life. She pulled herself together and went back upstairs to her mother's room. She sat quietly by her bedside for several more hours. When the sky began to darken outside the window, the nurse returned with some more pain medication. Then Lois finally left.[9]

There was much to think about on the bus ride home. Even though every nerve in her body and every thought in her brain told her to move from Clinton Street as quickly as possible, down deep she knew how foolish these urges were. Where could they go? What could they afford? Even a furnished one-room flat was out of the question right now, even if they sold all their clothing, silverware, dishes, and furnishings that Bill said were being shipped back from Canada. Besides, this was something she didn't want to do. She would put those things back into storage and find some way to pay for it. She would simply have to swallow her pride for the moment while trying to find a way out of this terrible mess.

By the time she reached Brooklyn Heights, this young woman who felt that she was carrying the weight of the world on her shoulders had already made two very important decisions. First, tomorrow she would begin looking for a job in order to pay her father a modicum of room and board for her and Bill. And if he wouldn't accept it, she would quietly pay for the food, the utilities, and other such bills without him knowing about it. Second, when she was financially able, she would go back to school and start studying for a career that had always fascinated her and one in which she truly believed she could excel—a career in interior decorating.[10] As Lois stepped from the bus into six inches of snow, the stark beauty of the streetlights glistening onto the white roadways and swaying trees, along with her newfound resolve to change the course of her life, somewhat lessened her feelings of shame and anxiety. However, by the time she trudged through the drifts and arrived at the steps leading up to the brownstone, her thoughts of her mother's pain, her father's troubles, and her husband's drinking quickly brought some of the world's weight back onto her sagging shoulders.

Her father had already left for his rounds the following morning when Lois entered the kitchen to find her husband bent over the table sipping a cup of coffee. His hands were trembling too much to lift it to his lips. Joining him at the table, she calmly explained her mother's condition, her father's predicament, and the decision she had made about finding a job. But Bill, who always prided himself in being the great provider, wouldn't hear of it. He said he had already made some phone calls before leaving Montreal and would have a new position himself before the week was out.

For a short while, Lois remained insistent. She wouldn't allow them to be a burden on her father. Then, even though she didn't believe Bill's continuing assurances of getting a new position, she decided to briefly postpone her own job search. After all, the holiday season was already here. She could put up a few Christmas decorations and spend more time with her mother while at the same time combing through the newspapers' employment ads, sparse as they were.

As for Bill, the truth was he had an old drinking buddy at a company called Stanley Statistics who said he could always find him a spot there. For a former Wall Street big shot, the "spot" in question was a rather nondescript job as an assistant bookkeeper for one hundred dollars a week. For many at that time, this was a rather goodly sum, but not for the still-haughty Bill Wilson. However, given the circumstances, he knew he had little choice. He accepted the job as "temporary." Lois was both surprised and pleased. Dr. Burnham was skeptical, and rightly so.

Just three days before Christmas, Bill got himself involved in a barroom brawl. The altercation wasn't much different than the many other drunken fights he had been in over the past several years—a torn jacket, a black eye, a bloody lip. But this time when he woke the following morning, he suddenly realized that the set of company books he had taken with him to work on over the holidays was missing. He must have left the books in the speakeasy after the fight. But which speakeasy, and where? He began searching his favorite haunts all over Brooklyn and lower Manhattan. He even called a number of places where he was now persona non grata. The company books never turned up. He was finally forced to call his drinking buddy at Stanley Statistics, who immediately informed his manager, who immediately fired Bill. So he cashed his last paycheck and set off on another binge—the day before Christmas.[11]

Matilda Spelman Burnham died that Christmas evening, 1930, surrounded by her husband and her children. The only close family member who wasn't there was Bill Wilson. In spite of the fact that he truly loved and respected his mother-in-law, and in spite of the fact that his wife needed his solace and his arms around her at the time, he never made the wake nor the funeral. He was in his own private, drunken world, oblivious to anyone else's pain and sorrow except his own.

For some baffling reason, the more her husband hurt and disappointed her, the more Lois seemed to understand the depth of his illness. Recalling her feelings at that tragic time in her life, she said:

> *As much as I was hurt and embarrassed, deep down I felt that for anyone to do such a thing—especially a man whom I knew sincerely loved my mother and myself—he had to be very sick and in need of much help.*
>
> *My family and friends kept wondering why I didn't express my anger and condemnation of my husband for not being with me at the funeral. But at least there was no longer anything to hide, nothing more to cover up. Now everyone close to me knew what I had tried so hard to keep secret—that Bill was a terrible drunkard who did things few could understand or tolerate.*
>
> *It took me a lot of years and a whole lot of soul-searching before I finally came to understand that I had been trying to hide and cover up his drinking problem mostly for myself— because of my own shame and humiliation. But now with people finding out, especially those who knew and cared for me, I found myself playing the martyr. Although, to be perfectly honest, I didn't realize I was doing it at the time. But Bill would go on his binges and I would bathe in the pity and admiration of others for being such a loving and self-sacrificing wife. I never understood until much later how sick that was.*[12]

Perhaps the shock of Bill's absence at the funeral, and his terrible condition when Lois brought him home from the drunk tank four days later, helped Dr. Burnham comprehend that it had to be more than a weak will and a bad case of immorality to make a man act this way—a young man he once knew as charming, kind, caring, hardworking, and courageous. As a result, and despite his lack of understanding, the good doctor's attitude toward his son-in-law began to soften from that point forward. He sought, almost against his better judgment, to help his daughter care for her husband, particularly in times of crises.

As the new year of 1931 rolled in, Lois found a job at Macy's department store in Manhattan. Since she had no experience at selling, she was hired to demonstrate folding card tables and chairs for the Leg-O-Matic Company. They paid her a salary of nineteen dollars a week while Macy's chipped in a 1 percent commission on sales. But her goal was still to become an interior decorator, a goal she had now shared with her father, who offered his encouragement and his blessing, in addition to any financial help she might need. She insisted she could do it on her own.

One day when Dr. Burnham found his daughter paying some household bills out of her meager salary, he became rather cross. Actually, it offended his pride. He insisted she use her hard-earned money to pursue her career goal and offered again to help her. With her father's encouragement, Lois enrolled in the advanced course at the New School of Interior Decorating in Manhattan. Because of her training and experience in painting and design, she only had to attend classes two nights a week for two semesters; she could be home most evenings. The very idea of moving in the direction she and her mother had discussed boosted Lois's morale greatly and also bolstered her confidence that, should it be necessary, she could make her own way in life.

Bill, on the other hand, was getting occasional "handouts" from some old friends on Wall Street, which usually entailed some simple research projects. As soon as the task was completed or as soon as he got paid, he'd be off on another toot. Often he'd come home so physically ill that Dr. Burnham would have to inject him with a sedative to calm his nerves and put him to sleep.

But Lois kept plodding ahead. By early 1932, she had not only finished school, but she had proven to be such an effective Leg-O-Matic demonstrator that Macy's offered her a sales position in the novelty furniture department, raising her salary to twenty-two dollars a week. However, she now found herself with a department manager who tried to become much too friendly. In fact, when he somehow discovered she was supporting a drunken husband, he became quite forward and overt in his propositions. Despite her angry protestations, the man was relentless. Finally she realized she would either have to file an official complaint and chance being fired, or she would simply have to quit.

Fortunately, her hard work and excellent sales results had come to the attention of the store manager, a gentleman named Guy Kolb. When Lois also told him she had studied interior decorating, he immediately moved her into the home furnishings department, two floors removed from her would-be paramour. His attentions toward her soon ceased, especially when he saw Lois now in the good graces of top management.[13]

It was around the middle of June when Lois came home one evening to find her father pacing the living-room floor. Asking her to remain calm, he explained that Bill had staggered in that afternoon sweating and shaking. He appeared on the verge of delirium tremens, so he rushed him to Kings County Hospital for treatment. He would be there for at least a week to "dry out."

As his daughter sank onto the sofa weeping, her father quietly suggested that Bill might require much more than a week of detoxification from alcohol. For a long time now, the good doctor posed, his actions seemed to border on the edge of sanity. Perhaps Lois should at least consider the idea of committing him for a while to a mental institution for psychiatric help. He said he was so concerned, he would be willing to sign the commitment papers—for her sake as well as his.

"You can't keep going on like this," Lois recalled her father saying in a voice filled with utter frustration. "There's nothing more you can do for him, not if he wants to keep on drinking like this."[14] Lois was shocked to hear her father even suggest such drastic measures. She would not hear of it and told him so. Bill was sick, yes, but certainly far from insane. What he needed was to get out from under all this pressure, his constant struggle to find a position back on Wall Street to prove he wasn't a failure. He needed to get away from people who were whispering behind his back, always putting him down. She would take some time off from work, that's what she would do. They would go back up to Vermont, back to the lake and the mountains he so loved. There he could find some peace and solace and get well again. Then he could start over. They could start over again. It was not too late. She would be there with him, to help him, to convince him that all was not hopeless—that he was still young and bright and capable and could begin a whole new life.

Dr. Burnham simply shook his head. He tried to explain to his daughter that she was simply doing the same things over and over and expecting different results. If it didn't work before, why should it work now? But Lois wouldn't listen. The good doctor finally threw up his hands and left the room. As she sat there all alone, something deep down inside whispered that her father was possibly correct, but she wasn't ready to hear it—at least not right now.

Because summer was the slow season at Macy's, exacerbated now by the Great Depression, Guy Kolb was willing to give Lois a three-month leave of absence, especially when he learned her husband was ill and needed to be nursed back to health.

Since Dr. Burnham was now negotiating to sell the cottage at Emerald Lake, Lois called Bill's sister, Dorothy, and her husband, who had purchased a farm in Green River, Vermont, not far from Manchester. Because they had managed their finances well, the Strongs planned to be abroad with their children for the summer, so they were delighted to have her and Bill use the place.

Fearing Bill might try to wiggle out of the trip, Lois showed up at the hospital with their bags already packed. The next stop was Vermont. By the time they arrived at Green River, Bill was smiling again, happy to be back out in the country he so loved. Soon Lois felt hope return as her husband seemed to have no trouble staying sober for the next four months.[15]

As the weeks went by and Bill regained his strength, both he and Lois began to adopt Dr. Burnham's philosophy that hard work in the clear Vermont air makes for a healthy body, a healthy mind, and a healthy spirit. The couple began fixing up the farm as though it were their own. They repaired the plumbing pipes, refurbished the water system, and created a beautiful waterfall by damming up the brook that ran across the meadow below the house. As they hiked through the mountainside, they gathered wildflowers, which they planted in a garden near the front porch. And in the evenings after frolicking in the brook, they made love in front of the fireplace.[16]

"Bill's sister and her husband were pleased as punch when they finally returned and saw all the improvements we had made," Lois recalled years later, "but it was the new start I had hoped for. Bill never thought about drinking all the time we were there. At least he didn't mention it if he did. A friend of mine had given me a copy of Mary Baker Eddy's book, *Science and Health,* which I left next to Bill's pillow the first night we arrived. He read it and reread it and told me before we left for home how much it helped to strengthen his willpower and resolve to stay sober once and for all. That summer our love was renewed once again as we camped in the mountains and made love under a heaven filled with radiant hope. Both of us regretted the day we had to pack up and return to Brooklyn."[17]

Had they known what was about to happen, however, those regrets would have turned into shouts of joy. For almost immediately upon arriving back at Clinton Street, Bill was given one more tremendous opportunity that could have changed the direction of his entire life—had he parted company with John Barleycorn once and for all.

Lois's sister Katherine had married a gentleman by the name of Gardner Swentzel who also happened to be a Wall Street financier. Despite the crash, Swentzel was still doing quite well at Taylor, Bates and Company, a firm closely connected to J.P. Morgan and its far-flung financial enterprises. Katherine's husband had always liked Bill and, more importantly, had always respected his research theories and his ability to make money. Still, he was puzzled by Bill's willingness to throw it all away for booze. But now he heard his brother-in-law was sober and that the whole family was buzzing about the "miracle" that had taken place in Green River, Vermont. Even Dr. Burnham was amazed and told his oldest and dearest daughter so.

One of Gardner's closest friends and clients was Arthur Wheeler, the only son of the president of American Can Company and a man he considered one of the gutsiest investors he had ever met. He knew that Wheeler and another wealthy gentleman from Chicago named Frank Winans were putting together their own private investment syndicate. They had the notion that if one could overlook the present timidity on Wall Street, gather enough capital, and take a long-term view, a vast fortune could be made from the stock market recovery that was bound to come eventually. They sought Swentzel's advice about choosing the right companies to invest in. That's when he suggested they meet his brother-in-law, Bill Wilson, whom he described as an "analytical genius."

The first meeting in Gardner's office went swimmingly. Wheeler and Winans, however, while gutsy investors, were cautious when it came to choosing partners. It didn't take them long to discover Bill's rather unsavory drinking background. Still, they were enormously impressed with his credentials, his past record of success, Gardner Swentzel's recommendation, and the fact that Bill was now sober and obviously eager to give his all to this new venture. So they offered him a handsome long-term contract with their syndicate with only one proviso—that if he ever drank again, the contract would become null and void. Bill had so much confidence in himself at this point and was so excited about his prospects that he readily agreed.

Lois was overjoyed upon hearing the news. She clearly recalled their talks about finding their own place just as soon as the syndicate's deals started paying off. It would be a while but they could be patient now; life at Clinton Street had become far more comfortable and hospitable with everyone getting along. In fact, over dinner each night when Dr. Burnham eyed his son-in-law, he would lose a little more of his skepticism. He shouldn't have—for everything came apart suddenly, unexpectedly, and incomprehensibly.

Arthur Wheeler had gotten a line on a hot new investment possibility in Bound Brook, New Jersey: the Pathe Company. He asked Bill to round up a few engineers and investigate the firm's new photographic process and growth prospects. Staying at a small hotel near the company, the engineers began playing cards after dinner one night. Bill hated card games. He found them boring. Lois had once tried to teach him bridge but he had trouble distinguishing between the jacks and the kings. So instead of joining the engineers, he sat in the corner reading a book.

Soon he found himself distracted by the card players passing around a large jug. Curious, he inquired as to its contents. One of the engineers described it as real applejack, better known as Jersey Lightning. He was offered a swig but turned it down and went back to his reading. Suddenly he found himself thinking about all the various kinds of drinks he had had in the course of his thirty-seven years. He recalled that first Bronx cocktail during his encampment in New Bedford, Dr. Burnham's finest Scotch whiskey on his wedding day, the brandy he had on the ship to Europe to prevent seasickness, and of course those fabulous French wines that fortified him at the Front. But he never remembered drinking Jersey Lightning.

Just then another one of the engineers leaned toward him and offered a sip from the jug, which now seemed sparkling and alluring. *What harm could one small sip do?* thought the maniac in his head. So he reached out, grabbed the jug, and took a long swig.

That night in Bound Brook, New Jersey, Bill Wilson learned one more important lesson about the disease of alcoholism—that for a drunk, there is no such thing as just one drink.

The engineers could not rouse him the next morning after he had helped finish their jug and then some. They left to check on the company themselves and then reported directly back to Arthur Wheeler, who naturally inquired about his chief investigator. When Bill finally arrived back at Clinton Street, Lois was standing at the front door, her face pale, her eyes red and filled with despair once again. She handed her husband a telegram. His contract with Arthur Wheeler and Frank Winans had been cancelled.[18]

At that moment, it seemed as though Bill Wilson were standing on a trapdoor that suddenly opened beneath him. He plummeted into the deepest abyss of alcoholism he had ever known and continued that downward plunge over the next two years. He went from speakeasy brawls to drunk tanks, from park benches to jail cells, from pitiful crying jags to horrible hallucinations. As Lois recalled that period in her life, her words were frank and direct:

"[He] became a drunken sot who didn't dare leave the house for fear that Brooklyn hoods or the police would get him."[19] She wrote, "I became more and more discouraged, and I feared I would have to look after him and support him all the rest of our lives."[20]

But if things were bad while Dr. Burnham still resided at Clinton Street, one could imagine just how much worse they got once he moved out. In May of 1933, to Lois's great displeasure, Clark Burnham married a lady by the name of Joan James, the ex-wife of their former minister. Concerning that relationship, Lois once commented to a very close friend, "My father had become interested in Joan while my mother was ill. At the time, he and his lady friend went together to church functions she had never attended when married to her minister husband. When I spoke to him about hurting my mother so, he said he loved mother more than anyone else in the world, that he always would, and that she understood his attention to Joan.

"Perhaps my mother did understand as she lay dying, but that was certainly not true of others in our family. They were greatly distressed by the relationship. In fact, I was the only one in the family who accompanied our father to the civil wedding ceremony, joined him and his new wife for dinner afterward, and wished them well as they left for Florida. When I returned home that night, I realized that it would be just Bill and I alone together now in the large brownstone. That much of the financial burden would be on our shoulders and that I would have to care for him all by myself. I suddenly felt overwhelmed."[21]

Bill now drank to escape and to block from his mind all the terrible, pathetic, inexcusable things he had done and the mistakes he had made. He was unemployed and unemployable. To him, in his sodden, alcoholic brain, his whole life was blown apart, and in the days and weeks and months that followed he could gather no inner strength to think about or create new ideas or plans for his existence. Nothing but guilt-tortured episodes of the past and horrific fears of the future filled his very being.

He continued to bum handouts from old buddies to pay his "admission fee" into speakeasies where he still had a tab; he talked "softies" like neighborhood druggist Barry Slavin into one more bottle of booze even though last week's "fix" hadn't been paid for yet; he stole money from Lois's purse, pawned her and her mother's jewelry and silver, and hid bottles all over the house. Finally, when all else failed, he wrote his mother,

Emily, the sob story of his bad luck and failed attempts to start anew on Wall Street. Sure enough, she sent him some money "to tide him over." When Lois found Emily's letter on their dresser, minus the cash of course, she was furious. She screamed and hollered and beat on her drunken husband when he staggered in two nights later.

When Bill was off on a binge, Lois created many ways to keep herself busy. She might make over one of her mother's discarded dresses, reweave a frayed oriental rug, find some of Matilda's old fabric in a dusty closet and sew herself a new blouse, or reupholster an old chair from the webbing to the finishing gimp. Through her work in Macy's home furnishings department, word soon spread of her expertise in interior decorating. She was offered occasional jobs, which she undertook during the evenings or on weekends. But as much as she needed the money, when Bill's drinking grew worse and the resulting problems escalated, she became more and more hesitant to do anything but hurry home from work and be there as much as possible. Soon, she began missing work on days when Bill was climbing the walls, hallucinating, or shaking so badly he couldn't eat or drink by himself. Embarrassed by her absences, she resigned her job early that summer. She still had some jewelry left to pawn and things to sell if it came to that. But she was absolutely terrified of leaving her husband in his worsening condition.

"Bill had become very careless the more he drank," she once confided to some friends. "He wouldn't bathe unless I forced him to or put on clean clothes unless I did it for him. And he was still a very heavy smoker which frightened me no end. There were more than several occasions when he fell into a drunken sleep with a lit cigarette in his hand and almost set the bed on fire. Because of that and his threats to leap from our bedroom window should 'those people' come after him again—he was now hallucinating quite frequently—I decided to drag his mattress down into the basement where he would be safer and I would have more peace of mind."[22]

In spite of these nightmarish episodes, there also were, strangely enough, some days when Bill was so sick he couldn't drink. He would sit in the kitchen trying to sip coffee or stand at the parlor window staring out at people passing by. After a while, they would talk, he and this woman who put up with more than even he could comprehend. It was always the same conversation, perhaps using slightly different words. In those moments, those times in between hope and hopelessness, she would caress him, hold him. He would kiss her and gently run his fingers through her hair. They would always pledge that somehow, together, they would find their way out of this alcoholic malaise.

Lois still had her needs and desires, and when he held her close, her feelings were aroused. She wanted him. She needed him. He would try to make love to her. He wanted to make love to her—but the huge amounts of booze still in his system kept him impotent. For her, it was more than mere frustration. It was emotional torture.

It was even worse when he was drunk and would awaken in the middle of the night filled with his own lustful desires and sexual urges. He would roll on top of her, grunting and snorting until he himself realized the futility of it all. These were the kinds of experiences it pained Lois to share until later in life, when she came to understand how much it could help others in similar situations.

"There's very little sex life with an active alcoholic," she would say. "When he's in his cups, he's far from enticing sexually. I found it very difficult not to get filled with disgust, no matter how much I loved him when he was sober. For almost two years, from 1932 to the end of 1934, there was no sex at all."[23]

When asked once if, being married to a hopeless, loveless, sexually impotent alcoholic, she ever had the desire or felt she had the right to seek another man's arms, Lois replied, "I can understand some women using this as an excuse, but no, I was never interested in any other man in that way—in a sexual way I mean. Yes, there were many times I yearned for affection. I would see young couples holding hands on the subway train or embracing in the park and I would feel empty and angry. Perhaps I knew deep down that if I ever sought the emotional support of another man, it might lead me to places I was afraid of going. So I simply continued to hope and pray that things would somehow get better—even just a little bit better."[24]

And she continued trying to make them better, sometimes in strange or even stupid ways, she later admitted. For example, there was that one weekend when Bill was struggling again to get sober. While gathering the laundry together, she found one of his bottles of gin stashed behind the laundry basket. She took a glass from the kitchen cabinet, walked into the parlor with the bottle, sat across from her husband and proceeded to fill her glass and drink it. As she later said, "I wanted my husband to see for himself just what liquor does to you. How foolish you look and act after drinking it. He tried to stop me. I don't know if it was for my sake or because he wanted the bottle for himself.

"Anyway, I told him since I was never able to stop him from drinking, he wasn't going to stop me. So he didn't. He let me drink until I got tipsy and then very sick. He carried me upstairs and put me to bed. The next morning I woke up with an atrocious hangover. Bill took very good care of me that day and it was the first time I heard him laugh out loud in months. However, it was all for naught. All I did was get sick and he was drunk again himself within a few days."[25]

It was early that summer, only a few months after her father's departure, that Lois reached out in desperation to her brother-in-law Dr. Leonard Strong. Bill had become so physically and mentally debilitated that Leonard took only one look and immediately insisted on having him admitted to Towns Hospital and put under the care of his good friend Dr. Silkworth. Seeing Lois's hesitation and knowing it had to do with her scarce finances, not his medical recommendation, Leonard insisted on paying for Bill's care since, over the years, he had made him so much money in the stock market—most of which the shrewd young physician had wisely withdrawn before the crash. For Lois, it was simply one more case of swallowing her false pride.

This was to be the first of four trips Bill would make over the next eighteen months to Towns Hospital, a well-known and well-regarded institution that specialized in the mental and physical rehabilitation of alcoholics. It was located at 293 Central Park West in New York City and had been owned and operated since the early 1920s by the strapping and effervescent Charles B. Towns, who was later to become one of Bill Wilson's greatest admirers and supporters in the formation of Alcoholics Anonymous.

Charlie Towns may have owned the facility, but Dr. William Duncan

Silkworth ran it. He was a white-haired, blue-eyed, soft-spoken Princeton graduate with a medical degree in neurology from New York University–Bellevue Medical School. By the time Bill was admitted to his hospital, Dr. Silkworth had already formulated his theory concerning uncontrolled drinking—a theory much disputed by many of his colleagues—that alcoholism was an allergy not unlike hay fever, whose sufferers gradually become sensitized to certain types of pollen.

As he described his beliefs in a 1937 article in the *Medical Record* entitled "Alcoholism as a Manifestation of Allergy," he wrote, "We believe . . . that the action of alcohol on . . . chronic alcoholics is a manifestation of an allergy; that the phenomenon of craving is limited to this class and never occurs in the average temperate drinker. These allergic types can never safely use alcohol in any form at all; and once having formed the habit and found they cannot break it, once having lost their self-confidence, their reliance upon things human, their problems pile up on them and become astonishingly difficult to solve."[26]

But it wasn't his theory so much that impressed Bill and Lois when they first met Dr. Silkworth; it was more his obvious love and concern for each and every alcoholic under his care. In fact, Bill was so impressed, he was convinced when he finally left Towns that he would never drink again. It was almost catastrophic when he did. As Lois recalled:

> *When Dr. Silkworth, such a highly respected specialist in the field, couldn't help my husband, I began to think that my whole life had been wasted. All my love, the affection I had constantly tried to show him, all the times I had forgiven and tried to forget, it was all for nothing. It made me realize that my love was not enough.*
>
> *No matter what, I kept ending up in the same old rut doing the same old things, and like my father had said, expecting different results. I felt like I was a complete failure in what I had tried to do just as Bill was a complete failure in what he had tried to do. Here we were just two complete failures sinking further and further down each day and not knowing any way out.*

> *But as I look back, my reactions to it all seem so strange*
> *now. Even though I saw no way out, I discovered that hope*
> *springs eternal. I don't know if it's like that for everyone who*
> *loves as deeply as I did, but every time I felt like I was ready*
> *to give up, a flicker of hope would return. Maybe I was so*
> *sick I didn't know how sick I really was. But I think, truly,*
> *it was my faith in God even though at times I was so bitter*
> *that prayers seemed like ashes on my tongue. Perhaps it was*
> *also my mother looking down on me, giving me strength to*
> *go on. Or maybe it was simply watching my dear husband*
> *weeping in despair as he came off another binge, begging me*
> *for the thousandth time to help him. Yes, in the face of*
> *absolute failure, hope always seemed to return. If it hadn't,*
> *I'm sure I would have given up for good.*[27]

In the summer of 1934, Lois was to receive news that would have left almost anyone else with no hope at all. It came as Bill was being admitted to Towns Hospital for the third time. His own confidence in any possibility of recovering was at its lowest ebb. He had even told his wife she would be better off without him and that if he came out of the hospital and drank again this time, she should divorce him.

It was a sultry summer night when she left her husband in the detox ward and found her way to Dr. Silkworth's office. By now they knew each other quite well and had always talked until now in very optimistic terms. Tonight, however, she needed to know the truth—the absolute truth. She sat in front of his desk and asked the kinds of questions the spouses of many alcoholics had asked him before. "How bad is this? Why can't he stop? Where . . . is he heading? . . . What's to be done now? Where do we go from here?"[28]

Dr. Silkworth, "the little doctor who loved drunks," as Bill was to call him later on in sobriety, came around his desk and sat next to Lois. He took her hand and in his quiet, gentle manner answered her questions honestly and forthrightly.

"I thought at first Bill might be one of the exceptions. Because of his very great desire to quit, because of his character and intelligence, I thought he might be one of the very few. But this habit of drinking has now turned into an obsession, one much too deep to be overcome, and the physical effect of it on him has also been very severe, for he's showing signs of brain damage. This is true even though he hasn't been hospitalized very much. Actually, I'm fearful for his sanity if he goes on drinking."[29]

Lois shuddered. She had heard all this once before, several years earlier from her own father's lips. She wouldn't believe him then and she didn't want to believe Dr. Silkworth now. It just couldn't be so. She was afraid to ask the next question. The doctor understood. He took both her hands, held them tightly, and looked warmly into her eyes.

"Just what does all this mean, doctor?" she asked, fearing with every fiber in her body what the answer would be.

"It means," he replied softly, "that you will have to confine him, lock him up somewhere if he is to remain sane, or even alive. He can't go on this way for another year."[30]

When Lois finally left Dr. Silkworth's office and walked out into the hot, humid night air, she had no tears left to shed. She was completely numb and totally oblivious to the many motorists and passersby on Central Park West. She took the subway back to Brooklyn, walked up the steps of the brownstone, opened the door, and entered the kitchen. The coffee Bill had tried to drink before leaving for the hospital that morning was still on the kitchen table. She carried it to the sink and simply stood there for a long moment.

That's when Lois Wilson found more tears to shed.

9

Recovery for Whom?

$\mathcal{L}$OIS WILSON WASN'T THE ONLY ONE WHO WAS FORCED TO SELL some of her treasured things during those dark days of the Great Depression, but like many others, she did so with great sorrow and reluctance. Perhaps it was the embarrassment of standing in long lines at sleazy pawnshops or being stared at in used furniture stores that finally convinced her to look for another job, regardless of the consequences. Besides, with all the bills piling up, she had little choice, especially with her husband still unemployable.

Fortunately, President Franklin Delano Roosevelt, who succeeded one-term President Herbert Hoover, had declared a "mortgage moratorium" in the summer of 1933 so that millions of citizens impoverished by the Depression wouldn't lose their homes. As a result, the mortgage payments on Clinton Street, which Lois had insisted on paying when her father married and moved out, had now been reduced to simply a small amount of interest for the next several years. It was something she could afford even if she earned only a pittance of a salary.[1] So, early in the fall of 1934, she found a new job as a salesclerk on the furniture floor of Frederick Loeser's department store in downtown Brooklyn, not far from the house. This led a few months later to the position of hostess in the company's interior decorating department, where she advised customers on the design and decoration of their homes and offices. While her salary was only nineteen dollars a week plus a 4 percent commission on everything she sold, having such a responsible position in a career she loved boosted her spirits enormously during a time when she needed it the most.

For at Clinton Street, it was once again the calm before the storm. After leaving Towns Hospital for the third time, Bill appeared so terror-stricken by Dr. Silkworth's admonitions—the same ones he had given to Lois—that he took every precaution for a while to avoid anyone, anything, or any place that could possibly tempt him to drink. He feared greatly being locked away in some dingy mental ward.

In fact, on their subway ride home from the hospital, Bill confided to his wife his memory of driving with his grandfather past the state insane asylum in Brattleboro, Vermont, a large, ominous-looking red brick building down by the river. Grandpa Griffith pulled to the side of the road so they could watch the mental patients through the heavy metal fence. For the young boy, it was an eerie and very scary sight.

Bill said he recalled seeing the inmates stumbling around and around in circles, bumping into each other and hollering so loudly that the guards had to pull them apart. Others were seated on rotting park benches mumbling to themselves or staring across the thick grassy lawn with dark, blank eyes. He said he saw several who kept pulling their gray bathrobes up over their heads as if to hide from the world or block out the hot sun beating down on them. After a few minutes, he couldn't bear to watch them any longer and asked his grandfather to drive away.[2]

Lois remembered urging her husband to hold on to those memories each time he thought about drinking and perhaps it would help dissuade him. As upsetting as that sounded, Bill agreed he had to do everything possible this time to stay sober.

For the first few weeks at home, Bill rose early and made breakfast for his wife, who had to leave for work by eight. They chatted about her job, the places she was decorating, and about how well he was looking and that soon he'd be back on his feet and working again himself. But then came the mornings when Lois would be up and dressed and ready to leave and he'd still be in bed. She'd smile at him lovingly and say, "Why don't you just go back to sleep for a little while?" The implication was, at least in his mixed-up head, "You don't have to get up for anything, you poor, hopeless thing."[3]

So Bill began to sleep later and later. His brooding soon turned to anger and resentment. The maniac in his brain told him his wife was putting him down, losing what little respect she had left for him. Soon he was twisting and turning in bed, trying to forget all he had lost and all he would probably never have again. Then he would think about the bottles of booze still hidden around the house in places Lois never thought of looking. Just knowing they were there would take the edge off, help him to breathe a little easier. But as soon as he felt the urge to get up and find one of those bottles and swung his legs onto the floor, the pictures of those faces at the insane asylum in Brattleboro would suddenly flash before him. He would break into a cold sweat and slowly ease back into bed, pull the covers over his head, and try to go back to sleep.

Armistice Day rolled around, November 11, 1934, and he was still sober. He was also feeling much better physically. In fact, Lois had been getting him out of the house for walks around the neighborhood. He did so a bit reluctantly, always feeling uncomfortable trying to avoid the stares of those who had all too often seen him hunched over on park benches or in doorways drinking from a bottle in a brown paper bag. Lois felt the same discomfort, but getting her husband healthy again was far more important to her than the humiliation swirling inside.

Lois had to work that holiday so Bill thought he might drop in on some old Wall Street connections "just to check the lay of the land." When she reminded him the stock market was closed for Armistice Day, he became pensive. Then, suddenly, the thought of playing golf occurred to him. He hadn't played since his stint in Montreal, but he remembered Rogers had an old set of clubs up in the attic.

Though apprehensive to see him going out alone to be with men who might hoist a few, Lois hid her fears and agreed the fresh air and exercise could be just what the doctor ordered. The family purse was rather slim, but there was an inexpensive public course he had heard about on Staten Island. All he needed was fare for the ferry and bus and a few dollars for greens fees.

They left the house together that clear, crisp November morning, their spirits high and hopeful. As they kissed good-bye, Lois suggested they celebrate the holiday by having dinner that evening at their favorite

Italian restaurant near the foot of the Brooklyn Bridge. Bill agreed.[4]

After the ferry ride to St. George, Staten Island, Bill boarded a bus to take him to the public links. The man seated next to him was also an army veteran headed for the same golf course, so they struck up a pleasant conversation. Halfway across the island, the bus broke down. They joined a number of other passengers in a nearby pub to await repairs. Here in this bar filled with World War I vets celebrating the holiday, the booze was flowing like water since Prohibition had finally been repealed earlier that year.

Prohibition, which had also been called the Volstead Act after the U.S. Congressman who had spearheaded passage of the legislation, had finally fallen of its own weight for two reasons. First, people began finding out they could be arrested for violating the act by simply having one drink. In other words, when the police arrested them for public intoxication and the courts sentenced them to the drunk tank or thirty days in jail, the offense was merely in the eye of the beholder—the authorities— because the rules and regulations were so confusing and there were no Breathalyzers back then. In fact, even a Catholic priest saying mass with sacramental wine or a druggist preparing a prescription that contained alcohol could be in jeopardy under the strict interpretation of the Volstead Act.

So soon a growing majority of the public, even those who initially thought Prohibition might be a good idea, was against the law. However, it wasn't until people began dying from rotgut booze, and mobsters battling for a stranglehold on the illegal whiskey business spilled blood into the streets, that ordinary citizens finally began to fear for their own safety. Then came a loud hue and cry for repeal—but it took fourteen long years for it to happen.

Now it had, and Bill's new friend from the bus bellied up to the bar and ordered a rye whiskey. He cast a strange glance at his companion when he ordered a ginger ale. Feeling a bit embarrassed and in need of explaining himself, Bill offered a brief history of his long ordeal with alcohol: his thwarted career, his trips to Towns, and even Dr. Silkworth's theory of allergy and obsession. It was when he dramatically commented that the next drink could put him in a padded cell that his new friend told him if he had it that bad, he sure as hell wouldn't drink either.[5]

Shortly after noon, a substitute bus arrived and took them to the golf course. The clubhouse restaurant was also teeming with the congenial holiday crowd. Across the way, a group of men surrounding a piano player were singing war songs, such as "Mademoiselle from Armentieres," "Over There," and "Oh Give Me Something to Remember You By," that spurred Bill's patriotic feelings. As he and his friend approached the bar, a red-faced bartender with a thick Irish brogue placed two glasses of Scotch in front of them and smiled: "It's on the house, me lads. It's Armistice Day. Drink up."[6]

It was almost a reflex action. Bill reached for the Scotch and put it to his lips. His companion stood there stunned, a deep frown on his face. "My God, is it possible that you could take a drink after what you just told me? You must be crazy." Bill simply replied, "Yes, I am," and then downed the whiskey.[7] When he turned around, his newfound friend was gone. He had disappeared into the crowd, perhaps fearful of being in the company of a potential lunatic. Bill swung back to the bar and nodded to the Irish bartender, who refilled his glass. He quickly forgot about golf and joined the drinking chorus at the piano. Before long he was back in France, back at the Front saving the world from the invading horde. He was in a small bistro in Paris, being idolized for his heroics by lovely French demoiselles. He was with his platoon on the transport ship home, all lined up at attention as a general pinned a medal on his chest for exceptional gallantry. Soon the singing began to fade as one by one the veteran choristers headed for the links or left for home.

Now he was back at the clubhouse bar, spilling down another Scotch in an almost empty room and being urged by the ruddy-faced bartender to go home—that he'd had enough.

But what is "enough" to an alcoholic when he can still stand, when he can still walk, when he can still dream those wild, racy, outsized dreams? It's when those dreams turn into memories and those memories turn into reality that the fear, anger, and self-revulsion set in. It's when he stares at himself in the mirror as Bill was doing now and the real enemy, the real provocateur, stares back.

That's when the panic hits. That's when Bill smashed his glass on the floor, stumbled off the barstool, staggered out into the cold, windy street and tried to find his way back home—back from the far reaches of Staten Island to the familiar streets of Brooklyn Heights.

It was very late that night when he finally arrived at 182 Clinton Street. Unable to climb the steps, he staggered and fell into the basement area below, cracking his head open on the iron gate. Lois found him there at five o'clock the next morning after a premonition had awakened her from a fitful night's sleep. Bill's scalp was still bleeding from the fall as she half-dragged him into the basement and plopped him down onto the mattress she had put there some time ago, fearing he might fall or jump from an upstairs window. She washed and bandaged his head, then sat next to him in a chair wondering who to call this time—Leonard Strong, Dr. Silkworth, or the Elmwood Sanitarium, one of the mental institutions she had been told about during her husband's last stay at Towns Hospital.

She sat next to him for several hours, dozing off and on. Finally she went upstairs and called Frederick Loeser's department store to inform them she needed the day off—telling another lie that only added to her own self-loathing. She made some tea and paced the kitchen floor, trying to pull her thoughts together.

How do you put a man you love but now also pity into an insane asylum? Must you do it to save his mind, to save his life? Should you get someone else to do it for you, like your father, for instance, or Leonard Strong or even Dr. Silkworth, whose opinion on the matter she already knew? Would the commitment to the asylum be for a month, a year, or possibly forever? How could she live with herself when she still believed deep inside that her own inability to have children was one of the reasons he still drank—and now she had completely failed to help this wonderful man who still had such great potential if only this curse were lifted from him? Would it be the courageous thing for her to do or simply the cowardly way out? What would he think of her for doing it, and if he were ever cured, would he forgive her? Could they ever have a life together again? Would he still love her?[8]

These were the kinds of anguishing questions that haunted Lois over the next several weeks as Bill hid away in the basement, sneaking out only when she was at work to beg, borrow, or steal more booze and then hide bottles around the house. She now guarded her purse and locked away what was left of her precious things. Where he got the money for his alcohol she never knew. When she came home, she'd search the house as usual to find whatever bottles she could and pour them down the drain, but it was a useless exercise. There was always that one bottle she could never find. He ate very little, and what he did eat she had to force into him. His clothes began to hang off his lanky frame as he lost more and more weight and more and more coherence each day that went by.

"I was at my wit's end," she recalled. "I think I was close to calling Leonard Strong again since he and Dorothy were always so kind and understanding and they knew things were only getting worse. Then something almost miraculous happened.

"I came home from work early one evening to find Ebby Thacher seated at our kitchen table talking with Bill. It had been more than a year or two since they had last seen each other, and I had heard several times that Ebby was also in terrible straights. But now here he was completely sober and I soon learned had been so for some time.

"For a brief moment my spirits rose, hoping that somehow he might share with Bill whatever he had found that was helping and then Bill would get sober too. To be honest, though, I really didn't hold out much hope for that, especially when I saw a half empty pitcher of pineapple juice on the table and Bill trying to hide the bottle of gin he had spiked it with. I was certain that before the night was over, both of them would be terribly drunk."[9]

But this time Lois was wrong. Little did she know until Ebby spoke with her on the front porch of Clinton Street later that night that this man she had known since her childhood in Vermont was actually here on a mission. He had come to help her husband find a way out of his alcoholic morass just as he had done himself, four months earlier, with the aid of two men from a religious movement called the Oxford Group. Lois had heard of the movement but knew little about it or its philosophy.

The Oxford Group was actually a nondenominational movement founded in 1921 by a Lutheran minister, Dr. Frank Buchman. Among his early followers was Dr. Sam Shoemaker, who was pastor of New York's Calvary Episcopal Church and also ran its affiliated Calvary Mission in lower Manhattan. Dr. Shoemaker, was to play a significant role in Bill Wilson's spiritual development and his writing of *Alcoholics Anonymous,* which became known as "The Big Book."

The religious movement focused on the need for people to change— that everyone must undergo a spiritual conversion in order to improve their lives. There was strong emphasis on personal housecleaning, that people confess their sins one to another, that they make restitution and amends in order to repair and restore personal relationships. Emphasis on prayer and meditation for at least one hour each day was also an integral part of the philosophy. The Oxford Group believed that if its followers, coming from any religious denomination, would adhere to such high moral standards, then God could and would enter and direct their lives. The movement's goal was to set up a worldwide chain reaction—one person carrying the good news of hope and recovery to the next.

Many people with serious problems and broken lives, such as alcoholics who had "hit bottom," were attracted to this stringent way of life almost as "a last hope." Many, such as Ebby Thacher, found help there, although admittedly most of them for only a short period of time. It has been said that the tremendous pain and despair from lost jobs, lost homes, and lost lives wrought by the crash of 1929 and the Great Depression was actually a boon to the Oxford Group, attracting to it society's poor and downtrodden, its alcoholics and Bowery bums. The movement hit its peak of popularity in 1936, and then its magnetism began to fade. In 1938, it changed its name to Moral Re-Armament and gradually lost the impact and influence it once had.

Still, when Ebby phoned Bill at Clinton Street two weeks after his harrowing Armistice Day experience and asked if he could drop by, he was bringing with him this dramatic message of change and conversion. Fortunately, his boyhood pal didn't know this at the time. Otherwise, as Bill said later with a big grin: "I would have told him to go peddle his papers somewhere else."

Instead, even though suffering his usual morning whiskey jitters, Bill was overjoyed to hear from his longtime drinking buddy who, as far as he knew, had dropped completely off the face of the earth. But now, almost as if he had risen from the dead, the marvelous, the fearless, the one and only Ebby Thacher would be joining him that very afternoon to toast the long-overdue reunion of two of nature's true survivors.

Despite washing up, combing his hair, and stumbling out of his pajamas and into a wrinkled pair of pants and a shirt for this special occasion, Bill still saw a pathetic-looking, red-eyed drunk staring back at him when he glanced into the bathroom mirror. But a few swigs from the bottle of gin he had stashed in the water tank above the toilet soon took care of those feelings. A few more swigs put him into just the right kind of affable mood to receive his long-awaited guest.

His mind began racing with anticipation. He started to reminisce about all those wonderful times he and Ebby had had together over the years—those practical jokes on their classmates at school; the exciting hayrides and barn dances in Vermont; those early drinking days when they were in the army together before shipping out; the many drunken blasts they shared after the war in speakeasies all over Manhattan. Even the trouble they got into back then—such as their infamous drunken airplane flight from Albany to Manchester five years earlier—seemed like fun now as the memories paraded through his sodden brain.

Bill wobbled downstairs and into the kitchen. After a brief search, he found what he was looking for—another untapped bottle of gin, wrapped in a towel and stashed amid the cobwebs under the stove. It was after two o'clock now and should Lois come home early, he didn't want her to see a naked bottle of booze on the kitchen table. That's when the thought struck him—a pineapple punch. It was one of Ebby's favorite "morning-after fixes." So what if it was already afternoon. He'd get a kick out of it, provided it contained more gin than juice.

The punch was now ready. The glasses were on the table. He had another quick swig, then lit a cigarette. His hands were trembling but not nearly as badly as they were an hour ago.

Then the doorbell rang.

No matter how many years went by, Lois could always clearly remember how her husband described the events that took place that afternoon when a man she once didn't particularly care for brought a message to her home that would save her husband's life.

"Bill always said he was absolutely stunned when he opened the door and saw the look on Ebby's face that day," she recalled. "He said there was something very different about him from the last time they had been together—in fact, from the many years they had been drinking together. It took Bill several moments to comprehend exactly what it was. Then he realized that Ebby was sober, not merely dried out, but completely sober. I can only imagine what went through Bill's mind at that point."[10]

One of those thoughts, which he later shared with his wife, was that he felt awkward and uncomfortable for a moment. He said he felt almost as he did when the police pulled him out of a doorway, drunk and covered with puke, and looked at him as if he were something less than human. That's the way Ebby seemed to be staring at Bill's red eyes and trembling hands as he stood at the front door. But Bill's uncomfortable feelings were only temporary, for somewhere in his head that ever-present maniac kept saying he could even the score by bringing Ebby into the kitchen and pouring him a few glasses of that punch.

There was something else different about his friend that afternoon. When Ebby smiled, it was a warm, serious kind of a smile, sort of an "I'm here on a mission" smile. And when he shook hands, it was a firm and clasping kind of handshake, not the slap-on-the-back type these two drinking buddies always used to exchange. It wasn't until Bill led him into the kitchen, offered him a seat, and poured him a glass of punch that he began to comprehend what was behind all these changes in his now-sober friend. Ebby pushed the glass away and said quietly but with great confidence, "No, thanks, Bill. I don't need this stuff anymore."

Bill laughed out loud, thinking at first Ebby was joking with him. But there was no laughter in return. So he poured himself a drink, chugged it down, and then asked, with a deep frown on his forehead, "Ebby, what on earth has got into you? What is this all about?"[11]

So Ebby told him. He told him that after his family's cast-iron stove business finally went belly-up, he drank so much that he spent more time in Albany's drunk tanks than he did in his own house. The local authorities, thanks to his straight-laced older brother, suggested he get some help for his problem, so he moved into the old Battenkill Inn in Manchester, Vermont, to dry out. The elderly owner had been a good friend of the Thacher family for years, so he helped by warning his employees not to serve his special guest any alcohol or they'd be fired on the spot.

Ebby managed to stay dry for almost six months. Then the owner of the inn suddenly died. Ebby had to mourn his passing. This led to another long drinking binge and total depletion of whatever family assets he had left. He went from one job to another, even working as a housepainter to get money for booze. After many more failed attempts to stay sober, he wound up in a vacant cabin in the Green Mountains, where he nearly drank himself to death.

Officials of the local lumber company that owned the cabin were about to ship him off to the insane asylum in Brattleboro when word reached two of Ebby's old friends in Manchester, men he used to drink with and who were now sober members of the Oxford Group. The two men brought him home with them, cleaned him up, and shared the newfound philosophy that was keeping them sober. Having hit bottom, Ebby began absorbing the movement's principles like a sponge, especially the four basic principles of absolute honesty, absolute purity, absolute unselfishness, and absolute love. He soon found sobriety, a new kind of sobriety he called "a sobriety of the soul." And now, just four months later, here he was trying to share what he found with his drunk and disbelieving boyhood chum.

"You mean . . . you got religion?"[12] Bill half-snarled, staring across the table at the man he suddenly decided had become a ludicrous convert and, even worse, seemed about to break one of the oldest laws in the book of scams: try to con a con artist. What Bill couldn't see was that Ebby was on a mission and wasn't about to give up that quickly, especially when he stared back across the table and saw a man he always loved and admired now desperately in need of help.

"It was really more of a spiritual than it was a religious movement," Ebby tried to explain. "It was what I had been taught as a child and what I inwardly believed but had laid aside."[13]

Because of their long history together and Ebby's obvious sincerity, Bill listened to his story for another hour or so while he himself continued to drink and smoke. Without his realizing it, something was penetrating, something was getting through, something was lighting a small flame that would eventually burst into a gigantic spiritual fire. But for the moment, the gin-laced punch was etching it all in his subconscious.

Finally, as Ebby rose from the kitchen table, he urged his friend one more time to seek the help of Dr. Sam Shoemaker at the Calvary Mission where he himself was staying while in New York. Bill promised to give it serious consideration while thinking to himself that he had heard enough about God and religion for one day and, with the pitcher of punch depleted, he needed to find another bottle hidden somewhere in the house to get him through the night.

On his way out, Ebby noticed Lois seated in the parlor, ostensibly sewing, although her mind had been focused on the happenings in the kitchen. He entered to say good-bye.

"I could hardly believe my eyes when I saw that Ebby was still completely sober," Lois recalled. "I wanted desperately to ask him how he was managing to do it and what he had said to Bill. So I walked with him to the front door and out onto the front porch.

"He told me briefly about the Oxford Group and where I could go myself to get more information. But then my heart sank once again when he said Bill didn't appear too receptive to the idea. When I asked why, he explained that as far as he knew, Bill had always wanted to stop drinking mainly to please me. Now the shame and guilt for not being able to do so only increased his need to keep on drinking, to drown out those feelings.

"Ebby also told me that night that Bill was never really concerned about hurting himself but that it tore him up inside each time he realized how much he was hurting me. Then, after the disaster on Wall Street when we lost everything and he really wanted to stop drinking for himself in order to turn his life around, he couldn't. By that time he was totally addicted mentally and physically just like Ebby had been until he found a spiritual solution in the Oxford Group.

"Then Ebby hugged me and said all we could do for Bill now was to pray for him. I thought to myself as I watched him walk down the steps, what good would more prayers do when they hadn't worked all these years. I didn't know at the time I had a soul-sickness too."[14]

When Lois walked back into the kitchen, Bill was still seated at the table, smoking. He appeared deep in thought.

"Without my even asking," she remembered, "he willingly related to me the story of Ebby's introduction to the Oxford Group. He admitted he was quite impressed that Ebby was sober and said he just might look into the things he told him about."[15]

Lois wanted to reply. She wanted to urge her husband to do just that . . . to do exactly what Ebby had suggested. But she was afraid of what his response might be, especially since she could tell he had been drinking rather heavily. So, not wanting to raise any more false hopes, she made herself a cup of tea, kissed him on the cheek, and then went upstairs to read herself to sleep.

Though inebriated, Bill could still recognize that all-too-familiar look in his wife's eyes, the look that said what's the use of trying anymore, of even attempting to share her painful thoughts and feelings with the very man who caused them in the first place. And now, Bill pictured her thinking, along comes their longtime friend from Vermont, sober and filled with hope and optimism. She has to be wondering why it can't be him, why this spineless, weak-willed excuse of a husband couldn't have found what Ebby found—and isn't willing to accept it even now.

He lit another cigarette, took a deep drag, and waited until he felt Lois was settled in her bedroom upstairs. Then he rose and quietly sneaked down into the basement. After another brief search, he found a half-empty bottle of booze hidden in an old storage bin. He sat down on the now-familiar mattress near the coal furnace, leaned back against the cold cement wall, and proceeded to ponder Ebby's visit as he poured the burning liquid directly from the bottle down his throat.

Sure, Ebby believed all that stuff he was spouting—but then his old drinking buddy often played it fast and loose with the truth. On the other hand, he, Bill Wilson, used to be a terrific professional investigator. He still could be if only some lame-brained idiot on the Street would give him half a chance. Anyway, maybe he ought to check out this Oxford Group himself, he thought. Go right to the source, the head man, this Dr. Shoemaker fellow over at this Calvary Mission place. As he continued to drink, his mind conjured up the deep theological and philosophical questions he would stump Dr. Shoemaker with. Soon the bottle was empty, and he passed out in the chilly cellar.[16]

Before leaving for work the next morning, Lois came down and covered her husband with a warm blanket. Then she briefly searched for more hidden bottles. She couldn't find any. As she stood there staring down at this man she once thought would conquer the world or at least achieve some kind of greatness, her head kept telling her she must soon decide about committing him to a sanitarium. If Dr. Silkworth couldn't help and now his closest friend couldn't get through to him, what hope was there left?

She remembered Ebby's last words to her. "All we can do for Bill now is to pray for him." But she had pleaded to God so many times she felt as if she had worn out her welcome. Nevertheless, she lowered her head and murmured the words she had said so often in the past: "God help me to help him, my husband, my boy."[17]

Then she wiped her eyes, tucked the cover up closer around his neck, and left for work. Lois was soon to learn that the God she had put her faith in often works in very strange ways—even in ways she might not agree with. But the prayer she had just uttered and the many prayers she had whispered, shouted, and cried out all these years were about to be answered . . . in a very strange and very powerful way.

It was around noon when Bill awoke, shaking and desperately in need of a drink. He could find nothing in the basement. He staggered upstairs and, despite his weakened condition, almost tore the kitchen apart looking for a bottle he knew he had hidden in one of the cabinets—unless Lois had found it. He wracked his brain but couldn't remember where he had stashed it. Then an idea struck him. Perhaps this was a sign, some kind of an omen, he thought. Maybe as a result of Ebby's visit, something was trying to tell him he didn't have to drink today. And if he turned himself over to that Oxford Group bunch, maybe he wouldn't have to drink at all, just like his old pal.

But then he remembered the kicker, the real stumbling block—this God thing. Sure, he believed there was something out there, some kind of unexplainable intelligence or power that ran the universe. But a personal God? One who watched over his life? He had given up on that idea a long time ago. Still, Ebby was sober. There was no denying that. So on that score alone it was something worth looking into, with a keen investigator's eye.[18]

He quickly washed up, threw on some clothes, and took off. He remembered Ebby saying Calvary Church was on Twenty-third Street, somewhere near Fourth Avenue in Manhattan. Back then, Twenty-third Street was a drunkard's paradise, with bars lining both sides of the busy thoroughfare. Bill managed to make it halfway down the block before some strange magnetic force emanating from an Irish pub pulled him inside. He was loaded by the time he staggered into the mission a few hours later, arm in arm with another drunk he met at the bar.

The mission was filled with men in every stage of decay, most bearded, filthy, and tipsy, seated on rows of wooden benches slopping down beans and bread from dented tin plates.

"I never will forget," Lois once said, "Bill telling me about his first impression of the old Calvary Mission. Even though he was quite drunk himself, he said all he could see was a roomful of victims and losers. Bill always had a great deal of pride. He never considered himself a victim since he was honest enough to admit he brought most things on himself. And while he might have been a loser at that time, he always believed he would one day turn things around and become a winner again."[19]

Dr. Shoemaker wasn't there that night, but Ebby was. He cornered his friend and forced some beans and black coffee down his throat and then began introducing him to a few fairly well-dressed men he kept referring to as "part of God's army."[20] This turned Bill off—this and the smell of society's rejects and discards, the bedraggled waste of a country in despair seated all around him . . . men who, his investigator's nose said, were as phony about their intention to stay sober as he was. He knew they came for the grub.

But Bill stayed anyway just to please his old friend. He even rose up and staggered to the front of the hall when "confession" time came. Standing among a crowd of sweating, stinking, but seemingly eager penitents, he shouted above the group for all to hear—that if Ebby Thacher could stay sober, so could he.

Lois was surprised when she came home that night to find Bill seated in the living room staring off into space. He was deep in thought. Ebby had brought him home from the mission, and they had talked for several hours over coffee until he left. Bill told his wife he might give the

Oxford Group a try, even though there was much about the movement he didn't like or agree with. He said he had to do something because he couldn't stand the hurt look in her eyes every time he got drunk.

"I remember how I hugged him and cried in his arms," she wrote. "As hard as I tried not to, I began to hope again. He didn't drink for the next several days even though he was shaking so badly I thought I would have to call Leonard Strong for help. But Bill got angry every time I mentioned it. He grew more and more restless and found it hard to sleep. Then I came home from work early one evening and he wasn't there. I didn't want to believe he was drinking again until I went upstairs and saw that he had gone though my bureau apparently looking for some of my jewelry to sell. I was devastated."[21]

Lois thought it was around nine or ten that night when she heard the front door slam and footsteps coming down the hall. She was in the den off the dining room sewing, trying to keep herself busy so she wouldn't have to think. She rose and started for the hall when Bill was suddenly there in the doorway. He was very drunk, angry, and incoherent.

"I don't know what you and Ebby have been cooking up," he ranted, "but nobody's shoving religion down my throat. Nobody! Not even you!"[22]

Then he began babbling about "God's army" chasing after him . . . that he wasn't like all those "bums and losers" at the Calvary mission . . . that she was among those religious fanatics who brainwashed Ebby but weren't going to brainwash him. He demanded she tell him where she had hidden all his booze and said he was sick and tired of living with someone who didn't respect him and always treated him like a helpless child.

Lois had witnessed many of her husband's hallucinations in the past, but nothing like this. It frightened her and crushed whatever hope she may have had left. But then suddenly something snapped inside her. Those emotions she had always tried to keep in check now loosened her bitter tongue.

All those years of loving and caring. All those years of living her life for him. All those years of people asking her why . . . why did she suffer this almost sick devotion to a man who showed her a thousand times that he didn't care to help himself so long as she was always there to comfort him and nurse him back to health? She had become not only his wife but his mother, his nurse, his excuse-maker, his caretaker, and his financial support as well. As he stood in the doorway raving at her, all those seething emotions rose to the surface and poured out in the most hurtful, vindictive words she could find.

"You are nothing but a drunken sot just like those other bums you keep talking about," she recalled screaming at him. "But I don't have to live like this anymore. I should have put you in a sanitarium a long time ago, when my father told me to do it and then Dr. Silkworth. That's where you belong—in an insane asylum—because you're crazy. You hear me! You're crazy!"[23]

Bill's eyes widened and his face filled with even greater rage. He glanced around the room, then charged toward the sewing machine. He picked it up and threw it against the wall. Lois had never seen him lose control like this before. She was petrified. She shrank into a corner and began crying hysterically. Her husband glared at her, then suddenly turned, ran down the hall, out the front door, and into the night shouting, "I'm not crazy! I'm not crazy!"[24]

Lois couldn't remember how long she sat curled up in the corner, weeping.

Bill rode the city's subways in a stupor that night and into the early hours of the morning. Then he panhandled enough from the rush-hour crowd to buy a pint of gin. That got him back to Clinton Street. Lois was gone when he entered the house. He had emerged from his blackout by now, and as he wobbled down the hall and past the den, vague glimpses of last night's harrowing episode began flashing through his troubled brain. He poked his head into the den. The cracked wall and broken sewing machine left little doubt about his irrational outburst.

He sank into a chair. Tears streamed down his face. Even in his half-drunken state, he realized there was nothing left for him anymore but madness or death. This was either the end of the road or the jumping-off place to a new start. No, not a start built on self-deception, but one like his pal Ebby had found . . . seemingly solid and sure. But he couldn't do it here, not in this house filled with so many ghosts, so many guilty memories, so many hidden bottles of booze. He knew in his heart there was only one place to go, that is, if Dr. Silkworth would allow him back. He must go to Towns Hospital at once to dry out—and then give the Oxford Group another try. Then maybe . . . just maybe . . .

He shuffled into the kitchen, found a pencil and piece of paper, sat at the kitchen table, and with his trembling hands wrote Lois a brief note. He admitted there was no way he could possibly apologize for his insane behavior but that perhaps this was what it had to come to for him to understand that she was right—that her father and Dr. Silkworth were right—that he truly was insane and getting worse each time he drank. He told her he was going back to Towns, where he hoped Dr. Silkworth would give him one more chance. He left the note on the table and hurried out the door.[25]

Bill's tremors were almost uncontrollable by the time he reached the train station. He needed a drink badly. He dug into his pockets but only found a nickel, the cost of the subway fare. Then he remembered a small grocery store down the block where Lois still had some credit. He talked the poor young clerk, who was stunned by Bill's appearance, into giving him four bottles of beer on account. He drank one of them on the street outside and then made it to the subway. He tripped and fell halfway down the steps. His head was cut and bruised but not one bottle of beer was broken. A drunk protects his booze with his very life.

Dr. Silkworth saw Bill approaching the hospital from his office window. He greeted him in the entrance hall. As the doctor later said, there was something in Bill's eyes that afternoon that spoke of desperation, that pleaded for one more chance at life. So the kind physician admitted him and allowed him to finish the beer before ushering him into the detox ward.

Despite the nightmarish incident with the sewing machine, Lois went to work the next morning to get it out of her mind. She loved her interior decorating job, and her involvement with customers helped her to relax and forget about her home life even if only for a few hours.

"I found Bill's note when I returned home from work that evening," she recalled. "I had planned to call Dr. Silkworth that day but kept putting it off. Once I told him all that had happened, I knew what his answer would be. When I read that Bill had gone to Towns Hospital, I was relieved for a few moments but then just as quickly my mood turned into one of deep despair.

"I thought, what good would it do anyway? He would only get drunk again the moment he left the hospital. And who was going to pay the bill this time? The money I earned was barely enough to keep us going. I had to ask my brothers to help pay the previous hospital bills. There wasn't much left in the house to sell or pawn. All I could think about over and over again was what possible permanent good could it do for Bill to go back to Towns again. I had so little faith left in the good Lord just when He was about to show me His miraculous power."[26]

Sweating and shaking to pieces in the detox ward, Bill received the usual Towns treatment to taper off—barbiturates to sedate him and paraldehyde to ward off the DT's. Two days later he was moved to a small private room and there fell into the deepest, darkest depression he had ever known. He was afraid to leave the room for fear of running out to find another drink. He was afraid to look out the window, at the cars and people struggling through the cold wintry night. He knew that out there he had only three choices left. He could stop drinking, something he deeply feared he could not do. He could go completely insane, a state he felt was very close at hand. Or he would die. For an alcoholic in the final stages of his disease, there are no other choices.

Alone, lost, and terrified, he lay back on his small steel-railed bed, reached his arms upward, and mumbled through his tears, "If there be a God, let Him show Himself!"[27]

What happened next was something few have experienced, a spiritual event of remarkable consequence. Bill Wilson would later try to explain it in his own words:

> *Suddenly, my room blazed with an indescribable white light. I was seized with an ecstasy beyond description. Every joy I had known was pale by comparison. The light, the ecstasy—I was conscious of nothing else for a time.*
>
> *Then, seen in the mind's eye, there was a mountain. I stood upon its summit, where a great wind blew. A wind, not of air, but of spirit. In great, clean strength, it blew right*

through me. Then came the blazing thought, "You are a free man." I know not at all how long I remained in this state, but finally the light and the ecstasy subsided. I again saw the wall of my room. As I became more quiet, a great peace stole over me, and this was accompanied by a sensation difficult to describe. I became acutely conscious of a Presence which seemed like a veritable sea of living spirit. I lay on the shores of a new world. "This," I thought, "must be the great reality. The God of the preachers."

Savoring my new world, I remained in this state for a long time. I seemed to be possessed by the absolute, and the curious conviction deepened that no matter how wrong things seemed to be, there could be no question of the ultimate rightness of God's universe. For the first time, I felt that I really belonged. I knew that I was loved and could love in return. I thanked my God, who had given me a glimpse of His absolute self. Even though a pilgrim upon an uncertain highway, I need be concerned no more for I had glimpsed the great beyond.[28]

It was December 11, 1934. Bill had just turned thirty-nine. He would never again doubt the reality of God. He now had a whole new life ahead of him but, as it would turn out, not the life of money and privilege he had once envisioned.

And as for Lois, she recalled, "I knew something overwhelming had happened. His eyes were filled with light. His whole being expressed hope and joy. From that moment on, I shared Bill's confidence in the future."[29]

"He told me he first thought he might have had another hallucination but that Dr. Silkworth assured him it wasn't so. He told Bill he had experienced some great psychic occurrence, some kind of conversion experience he had only read about and that he should hang on to it for it was a great gift, a great blessing. I had no idea which way our lives would go but I now had a strong reason to hope he was finally freed from his addiction. It never occurred to me that I was still trapped in mine."[30]

When Lois brought her husband home from the hospital on

December 18, he was filled with an insatiable desire to help other alco-holics like himself. He could not stop talking about it. He kept saying that since a miracle had happened to him and to Ebby, why couldn't it happen to others as well, to all the drunks in the world perhaps? He could help make it happen by spreading the message. And because her husband was finally back home, not just in body but in mind and spirit as well, Lois went right along with his idea enthusiastically, even accompanying him to Oxford Group meetings at the Calvary Episcopal Church. As usual, she wanted to help and support him all she could.

Lois was content enough attending Oxford Group meetings to sup-port her husband, but she never even considered applying the spiritual principles to her own life. She felt Bill's drinking and the troubles that ensured were her only real problems and now after his spiritual experi-ence at Towns Hospital coupled with the Oxford Group program, those problems were taken care of. After all, she had been raised to love God and her fellow man, and now that her prayers for her husband's recovery had been answered, she didn't require any further spiritual guidance.[31]

"My sheer arrogance told me I was fine and didn't need to change in any way," Lois later recalled. "Was I due for a serious comeuppance."[32]

Indeed, only after that serious comeuppance would Lois change her attitude toward the Oxford Group and realize the need to apply its prin-ciples to her own life. She eventually became a great admirer of both Dr. Shoemaker and Dr. Frank Buchman, who founded the movement, and of their belief that by changing each individual person, the whole world could be changed for the better. In fact, she and Bill would later use the essence of the principles that Dr. Shoemaker and Dr. Buchman preached in the development of the Twelve Step recovery programs used today in both Alcoholics Anonymous and Al-Anon.

Later in life, Lois Wilson would often profess the great aspirations of these men in her own words as they applied to the worldwide programs she and her husband cofounded: "If everyone could somehow learn to live by the principles incorporated in the Twelve Steps to Recovery," she would say, "then some day there could truly be peace and joy in the entire world."[33]

In the meantime, Bill began learning much about the physical side of his disease—the mental obsession coupled with a physical allergy—each time he visited his mentor, Dr. Silkworth. The doctor always allowed Bill to share his God-experience with some patients, hoping somehow it might help. And Bill began learning about the mental and spiritual part of his alcoholic malady from Dr. Shoemaker, who had now befriended the former Wall Street analyst. Dr. Shoemaker encouraged Bill to spread the message of change and spiritual recovery to others like himself.

Bill took the preacher at his word. With Lois's full support, he was soon walking through the gutters of the Bowery, into the nut ward at Bellevue Hospital, down the slimy corridors of fleabag hotels, and into the detox unit at Towns with a Bible under his arm. He was promising sobriety to every drunk he could corner if they, like he, would only turn their lives over to God.

"He was even bringing some of these poor souls home with him," Lois explained. "He thought a good home-cooked meal plus plenty of inspirational talks about the Oxford Group's principles of honesty, purity, unselfishness, and love would get them sober. Ebby had also moved in with us by then but between the two of them, it was obvious to me that all their preaching was only turning off our rather inebriated guests."[34]

After a while, the whole experience slowly began having a negative impact on Lois's life and her life together with Bill. The simple fact was they had no life together. Yes, Bill was sober, but it wasn't what she had envisioned. She thought that if she went along with his religious revival for a while, he would soon come back down to earth and things would return to normal—at least normal by other people's standards. But the revival continued, the drunks were constantly dragged in and out of Clinton Street, and there was no end in sight. Gradually she became deeply frustrated and less affable about hosting a household full of itinerants. Bill sensed her feelings.

Every now and then she overheard her husband talking with Ebby about his dream of building a movement separate and apart from the Oxford Group, one focused solely on saving alcoholics. He saw so many drunks in the Oxford Group fall by the wayside while few nonalcoholic members seemed to care. But during the first five months of 1935, he encountered his own frustrations on the "preaching circuit." None of his prospective converts were staying sober.[35]

Early that May an old friend of Bill's, Howard Tompkins of Beers & Company, a Wall Street stock brokerage firm, called and invited him to lunch. He wanted to discuss a prospective project. Tompkins had bumped into Bill from time to time and was impressed with his recovery and newfound zest for life. Over lunch he explained that one of his clients planned to launch a proxy fight for control of the National Rubber Mold Machinery Company in Akron, Ohio. He thought this former financial hotshot would be the right one to organize and lead the battle. So Tompkins offered him the project, a modest fee, and a handsome bonus if he could pull it off. Under growing pressure at home, both financially and emotionally, Bill reluctantly accepted the offer over Ebby's strong warnings and objections. Ebby was concerned about his friend's sobriety, alone in a strange town and among heavy-drinking stock promoters.

Lois was also concerned when Bill first told her the news. The thought of being so many miles apart, absent if he needed her, caught her off guard. She had always been the mainstay in her husband's alcoholic existence, and now suddenly she was about to find herself an almost unnecessary part of his sober new life. It took the wind out of her sails and gave rise to a sudden feeling of resentment she could not quite understand. But as the day of his departure for Akron drew near, she began to satisfy herself with the thought that perhaps this was God's way of returning her husband to normalcy, getting his foot back into the door on Wall Street, and restoring some balance she so desperately yearned for in their lives.

It was the day before Bill was due to leave. Lois was packing his suitcase, and he was huffing and puffing about having only one decent suit to wear, that the collar on his favorite dress shirt was frayed, that his black shoes needed new heels. Suddenly he burst out in anger that his whole damn life was a mess, that he'd never amount to a hill of beans, and that it was a sheer waste of time going to Akron to handle some lousy proxy battle he'd probably only lose anyway.

Lois was taken aback by her husband's attitude and remarks. Here was the man who had seen the face of God, now angry, bitter, and filled with self-pity again—when he had ruined his own life by drinking. She couldn't understand his outburst and told him so.

All those men he had brought home to sober up, she reminded him, were back out in the streets drunk, yet here he was sober for more than five months and with an opportunity to earn some decent income by doing something he was good at. What was wrong with that?

"Sober!" he shouted back at her. "You call this sober? I'm still a drunk who hasn't had a drink yet!"[36]

Then he stormed out of the bedroom leaving his wife bewildered and fearful that he would be back on the bottle again before ever reaching Akron.

The truth was, Lois's remarks and his angry response stuck in Bill's craw on his train ride west—the fact that he was still a drunk who hadn't had a drink yet. He would soon come to realize that booze was merely the symptom of his disease. That alcoholism runs much deeper than its obvious physical signs. That it's made up of all the low self-esteem, self-pity, anger, resentment, greed, jealousy, and other character defects and shortcomings that drive the alcoholic to find comfort and relief from such feelings in another drink. And Bill was soon to understand something else from his New York "preaching" experiences . . . that by trying to help other drunks, he was focusing less on himself and his own problems and thus had no thought or desire for a drink himself. He was bringing this newfound knowledge and understanding with him to Akron where he would desperately need it, for his five months of sobriety were about to be severely tested.

Lois admittedly felt lost as she watched her husband's train pull out of Pennsylvania Station. It wasn't that she would miss the frenzy and bewilderment that alcoholism brings into the household. It was simply the vacuum she now faced in her life and the wonder of where it would all end.

All she ever wanted was a peaceful life with a sober man she had always deeply loved. Now all she had was concern and confusion. Yes, he was sober and maybe he would stay that way in Akron. God only knew. And yes, he had recovered from his addiction, at least for now. But was that recovery only for himself, for his own desires, his own happiness, his own ambitions? Where did she fit in? After all she had given, all that she had sacrificed for their marriage, what was to be her reward?

"I thought I'd be glad once he stopped drinking," Lois would often share later in her life. "I thought we'd be happy and close and loving like we once were earlier in our marriage. Now I just sat and wondered and waited for his letters to arrive from Akron. I waited and I waited."[37]

10

Great Dreams in Akron

F IVE LONG DAYS WENT BY AND LOIS DIDN'T HEAR A SINGLE WORD
from Bill. She would rush home from the department store and
hurry up the front steps of Clinton Street to check the mailbox. All she found
were a handful of payment notices and, one day, a note from her sister-in-law
Dorothy inviting her to dinner. Her thoughts were always the same as she
stepped into the vestibule and hung up her coat and hat. She imagined he
was off on another binge and nowhere to be found. But by the time she
entered the kitchen and put the kettle on for tea, she would be angry at herself for having so little faith in her husband and especially in her God.

After all, she asked herself, why would the Almighty raise him up to
such a high spiritual place if only to let him tumble back down again?
That is not the work of a loving and merciful God.

Even Ebby Thacher kept calling and asking if she had heard anything
from Bill. Ebby had moved from Clinton Street back to the Calvary
Mission to work with Dr. Shoemaker once his friend had gone to Akron.
He told Lois not to worry, that "God's army" was praying for their boy.

Still, before the end of the week, Lois had left four messages for Bill
at the Mayflower Hotel, where he was staying. Yes, he had told her he
would be spending considerable time lining up brokers to solicit proxies
from company shareholders, probably working late into the night at their
respective firms. However, she thought, just a call or a brief note was in
order to let her know he was all right.

The call came Saturday morning. It was brief, but Bill sounded excited and upbeat. His whole demeanor seemed different. All was going well; he had written a letter that she should be receiving shortly. Then he had to run off to a weekend-long meeting with his financial team.[1]

The letter arrived on Monday. Bill said that in barely a week, his group already had put together more support among the shareholders of National Rubber than either management or another faction had done. He said he was already beginning to feel the rising excitement of prospective victory:

> *It is by far the greatest opportunity to do a fine piece of work that I have ever had, and I don't see how anything can be too much to sacrifice temporarily. Think of it, darling—the opportunity to be president of this company and have some real income to pay bills with, a new life, new people, new scenes. No more Loeser's—a chance to travel, to be somebody; to have you rested at last after your long wait for me to get somewhere. All these things are at stake. Is it not worth the worry, dear heart? I have never tried to do my best before, but I have this time, and I shall not have any regrets if I lose.*[2]

Lois could tell from the bold confidence behind her husband's words that he had no intention of losing. In fact, he not only intended to lead the takeover of this rubber machinery firm but to use it as a stepping stone to much greater things. As Lois penned in her memoirs, "After years of defeat and failure, Bill finally saw the door to victory and success opening wide for him. He wrote me from Akron that the take-over of the National Rubber Mold Machinery Company would only be his start. He said he might yet build that illustrious career he had envisioned years earlier, controlling vast enterprises and reaping great rewards. He was dreaming great dreams again and without realizing it, I became swept up in those dreams too. I would go to bed thinking all about his exciting work in Akron and wake up smiling and happy, feeling better than I had felt in years. And yet I wondered why I still had those old butterflies back in my stomach."[3]

Proxy battles can often turn into mean-spirited, dirty campaigns with adversaries digging up the past and hitting below the belt—"All's fair in love and war." And Bill, together with his primary financial backer at Beers & Company in New York, had underestimated their competition.

Those allied with the company's management group turned out to be no "hicks from the sticks," as some of Bill's proxy solicitors liked to describe them. They began spreading stories about Bill's drinking history and his power drive and probable ambition to be president of the company. They warned shareholders not to place their trust in a drunk who had been fired from several large, respected financial institutions and was washed up on Wall Street. Lois learned that the climate in Akron was worsening when she received another letter from her husband about ten days later: "There is an enormous load of internal dissension, hate, fear, envy, etc. And it is a question of adjusting personal relationships and restoring confidence. In this case in particular, confidence is the key to the whole matter. This thing has been a racket for so many years that the townspeople haven't a spark of confidence in it, and I am staying here so long as I am able to sell them on our good intentions as to them and to National Rubber."[4]

Reading between the lines, Lois could tell that the big deal Bill had hoped to pull off, the victory that would rocket him to success, was in trouble and likely not to happen. For Lois herself, it was one more punch in the stomach, one more balloon bursting, one more slide from the mountaintop of hope into the valley of despair.

But her main concern, as always, was Bill himself. If things didn't work out, how would he face still another terrible disappointment after building his aspirations up so high? His other painful failures had always led to another bottom with the bottle. She prayed that this time it would be different.

As hard as he tried, Bill was not able to allay the assault on his reputation. Soon the momentum shifted and things began heading south. Shareholders started changing their allegiances, Bill's proxy solicitors packed it in, Beers & Company pulled out, and Bill found himself pacing the lobby of the Mayflower Hotel one rainy Saturday afternoon on the eleventh of May, 1935, alone, defeated, angry, and depressed. He had a ten-dollar bill left in his pocket, and the entrance to the Mayflower bar with its sleek art deco facade was less than one hundred feet from where he stood.

There was a festive air in the lobby of Akron's finest hotel that particular Saturday afternoon as a crowd gathered for the annual May Ball given by the St. Thomas Hospital Guild. People were also arriving to dine at the Mayflower and then see a movie at the Rialto down the block where Ginger Rogers and Fred Astaire were starring in *Roberta* or at the Clover Theater around the corner where James Cagney was featured in *G-Men*. But Bill Wilson was totally oblivious to the festive air and the crowds around him. His eyes were fixated on the door to the barroom. He wanted to ease the pain, remove the fear and anger.

He watched a young couple enter the cozy saloon and heard the familiar sounds of tinkling glasses and laughter echoing back at him. That maniac in his head that had been dozing for six months was suddenly awake and whispering in his ear: What harm would one little drink do? You know how to handle it now. Why not? Who would know? Besides, you're miles from home and you could use a pick-me-up. Lois would never be the wiser.

It all made sense to a man who admitted to his wife he was still a drunk who hadn't had a drink yet. Then he noticed his hands were trembling slightly. He felt weak in the knees and beads of cold sweat began running down his arms. In his mind's eye he was back at Towns Hospital pleading for his life. He saw the faces of all the losers and victims at the Calvary Mission, the Bowery derelicts he had preached to, the itinerants he had dragged home to Clinton Street. Suddenly a thought struck him. They were the ones who had kept him sober all those months. He must find one to talk to now. Right now.

He glanced around and spotted, near a bank of phone booths, a glass-encased hotel directory that listed all the major churches and their ministers in the Akron area. Yes, preachers minister to drunks, he thought. Surely if he called, one of them should be able to help him.

One of them did—a Reverend Walter F. Tunks of the First Episcopal Church, who just happened to be familiar with the Oxford Group movement when Bill mentioned it and knew some of its members in town.

After phoning several with no response, Bill found himself speaking with Mrs. Henrietta Seiberling, the daughter-in-law of Frank Seiberling, who had built the Goodyear Tire and Rubber Company in Akron. When he explained he was a drunk from New York who needed to talk to another drunk in order to stay sober, Henrietta was taken aback at first. But her attendance at local Oxford Group meetings had brought her in contact with a number of inebriates, one in particular whose wife had become her good friend—one Dr. Robert Holbrook Smith. He, like Bill, had given up everything for another drink and was now surviving, with his wife, Annie, and their two children, on bare necessities and a history of broken promises.

As it turned out, these two drunks had several other things in common. They were both natives of Vermont, Dr. Bob Smith having been born in St. Johnsbury, Vermont, on August 8, 1879, only seventy-five miles from Bill Wilson's East Dorset home. They had both attended meetings of the Oxford Group movement. And they had both hit their alcoholic bottoms in late 1934, although Dr. Bob was still struggling to find his way out.

Henrietta Seiberling, a religious woman who relied heavily on God's guidance, invited Bill to her home that day. It was a modest but warmly decorated house at the entrance to the Seiberling estate and had once been used by a gatekeeper and his family. That is why it was often called the "gatehouse." Her invitation to an odd-sounding stranger was quite remarkable in itself since she had three teenage children in the house.

Upon meeting Bill and after a brief discussion, she called her friend Annie Smith and insisted she bring her husband over to meet this charming man who described himself as "a rum hound from New York."[5] Like Lois Wilson, Annie Smith, also a very religious woman, was willing to do almost anything to help her husband. She told Henrietta that Bob had passed out on the couch but that they would come the next day around five o'clock.

That was Mother's Day, May 12, 1935. Lois remembered going to church in Brooklyn Heights that day as she did almost every Sunday, only this time she had to listen to the minister extol the wonderful work mothers do, raising their children, caring for their husbands, and holding their families together. She left feeling blue. Even after all these years, she still had pangs of guilt for not being able to have a family of her own.

Recalling that day later, Lois thought she might have phoned Bill again that afternoon, leaving him another message. It had been several days since his last call and his most recent letter had been rather brief and not very optimistic. She was worried. She felt alone and helpless. If only she were there with him, to comfort him, to help see him through this depressing affair. For a while she thought about visiting her sister Barbara or perhaps Katherine, whom she hadn't seen in weeks. Instead she simply sat in the living room sewing and waiting for Bill to return her call. Lois had no idea or intuition that as she sat there in the quiet waning light at Clinton Street, her husband was about to embark on a momentous, world-changing journey that would begin that very afternoon hundreds of miles away in the gatehouse of Henrietta Seiberling in Akron, Ohio.[6]

Bob Smith woke that Sunday morning with a pounding headache, tremors, and an upset stomach. He drove with his wife to the Seiberling estate that evening mainly to please her. After all, it was Mother's Day, and he had already spoiled most of it for her by sleeping late and missing church. But Annie was used to that by now. She was with him on the pretext of owing Henrietta a visit, but in truth it was to make sure her husband got there. Bob also felt somewhat shamefully indebted to Mrs. Seiberling for her quiet generosity to his family and her personal kindness and concern toward him. However, on the drive over, he told his wife he wasn't feeling very well and could only give this "mug from New York" fifteen minutes of his time. As it turned out, he and Bill talked for almost seven hours.

Dr. Smith was fifty-five, more than fifteen years older than the man he was about to meet. A surgeon by training, he almost drank his way out of medical school as a young man. Thanks to his father, who was a stern probate judge, and to a college professor he greatly respected, young Bob stopped imbibing altogether until after he graduated, completed his internship at City Hospital in Akron, Ohio, and set up his medical practice in the Second National Bank Building there in 1912. He remained in the very same office until he retired in 1948.

A tall, broad-shouldered, somewhat reserved man, Bob Smith married a lady he had met seventeen years earlier, Anne Robinson Ripley of

Oak Park, Illinois, and brought her to Akron in January of 1915. She was a small, quiet woman whose charm, cheerfulness, and calm ways would stay with her all her life.

Reared in a family of railroad people, Anne found there was never enough money for the finer things in life. But she abhorred ostentation and pretense anyway. When she was admitted to Wellesley College, it was on a scholarship, not on the family fame and fortune that ushered many students into this elite institution.

Anne had been spending a holiday break with a college friend in St. Johnsbury, Vermont, when she met Bob Smith, a medical student at the time. They had gone to a local dance. He was quite shy until he had a few drinks, and then she couldn't get him off the dance floor. He and his drinking crowd made an impression on her. The way they acted reminded her of some heavy drinkers in her own family.

Nevertheless, while they fell in love right from the start, their romance was hardly a whirlwind courtship. It would culminate in marriage only after many years of school, hard work, and Bob's medical internship. But they corresponded frequently and dated whenever they could during this period, while Anne taught school.

Perhaps another reason for their long courtship was her healthy fear of walking down the aisle with a man she felt drank too excessively too often. She even learned about his almost being tossed out of medical school because of his drinking habit. So she waited until he finally graduated, completed his internship, set up his practice, and gave solid evidence of being sober for quite some time before agreeing to marry him.

They bought a two-story clapboard house at 855 Ardmore Avenue in Akron and proceeded to raise two wonderful children—a biological son, Robert, Jr., and an adopted daughter, Sue. Now hardworking and very professional, Dr. Robert Holbrook Smith had a flourishing practice and soon became a trusted and admired member of the community. Life was good.

In the spring of 1918, the young doctor attended a state medical convention with his wife, who was expecting their first child. He and the others at their table toasted her with a glass of wine. Annie never even thought about her husband's past drinking problem. That was when he was young and sowing his wild oats, she had told herself. Now he was sober and successful, so she paid little heed to the incident. Besides, she thought, a small glass of wine is not really "drinking."

That very same year Congress passed the Eighteenth Amendment—Prohibition—and Smitty, as his close friends now called him, thought it was his insurance policy to imbibe with impunity. After all, he told himself, how could anyone buy enough liquor to get into any real trouble now that the whole country had gone dry? He would soon discover how easy it was for an alcoholic to deceive himself.

He started drinking very moderately. Annie hardly noticed at first. In fact, it was almost a year before she learned her local druggist was also her husband's local bootlegger. But within a relatively short time, the respected physician's intake was drifting out of control. Only his past experience with booze and two "conflicting phobias" kept things in check for some time. He was afraid of running out of liquor, which he now needed in order to sleep, and was also afraid that if he didn't stay sober enough to earn a living, he couldn't buy the alcohol he needed to sleep. For the next seventeen years he led this squirrel-cage type of existence, which gradually eroded his abilities as a doctor, his medical practice, his reputation in the community, his spiritual beliefs and actions, and his financial and emotional responsibilities to his wife and children.

His son, Robert, Jr., was a teenager then. Before passing away on April 22, 2004, the younger Smitty recalled how bad things were by the time Mother's Day, 1935, rolled around. "My father had almost no practice left to speak of," he said some sixty years later. "When he wasn't hiding out somewhere, he would be at home, indisposed. My mother would lie to his patients for him. So did Lily, his assistant at his office.

"It seemed every time he came home, my mother always tried to frisk him. She wanted to see if she could possibly keep him in good enough shape to get him into the office the next morning. But my father always had his ways of fooling her. For example, he wore heavy driving mittens during the winter since car heaters didn't work very well back then. He would put a half pint of medicinal alcohol into one of the gloves and toss it up onto the second-story sun porch of our house.

"After mother had frisked him, he would go upstairs and get his whiskey from the porch. When he came down again, it was obvious to everyone he had been drinking. My poor mother never did figure that one out. If it wasn't for President Roosevelt's mortgage moratorium, we would have lost that house."

Then, remembering how sick his father felt before leaving for Henrietta Seiberling's home that historic night, the younger Smitty said with a smile, "He probably had his usual big glass of bicarbonate of soda before he left. I was at least twenty-one before I knew there was any other kind of medicine than bicarbonate of soda. My father had it in practically every room in our house. I found out why as I grew older when I saw how his heavy drinking was affecting him physically."[7]

The meeting began on an awkward note. It was obvious that Dr. Bob didn't want to be there as he stuck out his trembling hand to this much younger stranger. And Bill was now having second thoughts about imposing himself on these most generous people.

Henrietta had prepared dinner but both men politely declined, Bill apologizing for his lack of appetite, and the red-faced physician explaining his stomach was "on the fritz." So their hostess led them into her library, sat them before a large brick fireplace, placed a pot of coffee and two cups on the table in front of them, and quietly left the room.

It was a few moments before either of them spoke. Finally Dr. Bob leaned forward, squirmed a bit, and then said firmly that he could only spare fifteen minutes. He suggested Bill get right to the point. Why was he there? What did he want, exactly? And what did he possibly think he could do for him? He made it clear his drinking was a personal matter and besides, he had been worked over by the best—several well-meaning ministers, a so-called spiritual healer, and even a prominent psychiatrist a doctor friend had recommended to him some time ago. So what new cure was this interloper from New York offering?

At that juncture, Bill leaned forward. He nervously apologized if he seemed to be intruding into the doctor's private affairs. That was not his intention. He frankly admitted he wasn't there to help him, as his new acquaintance most likely assumed. Instead, staring deeply into Dr. Bob's eyes, he said with the utmost sincerity that he had come because he, Bill Wilson, was the one who needed help. They looked at each other for a long moment. Dr. Bob frowned, then eased back into his chair and began to listen.

Bill told his own story, playing down his spiritual experience, as Dr. Silkworth had always suggested, and describing in every painful detail the horror of his obsession with alcohol and the physical addiction that condemned him to the out-of-control drinking and irrational behavior that had destroyed his life. He even quoted some of what Dr. Silkworth had told him about the progress of the illness and its eventual prognosis—insanity or death. Being a doctor himself inflicted with the same malady, Dr. Bob found it all made sense.

Finally Bill explained that working with drunks in New York was probably the main factor that kept him sober all those months. Faced with the failure of his proxy battle, something he had pinned his hopes on for the future, the urge to drink returned with a vengeance. He felt if he could only find another alcoholic like himself to talk to, perhaps that would help him fight the obsession. That's why he had called and was here now.

Dr. Bob later recalled realizing that Bill understood alcoholism from actual experience. "In other words, he talked my language," said Dr. Bob. "He knew all the answers, and certainly not because he had picked them up in his reading."[8]

Suddenly, this helpless, almost hopeless inebriate began to see dimly through his fog. Dr. Bob, like Bill, had tried to stay sober through religion by attending Oxford Group meetings. But, also like Bill, he had failed. Now he was being offered a new solution, one his young friend from the East had already tried and so far found successful—turning to God while also working with other alcoholics. Perhaps it could work for him too. Perhaps talking with, being with, working with this newfound compatriot, he could stay sober too.

This recognition, this coming together of two desperate drunks seeking sobriety, was no mere coincidence. As they would both acknowledge, it was an event far beyond their comprehension. It was also the beginning of the worldwide Fellowship of Alcoholics Anonymous.

They talked on for hours over two more pots of coffee. Dr. Bob began to open up. He spoke frankly, as unashamedly as Bill. When they finally parted at eleven fifteen that night, they knew something had radically changed in them both. Although they couldn't explain what it was at that moment, a spark that was to light future fires had been struck.

Much to Lois's dismay, Bill decided to extend his stay in Akron for two reasons. First, his pivotal meeting with Dr. Bob, another failed Oxford Group drunkard, had revived the dream he had back in New York of creating a movement separate and apart from the "Groupers" as he now called them—a movement that would be focused solely on saving alcoholics. Second, with renewed confidence in his ability to stay sober in difficult times and situations, he had phoned Howard Tompkins at Beers & Company and talked him into an additional modest advance so he could try a new angle to win control of National Rubber.

Since he and Dr. Bob found themselves meeting almost daily, Annie Smith invited her new ally to be their guest at their Ardmore Avenue home. Bill gratefully accepted.

Back in Brooklyn Heights, Lois knew nothing of what had taken place at the Mayflower Hotel or at Henrietta Seiberling's gatehouse. All she knew from her husband's last letter was that he was in trouble, and she wasn't there to help him. On the one hand, she was angry he hadn't called, and yet on the other, she was fearful of his present condition. She wanted to catch the next bus to Akron, yet she wanted to believe that her God was taking care of him. She found herself tired and short-tempered from worry and lack of sleep, both at work and with her family.

Her father, who was now eighty, was retired and living in New York City with his new wife. He dropped by for a visit one evening as he did on occasion. This time it was to pick up some belongings he had stored in the attic. Lois had already told him about her husband's exciting exploits in Akron and their high hopes for the future. Dr. Burnham simply commented that he was pleased his son-in-law finally had a paying job somewhere, even if it was out West.

But this particular night he could tell by the familiar sadness in his daughter's eyes that all wasn't going very well. The good doctor had promised himself he wouldn't interfere any longer in her and Bill's life together. Besides, he wasn't feeling well himself and hoped to avoid any additional stress in his now rather uncomplicated existence. So he simply let his oldest and dearest daughter know as always that he was nearby if ever she needed him.[9]

This gave Lois some comfort. But the letter she received from Bill the following day only added to her confusion and concern. After stating that he planned to remain in Akron for a while longer to continue the proxy fight, his letter went on, "I'm writing this from the office of one of my new friends, Dr. Smith. He had my trouble and is getting to be an ardent Grouper. I have been to his house for meals, and the rest of his family is as nice as he is. I have witnessed at a number of meetings and have been taken to a number of people."[10] Bill went on to say that Dr. Bob was a prominent surgeon in town, but was in danger of losing his medical practice. His wife, Anne, was grateful that Bill and her husband had gotten together.

As Bill went on to explain his close call at the Mayflower Hotel and how his meeting with Dr. Bob had kept him sober, saved his life, and lifted his spirits, Lois felt a twinge of jealousy surge through her. It quickly turned into a strong feeling of resentment. Just when her husband needed her most, she thought to herself, some stranger comes along and does for him what her love and sacrifice all these years couldn't do. This drunken doctor, whoever he is, not only kept her husband from drinking, but lifted his spirits and renewed his resolve to fulfill his dreams, whatever they might be at this point.[11]

Lois put the letter aside as she rose from the living-room couch and walked to the small table where her Bible rested. She opened it and stared at the scrawled promises Bill had written on the page some time ago— promises she had prayed for years would come true. Now they had, only not in the way she had expected. Perhaps that's why all of these mixed emotions were now swirling inside her.

What is happening to me? she whispered to herself. *Why do I feel this way? This is not the kind of person I used to be, certainly not the kind of person I want to be. Why do I always seem so angry and afraid and now jealous and resentful of a man I have never met, a man I don't even know? I should be glad he was there, as Ebby was, to help my husband and that Bill was there to help him. But I was also there to support Bill, to go to those Oxford Group meetings with him, to be with him whenever he wanted to talk, to question, to share my strength and hope.*

As she touched Bill's handwriting in her Bible, the most fearful thought of all now struck her. Bill was hundreds of miles away, yet he was sober, happy, and filled with self-confidence. This she could tell from his letter. And he did it without her help. *What if he doesn't need me anymore?* she suddenly thought. *If that's so, then what is my life all about? What is the meaning of it all?* She closed the Bible and stared at it, afraid of what the answer might be. She began to weep.[12]

Bill knew his drunkenness over the years had seriously eroded his wife's faith in him. There were days, weeks, even months when they almost seemed like strangers to each other. At the same time, he was aware that she wanted him back in New York, especially after he informed her the proxy battle was all but lost. He was determined now to restore her faith in him even though he understood it would take time. He believed the deep love they still had for each other—tested by the years—would win out in the end. He felt certain of that, provided he didn't drink again. That was foremost in his mind.

When Bill received the cash from Tompkins, he immediately hired a shrewd local attorney to investigate the possibility of fraud in the stockholders' vote involving National Rubber's management group. But as much as he wanted financial success, he was now even more eager to pursue his talks with Dr. Bob and his dream of building a fellowship of drunks. He thought Dr. Bob was equally enthusiastic about the idea until along came another serious setback, another near disaster. Dr. Bob had been sober about ten days when he casually mentioned he planned to attend the annual American Medical Association convention in Atlantic City, New Jersey, four days hence. He had never missed one of these important gatherings, he said, and now it was even more essential to reestablish his reputation in the community. Bill saw the worried look on Annie's face but found it hard to argue the importance of the trip.

The Akron physician was drunk before he reached Atlantic City. He stayed drunk throughout the convention. Several of his colleagues put him back aboard the train for Akron drunk. Bill felt he had failed his good friend when he received a phone call from the Akron station master to pick up Dr. Bob at the depot at four o'clock the morning of June 9. Back at Ardmore Avenue, Bill put him under a cold shower, fed him black coffee throughout the day, and continued to talk to him late into the evening. Dr. Bob went to bed that night humbled by the experience and promising his dedicated friend he would never let him down again.

When he awoke the next morning with a terrible hangover, Bill gave his friend a bottle of beer to calm his shakes. That was June 10, 1935, and that was Robert Holbrook Smith's last drink. That is also the day the Fellowship of Alcoholics Anonymous celebrates as "Founders Day" because both Dr. Bob and Bill Wilson never had another drink for the rest of their lives.

But now they both realized they must take what they discovered to others in order to strengthen their own sobriety. They found their third candidate strapped to a bed in City Hospital, where Dr. Bob had once been on the staff. The man's name was Bill Dotson, a disbarred attorney who had blackened the eye of a young nurse who was caring for him. Depressed and remorseful, the lawyer listened intently while these two drunks told their stories. He totally identified with them and became the third sober member of this embryonic cluster of alcoholics who now had a much clearer view of their future together.

Bill had been imploring Lois to come to Akron for a visit. She had taken time off from work when he was drinking, he told her on the phone. Why couldn't she take some time off to spend with him sober?

"But all I did was nag at him to come home," she later recalled. "I kept saying we lived in Brooklyn, not Akron, Ohio. He said he wanted to show me he could succeed at something. He felt he had always failed at whatever he had undertaken when he was drinking. I thought he was talking only about the proxy fight. But he wasn't. I could tell there was something else happening so I became more patient with him each time he called. Besides, I hated myself for being a nag."[13]

Finally Annie Smith wrote Lois a warm personal letter. She told her what Bill's efforts meant to her and her family, how they had changed their lives. She said she would be honored if Lois could see her way clear to come for a visit so she could thank her in person. A short while later, Lois boarded a bus for Akron for a week's vacation. It was early July and she was still fighting her own mixed emotions.[14]

Bill met her at the bus depot. He kissed and hugged her warmly. She was pleased to see the light in his eyes and the happiness on his face, but

wished she had been responsible for making it happen, instead of someone else. If only those mixed emotions could have let her see the truth—
that her husband's sobriety at that very moment was in reality the
culmination of all she had given him in their life together. If only he had
said something then and there to let her know. But the assault of alcoholism on her own psyche, the fact that spouses and families grow equally sick from the disease, blinded her then to the role she had played and
all she had done just to keep him alive, to keep him sane. One day she
would be able to see through the pale and understand.

With the Smiths, however, it was a different story. The trepidation
and resentment Lois had carried with her on the bus all but vanished as
Annie and Bob greeted her on the front porch of their modest home.[15]

"I loved Annie and Bob from the moment I saw them," Lois remembered. "They were so warm, so gracious, so *good.* Bob was a tall, lanky
Vermonter like Bill and, like him, yearned to be of use to others. In other
respects they were very different."[16]

Lois said that "Bob and Bill were very busy at the time [I arrived].
They had just gotten Bill D. into the program. So Anne and I spent a lot
of time together. Anne was the person I related to as the wife of an alcoholic, even though we didn't talk too much about our problems."[17]

Lois later talked about how she was disappointed not to be spending
time with Bill, but she enjoyed her time with Annie. She noted that
Annie was as good a listener as she was a talker. The only sad thing was,
she was a heavy smoker like Bill.[18]

Bob Smith, Jr., was sixteen at the time of Lois's visit. "I remember
seeing Lois the day she arrived," he said. "It was a weekend and she was
as cute as Christmas, she was. She had this wonderful warm personality
that made you feel right at home with her. Maybe that's why she and my
mother hit it right off. But I think I grumbled the whole week she was
there because I had to give up my room for her and Bill and sleep in the
attic. Bill had been sleeping on a Murphy bed in the den."[19] Annie, who
was more than ten years older than Lois, filled her new friend in on all
that had happened—Bill's call to Reverend Tunks, the gathering at
Henrietta Seiberling's home, even her husband's relapse and how Bill
patiently got him sober again. She said it almost seemed like a miracle

after so many years of hardship and degradation. Perhaps that's why she still carried this sense of doom, something she couldn't quite overcome. And when Annie remarked that she still walked on eggshells when Bob was around and kept all her toes and fingers crossed, Lois smiled and nodded in agreement. She fully understood and began to share her own experiences.

Though affable and outgoing, Lois had always been a private person when it came to her feelings and especially with regard to her husband's drinking and all the shame and humiliation involved. But here she talked openly and freely about these things to a woman she had only just met, yet a woman she felt she had known forever since they had so much in common. In that one short week, Lois Wilson and Annie Smith developed a strong, close bond that would grow and last for more than a decade, right up to Annie's passing. It would help each of them through difficult times and produce the kind of self-discovery that would also help others who followed in their footsteps. But for now, their warm and loving friendship was enough.

Annie knew Lois wanted her husband to return to New York as soon as his proxy battle was over, which seemed only a matter of weeks at the most. At the same time, she admitted she was being selfish for wanting him to stay in Akron. She feared what could happen once he left. Lois remembered Annie telling her, "Having Bill here has been a godsend. Bob's practice has picked up. The bills are getting paid. There's peace in the house once again. I have a semblance of hope back in my life and I owe all that to your husband . . . and to God answering my prayers."[20]

While Lois was happy and a bit proud that her husband had done so much for this wonderful family, Annie's words actually prompted another twinge of jealousy, followed by that now familiar feeling of resentment. Here was a woman who, like herself, had put up with a terrible alcoholic, but now she was beginning to get some good things back in her life again—the kinds of things Lois herself yearned for. *If Bill could help strangers in Akron find them again, why couldn't he bring them back into our own lives?* she thought. Annie would have understood, but Lois kept these feelings to herself, at least for now.[21]

By the time Lois returned to Brooklyn, she had a very strong sense that her husband's main priority was working with alcoholics. She had seen him applying very little effort to the proxy battle even though it was currently putting bread on the table and its outcome was important to their future, or so she thought. She still had no idea where his work with drunks would lead even though she knew how important that was for all of them—her and Bill, Dr. Bob and Annie. But Dr. Bob had his practice. He had a growing income now. How did Bill plan to earn a living? What about the dream he came here with—to build a financial empire? He had no answers whenever she asked. He would only say it depended upon the outcome of the proxy fight . . . "and other things."

Lois rode the bus back to New York still filled with anxiety about the future and carrying all the mixed emotions she had brought with her to Akron.[22] Bill and Dr. Bob continued to go almost daily to City Hospital to talk with drunks. Afterward, they worked to formulate a program that would keep their new candidates sober, a program based essentially on the Oxford Group principles in which they both still believed. Soon they added a fourth sober member to their clan, and then a fifth. Bill was beginning to think that few men of forty could find a vocation more fascinating, more challenging, more absorbing of their energies than trying to sober up complicated, denying, angry, self-pitying, hopeless alcoholics. Just where it would all lead to he had no idea. But it was what he felt compelled to do—absolutely.

By the middle of August, the shrewd lawyer he hired had actually convinced a federal judge that National Rubber's management group had solicited fraudulent proxies in an attempt to gain control of the company. The judge ordered a revote. It was very close. Bill's group lost by a mere 2 percent.

The battle was over. Bill's business venture in Akron had failed. All he had to show for his four months there was the work he had done with Dr. Bob and the small group of now-sober alcoholics following in their footsteps. So on August 25, 1935, he caught the train back to New York leaving behind his dreams of building a financial empire—but having his dream of creating a fellowship of sober alcoholics ahead of him.

Lois met her husband at Pennsylvania Station. She was grateful he was still sober but worried about what their life together would be like from this moment on.

*Lois Burnham, "pink, bright-eyed, and healthy,"
as a six-month-old child in 1891*

*Dr. Clark Burnham as a young
physician in Brooklyn, New York*

*Matilda Spelman Burnham as Lois's
young mother*

Lois with her parents at Clinton Street, Brooklyn, 1891

Barbara Burnham, Lois's youngest sister, who was badly burned as a young child

Katherine Burnham, Lois's other sister, whom the family called Kitty

Lyman Burnham, the brother who became a doctor like his father

Rogers Burnham, the brother who was one of Bill Wilson's good friends

*Lois Burnham (second from left) with the Packer Collegiate Institute
1912 girls basketball team*

*Dr. Clark Burnham sitting on the front porch of the family cottage
at Emerald Lake in East Dorset, Vermont*

Lois (above) as a young woman frolicking at Emerald Lake,
one of the places closest to her heart

After graduating from Packer Collegiate Institute, Lois went on to study art.

Pictured here in an art class at age twenty-two, Lois loved this photo of herself.

Dr. Clark Burnham always enjoyed working on the family cottage at Emerald Lake.

Second Lieutenant William G. Wilson poses with his new bride shortly before leaving for World War I.

Lois was proud of this window she sewed in the tent they used on their cross-country motorcycle trip.

While Bill was overseas, Lois worked as a medical aide at Walter Reed Army Hospital in Washington, D.C.

Lois and Bill are caught relaxing during their first visit to AA groups in California in the late 1940s.

*This is the desk where Lois began to organize what became
the worldwide fellowship of Al-Anon. It is still in the large
upstairs room at Stepping Stones in Bedford Hills, New York.*

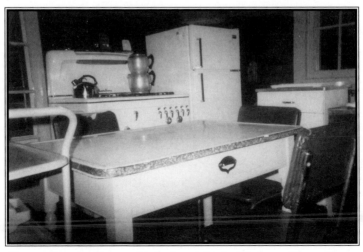

*Now at Stepping Stones, this is the original table from Clinton Street,
where Ebby Thacher sat with Bill, bringing him
the sober message of the Oxford Group.*

Bill Wilson and Dr. Bob Smith, the cofounders of Alcoholics Anonymous

Bill with his lifelong friend and sponsor Ebby Thacher

Bill and Lois often entertained guests at their home in Bedford Hills.
This photo was taken in the late 1960s.

Dr. Bob with his wife Anne Smith, who became Lois's closest and dearest friend

This is Stepping Stones, the lovely brown-shingled home Lois and Bill moved into in 1941, now surrounded by the beautiful gardens she planted.

Lois and Bill enjoying their gardens at Stepping Stones in the 1960s

*Lois visiting the Clinton Street brownstone where she was born
and later shared Bill's ordeal with alcoholism*

*This is the upstairs room at Stepping Stones, which Lois turned into
an AA and Al-Anon museum.*

Al-Anon cofounder Anne Bingham, who died in 1984

Harriet Sevarino, Lois's longtime friend and housekeeper

Lois with Bill in the spring of 1970, only a year before he passed away

Lois cutting her cake to celebrate
her ninety-fifth birthday

Lois with Nell Wing at Stepping Stones
in 1988, only months before Lois died

Every year Lois hosted a picnic at Stepping Stones, and this tradition continues today.
Here in 1986, author Bill Borchert leads Lois to a podium to address the large crowd.

II

Nightmare on Clinton Street

*I*T WAS THE WEEK BEFORE THANKSGIVING, 1935. CLARK BURNHAM had been in Vermont for some months selling his beloved cottage and the surrounding property on Emerald Lake, a sad and painful event for him and his entire family, who had so many happy memories of growing up there. But retired now and with little income, he and his wife needed the funds to support themselves. Upon getting word that his son-in-law was back from Akron and filling the Clinton Street house with a swarm of his drinking buddies, the good doctor decided to pay his daughter a visit upon his return to the city. Yes, he had promised himself he wouldn't interfere in their lives, but these ghastly rumors had to be looked into.[1]

Lois was in the kitchen making another large pot of coffee when she heard the doorbell. Drying her hands on her apron, she pushed her hair back from her forehead and headed down the hall to the front door. She was taken aback to see her father standing there. Dr. Burnham was also taken aback to see his daughter in a stained apron, her hair awry, and perspiration covering her weary face. He hadn't seen his oldest and dearest daughter looking this way since the time her husband returned drunk and broke from his failed excursion to Montreal. So Dr. Burnham stood with his mouth hanging open until Lois collected herself, grabbed him by the hand, and ushered him inside.

The good doctor couldn't believe his eyes as he glanced around at what he would later describe as "the alcoholic ward at Bellevue Hospital." He spotted two drunks shaking it off in the living room, two other fairly sober gents playing checkers in the dining room, and another staggering slowly down the front hall stairs. Ebby Thacher was chatting with another half-sober individual over a cup of coffee in the kitchen.

As Lois recalled, her stunned father leaned close and whispered quite loudly: "Tell me . . . what in God's name is going on here?"[2]

Knowing they couldn't have a private conversation in the kitchen, she led him out into the small yard behind the house. But before she could begin explaining, her father demanded to know why she was apparently nursing a house full of inebriates. Hadn't she gone through enough with her own husband? Had she, too, lost her mind? He had warned her what could happen if she stayed with Bill.

Lois waited until her father ran out of breath and was now only huffing and puffing. She had tried to remain calm as she fidgeted in the cool autumn air.

"I still love him very much, Father," she remembered saying.[3] Then she took his hand again and tried to briefly detail what had happened to Bill during his trip to Akron, how he finally found a way to stay sober and help others at the same time. That while he wanted to get back on Wall Street if he could, his life was now mainly about working with alcoholics to help them find permanent sobriety. She decided to stay with her husband, she confessed, because, well, he finally seemed to need her help once again—and she needed to be needed. That's all there was to it.

"But you deserve better than this," she recalled him saying as he stared at her in a very strange way.[4] She could tell he felt there was something definitely wrong with this need of hers to be needed, but he never said it. He was too kind and loving for that. Instead he remarked that if her husband was really cured of his drinking problem, he should be providing a much better life than this for his long-suffering wife.

Before her father left that day, Lois assured him she was doing exactly what she wanted to do at the moment and would continue down that path until she felt she couldn't go any further. While Dr. Burnham departed still worried about his daughter, Lois was even more concerned about him as she watched this once robust man, now eighty, shuffle feebly down the steps of his beloved Clinton Street brownstone.

Lois wanted to explain all that had happened—and happened so quickly—since Bill's return from Akron only three months earlier. But she sensed her father didn't have the patience to listen and probably wouldn't have understood anyway. After all, she herself was only beginning to comprehend the importance of the work her husband was doing. She even felt a growing pride in it. However, while living in the same house, his zealous dedication to his drunks was keeping them apart. He simply had no time for her, and this she found hard to accept.[5]

Almost immediately upon returning from Ohio, Bill had gone to Towns Hospital to fill Dr. Silkworth in on what he and Bob Smith had discovered together. Dr. Silkworth gave his prized patient the opportunity to try it out on some men in his hospital as he did once before, reminding Bill as he had in the past to "go easy on the God stuff. It turns a lot of drunks off."

By now, Bill understood this completely from his own experiences both in New York and Akron, although he never wavered from the belief that spirituality or a connection with a "Higher Power" was the real key to long-lasting sobriety. But he also understood that it took time, pain, and change for most alcoholics to accept this. This is the reason Bill used the term *Higher Power* when writing AA's Twelve Step program, since it was acceptable to those who had difficulty with the word *God*.

So, with Dr. Silkworth's help and Lois's reluctant consent, he began bringing a few willing candidates home to Clinton Street as he had before, only this time he had confidence that he could show them how to stay sober and that they, in turn, could show each other. As he and Dr. Bob now knew, it had to be one drunk helping another.

Lois remembered the first alcoholic her husband dragged in from Towns. He was Hank Parkhurst, a once high-powered promoter who lost his top management position with a major oil company because of his boozing. From the moment he heard about Bill's plan to build a large fellowship of drunks, he wanted to go right out, raise a lot of money, sell the idea to the whole world, and make Bill a fortune. But the air quickly came out of Hank's balloon when his mentor informed him the movement would be based on the Oxford Group principles, which called for everyone turning

The LOIS WILSON *Story*

their lives over to God. Hank didn't believe in God—at least not then.

John Henry Fitzhugh Mayo from Cumberstone, Maryland, was the second candidate from Towns. The son of a minister, Fitz, as everyone soon came to call him, said he always felt inferior, incompetent, and unworthy until he got smashed. Then he felt he was the greatest at everything. Lois soon dubbed him "the impractical, lovable dreamer."[6]

More came. More went. There was Freddie the chemistry professor, Herb the golf pro, Alec the accountant, Charley the plumber, Wes the obese advertising executive, and Chris the rugged wire-rope salesman. While many others tried Bill's wares for short periods of time, these men, along with Hank, Fitz, and Ebby, all of whom were living at the house, were the mainstay of the early developing Fellowship.[7]

Bill and Dr. Bob remained in very close contact and were basically taking the same approach—carrying their message to alcoholics in hospitals, nut wards, and drunk tanks while opening their homes as halfway houses or hostels to homeless men or men temporarily estranged from their wives and families. Since Clinton Street was much larger than the Smith's Ardmore Avenue residence, it could accommodate more "guests." Lois and Bill occupied the second floor, and the rest of the house—the first and third floors and the basement—were made available to "recovering" alcoholics.

As Lois would often share with friends later on, this was a period in her life where she felt very much alone and shut out of Bill's companionship. He was so busy trying to earn some money doing investigative work while also trying to care for his alcoholics that he had little or no time for his wife or those weekend trips to Vermont she so yearned for. Still, Lois tried as hard as she could to convince herself that she was not really that unhappy and that things would soon change for the better.[8]

For a while, her work with the drunks helped Lois ignore all those mixed emotions she still had inside.

Charley Baker, one of the early "Clinton Street boys,"[9] as Lois nicknamed her guests, whose drinking had cost him a very profitable plumbing business, reportedly told some friends back then, "All of us were living rent-free, food-free, everything-free in Clinton Street, and Lois doing all the work. She was working in a department store during the day and cooking for us and providing all the money the whole house had."[10]

While Lois may have enjoyed all the praise heaped on her by her "boys" for her perceived heroics, she was also well aware that some people, including her own family and her neighbors, looked upon the situation at Clinton Street as a nightmare and Lois's work as a seeming charwoman foolish and insane. Noting this in her later years, she commented, "I certainly thought I knew what I was doing and why I was doing it. I wanted to help Bill because I loved him and wanted to be with him. But I also received tremendous joy and satisfaction from helping the other men who were staying with us and watching some of them get sober and rebuild their lives. Of course, it didn't happen to everyone, I'm sorry to say."[11]

Most of the time their guests caused little trouble, but there were occasions when, with no warning, the house was overrun with six or seven men in various stages of recovery. One might get the urge and find a bottle he had stashed away for "emergencies." Then he and several buddies would proceed to get royally soused. Sometimes a fight broke out over the last few swigs. Bill, Ebby, and some other sober men would drag these "slippers" off to Towns or Bellevue or wherever they could get them admitted.

"The rule in the house was always no drinking or you would be evicted," Lois explained of that challenging time. "And Bill made sure it was strictly enforced because he was often gone, visiting needy alcoholics around town or in New Jersey or Connecticut and I would have to cope with the boys on my own. One could see in those instances another sort of trouble might have seemed likely, but I encountered it only once.

"My theory that advances from men were often caused by the woman's attitude held water through all my experiences with alcoholics—with just one exception. The exception was a man Bill and I had come to love and trust a great deal. This man must have misinterpreted my expressions of gratitude for his sobriety.

"One night while Bill was away, the man, much to my dismay, came into my bedroom. However, he did not make too much fuss at being rebuffed as he knew there were others nearby who could have been alerted. Perhaps knowing I would tell Bill, the man left quietly the next morning. We never saw him after that."[12]

Bill had now started holding meetings or, as some called them, "sharing sessions" at Clinton Street both for those at the house as well as for other alcoholics he had met at the Calvary Mission and elsewhere who decided to try his approach to staying sober. Here they openly discussed the serious problems drinking had caused in their lives and their current strategies for staying sober, such as trying to be more honest and caring, making amends for the past, and looking for ways to help their fellow drunks. While Bill and Lois also brought their guests to the regular Oxford Group sessions at Calvary Church, many felt looked down upon there by the nonalcoholic members of the movement. They much preferred their own gatherings aimed solely at the alcoholic and his particular requisites.[13]

"Bill and Dr. Sam Shoemaker, one of the leaders of the Oxford Group movement, had become very good friends by this time," Lois once explained. "But one of Dr. Shoemaker's assistants did not approve of Bill working only with alcoholics. He particularly did not like my husband holding meetings in our home away from the church's influence.

"That assistant gave a talk one Sunday at an Oxford Group gathering and said certain special meetings being held surreptitiously were not good for the overall movement. He was referring of course to Bill. The atmosphere of the Group toward us from then on became slightly chilly."[14] On the one hand, some of the Oxford Group's nonalcoholic members simply could not understand why Bill's followers had special needs and required special attention since they believed faith in God could cure anyone or anything. On the other hand, the more snobbish members felt that drunks lowered the overall image of the movement. After all, they said, wasn't one of the Oxford Group's main goals to attract the more powerful of society, the political and business leaders who could have a great impact for change in the world? Instead, here were rooms filled with inebriates, some of whom, like Hank Parkhurst, even questioned the very existence of God.

But the underlying concern was Bill Wilson creating his own "faction" by having his own meetings separate and apart from the Oxford Group. By the middle of 1936, the alcoholics who came to the Calvary Mission were instructed not to attend any more meetings at Clinton Street. Bill soon realized that such growing dissension could only have a negative effect on his goals. So quietly and without fanfare, he severed his relationship with the movement but continued to foster and incorporate many of its principles into the program he and Dr. Bob were developing for their fledgling Fellowship.

Even Dr. Shoemaker eventually became disenchanted with the back-biting and small-mindedness within the Oxford Group. He later resigned himself and ultimately became a great admirer of Bill's work. He even spoke in strong support of that work before thousands at two International Conventions of Alcoholics Anonymous, in 1955 and again in 1960.[15]

And so the work at Clinton Street continued, often at the pace of one step forward, two steps back. But it continued, and as it did, it produced many memorable episodes in the ever-changing lives of the men involved—some comical, some tragic, some inspirational. And Lois was involved in many, which she often recounted in her later years.

Lois loved to recall several humorous incidents involving Wes Wiley, the roly-poly advertising man who struggled as hard as anyone she ever knew to stay sober. But even after he took up residence in the basement at Clinton Street, he kept slipping and sliding. She still had great empathy for him and always tried to help wherever and whenever she could.

"Wes knew the rule that anyone who was drinking was not allowed into the house," she related. "So one night half-drunk Wes, nearly as wide as he was tall, decided to get in by sliding down the coal chute. Why his great bulk didn't get stuck in the chute, I'll never know. But then he decided to take a bath to get the coal dust off and believe it or not got stuck in our old-fashioned, soapstone washtub in the kitchen.

"He began yelling and screaming so loud he woke up the entire house. When I dashed down to see what was the matter, there was Wes folded up like an accordion, with his chin on his knees, yelling for me to get him out. I brought him a large towel to cover himself and with the help of a few other men we managed to get his arms out from under the faucets and finally pull him free. The incident chastened him for a while."[16]

But only for a while. Less than a week later, a friend set him up with a job interview at a large advertising agency in Manhattan. Still very shaky from his last binge, he asked Lois if she would call a doctor to give him something to settle his nerves. He wanted to be in good shape for his appointment the next morning.

"It was already late in the evening when he asked and I couldn't get anyone on the phone," Lois recalled. "There were many doctors in Brooklyn Heights at the time so we set out on foot to find one. I helped this rather rotund gentleman up and down front steps, held his arm steady as he lit cigarette after cigarette and rang a dozen doorbells, all with no success. One doctor in a nightshirt yelled from his window that he'd call the police if we didn't get off his front porch immediately."

After several more futile attempts, Lois found a policeman who, apparently impressed by her Florence Nightingale grit, suggested she try the physician who resided at the nearby Hotel St. George. When she called the doctor on the house phone and explained the situation, he told her there was nothing he could do to help.

"Wes was becoming shakier and shakier," she remembered. "When he said he needed a drink, I was afraid he might go into the DT's. So I took him to the Childs Bar & Grill where he had a whiskey. Then when I tried to coax him back to Clinton Street, he grinned and said a bird can't fly on one wing. He ordered another whiskey. That's when I had it. I left him sitting on the stool in Childs and went home. Of course, Wes never went for the job interview the next day and it was several more days before we saw him again."[17]

Then there was Joe Brawley, who perhaps had the briefest stint at Clinton Street. He had been sent over by Dr. Silkworth, spent the night, and was found terribly ill in the kitchen by Lois the next morning.

Lois laughed every time she told the story of how the man thought he discovered a bottle of booze in her kitchen simply because the bottle was filled with a brown liquid and was wrapped in Christmas paper. She said it was actually homemade Vermont maple syrup. How the man was able to swallow so much of the sweet stuff Lois never understood. Anyway, the man got terribly sick to his stomach and fled Clinton Street as soon as he was well enough to travel.[18]

Bill Corbett was one of the tragedies at Clinton Street. A brilliant Canadian-born lawyer, he was arrogant when he first arrived from Towns Hospital at Dr. Silkworth's urging. He agreed to stay for one night—but then stayed for almost a year trying to find some peace and contentment in his shattered life.

After sobering up, he soon found a job with a law firm in the city and began doing quite well. But he worked all day and gambled at bridge most nights—for a substantial amount of money—so he didn't make many meetings at the house with his fellow alcoholics.

Lois remembered how aloof the man was, even around her and Bill. She also recalled how those in the house would talk about his great obsession with gambling and how he always walked around with a deck of cards in his hands.[19]

She remembered when she and Bill had finally gotten away for a weekend together. Bill had borrowed a car to visit an old friend of his in Delaware to discuss a business proposition, hoping to generate some income. Lois was disappointed they hadn't run off to Vermont and camped out in the mountains as she had wished. But she was grateful she at least had this brief respite alone with her husband. That Saturday night they made love for the first time in many, many months. Returning home the next evening, they both smelled gas immediately upon opening the front door. The men inside were rushing around trying to discover where it was coming from, checking the basement, the kitchen stove, the gas jets used for lighting. Bill calmed everyone down, then sensed the odor could be coming from upstairs.

He followed the gas smell up to the third floor and began pushing open the bedroom doors. He found Bill Corbett's body stretched out on his freshly made bed. He had committed suicide by running a tube from the gas jet in his room into his mouth. He reeked of booze. The disease of alcoholism, together with his huge gambling debts, were apparently too much to handle by himself. And he never let anyone get close enough to help him. Then came the aftershock.

"It was several months before we realized that Bill C. had been selling our dress clothes, which hung in a closet near the hall bedroom he occupied," Lois explained. "Among the missing articles were Bill's dress suit, his evening jacket, my black velvet evening wrap, lined with white velvet, and several evening dresses. Suitcases had also disappeared. All these were relics of our well-to-do days." Lois felt that stealing and selling these things must have added to this man's sense of guilt. She said Bill was very depressed that he hadn't been able to do more to help him.[20]

But then there were the many inspirational stories, the men who made it, those who proved that Bill and Dr. Bob's way of staying sober really worked. One of those was Chris Hopkins, the rugged wire-rope salesman who wanted desperately to recover from his alcoholism but didn't believe he could.

Lois remembered that her husband often sat with Chris for hours, telling him about his own drinking experiences, talking to him about Dr. Bob and the others who were making it. He always concluded these talks by remarking that if those men could stay sober, Chris could too. One day Bill decided to share his spiritual experience, finally suggesting that only by accepting a Power greater than himself could his friend have his obsession removed and his sanity restored.

Chris's face filled with skepticism. He shook his head and admitted this was a concept he found almost impossible to understand or put into his life. He had grown up in a broken home where there was never any talk of God, only that one had to believe in and trust oneself if he were to make it in this world. Now Chris became so upset that he darted out of the Clinton Street house and was gone for several hours. Bill was convinced he had made no headway at all. Later Lois shared what a great privilege it was to see how it all turned out.

She remembered watching Bill pace up and down the hallway, fearing his talk of a Higher Power might have set his young friend off on another spree. It was dusk when the doorbell rang. Lois recalls her husband opening the door and Chris standing there with tears streaming down his face, telling Bill that he finally understood. That he had found his Higher Power. Lois said she began to cry too.[21]

Chris sat with Lois and Bill and explained that after he ran out of the house, the thought came to him: "If Bill has discovered a Power greater than himself, so can I!" He said he began to pray, perhaps for the very first time in his life. He suddenly was so overcome with a feeling of joy that he had to cling to a lamppost as he started crying like a baby. Lois said Chris became a stalwart member of AA, married a short time later, and never took another drink.

By the end of 1936 and into 1937, men were joining the Fellowship from all walks of life. Many of them still had jobs, others had wives and children. As a result, Lois recalled the growing concern at Clinton Street about the stigma of alcoholism—the fact that most people still regarded inebriates as weak-willed, immoral, unreliable, and usually nonproductive. Once a drinking problem was suspected on the job, for example, the man would often be fired. Neighbors would look upon drunks next door with disgust. Mothers would warn their children to beware of them. Even though sober now, many of these men feared their pasts might be revealed, especially since they were now gathering publicly with other alcoholics at Clinton Street meetings. They feared their names and past drinking behavior might somehow become public knowledge, and their jobs and reputations would be in jeopardy.

"They had every right to be concerned," Lois recalled. "The men at the house were good people but every alcoholic I ever met loved to gossip. And I remembered how people used to whisper about Bill when he was drinking, how they would look at him, trying to understand why he did the things he did and acted so strangely at times. How it affected his reputation on Wall Street. Even after he was sober for a good while, many people would still only remember what he used to be like."[22]

Bill finally came up with a suggestion that was approved overwhelmingly by everyone who attended the meetings. It was the concept of anonymity. No one in the Fellowship would have the right to reveal the name of any other member. All gossip would stop and there would only be great respect for each other's sobriety—whether a man was sober one day or one year. It relieved the anxiety of many, especially newer members who still had jobs and families to protect. Soon members were using their first names only.

As the Fellowship continued to grow, Bill found less and less time to seek gainful employment. The investigation work he did for some Wall Street firms in 1936 and 1937 was his last serious effort to reestablish himself in the securities field. He did try a few small business ventures over the next several years as the financial situation at Clinton Street became acute, but nothing came of them.

Lois now found herself worrying a great deal when traveling to and from work, out walking, or in bed late at night. The bills were piling up and her small paycheck only went so far. Hank, who was now one of the more respected of the "Clinton Street boys," became aware of the money problems and started passing the hat at meetings. However, since most members back then were only beginning to get on their feet, these collections barely paid for the coffee and cake Lois served.

Despite the lack of resources, Bill found ways to travel to Akron to discuss with Dr. Bob the need to put down on paper everything they had found that was keeping more than fifty alcoholics in New York sober and almost the same number in Ohio. With Dr. Bob's encouragement and blessings, Bill finally decided to try his hand at writing a book, one that would describe in detail how their Fellowship started, how and why it was growing and becoming more successful. When Hank heard about Bill's decision, he promised he would make the book a national best seller. But he, like Bill and Ebby and the other mainstays, clearly recognized this was no immediate solution to the serious financial problem at hand.

Lois often shared later in life that there were times she thought about throwing in the towel, particularly as the financial pressures grew and her husband didn't appear overly concerned. It was then she felt anger over her seeming role as a drudge, a nursemaid, and a financial patroness to a cause that seemed to succeed one day and fail the next. She had periods of maudlin self-pity and of deep fulfillment and satisfaction seeing that the work she was doing, the effort she was contributing, was truly helping others.

There were two things Lois always said helped her get through the bad days. The first was her close friendship with Annie Smith. While they saw each other only occasionally since their first meeting in Akron, they remained in constant touch by letter and telephone.

Lois shared that Annie was a most loving and understanding person. "She had a lot of wisdom and a wonderful insight into people. Not only wives and families came to her for advice, but many A.A. members did, too."[23]

"When I thought I couldn't take any more and would even hint to her I was considering leaving it all, she would say half jokingly: 'You've already been through the worst. If you leave now, someone else will get the best.' Then we'd both have a good laugh and I would start to feel a little better."

Lois was always concerned about Annie's health. "She had very weak eyes and smoked too much. Often when I would visit her, she would sit in a dark corner of the living room to avoid the light, smoking endless cigarettes. In the years that followed, that little dark corner of 855 Ardmore Avenue became a haven for many troubled wives."[24]

The other thing that helped Lois through those difficult times was a phrase her husband used when trying to persuade an obstinate newcomer that he could stop drinking and stay stopped. Bill would tell him that every alcoholic he ever knew, including himself, had at least one day or more of dryness at one time or another. All the newcomer had to do was not take a drink today—and not think about tomorrow or yesterday. Just not drink today. That anyone could handle almost anything if they did it one day at a time.

"So I decided I would try to handle my life that way—one day at a time," Lois concluded. "I wasn't always very successful at it, but just the attempt seemed to make things a whole lot easier at times."[25]

Then something happened at Clinton Street that took her mind, Bill's mind, and practically everyone else's mind off their own problems. It shook Bill deeply and even made him question the strength of his own sobriety.

While Lois had never cared much for Ebby Thacher during their growing-up years in Vermont, and certainly not when he became her husband's drinking buddy during the Roaring Twenties, she had by now developed a warm relationship with him, especially after the landmark visit he had paid to Bill a few years back. She knew the message he brought to Clinton Street that day led to her husband's spiritual discovery and his dramatic recovery from alcoholism. She was very grateful to him for that and everything else he had done to support Bill since then.

However, upon Bill's return from Akron with his reenergized zeal to build a special fellowship for alcoholics, Lois began to notice the frown on Ebby's face and the hurt look in his eyes every time his boyhood friend talked about Dr. Bob Smith. He seemed to feel put down, ignored for what he considered his vital contribution to all that was now happening.

That it should be him and Bill leading this movement, not Bill and some old drunk doctor in a godforsaken town in Ohio. Lois sensed Ebby's growing resentment over his backseat status when he thought he should be driving the bus or at least helping to navigate the course.

She also knew Ebby was shaken by Bill's decision to break with the Oxford Group. In fact, he was still attending some of their meetings. After all, these were the people who had saved his life in the first place and had given him the message to carry to his longtime friend. While he couldn't argue about the reasons for the separation, especially since Dr. Shoemaker also seemed to be in Bill's corner, he simply felt confused and a bit anxious about how it would all turn out.

Now, however, with the financial crisis at Clinton Street, Ebby saw a chance to shine again. He told Bill he still had some good money connections in Albany, some old family friends who might be willing to donate to their cause. He thought he'd spend a few weeks there raising some needed funds. Lois remembered her husband cautioning him not to go, that his old drinking crowd was still there, and he could easily find himself involved with them again. Ebby said he only wanted to do his part to keep the fellowship growing and to ease the financial burden on Bill and Lois. Hank and Fitz and the others patted their cohort on the back and wished him good fortune in Albany.

Ebby got drunk a week after arriving in his old hometown. After almost two-and-a-half years of sobriety, the man who had been Bill's sponsor in the Oxford Group, the man who had been Bill's rock to lean on before Dr. Bob, the man who first showed Bill that sobriety was possible had now fallen. No one knew exactly what had happened, but everyone at Clinton Street was certain that this proud man simply could not make it on his own. That Ebby Thacher, like they, needed the fellowship of other alcoholics in order to stay sober.

Lois and Bill both had a difficult time from then on handling Ebby's long periods of drunkenness mixed with his short spurts of sobriety, especially when he came around looking for a handout. Lois vividly recalled one time when she refused to give him money and he crawled around the vestibule at Clinton Street all night cursing her and calling everyone in the house terrible names. Sometime in the early morning hours, after he had passed out, several men took him to Bellevue Hospital. Bill was terribly shaken by it all, Lois remembered. He told her once that the lesson he learned from this tragic situation was that one can still have faith in the message if not always in the messenger.[26]

Bill never lost his deep gratitude toward his cherished friend. After moving from place to place over the ensuing years, taking a job here, losing one there, Ebby wound up in Texas. He eventually became very ill, so ill in fact that he wasn't able to drink alcohol the last few years of his life. Bill established a fund to pay all his expenses and contributed significantly to it himself. Ebby died sober in 1966.

As if Ebby's slip, the financial pressures, and the growing distance between her and Bill as he became obsessed with writing his book were not enough stress on Lois, her father suddenly took ill in the late summer of 1936.

"He was hospitalized and could barely speak as I sat at his bedside," Lois shared with a close friend. "I could tell from the look in his eyes that he was still worried about me so I kept assuring him that everything was fine. That I was doing all right. I don't really know if he believed me or not.

"I think it was the strong will that I inherited from my father together with the strong faith my mother instilled in me that kept me going all those years. I was grateful I was able to thank this kind and wonderful man for all that he had given me before he passed away."[27]

Dr. Clark Burnham died in September of 1936 at the age of eighty-one. Unlike when Matilda Burnham passed away, Bill Wilson was with his wife at his father-in-law's funeral.

Lois now felt even more alone. Indeed, losing both parents often leaves one with a great gap, a sense that the strength once there to lean upon is now gone. And when she tried to turn to Bill for comfort, he was often away or busy writing or counseling one of his drunks. There were even nights when they were in bed together and someone would pound on their bedroom door because there was trouble brewing in the house and they needed Bill to settle it. She hated those interruptions but knew the problems could be serious. One night, for example, Bill had to take a carving knife away from an angry newcomer who had accused another man of stealing the bottle he had secreted in the basement. The day Lois felt most alone happened to be the day Bill brought home a new man from Bellevue Hospital. He was in his late thirties, tall and handsome with a touch of an Irish brogue. He seemed lost and confused, as if trying to figure out what had happened to his life and how he had wound up in a Brooklyn brownstone filled with a bunch of crazy drunks.

This newcomer didn't take to the other "boys" right off, and Bill was frequently out rounding up another prospect. And with Ebby now gone, Hank was doing his best to cocaptain the ship, but even this talkative promoter found it hard to reach the new guest. It was Lois who sensed he desperately needed to talk to someone he could trust, to have someone convince him that if he didn't drink, everything would work out. He needed someone he could believe in—so he turned to Lois.

Soon they were spending time together, Lois and this tall, handsome newcomer. They would chat in the kitchen before she left for work in the morning, then walk in the evening along the East River by the Brooklyn Bridge, talking about their hopes and their dreams. Lois began to feel an attraction to this charming man, the kind of attraction she hadn't felt since she first met Bill. And she didn't know what to do about it—nor did she know where this infatuation might lead. At the moment, she really didn't care.[28]

12

Facing Her Own Addiction

*H*E NEARLY BOWLED OVER SEVERAL LADY CUSTOMERS THAT afternoon as he rushed excitedly into Loeser's department store to tell Lois the great news. For Bill, it was the answer to all their problems. Lois would no longer have to work. He could pay off all their creditors. And the Clinton Street gang would have a large and comfortable facility in which to meet, one that would accommodate their growing needs.

Heading straight for the home furnishings department, Bill could still hear the startling words of Charlie Towns, the owner of Towns Hospital, asking him to be his partner.[1] It all happened less than two hours ago, and he was still shaking his head in disbelief. He could hardly wait to see the joy and delight on his wife's face when he told her.

Just yesterday Charlie had called Bill at the house and asked him to drop by, that he had an interesting business proposition to discuss with him. When they met this morning, the flamboyant owner didn't have to explain the history of his well-known establishment nor its lucrative past, when famous celebrities such as John Barrymore and W.C. Fields poured thousands of dollars into Charlie's coffers for a few discreet weeks of drying out. Bill had heard those stories over and over again during his own turbulent visits there. But what he didn't know until Mr. Towns opened his books and disclosed his recent financial statements was just how seriously the business had declined in recent years. The nationwide Depression had taken its toll on jobs and expendable income.

Then Charlie laid out his proposal. He said that both he and Dr. Silkworth had developed enormous respect for Bill as they watched the "cures" he wrought on helpless drunks, many of whom were now rebuilding their lives at Clinton Street while others were already back out in society, sober and prospering. He and Dr. Silkworth, he added, were convinced their former patient's program was not only a proven success, but—and now Charlie was speaking strictly for himself—it could become a real "cash cow," if handled properly. The owner then patted Bill on the back and proposed that he move his entire operation into the hospital and make Towns his headquarters. He was prepared to give him an office, a very decent drawing account, and a generous share of the profits engendered by all the paying patients he was bound to attract. In no time, Charlie remarked, he expected Bill to become the most respected and successful lay therapist in New York with the opportunity to launch similar facilities around the country.

The washed-up Wall Street genius who only moments before was convinced he had little or no hope of rebuilding his business reputation did not have to ponder Charlie's proposition for very long to realize its tremendous upside potential. It even surpassed the dreams he had in Akron before the proxy battle turned against him. It appealed to all those egocentric instincts he thought had run their course—his drive for money, power, and prestige. They were all back now in force. He told his smiling suitor he'd have an answer for him in twenty-four hours, adding that he saw no major obstacles.[2]

Lois was with a customer when he finally arrived at her department. She was surprised to see him and waved that she'd be finished shortly. He paced impatiently back and forth, casting urgent glances in her direction. Fearing something might be amiss, Lois excused herself and led her husband off to the side. There he exploded his news on her.

The look of sheer joy and delight he expected to see on her face didn't appear. Instead, she reacted calmly, mulling over what she had just heard as though she hadn't fully understood. So Bill repeated himself. She smiled politely, gave his comments some further thought, then looked up at him and asked:

"Have you talked to Bob about it? . . . What does everyone else think?"[3]

Bill frowned down at her. *Why should she be asking about Dr. Bob?* he wondered. Surely his Akron colleague would see the obvious benefits to such a move. And besides, who launched this ship in the first place? And "everyone else"? If Lois was referring to his recovering alcoholics at Clinton Street, what doubt was there that they'd go along with whatever he suggested? They always did. Well, maybe not always, but certainly most of the time.

The real enigma for him was his wife's attitude. Bill simply could not understand why Lois was not overjoyed at the prospect of his success and the financial rewards it would bring. Then he thought, perhaps it's because she'd heard all of this before, at other times and in other forms. And once booze had taken over his life, it had never panned out—his grandiose schemes, his promises of laying the moon and stars at her feet. So why should she believe him this time?

But as he stared into his wife's eyes, he sensed it was more than that. She seemed preoccupied, distant, not the woman who would always throw her arms around him anyway and root him on no matter what. He suddenly began to realize how much about her he had taken for granted all these years. When he left the department store that afternoon, not only was the bloom slightly off his rose, but he had a strange feeling in the pit of his stomach, a worrisome overall sense that his wife's feelings toward him were changing.

If the offer from Charlie Towns had been a surprise to Bill, and Lois's reaction to the news a deep disappointment, that was nothing compared to the stunning, cold silence he received from the group that evening when he tried with as much enthusiasm as he could muster to depict the benefits he saw in this proposal for all concerned. But halfway through his pitch, he regretted not securing Dr. Bob's endorsement first. It would have reinforced his stance.

Lois stood in the back of the living room listening. The new man with the Irish brogue was sitting nearby. The place was packed. Another woman was also in the room that night, Marty Mann, the first female alcoholic to join the Fellowship. After several "slips," Marty had become a firm believer, a sober member, a good friend of Lois, and a very successful businesswoman who, twelve years later, went on to found the

National Council on Alcoholism—an educational organization still
working in the recovery field today. Recalling her initial reaction to Bill's
news, a skepticism that the group members were now about to share,
Lois once told a close friend: "As much as I realized Bill needed to earn
some money to pay our bills and get us out of debt, I felt like the others
that night. This didn't seem to be the way."

After a while Bill found himself addressing a roomful of impassive faces
all frowning up at him. Long before he finished his presentation, Lois
noticed her husband's voice wavering. He was stumbling over his words.
When Bill finally finished, Fitz slowly rose to his feet and began shifting
nervously. He admitted that everyone at Clinton Street and all those who
came from the outside to the meetings were sympathetic to Bill's financial
needs and had been for some time. But, he added, while he couldn't
speak for the others, he felt what was being suggested didn't seem like the
best answer and could possibly lead to complications of all sorts in the
future. Fitz wasn't challenging Bill. He was simply expressing his anxiety.

"Bill, you can't do this to us," he said. "Don't you see that for you,
our leader, to take money for passing on our magnificent message, while
the rest of us try to do the same thing without pay, would soon discour-
age us all? . . . Why should we do for nothing what you'd be getting paid
for? We'd all be drunk in no time."[4]

Chris then stuttered from his chair that Charlie Towns was not an
alcoholic and therefore couldn't possibly know what makes their
Fellowship work. Why was it that he himself could get sober among the
drunks at Clinton Street when he was never able to stay dry anywhere
else? Because of their trust and support, that's why. Chris wanted to say
more until Bill's challenging stare sat him back in his seat.

Everyone began whispering to each other when suddenly a short,
squat fellow with a graying beard slowly rose from the other side of the
room. His name was Buddy Hackler, and he was a former derelict who
hadn't had a drink now for almost five months. Bill knew that Buddy's
sobriety meant everything in the world to him. He had great respect for
this middle-aged man whose words whistled through three broken teeth
as he apologized for not being a very good speaker. That night, however,
he held the entire room in rapt attention, trying to explain in simple

terms why the proposal at hand could never work.

Everyone around him had this "thing" that bound them together, one to the other, the short, nervous newcomer said. He couldn't find the right words to describe it, Buddy went on, with all heads nodding at him in support, but it was something that could not be bought and paid for. No doctor or nurse or therapist ever got him sober. He doubted if they ever could, because drunks were not "cases." Drunks were people with an addiction to booze that few understood except here at Clinton Street and on Ardmore Avenue in Akron. What Bill and Dr. Bob discovered, Buddy summed up in a voice now filled with confidence, what this "thing" was based on, was one poor drunk bastard coming eyeball to eyeball with another drunk bastard and telling it like it was. With no BS, they could trust each other, bare their souls, and stay sober—and that was something you couldn't put a price tag on, he concluded.

Before sitting back down, the relative newcomer reminded Bill of something he was always telling others—that the good was often the enemy of the best. Drunks, Buddy said, needed the best and they had it in spades at Clinton Street.[5]

It was after midnight when Bill finally came into the bedroom. He stood at the window looking out at the full moon. Lois was still awake. She watched him for a moment, then climbed out of bed, walked over, and stood next to him. He told her he had phoned Dr. Bob after the lengthy meeting broke up and everyone had left, some offering their apologies for speaking out against the Towns proposal. He said Bob reminded him of something they had discussed very early on in Akron when laying out their ideas for the Fellowship. They had agreed that the only authority would be the group itself. Bill admitted he had forgotten that in his desire to solve his economic problems and probably also to satisfy his own big ego.

Lois squeezed his hand to let him know she understood. She told him it was probably all for the best, and they'd find their way out of their financial maze somehow or other.[6] Bill wanted to reach out and take his wife into his arms and ask her why he felt they were growing apart. Where was the warmth she had always exuded toward him even in the worst of times? Yes, he was constantly busy with his drunks and now his book, but she always said she understood. Was he simply taking her for granted again? Was it his imagination, or was her seeming preoccupation the result of her being the breadwinner, the one who was truly keeping things together? So he hesitated. He simply stood there holding her hand and sensing this was not the right moment, especially since the evening's events—whether he agreed with the outcome or not—made him feel like a huge failure.

The next morning Bill phoned Charlie Towns to thank him and to say rather reluctantly that he couldn't accept his generous offer.

Lois could also sense the distance that was opening between her and her husband and wondered just when it began. Yes, she was often hurt when he paid more attention to his drunks than he did to her, but by now she was used to that. Yes, he needed her, but was it more for her cooking and cleaning and financial help than for her emotional support? It sometimes seemed that way. But somewhere deep inside she sensed her feelings toward Bill really began to change the day the tall, handsome newcomer from Bellevue Hospital showed up at Clinton Street.[7]

His name was Russell, and she remembered how, as the days went by and he became more sober, his delightful gift of gab returned and she found him great fun. They were drawn to each other so quickly that she never gave it a second thought. However, the more she saw of him, the more she began to question her every thought, her every action, her every feeling, especially the guilt that suddenly came over her each time she was with Bill.

A County Cork man from a well-to-do Irish family, Russ decided America offered a more challenging and exciting life. So after college in Dublin, he came to the states and settled in New York City. He became an apprentice at Time-Life. He moved up the ladder quickly, and soon he was a correspondent for *Life* magazine, writing about everyone from Al Capone to J. Edgar Hoover. But the bright, good-looking Irishman loved the night life and the ladies. Soon he was known in every speakeasy from Manhattan to the south side of Chicago. Then one day a wealthy uncle died back home and left Russ a considerable sum. He decided to quit his job and play—and for him, playing meant drinking up a storm.

Before long, instead of being well known in the most popular saloons, he was becoming well known in drunk tanks, drying-out hospitals, nut wards, and finally among the lowest of the low at the Bowery Mission. By the time his money was almost gone, he had become a frequent guest at Bellevue Hospital. That's where Bill found him, believed he sincerely wanted to stop drinking, and brought him home to Clinton Street.

"He was not only quite handsome," Lois once shared with a close friend, "but he was also very intelligent. He could do a crossword puzzle in no time. He was perhaps one of the brightest men I ever met.

"After getting sober, he was so happy he had another chance at life that he seemed to be laughing all the time. He was so much fun to be with. He once told me he played the piano in a college band, a dance band. He asked me if we could go out dancing some time. Just the thought of it brought back so many wonderful memories. The dances we would go to in Vermont. The hayrides. But he knew by the look on my face that I couldn't go so he just laughed again and pretended he was just joking all along."[8]

Russell often dropped by Loeser's department store unexpectedly. He waited for Lois if she was busy, and then they would sit and have lunch in a nearby park. Afterward they walked along the street window-shopping until it was time for her to go back to work. One day as they were walking, Lois recalled, he took her hand. She felt awkward and nervous. After a few moments, she eased her hand away, turning a soft shade of pink in the process. Russell simply grinned and began chatting about something or other to quietly dismiss the unease of the moment.

Here was a warm, charming, caring man who wanted to be with her, to be near her, to spend time with her, who needed her trust and confidence so that he could share his innermost feelings. And here was a fragile, vulnerable, unhappy lady who needed someone to care about her, to pay attention to her, to let her know she was lovable, attractive, and sensuous still. That she was a woman.

"I was so terribly unhappy at the time," Lois admitted later. "I tried so hard to hide it from myself but deep inside I was terribly unhappy. And now this emotional feeling I suddenly had for this man began to frighten me because it went against the ideal I knew I should be living up to, the ideal I was raised with."[9] One belief that Lois still clung to was that advances from men were most often caused by the woman's attitude, so now she questioned her own attitudes. Was she encouraging Russell's affection by her willingness to spend so much time with him? Was she less concerned about her husband's needs now that she had another man to look after? Or was she unconsciously playing a game, hoping Bill would notice, get jealous, and finally give her the love and consideration she craved? One of the most important traits Lois inherited from her mother was self-honesty. She might be able to fool herself for a little while but not for very long, not with that gnawing feeling in the pit of her stomach. And so it was this time. She was forced to admit to herself that the answer to all these questions was yes. The only question that remained was, what should she do about it?

"Looking back," she once said, "I must admit that for a woman of my age then, I was still very naive. I smugly thought I knew so much about life and the world, love and relationships and how it should all be. But when it came right down to it, I knew very little.

"I soon became convinced that Bill suspected something the way he would look at Russell and then at me. So to get rid of this guilty feeling and that gnawing inside of me, I decided the best thing to do was to tell him all about it without mentioning anyone's name, although I felt sure he knew.

"I told Bill I was very upset with myself for becoming so interested in another man regardless of the reasons. I said instead of it making me happy, the guilt I felt was making me even more miserable. I told him I didn't plan to spend any more time with this man ever again."[10]

Looking back at this whole affair some years later, Lois said she could see more clearly that, while she had come to care for Russell rather deeply, she was mainly screaming out for her husband's attentions. She might as well have been shouting, "Bill! Pay attention to me. I'm your wife and I have a problem. I want you to think about me for a moment instead of yourself, your drunks, your Fellowship, and your damn book! This is me, Lois, and I have something going on here that could get out of control. You better pay attention to me. I need you to pay attention to me!"[11]

As she suspected, Bill had been paying attention. But perhaps his own guilt, the recognition of his own failures, and his seeming lack of concern about their relationship prevented him from saying anything right away—from asking questions and getting answers he didn't want to hear—or quite possibly being afraid of how he might react. As it turned out, he was right, for when Lois finally told him what had been going on, even she was shocked by his sudden and bewildering reaction. Lois had no idea she was reminding him of his past, those times when people had left him, walked out of his life—his father, his mother, Bertha Banford— and he had felt "unlovable" all over again.

"We were in the bedroom," she recalled. "I had just gotten home from work and said I needed to speak with him. I had been thinking all day about how I should put it. As I began to tell him, he turned away and faced the wall. When I finished, he yanked open the door, shouted that he might as well be drunk and ran down the stairs. I was desperately afraid that he meant it—that he was going out to get drunk. All I could do was cry."[12] After more than two years of not drinking, after leading dozens of helpless alcoholics along the path to sobriety, after creating so much hope in the lives of so many, Bill Wilson was about to follow in the footsteps of his sponsor, Ebby Thacher. He was about to let those character defects of anger, jealousy, and resentment get him drunk. As he would later share with Lois and a few members of the Fellowship, he ran through the streets of Brooklyn Heights until he found a bar. He went in and stood looking into the barroom mirror. As he stared at the rage filling his face, he saw out of the corner of his eye a man flopped over a corner table in a drunken stupor. In an instant, the sight brought back his every binge, every hangover, every catastrophe in the company of John Barleycorn. Then, as the bartender approached, he turned and rushed out the door.

Bill wound up that evening at the Hotel St. George, where Charley the plumber had restarted his business and now roomed with another Clinton Street graduate. They all talked late into the night. Bill left grateful to his friends for reminding him of his own words to them—that alcohol was only the symptom of their disease and that unless one works on his character defects and shortcomings, he would always be in danger of drinking again.

Lois was so worried and regretful for having opened Pandora's box that she couldn't sleep. It was very late when Bill walked into their bedroom.

His eyes were red, but she could tell immediately that he hadn't been drinking. As she started to beg for his forgiveness, he took her gently into his arms and said he was the one who needed to be forgiven. He was the one who had to make amends for his selfish, insensitive behavior, for not showing his love and gratitude often enough for all she had given to him. They hugged and they kissed. Then they got undressed, turned out the lights, and went to bed. They made love again for the first time in many, many months.[13]

Russell heard the buzzing going on around Clinton Street that evening, talk that Bill had stormed out of the house red-faced and angry and no one seemed to know why or where he went. Later, when he saw Lois going upstairs crying and avoiding his glances, Russell sensed that whatever might have happened had something to do with him. After all, he was a very bright man who by now had seen the jealousy in Bill's eyes whenever they passed each other. So the charming Irishman went upstairs himself that night, but not to see Lois. He went to pack his suitcase. He was gone before Bill returned from the Hotel St. George.

A few weeks later, after everything had settled down, Lois wrote a poem for her husband, a tongue-in-cheek ditty to let him know that she not only still loved him, she was very proud of what he was accomplishing.

> Once there was a funny man
> Who lived at 182.
> He had so many drunks around
> Who didn't know what to do.
> He nursed some, he razzed some,
> He taxied some to Bellevue.
> But the funniest thing about him was,
> He really "fixed" a few.[14]

Bill remained quite attentive for a while despite his heavy workload. He put his book project aside for a short time to take on several small stock analysis jobs for an old Wall Street buddy, which produced a few thousand dollars of income. One involved Loft's Candy Company and the other Pepsi-Cola. He later told Hank and Fitz that if he had some money to spare at the time, he could have made a killing. Loft's stock quadrupled.

At the same time, Bill began encouraging his wife to "go out on your own as an interior decorator."[15] He said everybody raved about her work and "that damn department store is taking advantage of you."[16] He said with all her talent, she could probably build a nice business for herself and enjoy the satisfaction of doing it.

Lois finally acquiesced to her husband's wishes. She had been anxious to see how well she could do on her own. And now with Bill bringing in a few more dollars, the time seemed right. She quickly found two customers. One was a rather wealthy lady who was redecorating her entire house. The other, a speech teacher.

While Lois felt no compunction about billing the Loeser customer, she did have qualms for some reason about sending her bill to the teacher with whom she had now become quite friendly. So she made an agreement instead to take speech lessons from her as payment, but then never took the lessons.[17]

Even when Lois redecorated the offices of her brother-in-law, Dr. Leonard Strong, she sent him a very small bill, greatly underestimating the value of her services. Knowing this, Leonard gave her a large gratuity, which embarrassed her to no end.

Perhaps it was Lois's upbringing that stood in the way of her turning her interior decorating skills into a profitable enterprise. Her parents had always insisted that she and her siblings were to help people without seeking payment in return—that being of assistance and the good feelings that come from it were reward enough. As a result, Lois started bringing less money into the household than she did before leaving Loeser's.[18] By the autumn of 1937, Bill had become quite dispirited by having painted himself into a very tight corner. He had a wife who deserved far more than he was giving her. He had a house full of drunks who demanded more of his time. And he needed to find a way to earn considerably more than he was from his infrequent Wall Street assignments. He felt he had to talk with someone, to get some fresh ideas, some new suggestions. So he went to see Leonard Strong to seek his advice. They were now even closer friends, and Bill always had great respect for Dr. Strong's counsel.

"The very first thing Leonard did was offer Bill some money," Lois remembered her husband telling her. "Trying not to show his embarrassment, Bill said he joked and told Leonard he was no longer hustling family and friends since getting sober. He also told Leonard he already owed him more than he could possibly repay for all the help and support he gave both of us while he was drinking. He turned the money down."[19]

Dr. Strong, like his good friend Dr. Silkworth, had become very impressed with what Bill had been accomplishing with his drunks and was convinced his work must go on. So he volunteered to call a man he had met several years earlier, a Mr. Willard Richardson, who headed the board at the Rockefeller philanthropies. He thought Bill might approach him about some sort of grant to support his growing group of alcoholics. After all, everyone knew that John D. Rockefeller, Jr., had been one of the major forces behind the passage of the Volstead Act, which gave the country Prohibition. He might possibly be sympathetic to Bill's cause.[20] Within a matter of weeks, Leonard and his nervous brother-in-law were seated in John D.'s private boardroom at a huge, beautifully carved mahogany table, directly across from Mr. Richardson. As Bill described the program he and Dr. Bob had created to help alcoholics, both he and Leonard could tell the philanthropic foundation's chief executive was moved by what he heard, so moved in fact that he promised to have his committee look into this "evangelical society," as he called it, just as soon as possible. And, he added, if they approved of the movement and its monetary requirements, Mr. Rockefeller would probably give it his financial support.

Lois remembered her husband coming home that night "riding on a pink cloud."[21] She said he called everyone in the house together and urged them to be on their best behavior when Mr. Richardson and his committee came to call the following week. Lois said Bill then phoned Dr. Bob in Akron and explained all that had happened. He told him it was important that he come to New York to be on hand to meet the Rockefeller people.

Dr. Bob would later remark that his good friend and partner was "higher than a kite" when he spoke to him that evening, even though he was stone-cold sober. Dr. Bob was concerned, however, when he heard Bill say, "The cat's in the bag." While he promised to be there for the meeting, he warned Bill not to count his chickens too soon.

As usual, Dr. Bob's advice was right on target. The philanthropic group came to Clinton Street, where they greatly admired the work being done. Some of them remarked it was comparable to "first century Christianity." One committee member, a gentleman by the name of Albert Scott, chairman of the trustees for Riverside Church in New York, even went so far as to ask, "Won't money spoil this thing?" His remark disturbed Bill and momentarily blurred the vision of sugarplums dancing in his head. However, he started smiling again when the others decided they wanted a closer look to better understand what this growing Fellowship was all about and the extent of its future success.[22]

Christmas came and went. Bill's spirits were up one day and down the next as the committee's investigation dragged on. The new year of 1938 was now already underway. Then, in the middle of January, Willard Richardson phoned and asked Bill to meet him in his office. Lois admitted she was on pins and needles waiting for the news.

Committee member Frank Amos, a well-known New York City advertising executive who had taken a shine to Bill and his work, was with Richardson when he arrived. Amos said he was recommending that the Fellowship be given an initial grant of fifty thousand dollars, adding that the committee was in general agreement. It only awaited Mr. Rockefeller's final approval. While it was nowhere near the hundreds of thousands of dollars Bill had dreamed about, it was an enormous sum and a fantastic solution to the immediate and pressing problems both at Clinton Street and in Akron, where Dr. Bob was now having some health problems.

By the time Bill arrived back in Brooklyn that night, he was floating on air. He phoned Akron to give his friend the good news and was unpleasantly surprised by his response. Bob was still warning Bill not to count his chickens too soon. Lois recalled they almost had their first knock-down, drag-out fight on the telephone that evening when Bill accused Bob of always being "too damn negative."

A few days later, however, those chickens Dr. Bob had been talking about finally came home to roost. Albert Scott, the committee member who from the beginning felt that alcoholics who helped other alcoholics were like the early Christians, had convinced John D. Rockefeller, Jr., that indeed "too much money could spoil their work"—and that fifty thousand dollars was too much money. The wealthy philanthropist agreed. He and the committee finally decided to place five thousand dollars in the treasury at Riverside Church for Bill and Bob to draw upon as needed. But that would be all. The letter from Mr. Richardson informing them of the decision said the committee came to believe in the end that the alcoholic movement should become self-supporting in order to achieve and maintain its magnificent goals.

Despite such flattering comments, Bill was devastated at first. As usual, he had projected a momentous outcome only to be crestfallen when it failed to come to pass. In time he would learn another great lesson from all of this, but for now he had to fight his way out of another depression. While the five thousand dollars would help temporarily, he saw it as a mere drop in the bucket. That's how deep an emotional pit he found himself in.

Lois recalled what a bitter disappointment this was to her husband, mainly because he was torn between not having the time to earn money and continuing to direct and grow his struggling fellowship of alcoholics. But Lois also remembered how Bill felt sometime later when he came to recognize that a great influx of money at that point would have finished Alcoholics Anonymous just as it was getting started. It was then that Hank Parkhurst tried to ride to the rescue.[23]

The second man to sober up at Clinton Street, Hank had since moved out, reconciled with his wife, Kathleen, and was living in New Jersey, although still attending all the meetings in Brooklyn Heights. Now feeling his oats after more than a year and a half without a drink, he had started an entrepreneurial venture in the Garden State, where he had worked for many years in the oil business. Through his former connections, Hank was organizing gasoline service station owners into a cooperative buying syndicate that he called "Honor Dealers." He had set up an office in Newark, hired a lady named Ruth Hock to run the place, and now invited Bill to join him in what he was convinced would quickly become a lucrative enterprise. He thought it would solve Bill's financial problems.

Miss Hock, a dedicated, hardworking German lady in her early thirties, didn't know what she had gotten herself into at first. Almost from the start she was shocked to see rather shabbily dressed men stagger into Hank and Bill's office in the rear of the building and not come out until the day was over. One afternoon she entered the office without knocking only to find Bill and some others on their knees praying, while Hank was at his desk pretending nothing was going on. She hurried back out blushing, then Bill took her aside and explained what they were doing and why— that it was a practice left over from his Oxford Group days. Before long, the office at 17 William Street in Newark became Clinton Street West, with Hank and Bill spending more time trying to sober up New Jersey's alcoholics than trying to help its service station owners. A native of Newark, Ruth would soon become Bill's trusted secretary, working with him on his "Big Book" project. She would also become a close friend and confidante of Lois.

"I remember Ruth telling me once," Lois recalled, "that the business could have been very successful had they given as much energy, thought, and enthusiasm to it as they did to helping drunks. She said she soon came to realize that the Honor Dealers business was really only a means to an end, that end being expanding the Fellowship of drunks. I could have told her that the very first day she started work."[24]

Soon Hank and Bill were finding it difficult to pay Ruth her twenty-five-dollar-a-week salary and the rent on the office at the same time. Ruth so admired what they were doing to help others that she often went without pay for a while. The landlord, however, was not as generous. In fact, he eventually forced them to leave. They set up shop in a smaller office in Newark, and that's where, with the aid of Ruth's typing skills, Bill went to work on his book in earnest. It was now May of 1938. He started gathering success stories from the men who had stayed sober thus far and discussed with Dr. Bob how to formulate the "steps" the first one hundred sober alcoholics had taken to achieve this goal.

While the financial pinch became evident in Newark as the buying syndicate failed to produce the profits Hank had hoped for, funds became even tighter at Clinton Street. The more time Bill spent outlining and gathering material for his book, as well as working with his drunks in Brooklyn and New Jersey, the fewer hours he had to dredge up income. And with Lois now earning less as an independent interior decorator, the financial cupboard was rapidly running bare. On top of all this, President Roosevelt's "mortgage moratorium" had now run out, and the bank that held the loan on Clinton Street was demanding a larger payment each month.

One evening Lois came home tired and discouraged, a mood she thoroughly disliked because it seemed to have become too frequent lately. While she and Bill had been getting along much better, Lois saw no end in sight to their economic malaise, no light at the end of the tunnel. She trudged up the steps of the brownstone only to find another letter in the mailbox from the bank, probably reminding her again how far behind they were slipping on their mortgage payments. She shook her head and slowly entered the house.

When she climbed the hall stairs and reached their bedroom, she found Bill dressing for his meeting. He didn't rush to her and take her into his arms, as she would have liked. He didn't ask her how she felt or how her day went. He didn't even ask her about the new interior decorating project she had started at a business office in downtown Brooklyn. He simply smiled, kissed her on the cheek, and finished buttoning his shirt.

Lois slipped off her coat, hung it in the closet, then sank down on the bed and opened the letter. It was exactly what she had expected. She glanced over at her husband. He was now knotting his tie in the dresser mirror. She wanted to talk to him about the problems with the bank, and some other troubles, but as she started to speak, he turned her off rather abruptly. He said he was running late and that they could talk after the meeting. Immediately she began to feel that now familiar anger rising.

No, she heard the voice in her head shout. She said it out loud. No! They had to talk now! He was always putting things off, putting his needs, his desires ahead of hers. It had been different for a while but now he was sliding back into his same old ways. At least that's what her anger and self-pity were telling her at the moment. So she said it again, this time more forcefully. They had to talk now!

Bill frowned and looked over at the clock. Then he turned toward his wife as he slipped into his jacket. There simply wasn't enough time right now, he pleaded. He'd be late for the sharing meeting at Calvary Church.

Lois had a shoe in her hand. She remembered her rage suddenly erupting like a volcano. Before she knew what had happened, she flung the shoe at her husband, shouting: "Damn your old meetings!"[25]

"This unexpected display of anger surprised me even more than it did him," Lois later wrote in her memoirs. "I might have had an excuse for losing my temper during his drinking years. But why now, when everything was fine, had I reacted so violently to his very natural remark?"[26] Bill was at a loss for words. He picked up her shoe and handed it back to her. She turned her head away. She couldn't explain her actions and she didn't want him to see her crying again. The tears were coming too often of late. Bill quietly left the room and went to his meeting.

Lois couldn't remember how much time passed after she heard the door close. Finally she slipped her shoe back on, turned around, and caught her image in the dresser mirror. *Who is this I'm looking at?* she asked herself, watching the tears roll down her cheeks. *What kind of person have I become? Why am I always so angry, so negative, so unhappy about my life when it's the life I chose?*

Suddenly the room felt very stuffy. She opened the window, but there was hardly a breeze. She decided to take a walk, to get some fresh air, to think about what had just taken place, and to try to find some answers that made sense. That sudden outburst of anger just would not leave her mind.

The following night, Bill was holding one of his regular gatherings of drunks in the parlor at Clinton Street. Still thinking about her outburst the night before, Lois walked out onto the front porch trying to relax, to put her mind at ease. That's when she glanced toward the street and noticed a long line of cars parked along the curb. Only the wealthier people still living in Brooklyn Heights had automobiles in those days, and most had garages for them. The regular folks in the neighborhood rode the subways and the buses. But on Fellowship meeting nights at Clinton Street, people would drive their cars in from the suburbs. For some reason, this was the first time Lois had really taken note of them, perhaps because in most of the vehicles she saw ladies sitting uneasily in the passenger seats, all appearing stoic or sad.

Recalling that important evening in her life, Lois said she had no idea what possessed her to approach those ladies except that she suddenly realized their husbands were probably attending Bill's meeting.

They were simply sitting there all alone, waiting for it to be over. She walked down the steps and knocked gently on the window of the first car. The lady inside rolled down the window. She happened to be Anne Bingham, an attractive, auburn-haired lady in her early forties, who would become one of Lois's closest and dearest friends. She would eventually help Lois organize the fellowship of the Al-Anon Family Groups. But on this particular night, Anne Bingham was in the same kind of mood Lois had brought home with her only a short time ago—tired, discouraged, and frustrated. She had driven again with her husband, Devoe, all the way from their home in Westchester County for him to attend this AA meeting. He had tried everything, and this gathering of alcoholics was the only thing that seemed to work. It was keeping him sober.

It wasn't as though Lois had never befriended the spouses of alcoholics before. She had always welcomed them into her home just as Annie Smith had done and was continuing to do in Akron. It was simply that her work schedule and her household chores gave her little time to spend with them to develop close and meaningful relationships. Then again, perhaps she didn't really want to. Perhaps she preferred to isolate and enjoy the sickly warmth of her self-imposed martyrdom and self-sacrifice. But this night was different. This night she needed someone to talk to, someone who could understand and possibly even help her find some of the answers she was looking for. This night Lois was to find once again that God does work in very strange ways indeed.[27]

After introducing herself, Lois invited Anne Bingham to join her for some tea or lemonade in the kitchen. The offer was gladly accepted. Then Lois glanced toward the other cars. Almost without hesitation, she and Anne invited the other eight ladies in waiting to join them. While a few were shy and a bit reluctant at first, a short time later they were all seated around Lois's kitchen table asking themselves what brought them there in the first place.

"If I didn't drive him here and wait outside, he probably would never come to these meetings,"[28] Lois recalled one dour-looking woman commenting as several others nodded in agreement. Most continued to fidget uncomfortably, not knowing what to do or say until Lois quietly remarked, "I threw a shoe at my husband last night. I'm still trying to understand why I did it, why I'm still so angry when he's been sober now for over three years. I guess I thought that once he stopped drinking, everything would go back to what it was like before, happy and loving. But it hasn't and I'm not sure whose fault it really is."

That's when Anne Bingham turned to her and said: "It's because of all the things they did, that's why. You can't forget so easily. At least I can't."

"I think it's more than that," Lois replied, admitting at the same time she couldn't put her finger on exactly what it was.[29]

As the moments passed and the initial discomfort of being among strangers started to ease, these ten ladies from all walks of life—some with children; some living in nice homes, others in hovels; some filled with shame, others with rage; some attractive, others pale and sickly—began to share their anger, their fear, and their frustrations. Lois listened, and as she did, she slowly came to realize how much they all had in common. She felt as she had when she first met Annie Smith. Lois also came to realize that night that, like these other ladies, she had the same addiction—only hers went by the name of Bill Wilson.

"Even though I had known it deep down inside," Lois would later share, "it struck me so clearly that night that I was as addicted to Bill as he was to alcohol. But I also now saw that I wasn't alone in how it had affected me. That every spouse of every alcoholic I have ever known also becomes terribly affected by this disease."[30]

At one point during this kitchen gathering, the ladies heard the roar of laughter coming from the Fellowship meeting in the parlor. Lois remembered one very thin and peevish lady remarking with a deep frown: "Listen to them in there having a good time while all of us sit out here stewing from all their garbage!"[31]

Lois remembered looking at her and replying: "No. I think they're all in there getting well while we sit out here sick and getting sicker."[32]

While her retort didn't go over well with some of the ladies, it didn't stop any of them from joining Lois and Anne around the kitchen table at Clinton Street again a few nights later. The women were more open this time. One talked about being sick and tired of lying to cover up for her husband when he missed work or disappointed the children. Another said her children were too embarrassed to bring their friends into the house anymore because their father was either drunk on the couch or staggering around in his bathrobe.

Some expressed their fear of financial insecurity. A very pale and nervous lady remarked that her husband was into his third job in the last six months, and she was worried he might soon lose that one too. And another woman's husband had such a violent temper when he drank that one night he kicked in the bathroom door because their son was taking too long in the shower.

A rather stout lady with very sad eyes seemed to sum it all up when she confessed she would get so depressed over her husband's drinking and its effects on her family that she kept the window shades down all day. She said sunlight was only for happy people.

Lois could only reply that since throwing her shoe at Bill, she had started taking a closer look at herself. It seemed she had always depended upon her husband for her happiness, her contentment, her reason for being. Maybe she had better consider more seriously what her mother had told her as she lay dying in the hospital. "Lois," she said, "you have a life of your own to live, and you must live it. You must find out what can truly fulfill you, otherwise one day you will wake up and be consumed by anger and resentment for being cheated out of that life."

Soon this gathering in Lois's kitchen became a regular affair. It planted the seeds from which Al-Anon would eventually blossom. However, at the start, it began to bother some of the newly sober alcoholics coming to the house. In fact, one evening as the ladies were straggling down the hall toward the kitchen, a newcomer asked Bill if he thought it was a good idea for Lois to be meeting with members' wives. Some of the "boys," he said, thought the women might be comparing notes.

Bill laughed, put his arm around the newcomer, and replied, "What can they find out that they don't already know or suspect? Besides, I don't think they're spending their time chewing us over. So relax."[33]

Lois came to realize increasingly, as these kitchen meetings continued, just what a toll the disease of alcoholism had taken on her life, how it had changed the very ideals and virtues she had grown up with, and how it had turned her into the kind of person she never wanted to be.

Looking back at that extraordinary evening when she invited those ladies into her kitchen, Lois recognized that it marked one of the most important turning points in her life.

When she began to share her innermost thoughts and feelings with others, she came to understand how much she had really believed she could control her husband's life from the very beginning of their relationship, when he first started his heavy drinking. She was totally convinced that her love and inspiration was all that was required to fulfill his every need, that her own willpower and steadfast guidance was all that was needed to quench Bill's thirst for alcohol.

But as her husband's drinking grew worse and their lives spiraled into chaos, she then turned to prayer and her relationship with God, believing that this would cure Bill of his affliction. She never thought about what God's will might be. She only thought about her own will—what Lois wanted and what Lois's sheer determination should be able to achieve.

Then came the crushing blow: Bill finally found sobriety through the help of Ebby Thacher, Dr. Robert Holbrook Smith, the Oxford Group, and now his small but budding band of fellow alcoholics. She felt she played no role in the most important goal of her life—getting her husband sober—and now was playing no role in helping him stay sober. Her own inner needs had always been fed by being her husband's nurse, his mother, the breadwinner, and the decision maker. Now she was on the outside looking in.

Since throwing her shoe in anger and now meeting and sharing with her "kitchen group," Lois was discovering how resentful and jealous she had become of her husband's newfound friends, and how filled with anger and self-pity she was. But most of all she had come face to face with a woman who was smug and self-righteous, a lady who thought she had all the answers for Bill and the rest of the world but now saw she didn't even have many answers for herself. She was now determined to find them.

So Lois set out with her own newfound friends to take an honest and searching look at herself in order to change—to rid herself of those painful traits and defects she was now uncovering. At the same time, Lois was recognizing that often her will and God's will were in conflict and that true peace and comfort only comes when these two meet and she accepted God's plan for her life.

In a wonderfully strange way, as Lois began to walk down this new path, she came to realize more and more that she and Bill were walking along similar paths and that hopefully those paths would converge one day at a juncture where she and Bill would find an even deeper and more loving relationship. She hoped it would be soon.[34]

As Lois Wilson met with her fledgling kitchen group, she slowly but surely began to find some of the answers she was looking for. And it was important that she did, for soon her mettle would be tested even more. The next letter she would receive from the bank would warn that unless the payments were brought up to date soon, the bank would have no choice but to foreclose on the mortgage and have her and Bill dispossessed. This time her husband listened to her plea and sat with her as they both tried to figure out what to do next.

13

An Unsettled World—
An Unsettled Life

S INCE HIS INAUGURATION IN 1933, PRESIDENT FRANKLIN D. Roosevelt had subordinated any and all problems abroad to his enormous battle to pull America from its deepening economic crisis and restore its people to the life of abundance and security they once enjoyed. To help achieve this end, the president and his Congress had initiated and passed the most stringent neutrality legislation in the nation's history.

As a result, throughout the 1930s, the entire nation practically wore blinders when it came to distinguishing between "aggressor" and "non-aggressor" belligerents overseas. America focused inward instead, on the needs of its own people. Fathers had to have jobs, not guns. Mothers cried out for food, not tanks. And families yearned for homes, not battle-ships. So when Adolf Hitler rose to power in Germany, threatened his European neighbors, joined forces with Italy and Japan, and pointed his storm troopers in the direction of Austria and Poland, the United States was ill-prepared to meet the pending crisis. The ensuing result was an increasingly frightened and unsettled world.

On the home front, however, President Roosevelt's tactics, both tough and ingenious, were beginning to win the war against the Great Depression. His often-controversial New Deal program was pumping new life into an almost moribund economy. First he cut federal salaries and government overhead generally. Then he signed into law the Agricultural Adjustment Act, which through price increases and loan guarantees relieved farmers of a mortgage indebtedness of more than eight billion dollars, a burden that could have threatened the nation's food supply.

FDR then forced passage of his most contentious measure, the National Industrial Recovery Act, which created minimum wages, fixed maximum hours, abolished sweatshops and child labor, and required business owners to open their books to government inspectors. In addition, the government began building new roads, bridges, and tunnels and financing the construction of huge public works projects such as the Grand Coulee and the Bonneville irrigation plants. Soon the country's wage earners were finding more jobs and steadier employment and bringing home bigger paychecks.

President Roosevelt won a second term in 1937 by a landslide and swept Democratic majorities into office with him. He now had an even freer hand. He continued to create more "alphabetical" government relief programs to subsidize the unemployed and provide lower interest rates and a greater money supply to business and industry. This helped stabilize companies and allowed them to begin growing once again. Now there were the FER, the RFC, the TVA, the HRA, and the NRA. Despite the enormous public debt piling up—almost four billion dollars more than the World War I debt at its peak—by the end of the 1930s the country was finally beginning to sense that the worst was over.

However, while the nation's economy was slowly starting to awake from its painful doldrums, such was not the case at 182 Clinton Street in the heart of Brooklyn Heights, New York. If the country had been wearing blinders so as not to see the growing menace overseas, the increasing difficulties in the Wilson household were so obvious they simply couldn't be hidden from view. This became even more evident when John D. Rockefeller, Jr., declined Bill Wilson's request for a major infusion of capital for his struggling band of alcoholics.

As Lois once shared with a close friend: "The small grant Bill received from Mr. Rockefeller was really a godsend. Even though it didn't solve our problems, it did help us a bit during a very difficult and trying period. Bill had hoped, however, that the five thousand dollars would somehow last until he finished writing his book. Hank was certain the book would be a best seller. They were both wrong. The money slowly ran out and the book didn't sell, at least not right away."[1]

But one important thing did emerge from the Rockefeller episode. Bill had made a number of important contacts with some very generous and very high-powered men who were now sold on his budding movement. Hank, who by now had become Bill's right-hand man, was the first to see the opportunity in such elite connections. He was convinced that most wealthy people only liked to donate to organizations or foundations they could brag about to their friends and associates—medical, charitable, scientific, the arts, and such—not a disorganized bunch of "raggedy-assed, low-bottom drunks." And he told Bill so. What they needed, Hank said, was to somehow find a way to directly involve these nonalcoholic movers and shakers in their Fellowship, perhaps as "advisory members." Bill cottoned to the idea at first until his friend suggested such prominent figures would make "great window-dressing."

Lois remembered the reluctance her husband initially expressed about the whole idea following Hank's remark. "Bill told me he didn't like the thought of 'using' people simply to gain your own selfish ends," she once shared. "He said he did that too many times when he was drinking and he wasn't going to do it now that he was sober. And he didn't."[2]

Besides, Lois went on to say, Bill was mainly interested in the objective counsel and experienced guidance such men could provide to help him build the Fellowship into a strong and lasting organization. Certainly he was open to whatever suggestions and support they could lend to raising much-needed income, but he had now come to believe that Mr. Rockefeller was right—that too much money in the hands of recovering alcoholics could, at this juncture, prove to be an absolute disaster.

After cooling Hank's "promotional instincts," Bill phoned Dr. Bob to discuss the concept of engaging outside advisors. His partner agreed that a small group of nonalcoholic men of good will and good repute could lend great objectivity to their efforts. He also agreed that "putting the arm on them" must not be the primary motive for their involvement.

Then Bill went to see his brother-in-law Dr. Strong once again for his trusted opinion. Leonard offered him similar advice. As a result, the Alcoholic Foundation, a tax-free charitable trust, was formed a short time later, and Leonard Strong was the very first person Bill asked to serve on its board of directors. He accepted. Then Bill went to Willard Richardson and Frank Amos, and they, too, graciously offered their services.[3]

When the new foundation held its first formal meeting in Richardson's office, Hank still hadn't changed his stripes. He insisted the first item on the agenda must be a plan to solve the movement's serious financial crisis. That there was no way to help and support any more alcoholics without additional resources. He urged the board members to show Bill and himself how they could approach other philanthropists and wealthy donors for financial grants—and possibly lend their influence.

Once again Bill had to politely chastise his friend for trying to move too fast. He told the board he had high hopes for solving the money problems himself by finishing his book about the Fellowship. He said many in the group strongly believed there was a vast nationwide audience of suffering alcoholics and their families just waiting for a treatise that could offer them an answer to their dilemma—an answer that almost one hundred alcoholics had already found in Brooklyn, New York, and Akron, Ohio.

When Frank Amos, the advertising executive, heard Bill's description of the proposed book, he excitedly agreed with his comments. He thought its potential to create the much-needed funding was significant and offered to help by contacting his good friend Gene Exman, the editor of religious books at Harper Brothers Publishing Company. Frank said once Bill had completed a few chapters, he would show them to Exman. If the editor liked what he saw and thought the book had good marketing possibilities, he might offer an advance against royalties, even though Bill was a first-time author. The other board members readily agreed with Amos that the book project was where the foundation's emphasis should be placed at the moment. It could lead to what each director firmly believed—that the Fellowship of alcoholics must eventually become self-supporting and not dependent upon outside financial support that could unduly subject it to external influence and dickering.

While Lois was pleased on one hand that her husband was now envisioning some daylight ahead, she was unhappy on the other hand that she would be seeing him far less as he dedicated himself to producing what would become the "Bible" of AA's teachings. He began spending much of his time in Newark dictating his prose to Ruth Hock, editing the personal success stories of his sober alcoholics, and getting comments back from Dr. Bob and others on the pages he had completed.

Lois often said her saving graces during this period, from the spring of 1938 to the end of January 1939, when the book was finally finished, were her meetings with her "kitchen group" and her frequent conversations with her dear friend Annie Smith in Akron.

Bob Smith, Jr., Annie's son, remembers traveling with his parents to visit Bill and Lois at Clinton Street around this time. He was seventeen then and excited about his first trip to New York City.

"My father came to spend a few days with Bill to go over the pages he was writing for AA's Big Book," he recalled. "Lois seemed to perk right up as soon as she saw my mom. They had developed a very close bond with each other. In fact, as I recall, they spent most of the time together while we were there and also went to meet with other ladies whose husbands were in the Fellowship. And with Dad off somewhere with Bill, I was basically on my own. Once I discovered New York's subway system, however, I had a ball. There was no graffiti back then. The trains were neat and clean and I rode all over New York seeing everything I could."[4]

Young Smitty said Lois appeared to be doing the same thing in Brooklyn that his mother was doing back in Akron—gathering spouses together to talk about living with an alcoholic, coping with the problems that result, and trying to find ways to improve their own lives in spite of it all.

"My mother was a Wellesley graduate," Bob liked to recall. "She was not only very intelligent but had great insight into people and could readily understand their problems and their situations. She was still a member of the Oxford Group at the time and would share those principles with the wives of other alcoholics as well as try to live by them herself. I know my mother and Lois would frequently talk about this and how they needed to change their old ways of thinking and acting or perhaps reacting.

"As the AA movement continued to grow," he said, "Bill and Lois would visit our home in Akron when they could and we would visit them at Clinton Street in Brooklyn. They became devoted friends. Dad told me that, although he and Bill often saw things from different angles, they never had a real serious argument and their minds seemed to mesh in developing an intelligent program which they could present to an alcoholic. I think my mom and Lois were on the very same path before my mother died in 1949."[5]

The day the Smiths were leaving for Pennsylvania Station to return to Akron, Lois remembers Dr. Bob took her aside and said to her with great warmth:

"Lois, I want to thank you for staying with Bill. You know what it's meant to me. For some reason, we alcoholics seem to have the gift of picking out the world's finest women. Why they should be subjected to the tortures we inflict upon them, and stay, I cannot explain."

Then he hugged her and left. Lois later commented about the incident, "Bob was not a flatterer. He was generally quiet and reserved. So I know he spoke those words from his heart. I was deeply touched."[6]

While Bill worked intensely on his book, he was always back at Clinton Street for group meetings, which were gradually attracting more and more people.

Lois came to recognize what a privilege it was seeing people change right in front of her eyes, witnessing the miracle of those crawling out of abject despair into the light of hope and leaving the anchor of alcoholism behind.[7]

But many of their wives continued to have a much more difficult time, it seemed. "Like myself," Lois would share, "they thought once their husbands stopped drinking, everything would be hunky-dory, that life would be beautiful. When it didn't happen, we only became more angry and resentful, always blaming our husbands for all of our problems."[8]

So Lois continued to meet with her "kitchen group," not only at Clinton Street but now at the homes of other ladies as well, some of whom couldn't always afford babysitters or couldn't travel for various reasons. Slowly but surely she was beginning to find some answers—mainly the calm and patience that come when you take your mind off your own problems for a while and try to help someone else, she would say. Without realizing it at the time, Lois was actually starting to walk in Bill's shoes, to discover the same principles, to find the same empathy for those suffering from the same disease of alcoholism. But again like her husband, it would be two steps forward and one step back before the real solution would become crystal clear.

Bill arrived at his small office in Newark each morning with a batch of crinkled yellow pads under his arm, all filled with scribbled notes. He propped his lanky legs up on a beat-up desk and slowly began dictating his thoughts to Ruth Hock. He spoke simply, honestly, and unashamedly about his own experiences with alcohol and the tools he and Dr. Bob had discovered that were keeping them and many others sober. With no hesitation he described his surrender at Towns Hospital and his miraculous communion with Dr. Bob at Henrietta Seiberling's gatehouse. He didn't worry about style. It was plain, homespun prose, the kind of straight talk one would hear sitting around a potbelly stove in an old Vermont general store.

In no time, Bill had completed the first two chapters—the first his own personal story and the second entitled, "There Is a Solution." Ruth typed them up and sent copies around for comment. There were many questions, a number of suggestions, and a few proposed changes, but overall there was general acceptance of the way Bill had begun his treatise. Frank Amos gave a copy to Gene Exman at Harper Brothers as he had promised. The editor liked what he read. After being convinced that Bill could write the entire book in the same simple, direct style, Exman said he was prepared to offer him fifteen hundred dollars as an advance against future royalties on book sales.

Bill was ecstatic. So was Lois. In the light of this sudden and delightfully shocking turn of events, they both celebrated two things: that the cash advance would help pay some bills, and that a major publishing enterprise was willing to print, promote, and sell the book worldwide. What could be greater than that? the board members said, admittedly surprised at how well and how quickly things were turning in the foundation's favor.

That night, however, Bill couldn't sleep. Lois recalled how he paced the bedroom floor, asking himself questions that suddenly occurred to him as the initial exuberance wore off.

"Bill began thinking about all the difficulties that might arise if the book were to be successful," Lois recalled. "If a commercial publisher owned the book, who at that company could answer the flood of inquiries that would undoubtedly pour in. Whereas if the Fellowship itself printed the book and handled its distribution, it would have the know-how to respond to questions and could control the number of books printed and distributed in order to control the number of inquiries. It all made sense to me."[9]

Besides, she remembered her husband saying, if this book was to be their basic text, and if the Fellowship were to grow as everyone had hoped, then it didn't seem right that its main asset should be owned by outsiders. It should be owned by the Alcoholic Foundation and provide the means of self-support the board had recommended.

All three trustees, however, argued against turning down Harper's offer, mainly on the grounds that they knew of no author who had ever successfully published his own works. Troubled by their stance, Bill went back to Gene Exman, thanked him for his offer and then told him about the controversy he found himself in. The editor immediately saw that the group would benefit in many ways by controlling its own published materials and generously advised Bill about having the book printed on his own. The foundation trustees quickly dropped their objections and turned instead to helping raise the four thousand dollars that would be needed to initially publish and distribute five thousand books.

Lois had hoped that with the publishing controversy now settled, there would be clear sailing ahead. Bill would finish writing the book, it would become the great best seller everyone seemed to anticipate, and the money would start flowing in to meet the bills and the mortgage payments so they wouldn't lose their home. But those old butterflies that had never left her stomach were now whispering loud and clear that if the past was any barometer, things would not be that simple, that easy, or that successful. And the butterflies were right, as usual.

All hell broke loose, particularly at Clinton Street, just as soon as Bill finished chapter five, which he called "How It Works." It began, "Rarely have we seen a person fail who has thoroughly followed our path."[10] The path Bill was referring to consisted of both the practical and the spiritual principles he and Dr. Bob had formulated and tried to practice daily in order to stay mentally, physically, and spiritually sober. These principles, which Bill developed into AA's Twelve Steps to recovery for millions of alcoholics around the world, essentially incorporated and expanded upon the Oxford Group's "Four Absolutes" of honesty, purity, unselfishness, and love. Bill's first draft of the Twelve Steps read as follows:

1. We admitted we were powerless over alcohol—that our lives had become unmanageable.

2. Came to believe that God could restore us to sanity.

3. Made a decision to turn our wills and our lives over to the care and direction of God.

4. Made a searching and fearless moral inventory of ourselves.

5. Admitted to God, to ourselves and to another human being the exact nature of our wrongs.

6. Were entirely willing that God remove all these defects of character.

7. Humbly on our knees asked Him to remove these shortcomings— holding nothing back.

8. Made a complete list of all persons we had harmed, and became willing to make amends to them all.

9. Made direct amends to such people wherever possible, except when to do so would injure them or others.

10. Continued to take personal inventory and when we were wrong, promptly admitted it.

11. Sought through prayer and meditation to improve our contact with God, praying only for knowledge of His will for us and the power to carry that out.

12. Having had a spiritual experience as the result of this course of action, we tried to carry this message to others, especially alcoholics, and to practice these principles in all our affairs.[11]

Lois vividly recalled the night she heard Bill read these steps to the
Clinton Street boys. She always seemed to turn up at opportune
moments with fresh pots of coffee to overhear her husband discussing
with the group the chapters he had just completed. She said there was
always a lively debate but none compared to what ensued after the reading of chapter five, "How It Works."[12]

"Bill had told me he was quite pleased with what he had written," Lois
recalled. "He said Dr. Bob had agreed with almost every word he had put
down. So he was in no way prepared for the violent reaction when he read
the steps to the group that night. I never will forget what happened."[13]

While a few men smiled with delight and bought the steps exactly as
Bill had written them, most members squirmed uncomfortably. And
much to Bill's dismay, a faction led by his friend Hank shouted that there
was too much God talk and it would scare drunks away.[14]

"It wasn't any God that got me sober," Hank argued. "It was you
guys. Being around all you guys and knowing what can happen if we
drink again."[15]

While Bill and Hank had often disagreed about "this God thing," it
was particularly disturbing that the one leading the anti-God stampede
was his right-hand man. Then others joined in. If Bill wanted to talk
about the spiritual, okay, they said, but religion? Never! The missions at
Calvary Church and on the Bowery did the God thing, and everyone
knew they always failed with alcoholics.

Bill argued back at first for he knew, as few men did, that his Higher
Power made everything else work, had brought him together with Dr.
Bob, and had given him this insatiable desire to help other alcoholics. But
the more he defied the group, the more the battle raged on. So he decided to sit back and hear them out, to keep an open mind. And as the hours
passed, he began to understand their anxieties, their fears, and their prej-
udices as he never had before. A compromise began to form in his mind,
a compromise that soon everyone would come to accept, including the
recovering drunks in Akron and elsewhere. And it was a compromise that
would enable the Fellowship to attract believers and nonbelievers alike,
the willful and the beaten-down, the citizens of all nations and the sons
and daughters of all "Gods."

First, they would label the steps as "A Suggested Program of Recovery." Everyone agreed that night that no drunk would rebel at a mere "suggestion." It was the "musts" that bothered them and Bill removed all "musts" from the steps.

And second—and this proved providential—whenever the word *God* was to be used in the steps or anywhere else in the book now and into the future, it would be followed by the phrase "as we understood Him." Once again there was a meeting of the minds, including Hank, that this would open the gates wide enough for all drunks to pass through, regardless of their belief or lack of belief. This settled the group controversy once and for all.[16]

But then came another bump in the road, only this one had nothing to do with the group. It concerned a hurtful misunderstanding between Lois and her husband. From the beginning of his book project, Bill had always felt it necessary to address the wives and families of alcoholics, to share with them the knowledge and insight he and Dr. Bob and the Fellowship in general had gleaned from their painful experiences and to offer whatever sage advice they could to those still living with this terrible disease. And Lois had always felt that Bill would involve her in this process. That, she felt, was only natural since she herself had lived through those harrowing times and had come to learn much from her own experiences. That's why Lois was certain her husband would want her to write the chapter in the book, "To The Wives" and even the following one, "The Family Afterward." When he didn't, she was devastated.

They had often talked about spouses not being as happy as should be expected after an alcoholic was sober for a while. They wondered together why the initial exuberance that comes with sobriety couldn't be sustained. What was it that impeded these relationships and what could be done to solve this disappointing problem . . . not just for the spouse of the alcoholic but for the entire family as well?

With Lois now embarked on her own journey of self-discovery and learning much from others similarly involved, who else could have greater insight and a more experienced perspective? So when Bill came up with the flimsy excuse that the book had to be written in the same style, Lois didn't buy it. Not only didn't she accept his rationale, but the hurt from his dismaying decision stayed with her for years.[17]

Lois simply buried the hurt inside where she had buried many other things in the past. Later in life, as she looked back at that incident, she shared with a close friend: "While the disappointment still remains, I finally came to see, when reading what Bill wrote in those chapters, that he did understand and appreciate all that I had gone through as the wife of an alcoholic, and all the pain and suffering the malady of alcoholism had brought into my life. That at least salved the hurt somewhat."[18]

By the middle of January 1939, Bill had finished the book. That's when the final controversy arose—what should its title be? Everyone in the Fellowship, both in New York and Ohio, seemed to have a suggestion. Lois once said that more than a hundred names were considered including Hank's tongue-in-cheek offering—"The Bill W. Movement." She noted with a smile that while her husband may have enjoyed the momentary flattery, he killed that notion very quickly. "He still had a big ego," Lois once shared, "but not that big."

In the end, six suggested titles led the pack. They were, *One Hundred Men, The Empty Glass, The Dry Way, The Dry Life, Dry Frontiers,* and *The Way Out.* The last one, *The Way Out,* seemed to be the favorite of most until Bill asked his friend Fitz to find out how many other books carried the same title. Fitz had a former business partner in Washington, D.C., who knew someone at the Library of Congress. When it was discovered there were at least twenty-five books called *The Way Out,* that name dropped to the bottom of the heap.

That's when one of the members at Clinton Street—nobody could ever recall exactly who—pointed out that they had been calling themselves "anonymous alcoholics" for some time. So he suggested that moniker as a book title. When Bill turned the words around to "Alcoholics Anonymous," the name was not only chosen unanimously as the title for the book, but soon became the name for the entire Fellowship—"The Fellowship of Alcoholics Anonymous."[19]

By March 1939, book pages were rolling off the presses at the Cornwall Printing plant in Cornwall, New York, an excellent company recommended by Gene Exman of Harper Brothers. Supersalesman Hank had talked Bill, Dr. Bob, and the foundation board into pricing the treatise at three dollars and fifty cents a copy, rather steep back in 1939. So to convince the buyers they would be getting their money's worth, Hank told the printer to use the thickest paper they had in the plant.

"The original volume proved to be so bulky," Lois would often share when talking about that historical event, "that it soon became known as the 'Big Book.' That's where the name came from and why it's still called that today even though it's not nearly so bulky."[20]

Hank's plan to sell books was publicity, publicity, and more publicity. He thought he had *Reader's Digest* talked into doing an article about the Fellowship, but that fell through at the last moment. So did everything else in his promotion plan. As a result, five thousand copies of the Big Book lay idle in Cornwall Printing's warehouse for months after their publication. It seemed they weren't worth the paper they were printed on. And as the books remained piled up in Cornwall, the bills continued to pile up at Clinton Street.

"I had difficulty sleeping at times," Lois once shared with a close friend. "I would walk through the house late at night wondering what I would do if I ever lost the only real home I ever knew. It was frightful to think about. Bill kept assuring me that things would work out. That soon the book would begin to sell. That it just had to."[21]

Then suddenly came more excitement—another hopeful light at the end of an ever-lengthening tunnel. A newcomer by the name of Morgan Rogers, who had only recently sobered up at Clinton Street, told Hank and Bill that he knew Gabriel Heatter very well and had worked with him in the past. Gabriel Heatter was an immensely popular radio broadcaster in the 1930s and 1940s whose nationwide program *We the People* focused on heartrending human-interest stories. Morgan, who had once been in the publishing business himself and was a very good speaker, offered to tell his own heartrending story on Heatter's radio show, talk about the Fellowship, and plug Bill's book.

Once Hank confirmed Morgan's appearance on the national radio program, he put together an elaborate promotion scheme to take advantage of the exposure. More than twenty thousand postcards were mailed out to doctors and related medical practitioners east of the Mississippi announcing Heatter's broadcast and urging them to send for a copy of *Alcoholics*

Anonymous while it was still available. Then he and Bill and the group sat back and waited for the anticipated avalanche of replies to pour in.

They waited anxiously for three whole days before going to the post office, carrying with them a large suitcase to collect the deluge of reply cards they had anticipated. They found twelve cards, two made out so illegibly they were probably from medics in their cups. Just two more replies dribbled in a few days later. The scheme turned out to be a total failure, and the rest of the five thousand books continued to gather dust in the Cornwall warehouse.

On Wednesday, April 26, 1939, the day following the *We the People* broadcast, Lois and Bill Wilson received an eviction notice from the bank, telling them they must vacate the house that had been the Burnham family home for half a century.

Lois's worst nightmare had now become a reality. She cried for days. Bill couldn't console her. In fact, his presence at times only made things worse, for as hard as she tried not to blame him, the words were always at the tip of her tongue. Finally she had to face the facts, and the facts were they had to move. But where? What could they afford? What could they take with them and what did they have to leave behind?

Then one day Annie Smith showed up on her doorstep. Though not in the best of health, she had come all the way from Akron to help Lois, to calm her, to convince her that God had a very special plan for her life, that everything she was going through at the moment had a purpose, a meaning, and that some day she would understand why. Annie then took her out on the town to shake her from her blues. They went to a movie, ate dinner at a nice restaurant, and had a banana split at Schrafft's. Annie picked up the bill. She said it was her way of repaying her dear friend for all she had given her.[22] The next day, Annie joined Lois's "kitchen group" for one last meeting at Clinton Street. While the ladies were thrilled to meet Dr. Bob's wife, they were sad about Lois's dire situation. Many offered to share their own homes and apartments with her and Bill for as long as necessary. By the time Annie left for Akron, Lois's spirits were buoyed a bit, and she was prepared to face the difficult tasks ahead.

The house was still filled with possessions her parents had accumulated since 1888, Lois said. She also had her own things to pack. It took her months to sort everything out, distribute some to friends and relatives, and pack up what they wanted to put in storage. They donated carloads of things to the Salvation Army and Goodwill Industries.

Lois labeled every single item in the house she planned to keep, whether it was stuck away in some bureau draw or sitting idly on a shelf. And her organizational skills had her put each item on a list—from silverware to blankets to books—so she could find them at the storage warehouse if need be.[23]

She said it was heartbreaking to leave Clinton Street. "Having no money for even a small apartment, we had no idea when or where we would ever again have a home of our own. But our AA friends, the sober alcoholics in the Fellowship and their wives, helped us out. Many invited us to stay with them until we were able to afford a place of our own. I soon began to feel like a vagabond, living off the kindness and generosity of others. If I wasn't familiar with humility before, I certainly was now."[24] Had it not been for the fact that Lois had already "lived around," having traveled across the country on a motorcycle with Bill, knowing how to pack frugally, camping out in all kinds of weather, accepting the graciousness of strangers to share their abodes in North Carolina, Florida, and New England, perhaps she could not have handled what she was about to face over the next two years—two years in which she and Bill were to move fifty-one times and often live in conditions that were both uncomfortable and humiliating.

What must Lois Burnham Wilson have felt that chilly, gray spring morning as she stood on the sidewalk outside of 182 Clinton Street and watched her possessions being carried out and packed into a van? What shame this proud woman must have felt when she and her husband found themselves almost penniless, without even enough money to pay the movers. If it hadn't been for their friends in the AA group setting up the "Bill and Lois Improvement Fund,"[25] which barely collected enough money to pay the storage company's bill for a single month, all their furnishings would have been left in the street.

As she stared at the stately brownstone one last time, she must have been thinking back to those wonderful childhood days when her mother dressed her so prettily for kindergarten, and their housekeeper, Maggie

Fay, led her to the front door and watched her bound down the steps and into the horse-drawn black brougham filled with her noisy classmates.

She must have thought about those disturbing nights when her little sister Barbara, still recovering from her terrible burns, awakened in their bedroom and sobbed in her arms from the fright and the pain. And about those wonderful parties and formal dinners when she squelched her giggles over the guests who squirmed and blushed holding hands with strangers as the family said grace.

She must have been remembering all the time she spent in the den, talking and studying with her best friend, Elise Valentine. Just the thought of their many years of friendship and their bitter parting must have added to her heartache that day.

And of course she had to be thinking of her and Bill's wedding in that lovely, ornate parlor filled with guests, he in his army uniform and she a blushing bride, and their hopes and joys as they looked forward to their exciting future. Yes, there was a war in Europe, and they both knew that Bill would be leaving shortly to help conquer the enemy. But then he would return home and conquer the world, to achieve the greatness she knew he had within him.

That's when Bill took her hand and slowly led her away from 182 Clinton Street in the heart of Brooklyn Heights, New York. They both were carrying their own suitcases.

The Clinton Street boys also had to find new abodes. Some buddied up in small, inexpensive apartments. Some moved into rooming houses. Others, particularly the newest arrivals, returned to places like the Salvation Army and the Calvary Mission, where at least they could get "two hots and a cot."

Since Bill and Hank were working on another book promotion deal with Morgan Rogers, for the first week Bill and Lois stayed in Morgan's small apartment on Fifty-first Street in Manhattan. A bachelor, Morgan slept on the couch while Lois and Bill snuggled in a twin bed. Lois remembered the place well, having bumped her knee painfully on a dresser while hauling her suitcase into the tiny bedroom.

But their second stop was much more pleasant for two reasons. First, Lois had decided to make the best of things for a while, turning her life over to her Higher Power and trying not to feel sorry for herself. Somehow, some way, everything would work out just as Annie Smith had told her. And second, she and Bill were back out in the country, the environment she loved. It seemed that Chris, the wire-rope salesman, had a small bungalow on Green Pond in northern New Jersey that he inherited from his parents. So he lent it to Lois and Bill until the end of June when others in his family would be using it. At least the "vagabonds" could now breathe freely for two months while deciding where to go next.

When she shared those times with friends later on, Lois would recall how much she enjoyed being out in the country again, even though it was just for a short while. She said honking geese would wake her and Bill in the morning. They would run outside the bungalow to see them flying north to nest, sailing across the pale blue sky in their usually orderly triangle.

Then she and Bill would hear a loud noise behind them like someone starting up an old motor. They'd turn to see a flight of ducks beating their wings as they rose from a nearby pond. Lois would then inhale the morning dew, smile at the new spring flowers, kiss her husband warmly, and saunter back inside to make him breakfast.[26]

Since they had no car, they had to walk four miles to the small town of Newfoundland for provisions. The grant from the Rockefeller philanthropies hadn't completely run out, so they were still receiving thirty dollars a week from the Riverside Church fund and twenty dollars every now and then from the "Bill and Lois Improvement Fund." It was enough for food and travel but little else.

Bill was still meeting with members of the Alcoholic Foundation, keeping in touch with Dr. Silkworth, gathering with his sober alcoholics at various homes around town, and working with Hank and Morgan and others on ideas to get the Big Book off the ground. So he frequently took the train into New York and sometimes spent a day or two there with some friends.

Lois became so enamored by the lovely place on Green Pond that the time just flew by. Soon their solitude and the fun things they did together came to an abrupt end. It was June and Chris's family was due to arrive. That's when Lois and Bill began another sojourn, one that would find them changing abodes fifty-one times during the years of 1939 and 1940.[27] Over the course of this "living around" period, Lois and Anne Bingham—the first woman she had met that night from the cars parked along Clinton Street—became very close friends as she and Bill spent several weeks at her Westchester home from time to time. Anne would invite the "kitchen group" ladies over for a meeting, or she and Lois would travel to one of their homes. By now the group had expanded and splintered into other groups. And the women were beginning to focus more on their own lives and their own problems and less on their husbands. Lois once said of those days that she could sense the principles of AA were starting to "rub off on them."

It was late January of 1940. Lois and Bill were staying with Marty Mann, the first recovered woman alcoholic, at her home in snowy Greenwich, Connecticut, when they received the news. Willard Richardson, who now chaired the Alcoholic Foundation board, said his boss, John D. Rockefeller, Jr., wanted to give a dinner for the AA Fellowship. He had been quietly following the movement's progress over the past three years and now wanted some of his wealthy friends to hear the marvelous story of how it was continuing to cure hopeless drunks.

Lois remembered her husband's initial reaction to Richardson's remarks. "He assumed that Mr. Rockefeller had changed his mind and had decided to give AA money and to ask his friends to do the same," Lois told a close friend. "He had just gotten used to the idea that the Fellowship shouldn't have a lot of money so now he had all sorts of mixed feelings about what was happening."[28] This was especially true when he learned the invitation list for the dinner was "a veritable constellation of New York's prominent and wealthy. Anybody could see that their total financial worth might easily be a billion dollars."[29]

Dr. Bob came to New York a few days before the dinner to discuss the prospects with Bill and the foundation trustees. They shared ideas on what the Fellowship might do were millions to be donated. That perhaps there could be AA hospitals for the sickest of drunks and halfway houses to help them get back on their feet. Perhaps there could be AA-financed clubhouses where alcoholics could gather for meetings as well as social events. It all sounded wonderful—that money properly spent could help thousands of recovering alcoholics in many meaningful ways. The foundation could also have its own office, it could have a staff to help manage the growing movement, and Bill could finally draw a salary that he and Lois could live on comfortably. After all, didn't they deserve it by now?

While the trustees all seemed to agree, Bill could tell that Bob had serious reservations. He told Bill as they left the meeting that he never met a drunk who could handle a whole lot of money very well—and besides, they were all once again counting their chickens before they hatched.

The Rockefeller dinner was held on February 8, 1940, at Manhattan's exclusive Union Club. It was an all-male black-tie affair. Of the four hundred prominent and influential people invited, seventy-five accepted. Using his characteristic promotional instincts, Hank placed one "very sober" AA member at each table, having rehearsed with them the story of their miraculous path to sobriety for their guests to hear. John D., Jr., had taken ill a few days earlier, so his son, Nelson Rockefeller, who was thirty-one at the time, chaired the proceedings.

As Bill and Dr. Bob told their stories that evening, supported by the testimony of Dr. Silkworth and others, it became obvious that the audience of millionaires was both sympathetic and impressed. Bill's hopes and expectations soared. At one point, Dr. Bob leaned over and whispered: "Keep both feet on the ground." Bill simply frowned.[30]

Did it occur to either one of them that this was déjà vu all over again, that they had been through all of this once before, only without the squab on toast that was served at dinner? Neither one ever said. But as it turned out, they had been.

When the guests had finished asking questions and offering flattering comments, Nelson Rockefeller returned to the podium. A hush came over the room. Bill could hear his heart thumping—then almost stop as he listened to the rich young man summarize the evening. He thanked his guests for attending and for witnessing with him what his family believed was the birth of an important movement. Then he underscored his father's faith in AA, and his belief that its power lay in the fact that the message was always carried from one man to the next without any thought of financial reward. For this reason, he concluded, he agreed with his father that AA must always be self-supporting as it was with the early Christians. That all they needed from the public and from the men gathered there that evening was their confidence and goodwill.

Then the guests rose and gave Bill and Bob and the AA Fellowship a thunderous round of applause. After hearty handshakes and pats on the back, Bill watched in disbelief as millions of dollars walked slowly out of the room. He slumped back into his chair and tried to figure out what this evening, what this elaborate dinner was all about. But for the moment, he couldn't come up with an answer. He would later understand, however, that the confidence and goodwill of such people contributed enormously to lessening the stigma of alcoholism. He would also realize once more, after thinking it through, that a whole lot of money really and truly would have unraveled the Fellowship sooner or later because, as his friend Buddy the derelict had said a few years earlier, "sobriety was something that could not be bought or paid for."

The Fellowship did receive a little money as the result of the dinner. Nelson Rockefeller purchased five hundred Big Books, which he sent to those on his original guest list and to some libraries around the state where he thought they might be of some help to families. And the Alcoholic Foundation received an additional two thousand dollars in anonymous contributions for a total of about four thousand dollars. But all this did was cover some foundation expenses and help provide Lois and Bill with the bare necessities as they pondered what to do next about their future—which certainly looked far bleaker than it had before February 8.

Then, just before the first crocus of spring fought its way into the sunlight, Bill was hit with still another deep disappointment that made him feel he was back in the dead of winter. His right-hand man, Hank, got drunk.

"First there was Ebby and now Hank," Lois said, recalling the incident. "Here were two of his closest friends he was sure would stay sober forever. He began to question himself all over again until he came to realize what made them start drinking again in the first place."[31]

She said Bill saw they were no longer helping newcomers, had drifted away from the group, and harbored resentments against certain people, which they refused to discuss. Lois also knew that Hank and his wife, Kathleen, weren't getting along in their second try at marriage. She had pleaded with Kathleen to attend some of her "kitchen group" meetings, but to no avail. Kathleen insisted that drinking was her husband's problem, not hers, and that she had been very patient in letting him attend all his AA meetings even though he wasn't paying enough attention to his business or to her.

On that score, the confused and upset woman was correct, especially about the business. The Honor Dealers buying syndicate had continued to evaporate as Hank spent more time on AA affairs than on his own. But, according to Lois, two other reasons may have led to his slip.

First, Bill had been sharing Hank's Newark business office to write his book and conduct some of the Alcoholic Foundation's work at the same time, contributing to the rent whenever he could. Now Bill was talking about finding a small office in New York for the foundation's headquarters when all along his friend felt it would remain in Newark. This misunderstanding created resentment between these two good friends.

Second, and probably the more important reason, Hank had become smitten with Ruth Hock. In fact, as his own marriage was crumbling once again, he proposed wedded bliss to Ruth. While she respected her boss for his dedication to helping the less fortunate, she was not in love with him and therefore not interested in his proposal. She turned him down.

Filled with anger at his wife, resenting Bill, hurt by Ruth's rejection, and with no God in his life, Hank had little or no defense against alcohol. He went out and got drunk, and he stayed drunk for many months. He tried to come back to the Fellowship on several occasions, but his false pride, anger, and other character defects always stood in his way. His drinking finally grew much worse and, in a few years, it ended in his death.

Hank's slip shook Bill to his very core. It forced him to take a good look at his own life once again and the utter failure he saw when measured against the world's standards for success. He recognized that the struggle he was waging to build a sanctum for suffering alcoholics only heaped more hardship on his loving wife and caused him great guilt. He decided AA could get along without him. That he had brought it along far enough and now it could survive on its own. He needed to put his own house in order and get a job, any sort of a job. He needed money and he needed it fast.

Bill thought about his young friend Chris who had lent him his bungalow on Green Pond. Chris was now making a good living selling wire rope for Paulson and Weber, a large industrial products distributor, and had always kidded Bill about being the best damn salesman he had ever met. The former stockbroker decided to put that to a test with Chris's help.

Although he knew nothing about wire-rope customers and had even less interest in the product itself, Bill spent that summer doing his best under very pressing and distracting circumstances. It barely put a few dollars in his pocket.

Lois also tried to find a way to bring in some money. With life being too hectic and disorganized to hold down a regular job, she tried her hand at writing. She had once sold an article about veneers to *House and Garden* magazine. However, when she submitted some tales to the magazine *Romantic Stories*, she received pink slips rather than greenbacks.[32]

In June of 1940, a group of New York AA's, concerned about Bill pulling back from his activities for the Fellowship, met with him to say that the movement needed his continued guidance and direction. Otherwise it would fall apart. Too many recovered alcoholics were already going in different directions, setting their own rules. They said they also needed a central place to meet as they once had at Clinton Street. So these concerned members came up with a proposition. Two of their number who had a few extra bucks were willing to guarantee the rent on a quaint little building at 344¹/₂ West Twenty-fourth Street in Manhattan. The building, which could be supported by passing the basket, would actually become an AA clubhouse and serve multiple purposes. It would be used for AA meetings, contain an office for Bill, and be a gathering place for members to pass their time and talk about their disease and their recovery. They said Bill and Lois could live rent free in the rooms on the second floor, which were neat and clean. They convinced him that in time, as the Fellowship continued to grow, the Big Book would sell and his royalties would be enough for him to live on.

Bill sat with his wife that night and talked things over. They had come this far together, Lois said; why turn back now? If God had wanted him to be a successful wire-rope salesman, He would have at least had him enroll in the navy, not the army, in order to get the right experience and contacts. They both laughed, something that they hadn't done for a while.

So they moved into what soon became known as the Twenty-fourth Street Clubhouse, and Bill dedicated himself once again to the task of saving drunks. He set up a temporary office there until the Fellowship could afford a larger central office some time later. Lois described the clubhouse in her memoirs. "It used to be a stable," she wrote, "so is set back from the street and entered through a covered passage with a doorway on the street. It used to be the Illustrators Club so is very attractive. One large room, with fireplace and paneled in knotty pine, and kitchen are downstairs. Upstairs there is a large room with skylights, and two small bedrooms and two toilets."[33]

Lois went ahead and fixed up the place. The ten feet square room, once used by the Illustrators Club of New York, had little privacy and few conveniences. Still, Lois tried her best to at least make it bright and comfortable. She and Bill painted the walls and found two fruit boxes that they used as lamp stands and bureaus. They screwed hooks into the wall to hang their clothes, which they had to get at by climbing across a bed without a footboard. And they ventilated the room by opening the door to the fire escape.[34]

After she and Bill moved in, Lois described how the clubhouse quickly became a beehive of AA activity.

"It was Clinton Street 1935," she wrote, "only more so. There were always visitors, people driving in from Westchester or Connecticut, winos shuffling in from the Salvation Army down the street, or out-of-towners far from the safety of their group, who needed the security of this crazy, solid oasis in the city. These were men from every rung of the social ladder, who never conceivably would have drunk together, never would have gone to the same bars, yet here they were in one room, helping each other to keep sober. Whatever hour Bill wandered in, there was a feeling of a meeting. In a sense they were all members of an exclusive club and only they understood what they had to pay to get there."[35]

These notes from her memoirs showed how much Lois had come to understand what AA was really all about and how much every alcoholic had in common. And she was coming to understand the same thing about the wives and the families of alcoholics.

Lois didn't write in her memoirs about the "accidental" break-ins in the upstairs rooms at the clubhouse, but she did tell a close friend. It seemed the upstairs bedroom was sometimes mistaken for one of the bathrooms since the doors looked alike. There were times when newcomers unfamiliar with the place mistook her bedroom door for the entrance to the toilet and barged in on her when she forgot to lock her door. It was embarrassing, to say the least.

Even after Bill made sure the toilets were clearly marked, there was yet another incident. A newcomer still in his cups and in a hurry to get to the men's room grabbed the handle of Lois's bedroom door instead. He jiggled and pulled and began banging on the door until Lois finally had to open it and scream at him to leave. The man slunk away red-faced, leaving her weeping over her unseemly circumstances. That was when Lois knew she couldn't go on like this much longer.[36]

Shortly after that incident, she and her husband were invited to spend a weekend with some AA friends, Ruth and Wilbur Slocum, in Chappaqua, New York, a small, upscale town in the heart of Westchester County.

"We were lugging our suitcases through Grand Central Station, hurrying to catch the train," Lois shared in her later years, "when suddenly I felt overwhelmed by the way we were living. I can't explain why it suddenly happened like that. I sat down on the cold marble stairs and burst out at Bill: 'I can't go on like this anymore! Will we never have a home of our own?' I wept oceans right there in public.

"Bill finally consoled me. He understood perfectly what I was going through. He wanted a place for us too. He asked me to put up with it for just a little while longer. He had said that before only this time for some reason I believed him."[37]

By now the AA Fellowship was more than five years old and had been spreading its wings far beyond New York and Ohio. Sober alcoholics traveling on business and finding themselves alone in a strange hotel in a strange city, as Bill once had at the Mayflower Hotel, sought out other drunks to help themselves stay sober. That's how the Fellowship arrived in Philadelphia, began to grow, and came to the attention of Judge Curtis Bok, the owner and publisher of the *Saturday Evening Post*, at that time one of the largest and most influential magazines in the country.

Curious to learn the truth behind the wild rumors he was hearing about "miraculous cures" of hopeless drunks, Judge Bok hired a well-known, hard-nosed reporter by the name of Jack Alexander to look into the movement. He wanted Alexander to investigate "this AA thing" as thoroughly as he had recently probed the New Jersey crime rackets, and then write an in-depth article about whatever he uncovered.*

The truth was, the reporter was extremely skeptical when he began his assignment in November of 1940 and expected to write a critical and derisive piece. "When did you ever meet a drunk who told you the truth?" Alexander cynically thought he'd never met a drunk who told the truth until he met Bill Wilson and Dr. Robert Smith. He was frankly impressed by their candor and stunned by what they were doing.[38] Lois remembered that both Bill and Dr. Bob were leery when the reporter first called to tell them of the *Post*'s interest in the Fellowship. The idea of a "full and complete investigation" sounded rather ominous. But then, they had nothing to hide, and a story about AA in a major publication like the *Post* could get their message out to thousands. So they decided to meet with the reporter.

Once Alexander agreed to protect the anonymity of his interviewees by using fictitious names, Bill took him in tow for almost a month. He brought him to Akron and Cleveland, to Brooklyn and Westchester County. He sat him down with Dr. Bob, walked him through the new alcoholic ward at St. Thomas Hospital in Akron, introduced him to Dr. Silkworth at Towns, and had him meet and chat with the nonalcoholic trustees of the Alcoholic Foundation in Manhattan. Every question Alexander asked was answered forthrightly and without reservation. He was treated almost like a member of the Fellowship in terms of openness and trust.

When his story was finished, it was not only approved but applauded by the editors of the *Post* and scheduled for the March 1, 1941, issue. It was a cover story of about seventy-five hundred words, headlined "Alcoholics Anonymous: Freed Slaves of Drink, Now They Free Others."[39] It detailed exactly how the program of AA worked, supported by the stories of some of the men it helped get sober, mainly Bill and Bob. And finally it highlighted AA's acceptance by many medical, legal, and social service professionals.

The effect of its publication on the still relatively small band of sober drunks was explosive. It stretched Bill and Dr. Bob and their fellow members almost beyond their capacity to meet the demand for help. Overnight, attendance at meetings rose dramatically. Older members were running wild trying to make "Twelfth Step Calls"—the term AA uses to describe sober alcoholics carrying the message to wet ones.

In the beginning of March, 1941, there were about two hundred members attending meetings at the clubhouse. Before the end of March, the membership more than doubled. Lois wrote in her memoirs, "It was the same everywhere. Groups outgrew their meeting places and had to be divided. Older members worked frantically with newcomers. These new-comers in turn, after a month or so of sobriety, were sent on Twelfth Step calls to help still newer-comers. It is estimated that 6,000 AAs owe the start of their sobriety to the *Post* article, and nobody knows how many more thousands were sparked by them."[40]

It can be said that Alcoholics Anonymous was firmly established in 1941 as a great American achievement.

And as new members poured into the Fellowship, they needed the program's "Bible" to learn from. So the piles of dusty Big Books sitting in the Cornwall warehouse were rapidly depleted and more books had to be printed. The royalties began to slowly accumulate. Bill could finally see the prospect of earning a decent income after his long struggle and dedication to helping his fellow alcoholics. And perhaps he could somehow make it up to his loving wife, who never left his side.

Lois remembered how her husband turned to her one afternoon as they were returning to the clubhouse to face another desk full of mail and pleas for help and smiled: "Maybe it's about time we started looking for a place of our own."[41]

She hesitated. She was waiting to feel those butterflies in her stomach again or hear them whispering in her ear. But they weren't there. Could it possibly be they had gone, had flown off somewhere to haunt some other doubting Thomas? She didn't know, and, for the moment at least, she didn't care. For Bill's words had just made her deliriously happy.

14

The Evolution of Al-Anon

৵

*T*HE TRAIN RIDE ALONG THE HUDSON RIVER FROM URBAN NEW York City into the picturesque countryside of Westchester County was something Lois always enjoyed. She would sit back and watch the scenery change from crowded Bronx apartment houses to sprawling landscapes dotted with suburban homes; from black-tarred city streets to winding country roads; from stark cement sidewalks to tree-lined paths. It was still only March, but she could tell by the yawning shrubbery and small patches of greening grass that spring was right around the corner.

Ruth and Wilbur, their dear AA friends in Chappaqua, had invited her and Bill up to their home for another relaxing weekend. As Lois stared out of the train window, her mind began racing again, excited about soon leaving their cramped and often too-public quarters at the Twenty-fourth Street Clubhouse.

Should they rent a small apartment back in Brooklyn Heights, she wondered, or one in the heart of Manhattan, since Bill would be spending much of his time there on AA business?

Certainly they had to have at least two bedrooms so that when Annie and Bob came to town or when other AA friends visited, they would have room for them. Of course, she would like a large living room for entertaining, maybe one with a skylight, and a nice kitchen and, oh yes, a big old fireplace like the one they had at Clinton Street. Then again, that might be overdoing it, at least for now. They could start small, and as

Bill's royalty income continued to grow, they could find something larger. But no matter what, whatever it was, it would be all their own.[1]

Ruth and Wilbur met them at the train station in their used Buick and, after hugs and kisses, loaded the bags into the trunk and headed off. They talked at first about Jack Alexander's article and its far-reaching impact on the Fellowship, even here in Westchester County. Then the conversation turned to the war in Europe, the fall of France, and Winston Churchill and the Brits' heroic stand against Hitler's blitzkrieg of London. Would the United States enter the fray or not? Wilbur was also a veteran of World War I, so he and Bill were both convinced that President Roosevelt, like President Woodrow Wilson before him, would soon be forced to abandon his neutrality policy and come to the aid of the nation's European friends.

The ladies also remembered the war that was supposed to end all wars. Lois and Ruth both hoped that somehow there could be a peaceful resolution to the growing crisis. It was 1941 and the entire country seemed to be holding its breath.

It was Bill who first noticed they had passed Chappaqua and were approaching the quaint little village of Bedford Hills. That's when Ruth smiled coyly and told her guests they had a surprise for them. She and her husband wanted to show their friends a charming house that was perfectly suited to their needs. Not only that, the house was owned by a widow who absolutely revered the program of Alcoholics Anonymous because of how much it helped someone near and dear to her.

A house! Lois looked at Bill. He simply shrugged. Lois had often heard Wilbur talk to Bill about someday moving to Westchester, only a forty-five-minute train ride to the city. But buying a house there was out of the question. In fact, buying a house anywhere was a prospect so remote they never even gave it a thought. After all, they were only now beginning to see their way clear to rent an apartment. Then again, "what harm was there in looking?" Bill whispered to his wife as Wilbur turned off a small road and headed up a long dirt driveway. There, sitting atop the hill on a two-acre estate, was a charming country house.

Secluded among the thatch of trees on a lovely knoll overlooking a valley, the brown cedar-shingled house seemed to enchant them into taking a closer look. Bill discovered an unlocked window around back, climbed in and hoisted Lois in after him. They found themselves gazing into a marvelous fieldstone fireplace that ruled a large, wood-paneled living room. Lois had always fancied a little white cottage so the place immediately struck her as too large and solemn. She later admitted that perhaps she didn't want to like the house at first because she knew they couldn't afford it.[2]

But as Lois walked around the house that day, she came to realize it wasn't all that big and formal. There were seven rooms: a living room, three bedrooms, and a kitchen downstairs, and a long, bookshelved library and one bedroom upstairs. When she stood in front of the fireplace, she felt warmth, friendship, and hominess. And when she stepped outside and saw the gardens and the surrounding woods, as much as she didn't want to, she fell in love with this enchanting place.

Lois had never really believed in coincidences, not since she was a child. She believed that everything happened for a reason—not by accident. She remembered her mother used to tell her that "happenstance was God's way of doing something nice for you in His own quiet and surprising way."[3] And at AA meetings she often heard some very spiritual members call coincidences "God shots." So why should she be surprised, then, to learn that the owner of this wonderful house and grounds had been to some AA meetings, not for herself but to accompany and support a very close friend? And why should she be taken aback when her friends Ruth and Wilbur told her this lady had often expressed great interest in meeting her and Bill?

It was all true. That Sunday they drove back to Bedford Hills, up the long dirt driveway, and there at the top of the hill standing next to her house was a warm and generous middle-aged lady by the name of Mrs. Helen Griffith—no relation to any of Bill's kin. When her husband had died several years earlier, Mrs. Griffith moved back into the city, leaving her country home locked and shuttered until just the right buyers came along. And now here they were.

The tall, stately woman knew that Lois and Bill were living at the Twenty-fourth Street Clubhouse and said she was frankly "appalled at the notion."[4] She insisted they have her home and proposed a plan they could hardly refuse. She would let this stunned couple have it for sixty-five hundred dollars, a significant decrease from her original asking price. There would be no money down, and they could pay her forty dollars a month against the mortgage with no interest at least for the first year. Bill quickly calculated they'd be saving twenty dollars a month by taking their furniture and possessions out of storage, so all they would need was another twenty each month. He felt certain the book royalties would more than cover that.

All Lois could do was cry, she was so overcome. Mrs. Griffith embraced her and said that for all she and Bill had done for others, the least they deserved was a comfortable home for themselves. Before parting, Mrs. Griffith said she felt very grateful they had accepted her offer. Lois and Bill moved into their new home on April 16, 1941.

Their "vagabond" days were over. They finally had their own place, a home where they could once again be together to enjoy the normal pleasures Lois yearned for such as music, reading, gardening, and other activities Bill also loved. And they could now plan their future together as Bill continued to guide and grow Alcoholics Anonymous.

However, since one of Bill's favorite sayings was "first things first," he recognized that the house was in need of significant repairs and improvements. For example, there was no furnace. One day he spotted an old coal-burning furnace stashed beside a bar in the town of Bedford Hills. The owner was changing his heating system over to oil. Bill paid the man ten dollars and had several of his AA friends help him install the old furnace in the house. It lasted until they could change over to oil themselves.[5]

Having moved out of the clubhouse and also out of his digs in Newark, Bill established a central office for AA activities at 30 Vesey Street in lower Manhattan. This gave the Fellowship, for the first time, a headquarters of its own. It was also where the trustees of the Alcoholic Foundation now gathered to share their thoughts on the objectives and direction of the movement. The office was actually one large room that Bill had partitioned off to hold meetings with some privacy. The total staff at the time consisted of himself, Ruth Hock, and Ruth's new assistant, Lorraine Greim, also a nonalcoholic.

At Vesey Street, the ripples from the *Saturday Evening Post* story turned into gigantic waves of activity—responding to a constant stream of inquiries; contacting members to go on Twelfth Step calls; answering questions from the many new groups sprouting up about how to organize and conduct AA meetings; and continually sending out copies of the Big Book across the country.

Then came that awesome Sunday of December 7, 1941. The Japanese attacked Pearl Harbor. President Roosevelt responded immediately. The United States was now engulfed in World War II.

Bill tried to reenlist, but at forty-six, he was not accepted. So he and Lois followed the war intently from the home front. Bill charted the battlefronts with pushpins on maps on his office wall. And as AA continued to grow through the war years, Lois recalled that her husband was intent on keeping the program strong for those returning soldiers who, like himself, would develop a problem with alcohol while overseas.

While Bill was running frantic at his new office in the city, Lois was busy with renovations in Bedford Hills. Being a creative person, she had always enjoyed working with her hands. And since there was still no money to hire help, she set about scraping and staining the wooden floors and painting the walls, highlighting the tops of them with the design of fancy drapery swags—something she loved to show off to her guests.

Lois then cut and laid squares of linoleum on the kitchen floor, creating her own pattern. She made valances for the windows, being careful not to obstruct the lovely views of their gardens and nearby hills. Each night she would soak in the tub to soothe her sore knees and aching muscles, yet she felt proud and happy that the house was taking on a life of its own.[6]

With Bill commuting to the city and busy working on other AA materials when he was home, he didn't have much free time to help out with the remodeling chores. But there was one big job he had to tackle since it required a bit of muscle: "the waterworks."

There was a pumphouse down the hill that pushed the water from a spring all the way up to the tank under the porch and then through the pipes in the house. The trouble was, the pump was slow to get the water upstairs, where their bedroom and bathroom were. So Bill purchased a large, open cattle-feeder tank from Sears & Roebuck and put it in the attic, reinforcing the supports in that area to hold the weight. The pump then filled this tank periodically, and gravity supplied the house with water. The problem was, Bill never knew when to turn the pump on and when to turn it off.

However, now sober and filled with creative juices, Bill devised a contraption that would signal when the tank was filled or empty. He connected a bell to a float he placed in the tank. When the tank was filled, the bell would ring and a red light would go on in the kitchen.

The contraption performed even better than Bill had hoped for, that is until one disastrous weekend when some AA friends dropped by unannounced. They all decided to go out for dinner. Bill forgot to turn off his contraption.

While Lois and Bill were enjoying a fine meal with their friends, the tank filled and filled and filled—and then overflowed. Upon their return, they could hear the bell ringing and ringing and ringing. Inside the house they found Niagara Falls. The parlor furniture was soaked, the kitchen linoleum curled up, and the water stains in the upstairs room could be seen for years after regardless of how often the ceiling was painted.[7]

Once the inside of the house was livable, Lois turned her attention to her first love—the outdoors. It was almost summer now, so she put in flower beds everywhere and manicured the rosebushes and shrubbery that surrounded the house.

Lois also planted a vegetable garden, hoping to grow lettuce, tomatoes, and corn. While she and Bill loved to watch the rabbits, deer, and other animals prance around their property, it became less enjoyable once they began to chew up Lois's vegetables.

Bill's creative juices came to the rescue once more. He put a battery-charged wire fence around the garden and the constant static noise from the battery kept most of the animals at bay.[8]

To get back and forth to the Bedford Hills train station, Bill needed transportation. So he bought an old Stutz from an AA friend in the city who had no more use for it. The car ran well and only cost him thirty bucks. Fortunately, there was a small garage on their property, but it stood at the bottom of a steep hill, reached from the house by a flight of rugged stone steps. Because of the constant climbing up and down, Bill turned to his wife one day and suggested they call their home "Stepping

Stones." Lois smiled and quickly agreed, perhaps because she knew her husband was implying a connection to the Twelve Steps of the Fellowship. So that's how the home of Lois and Bill Wilson fondly became known to millions around the world as "Stepping Stones."[9]

For Lois, the years from 1941 to 1949—aside from some friends losing sons in the war—were filled with many happy events. Their home was constantly overflowing with AA members and their families as the Wilsons continued to share themselves and their good fortune with others. Lois began traveling with Bill to visit AA groups in other cities. She often met with other AA wives, some of whom had started small gatherings just as she and Annie had done. But many others had not. And even when she would attend such meetings, she found many to be simply "gossip sessions" or places for wives to vent their anger and resentment against their alcoholic husbands.

At times when Lois shared about her own "kitchen group," which was continuing to expand and start new meetings, and how these women like herself discovered they had to change along with their husbands, she often got blank stares or comments such as, "You just don't understand." She found such experiences disturbing and kept them in her mind—and in her heart.

Lois, like her dear friend and compatriot Annie Smith, had always felt a part of AA, perhaps because both played such a major role in the lives of the men who launched the movement. In fact, Dr. William Silkworth of Towns Hospital once said in his later years when questioned by an interviewer about the success of AA: "I doubt if there would be a Fellowship of Alcoholics Anonymous, no saving grace for thousands of men and women suffering from this malady, without the likes of Lois Wilson and Anne Smith. One should never underestimate the importance of the love and support they gave their husbands that enabled them to eventually come to grips with their disease and find a solution."[10] Maybe it was the commitment these two women felt for the AA program, together with their own personal experiences, that led them to comprehend alcoholism as a family disease. It was undoubtedly their continuous contact and intimate discussions that pulled them both through some extremely difficult times so they in turn might show other wives the ways they had found to better cope with life.

So when Annie took seriously ill in late May of 1949, Lois rushed to Akron to be at her side. While Annie had been in bad health for several years, which her smoking didn't help, she rarely worried about herself. Her main concern as always was Bob, who had been diagnosed with cancer only the year before. As this generous and loving woman lay in her hospital bed with a serious case of pneumonia, her only worry seemed to be that her husband would be left all alone. She made Bill and other close AA friends promise her they would always be around Bob and watch over him.

Her struggle with pneumonia led to a massive heart attack. Annie Smith died in St. Thomas Hospital in Akron on June 1, 1949, at the age of sixty-eight. Lois, like Annie's family and many friends, was devastated. At that moment, she wished the whole world had known the wonderful things her confidante had done for so many people. Lois was pleased when she saw the editorial that accompanied Annie's obituary in the *Akron Beacon Journal.* It read, "It seems a pity Mrs. Smith's wonderful work could not have received the public's recognition while she was still alive, but she must have known the gratitude in the hearts of many people she had helped. . . . Akron should always be proud of the AA movement which was born here and proud of the fine woman who did so much to foster that movement."[11]

Recalling his mother's passing, Bob Smith, Jr., said, "After being involved with drunks for a while, nothing could ever shock or surprise her anymore. Even though their ways might be foreign to her own upbringing, Mother was extremely tolerant of others. She just would not criticize. She always sought to excuse their actions.

"Her advice was never given on the spur of the moment to anyone, but was reserved until she had time to pray and think about the problem. As a result, her answer was given in a very loving, unselfish way to whoever was involved."[12]

While deeply saddened by Annie's passing, Lois never forgot nor would she let anyone else forget the vital role her dear friend played in the development of Al-Anon. She would always point to the love and caring Anne Smith showed not only to the spouses of alcoholics but to their children as well. Dr. Bob's wife recognized early on that alcoholism is a disease that affects the entire family and that there needed to be a program to help the entire family recover.[13]

Regarding her own many warm and wonderful memories of her departed friend, there was one that stood out above all the rest. It was Annie's surprise visit to Clinton Street shortly after Lois received the dispossession notice. Over the banana split they had at Schrafft's, Annie emphasized how important it was that they share their personal experience with the wives of other alcoholics no matter what kinds of problems they might be facing themselves. Sharing with others helped lessen one's problems.

"You and I discovered that by living with this disease, we got as sick as our husbands," she recalled Annie telling her again that night. "The problem is, not many wives realize that. That's why we have to help them."[14]

What Lois and Annie had found, and what Lois was now passing on to other spouses, was that they needed the same tools of recovery their husbands had been given in the AA Fellowship. Once they embraced this set of principles, both spiritual and practical, they too could change and find the serenity and happiness they sought.

But the Fellowship and the program that was to become Al-Anon was very slow in evolving. It did not have the sudden and dramatic genesis of Alcoholics Anonymous, when Bill and Dr. Bob met at Henrietta Seiberling's gatehouse and miraculously understood that they needed each other to stay sober . . . and stay alive. Nevertheless, its gradual but certain maturation was just as important in the lives of suffering spouses and their families. One of the reasons for its slow evolution was, perhaps, the lack of that same sheer desperation alcoholics feel when they reach the point where they must get sober or die—or at least escape the hell of the Bowery, a mental institution, or jail. Or then again, maybe it was the denial factor of many spouses who truly believed that the drinking wasn't their problem. It was their husband or their wife, and once they stopped, everything would be fine.

Even Lois and Annie had taken a long time to fully recognize the impact the disease of alcoholism had on their lives—how living with and coping with an active alcoholic had changed their attitudes, their thinking, their actions, their morality, their very character.

Long before Annie's death, Lois and Annie had talked frequently about wives of alcoholics needing more help and direction than they were getting, but neither was in a position to do anything about it at that time. Annie was in very poor health, and Lois was either homeless or working to make ends meet.

But now, just when Lois had everything in her life she ever really wanted—a sober and loving husband, a home of her own, gardens to tend, peace and serenity—her Higher Power was about to request that she give all that up, at least for a while, and be of service to Him once again. That is, if she were willing to accept His request.

It all began with Dr. Bob's death. Even though expected, it stunned the world of Alcoholics Anonymous and sent Bill into another depression. Fortunately, he had spent considerable time with his partner in sobriety during those final days of his terrible bout with cancer. They had both agreed they must get out of the driver's seat and turn the Fellowship over to its members. That the "Group conscience" should, as it had from the beginning, run the most democratic society man had ever created.

Certainly the board of trustees, which was now made up of both alcoholic and nonalcoholic members, would continue to suggest policy and direction, but the membership would always have the final say. On that Bill and Bob had finally come to total agreement.

Lois remembered the look on her husband's face the day they left Akron in early November of 1950, shortly before Bob passed away. Bill couldn't envision his life without his "anchor," as he always called his closest friend. But Bob assured him his spirit would never leave his side.

Dr. Robert Holbrook Smith died on November 16, 1950, just seventeen months after his wife's passing. The funeral service was conducted in the old Episcopal church by Rev. Walter Tunks, whose answer to a telephone call made by "a drunk from New York" fifteen years earlier had opened the way toward the formation of the worldwide Fellowship of Alcoholics Anonymous. Dr. Bob was buried without great fanfare in Mount Peace Cemetery next to his wife, Annie. There was no monument, only a simple headstone. However, every member of AA, then as now, would argue that the Fellowship was the greatest monument he could have ever wanted.

To shake his depression over his loving friend's passing, Bill decided to travel the country, visiting AA groups new and old, in major cities and country hamlets. He talked about Dr. Bob wherever he went, letting everyone know about the important contributions his friend and cofounder had given this burgeoning Fellowship of drunks. He also talked about the need to hold a General Services Conference for AA in order to officially turn over the work and responsibility of the movement to its members, alcoholic and nonalcoholic alike, as he and Bob had agreed.

Wherever he went, he also noticed that Family Groups were sprouting up all over, usually small gatherings of spouses—both men and women— and their families who were trying to learn more about the terrible malady that had wreaked havoc in their homes and on their children. But Bill also noticed that most of these groups had no program, no organization. They were simply doing their best under very confusing circumstances.

Lois believed it was better that Bill go off on his own this time, that he be alone with his old friends in the Fellowship while meeting new ones along the way. By immersing himself totally once again with his fellow drunks he might find some much-needed solace. And he did. He returned home not only renewed, but with another vision—the vision that the work his wife and Annie Smith had started must be carried on, not just across the country, but around the world, where AA was now bringing sobriety to many lands, but still leaving families behind.

Lois said that upon his return home, Bill was bubbling over with excitement about all the family groups he ran into around the country, gatherings of spouses and children looking for direction, for some way out of all the hurt and confusion the alcoholics brought into their lives.

That's when he turned to his wife and suggested she might want to do something about it since she and others were already meeting and finding some kind of answers for themselves. He thought perhaps that Lois could open a service office to provide a place for these groups to register and share experiences and advice.

At this time, however, Lois loved being at home and working in her gardens, enjoying the kind of life she had always dreamed of. Now her husband was asking her to give it all up and get back into the fray of alcoholism. She found his suggestion far from appealing so she didn't respond right away. But the one thing it did was keep her awake for the next few nights thinking about it.[15]

Lois later said she realized how selfish she was. The more she thought about the need, something she and Annie had always talked about, the more she realized it had to be done. Recognizing this would not be a one-woman job, Lois immediately reached out for her close friend Anne Bingham. Anne also lived in Westchester County and had continued to be active in the growing Family Group movement. She quickly said yes to her friend's request for help although neither of them had any idea how they would begin to tackle such a challenging task.

Like Lois, Anne was also born in Brooklyn. She was, by her own admission, a sickly child. She once said she had every known childhood disease all in one year, including diphtheria. Her sister died of heart disease when she was twelve, leaving Anne an only child. When she herself was eight, she contracted Saint Vitus's dance, a nervous disorder, and it was the family doctor who suggested a move to the country for the sake of the young girl's health.

Anne always regretted that she never had a close relationship with her mother and admitted that was probably the reason she married so young. She met Devoe Bingham at a Baptist Sunday school when she was seventeen and married him two years later. They had one daughter, who was named after her mother. Devoe, who was a few years older, owned his own filling station and sold and serviced high-priced foreign cars as well, until the outbreak of World War II.

According to Anne, her husband did not start drinking until he was thirty. Delayed at a business meeting one evening, he decided to stop at a bar to phone his wife, telling her he would be late for dinner. It was a chilly night so he thought a highball might warm him up. He never arrived home until the wee hours of the morning—totally ossified. Devoe Bingham's progression into alcoholism was rapid and severe. During Devoe's four trips to Towns Hospital and his several stabs at AA before finally getting sober, Anne turned constantly to Lois for support and consolation. Lois often said Anne helped her more than she helped her friend. Be that as it may, the two became very close, and when Lois and Bill moved to Bedford Hills, the foursome spent many an enjoyable Saturday evening together.

Bill chaired AA's first General Service Conference in New York in April of 1951. At the close of the two-day event, Lois invited the wives of the member delegates for lunch at Stepping Stones along with a number of local Family Group members Anne had gathered together. More than three dozen came. All but two or three of the delegate wives said they attended gatherings of alcoholic families in their hometowns and that almost every one was conducted differently, with no established format. By the time the ladies departed, Lois and Anne had a growing list of Family Groups nationwide. Many other Family Group names were given to them by Ruth Hock from her files at the Vesey Street central office of AA. They wound up with eighty-seven contacts in all. Some of the delegate wives invited Lois and Anne to visit their groups to see how the meetings were conducted. They accepted their invitations. As Lois and Anne traveled by train, bus, and car, they soon found that most of the wives they met desperately wanted a program to live by, one that could help them better understand the disease of alcoholism and what they might do to improve their own lives and the lives of their children.

Upon their return in early May, Lois set up the first Family Group service office on the second floor of Stepping Stones and rented a post office box, number 1475. She acted as the temporary chairperson and Anne as secretary, since she knew how to type and had her own typewriter. They sent off letters to the eighty-seven groups, expressing the resolve of many they had met that the Family Groups should be unified under one organizational umbrella with one program for all its members. The letter asked for approval to use AA's Twelve Steps for the program and that the currently amorphous organization be called AA Family Groups. The letter also suggested adoption of AA's policy of anonymity—the use of first names only on the public level.

In less than three weeks, forty-eight groups responded and an overwhelming proportion of them voted in favor of adopting AA's Twelve Steps as their "Guide for Living." As for a name, there was little consensus. Suggestions ranged from "AA Helpmates" to "Triple A" and from

"First Step AA" to "Non AA." It was a Family Group in California that suggested the name "Al-Anon," a contraction of the words "Alcoholics Anonymous." Lois and Anne extended it to "Al-Anon Family Groups" and the name was adopted unanimously. Al-Anon had now "officially" been born.[16]

By July of that year, only three months after the AA General Service Conference, the number of groups registered at the Stepping Stones service office had risen to one hundred and forty five. Leading among the states were New York with twenty—many of them offshoots of Lois's original "kitchen group"—California with sixteen, and Texas with thirteen. However, thirty-nine states were represented and, in addition to eleven groups flourishing in Canada, others were registered from as far away as Australia and South Africa. And they all had questions and requests for information starting from how to conduct their meetings to the need for a better understanding of how the Twelve Steps should be taken and put into their lives.

Lois quickly recognized the need for literature as a helpful Al-Anon tool. So Lois and Anne wrote a pamphlet, *Purposes and Suggestions for Al-Anon Family Groups*, which included the primary principle she and Annie Smith had always talked about—focus on oneself rather than the alcoholic. She went on to say in that first simple publication, "To insure the success of the Family Groups, there should be no gossip, no complaints about the alcoholic's faults at meetings. Newcomers can quickly make friends with older members with whom they will invariably feel free to discuss their personal difficulties privately."[17]

From the outset, Lois and Anne funded their small service office out of their own pocketbooks. But they knew that should the Fellowship begin to grow and with it the expenditures for phone calls, literature, and mailings, they would be needing additional funds—hopefully voluntary contributions. But just how would they go about asking for them?[18]

Then spontaneously, but hardly by coincidence, contributions began to trickle in from grateful members. According to Lois's detailed records, the first one came in on June 22, 1951, from a Sam K. of Lynn, Massachusetts. It was a check for ten dollars. Then others started flowing in, from Syracuse, New York; Montgomery, Alabama; and Yankton,

South Dakota. Before long, the cramped office on the second floor of Stepping Stones was out of the red and in need of larger quarters. More space was certainly necessary if Lois and Anne and their growing number of volunteers were to keep abreast of the constant deluge of phone calls, correspondence, and requests for information and literature. The Al-Anon movement was coming together, and Lois wanted to be sure it spoke and acted with one mind and one voice.

When word got out that the recently organized Fellowship of Al-Anon was looking for a new headquarters office in a more central location, Lois received a call from the New York AA group that managed the old Twenty-fourth Street Clubhouse. They offered her the upstairs room she and Bill once used as a parlor. It now served as a recreation room for members at night, but Al-Anon, she was told, could use it as an office during the day. There was even a closet where they could lock away any valuables.

Lois smiled at the irony of being invited back to a place that held some rather unpleasant memories for her. But then, it had been a roof over their heads and an office where Bill continued his work of building AA. Then she smiled again when she realized it was the last place they lived "on the road" before entering the paradise of Stepping Stones—and for that she would be forever grateful.[19]

So, after thinking it over and learning the rent would be very low, Lois and Anne decided to make the move. They packed up the typewriter, a two-drawer filing cabinet, several boxes of stationery, and the little black book in which they kept the Fellowship's financial accounts, loaded it all in Anne's car, and headed down to New York City, where a small band of volunteers awaited their arrival. It was January 9, 1952, and Al-Anon had a new home.

"We could feel the excitement of all that was happening," Lois once shared with a close friend, "the sense that Al-Anon was beginning to reach out and touch many, many people across the country, and we were part of it. While our new headquarters would only be one room at the old clubhouse, it symbolized for us the growth that was taking place."[20]

Because of all the correspondence and literature moving in and out of the office, the cofounders decided to call it the Al-Anon Clearing

House. More than two hundred Family Groups were registered by now, so any and all volunteers were welcome to handle the workload.

Since the vast majority of Al-Anon members at that time were women, so were the volunteers. And they came from all over. Irma F., Dot L., and Sue L. from Westchester were the first. They were joined by Mag V., Eleanor A., and Jean B. from New Jersey and Evelyn C., Vi F., and Henrietta S. from Long Island. And as the overhead, the cost of mailings, and other expenses rose, the tiny band asked the growing number of groups to voluntarily support the Clearing House by donating one dollar per member semiannually. The contributions from grateful members surpassed the request.

Fifty years ago there was very little known about the disease of alcoholism, so many wanted to understand how they could tell if their spouse was an alcoholic or merely a heavy, willful drinker. One of the questions Lois was often asked, both over the phone and in letters, was, "How can I tell if my husband is a real alcoholic?"[21] Initially, even though she still bore the disappointment of not writing the chapter herself in AA's Big Book titled "To Wives," she urged her inquirers to read it. At times when the pleas seemed urgent or she sensed someone could not afford to purchase a Big Book, she sent them mimeographed copies of the two pages most pertinent to the subject at hand. They read:

> The problem with which you struggle usually falls within one of four categories:
>
> *One:* Your husband may be only a heavy drinker. His drinking may be constant or it may be heavy only on certain occasions. Perhaps he spends too much money for liquor. It may be slowing him up mentally and physically, but he does not see it. Sometimes he is a source of embarrassment to you and his friends. He is positive he can handle his liquor, that it does him no harm, that drinking is necessary in his business. He would probably be insulted if he were called an alcoholic. This world is full of people like him. Some will moderate or stop altogether, and some will not. Of those who keep on, a good

number will become true alcoholics after a while.

Two: Your husband is showing lack of control, for he is unable to stay on the water wagon even when he wants to. He often gets entirely out of hand when drinking. He admits this is true, but is positive that he will do better. He has begun to try, with or without your cooperation, various means of moderating or staying dry. Maybe he is beginning to lose his friends. His business may suffer somewhat. He is worried at times, and is becoming aware that he cannot drink like other people. He sometimes drinks in the morning and through the day also, to hold his nervousness in check. He is remorseful after serious drinking bouts and tells you he wants to stop. But when he gets over the spree, he begins to think once more how he can drink moderately next time. We think this person is in danger. These are the earmarks of a real alcoholic. Perhaps he can still tend to business fairly well. He has by no means ruined everything. As we say among ourselves, "*He wants to want to stop.*"

Three: This husband has gone much further than husband number two. Though once like number two he became worse. His friends have slipped away, his home is a near-wreck and he cannot hold a position. Maybe the doctor has been called in, and the weary round of sanitariums and hospitals has begun. He admits he cannot drink like other people, but does not see why. He clings to the notion that he will yet find a way to do so. He may have come to the point where he desperately wants to stop but cannot. His case presents additional questions which we shall try to answer for you. You can be quite hopeful of a situation like this.

Four: You may have a husband of whom you completely despair. He has been placed in one institution after another. He is violent, or appears definitely insane when drunk. Sometimes he drinks on the way home from the hospital. Perhaps he has had delirium tremens. Doctors may shake their heads and advise you to have him committed. Maybe you have already been obliged to put him away. This picture may not be as dark as it looks. Many of our husbands were just as far gone. Yet they got well.[22]

While this chapter in the Big Book went on to offer some general suggestions to wives on handling their particular situations, Lois and Anne both felt, based upon their own personal experiences, that most of these women needed much more specific advice and guidance. So they put together another pamphlet, *So You Love an Alcoholic*, adapted from a leaflet from the Texas Commission on Alcoholism. It offered suggestions such as "Detaching with love" and "Say what you mean and mean what you say." It pointed out that even when one tried to live by the principles of Al-Anon, coping with alcoholic behavior could often make one seethe with anger and resentment. The cofounders emphasized that while such emotions rarely affected the inebriate, they did considerable mental and physical harm to the spouse. So, they added, one must learn to work on and eliminate such rage whenever possible, for one's own sake.

As more questions, comments, and suggestions poured into the Clearing House, along with notes from members sharing their own personal stories, Lois decided a monthly newsletter would be the best way to communicate regularly with the rapidly expanding movement, which, by the end of 1953, exceeded five hundred groups.

A typical day found Anne busy typing at her desk, other women sorting the mail or packaging literature at tables lining the one-room office, and Lois seated in a corner by herself with a yellow pad in her lap, drafting another issue. It would contain responses to inquiries, news about Family Group happenings, and edited versions of the personal experiences sent in by members. This *Family Group Newsletter* eventually became Al-Anon's magazine, *The Forum*, which today disseminates information and sharings to thousands of groups worldwide.

In 1952, many of these groups still adhered to some of their old ways of doing things. Some, for example, refused to allow men or children at meetings. Others felt Al-Anon was strictly for spouses and no other relatives. And still others brought religion, psychiatry, medicine, and politics into their discussions, which often drove other members away.

Recognizing the problems and the need for unity, Lois decided to do exactly what her husband had done to solve similar situations in Alcoholics Anonymous. He had put together a list of suggested principles for all AA groups to follow called "The Twelve Traditions." While it took some time, they were finally approved by the membership and created the strong unity in the Fellowship that exists to this day.

Lois consulted closely with Anne and some of their trusted volunteers before penning a specific list of principles, which was then sent out to all Family Groups for their consideration. Most members responded positively. Over time and after some minor squabbling and nitpicking by some of the older groups, Al-Anon's Twelve Traditions were finally and unanimously approved. They read as follows:

1. Our common welfare should come first; personal progress for the greatest number depends upon unity.

2. For our group purpose there is but one authority—a loving God as He may express Himself in our group conscience. Our leaders are but trusted servants—they do not govern.

3. The relatives of alcoholics, when gathered together for mutual aid, may call themselves an Al-Anon Family Group, provided that, as a group, they have no other affiliation. The only requirement for membership is that there be a problem of alcoholism in a relative or friend.

4. Each group should be autonomous, except in matters affecting another group or Al-Anon or AA as a whole.

5. Each Al-Anon Family Group has but one purpose: to help families of alcoholics. We do this by practicing the Twelve Steps of AA *ourselves*, by encouraging and understanding our alcoholic relatives, and by welcoming and giving comfort to families of alcoholics.

6. Our Family Groups ought never endorse, finance or lend our

name to any outside enterprise, lest problems of money, property and prestige divert us from our primary spiritual aim. Although a separate entity, we should always co-operate with Alcoholics Anonymous.

7. Every group ought to be fully self-supporting, declining outside contributions.

8. Al-Anon Twelfth Step work should remain forever non-professional, but our service centers may employ special workers.

9. Our groups, as such, ought never be organized; but we may create service boards or committees directly responsible to those they serve.

10. The Al-Anon Family Groups have no opinion on outside issues; hence our name ought never be drawn into public controversy.

11. Our public relations policy is based on attraction rather than promotion; we need always maintain personal anonymity at the level of press, radio, films, and TV. We need guard with special care the anonymity of all AA members.

12. Anonymity is the spiritual foundation of all our Traditions, ever reminding us to place principles above personalities.[23]

Fortunately, the Al-Anon newsletter helped to communicate these principles on a constant basis and thus enabled the Traditions to foster unity throughout the Fellowship—at the local, national, and international level as well.

One morning, while Lois was on the train from Bedford Hills into New York City, a picture jumped off the society page of the newspaper she was reading. It showed her old friend Elise Shaw's youngest daughter coming out of St. John the Divine Church in Manhattan after marrying the son of wealthy New York socialites. She stared at the beautiful young bride as her mind tumbled back to her own wedding day when her then closest friend, Elise, was her maid of honor. Where had all the years gone? And what of those terribly divisive and confusing days that drove these two friends apart?

Lois had put it all out of her mind. During the long and painful ordeal of Bill's drinking and the perplexities that initially followed his recovery, it had all been washed from her memory. It wasn't until 1954, on that train ride to Manhattan, that Lois allowed herself to recall Elise's painful revelation twenty-five years earlier.

Now, as those remembrances flashed back, Lois thought it strange that her recollection of Elise helping to thwart her attempt to adopt a child no longer caused her pain. Sadness and disappointment, yes, but not the deep, bewildering anger and resentment that Lois had often used to fire up her old self-pity whenever she was running out of better excuses.

Seeing that picture of Elise's daughter may have prompted Lois to think about her own role in the hurtful break in their relationship. For Lois had to admit she never really tried to understand Elise's reaction to Bill's drinking. Only now, after all these years of suffering through it herself, did she finally realize how her husband's drunken behavior must have brought back so many onerous memories of Elise's childhood in an alcoholic home. Perhaps if they had talked more about it . . . although how could Elise possibly get through to someone who was in such denial? How many times did she attempt to discuss Bill's growing problem only to be quickly and totally turned off, dismissed for even raising such an embarrassing subject? Lois had been absolutely closed-minded, even with a loving and caring friend. How it must have hurt Elise when she could do nothing to help.

Lois had been trying her best for a long time to live according to AA's Twelve Steps. Now here she was faced once again with Steps Eight and Nine.

> Eight: Made a list of all persons we had harmed, and became willing to make amends to them all.
> Nine: Made direct amends to such people wherever possible, except when to do so would injure them or others.[24]

More than twenty years had passed. Certainly Lois was right in feeling that Elise had hurt her deeply, had taken away any chance she might have had to have a family of her own. But now she knew that raising a child under such conditions would have been wrong. She also knew she had harmed her best friend by her anger, her insensitivity, and her self-righteousness. It was time that she cleaned off her own side of the street. So she found Elise Shaw's phone number, called, and made an appointment to have lunch with her in the city.

Their meeting was awkward and uncomfortable at first. Then, after they caught up on news, it became almost pleasant. Elise had heard much about AA and was filled with praise for the good work Bill was doing. She said she knew her father would have been proud of him although, in all honesty, she herself thought Bill would amount to nothing and die a horrible death from drinking. Lois confessed that toward the end, she had felt the same way.

Elise appeared embarrassed at first that she knew nothing about Al-Anon. But, as she listened to Lois talk about it, one could see in her face she completely understood the great benefits such a program could bring to the families of alcoholics. "If only it were around in my day," she said rather sadly.[25]

Lois waited until they had finished eating before expressing her apologies to her old friend for the way she reacted. She wanted to thank her for her honest concern about Bill's drinking and the many attempts she made to help. Elise appeared shocked. She quickly interrupted to say she was the one who should be apologizing. After all, what she did was very cruel, even though she truly believed it was the right thing to do at the time.

Lois reached out and touched Elise's hand. She explained that she had finally come to realize that not being able to bear children or adopt a baby was all part of God's plan. That she had come to accept His will. Had they been blessed with a family, Bill would not have been able to devote all his energies into creating and building the Fellowship of Alcoholics Anonymous, nor could she have dedicated herself to the problems of the wives and families of alcoholics through Al-Anon.

Elise Shaw understood. One could see it in her eyes. After lunch, they walked back outside to her chauffeur-driven limousine. She offered Lois a ride downtown but her friend said the subway was faster. They hugged briefly and promised to have lunch again soon.

These two women who had grown up and spent their formative years together would never really be close again. Their lives had gone in very different directions. But the wounds had healed and the amends had been made. Lois Wilson went back to the old Twenty-fourth Street Clubhouse feeling comfortable inside, knowing that the program of Al-Anon really works—if you "work it."[26]

15

A Heart Attack Can
Be Good for the Soul

❦

HARRIET SEVARINO MADE THE BEST SOUTHERN FRIED CHICKEN in Westchester County. At least that was Lois's declaration the day she and Anne Bingham stopped for a bite of lunch at Harriet's roadside café in Golden's Bridge, near Bedford Hills. It was a special treat since she only made it twice a week, along with homemade mashed potatoes and coffee Jell-O. On other days the main staples were simply hamburgers, hot dogs, and french fries.

Lois had heard about Harriet's specialty from Ruth and Wilbur and decided to drop by the sweet, olive-skinned lady's place for two reasons. First, Lois loved Southern fried chicken and mashed potatoes, and second, she understood the hardworking mother of four was thinking about closing the local eatery and finding other means of contributing to the family's slim income.

Recalling that day much later, Harriet remarked with a warm smile, "She really loved my chicken. She even had a second helping. If I had more customers like her, I would have done all right. But one reason I wasn't making any money was because my children would always come by with their friends and eat me out of house and home without contributing a red cent. Also, we really needed more room in the place for more paying customers and we just didn't have the money to expand."[1]

Lois's life was now almost totally dedicated to Al-Anon, with most of her days spent helping wives and families recover from the disease of alcoholism. As a result, she had less time to cook, clean, and keep up the country house and grounds at Stepping Stones—much as she loved that part of her life. She needed help.

Since Bill's royalty income from the Big Book was gradually increasing, they both agreed they could afford to hire someone to help with the chores and some of the meals, at least one or two days a week. So that's what Lois discussed with Harriet Sevarino that day at her roadside café while munching on the best fried chicken she could remember ever tasting. Harriet accepted the offer to work part-time at Stepping Stones, planning to keep her restaurant open on weekends and make a profit by serving paying customers only, she hoped.

Lois's relationship with this kind and giving woman would last more than thirty-five years. Harriet became far more than a housekeeper and cook; she was a trusted friend and helpmate. Over the years, Lois came to rely on her as a traveling companion, a party-giver, a shopping confidante, and later, as a tender nurturer when she became elderly and ill.

When Lois and Bill could afford it, Harriet began working full-time at Stepping Stones and finally had to close her restaurant for good. It was a bit of a disappointment but, as she explained, she came to enjoy being around Lois and Bill, meeting their many AA and Al-Anon friends, and hearing about all their wonderful projects.

"I remember when Mr. Wilson would be home," Harriet recalled. "He and Lois would sit together on the couch and he would thank her for helping the wives and families of so many alcoholics. Then she would thank him for finally getting her such a lovely home. Then they would both thank me for working so hard, but particularly for my coffee Jell-O, which they both really loved."[2]

But life was not always so lovey-dovey at the Wilson household, their longtime housekeeper revealed. There were times when Lois got very upset over her husband's frequent absences, his constant traveling, or his failed promises to be home from town early for dinner.

"I remember several times how she lost her temper real bad," Harriet confided. "In fact, one evening she started throwing pots and pans at Mr. Wilson until he finally ran out the door and took a long walk. But before I left, I would see them making up and I could tell by the way Lois would look at me that she was ashamed for the way she acted."

Here once again Lois tried her best to work the program of Al-Anon in her life. After such outbursts, she would use the Tenth Step not only with her husband, but also with Harriet. The Tenth Step read:

"Continued to take personal inventory and when we were wrong promptly admitted it."[3]

Harriet smiled warmly once more as she explained:

"Lois would write me letters apologizing for her behavior, for losing her temper like that and getting me upset as well as Mr. Wilson. I guess I have four or five letters like that. But after a while they stopped coming because, well, to tell you the truth, she didn't lose her temper as much anymore."[4]

While Lois's impatience at times caused her grief, she was particularly upset by what it did to Bill and how it affected their relationship. He would simply get up and leave the house and take long walks. But sometimes his lack of attention to details, his forgetting to let her know when he wouldn't be home for dinner and his failure to put his dirty socks in the hamper would simply try her patience to no end and the outbursts would come. Lois worked harder and harder on accepting the things she couldn't change—her husband, for example. As a result, their spats became fewer and fewer.[5]

Another warm and caring lady, who would eventually become Lois's most intimate friend and companion, also entered her life about this same time. Nell Wing had joined the staff at AA's General Service Office in March of 1947 as a typist, and five years later was Bill's personal secretary and administrative assistant.

"Nell was just about the most generous and thoughtful person I ever knew," Lois said of the woman who became "the daughter I never had."[6]

Lois remembered that the AA Fellowship had only recently moved out of Vesey Street and into larger quarters at 415 Lexington Avenue when Nell first arrived, fresh out of the SPARS—the female arm of the

United States Coast Guard. A native of West Kendall, New York, a small upstate town near the shores of Lake Ontario, and the daughter of the local justice of the peace, she found the work at AA's central office "absolutely fascinating."

Alcoholics Anonymous was not quite twelve years old at the time and Nell was not quite thirty. She said it was such a privilege to watch it grow and help so many millions of people over the seventeen years she worked for Bill before becoming the archives director for AA. And then to watch Al-Anon do the same over the thirty-four years she knew and was close to Lois made her so grateful for just being there.[7]

Nell Wing came to consider Lois and Bill Wilson her family, and they felt the same about her. In 1954, she began going up to Stepping Stones an average of every third weekend because Bill preferred to work there. He and some of his AA buddies had built a small studio on a hill just above the house where he would write and meditate. Nell would take dictation and then type up his notes for the book or pamphlet he was working on at the time.

She became close friends with Lois, getting to know her more and more as they spent time together. After working on Saturdays, the three of them would take long walks.

In the evenings after dinner, they would have music—Bill playing the violin or cello and Lois or Nell accompanying him on the piano. Stepping Stones in time became Nell's second home, and Bill and Lois were her family, closer really than her real parents, as she relied on them for advice and counsel in her occasional "affairs of the heart" and any problems as they occurred.[8]

Nell noted that music always remained an important part of Lois's life. When home, Lois usually tuned the radio to WQXR, New York City's classical music station, Nell said. But she enjoyed popular music as well and could play many old tunes on the piano. Often, after Harriet had provided a special meal and a really scrumptious dessert, Bill would say to Lois: "How about playing some of those old chestnuts?"

Lois would sit down at the piano, Nell explained, recalling those lovely "family" moments. Bill would pick up his violin and they would get right into favorites like "Home Sweet Home," "Roamin in the

Gloamin," "Seeing Nellie Home," "The Wearing of the Green," and "It's a Long Way to Tipperary" from his war years.[9]

Nell pointed out that Lois and Bill were also both great walkers. When they first moved to Bedford Hills, they were practically the only people in the area, so they created their own walking trails, up and down the gently rolling hillsides. As time passed, and more people moved in, the Wilsons had the foresight to invest their growing income in the purchase of eight more acres of the surrounding countryside. So, even when the area became more populated, they managed to keep portions of their original trails intact.

While Lois loved the fall, Nell noted that Lois was also very fond of the spring season when she could view close up the tiniest baby leaves emerging on the trees and bushes of her gardens and sprawling lawns—the pink and white buds of the magnolias and the dogwoods.

"On those chilly days in late March," Nell recalled, "we would walk all around the property, always with the same sense of awe at the annual, mysterious unfolding of mother nature's fresh young season. We would inventory the winter's damage and clean out the debris.

"In the fall, when the air was soft and mellow, Lois and I would drink in the beauty of the autumn colors and would pick huge white and purple hydrangeas for the house—and some for me to take back to my New York apartment. I've learned so much from Lois—she was especially in harmony with her environment. She knew the names of all the trees, plants, and birds—birdfeeders all around the place. It was a constant battle of wits with the squirrels and usually the squirrels won."[10]

Remembering her many walks with Lois and Bill, Nell spoke of one particularly poignant moment toward the latter years of Bill's life. He had been ill but was recovering and having one of his good days. "The three of us started on a walk, deciding to try out a new, hilly road. At one point, Lois and I stopped to examine an unfamiliar species of flower. As Lois was telling me about it, I turned to see Bill walking on ahead of us, trudging along the upgrade, hands clasped behind his back, leaning forward as he always did.

"As his figure became smaller in the distance, I experienced a sudden but not unexpected premonition that this was to be the last walk the three of us would take together—which it was. I saw in that vision that Bill was literally and symbolically much ahead of us, while Lois and I were still attached to the things of this world, so to speak—to the roadside flowers and plants and nature. A moment later, Bill moved out of our sight."[11]

With Harriet now lightening Lois's cooking and household chores and Nell lending a hand with manicuring the outdoor floriculture, Lois felt both relieved and bolstered to carry on her Al-Anon responsibilities with Anne Bingham at her side.

Lois once wrote that, outside of New York and California, Al-Anon had expanded most rapidly in those days in Akron and Cleveland, Ohio, thanks to the seeds planted by Annie Smith. But Lois had another lifelong comrade too, who played a major role in carrying the message of Al-Anon to wives and families. Her name was Sister Mary Ignatia Gavin, a member of the Sisters of Charity of St. Augustine.

Lois had first met Sister Ignatia in 1935 during her trip to Akron shortly after Bill and Bob began their journey together to create a Fellowship for drunks. At the time, the diminutive Catholic nun with a giant-sized heart was working with Dr. Bob at St. Thomas Hospital and had been concerned about his drinking problem for years. Once she came to see the "miraculous" work her colleague and this "mug from New York" were doing with alcoholics, she immediately joined their crusade. In fact, among the medical community in both Akron and Cleveland, she led the parade, quickly setting up a special ward at St. Thomas for the treatment of alcoholic patients. By the time Al-Anon was officially launched, Sister Ignatia had moved to St. Vincent Charity Hospital in Cleveland where she had set up Rosary Hall, a special wing for recovering alcoholic men and women, with the close cooperation of local AA groups.[12]

"Sister used to interview the wives of the alcoholics in Rosary Hall," said Edna G., longtime Al-Anon member, of this dedicated nun who became known to many in both Fellowships as "the Angel of Alcoholics Anonymous." "She said that she didn't know who was more mixed-up, the alcoholic or the nonalcoholic. That was when she realized that we were sick too and needed help."[13] Sister Ignatia started an Al-Anon group at Rosary Hall that became the largest Family Group in the area.

Sister Ignatia is revered to this day in AA and Al-Anon circles for her work to hospitalize and treat inebriates as sick people at a time when alcoholism was seen as a weakness of character, rather than a disease. Both at St. Thomas Hospital and Rosary Hall, she carried on her crusade to help them become functioning and productive citizens once again. Before her death, she was recognized by President John F. Kennedy for her pioneering contributions in the field of alcoholism.

"Sister Ignatia," noted Lois, "always encouraged the wives of alcoholics who came to Rosary Hall to start Al-Anon groups in their own neighborhoods. By 1955, there were more than one hundred Family Groups in Cleveland and the surrounding area."[14]

In 1962, Lois printed in her Al-Anon newsletter a letter from one of the early Cleveland members. As timely now as it was then, the letter read:

> *When I first came to Al-Anon, I was 41 years old and the majority of women were also around that age. In the beginning, we had all women members, most of whom had spouses who were either in Rosary Hall or had recently gone through Rosary Hall. It seems to me that the problems today are somewhat different from the early days of Al-Anon. Women today are working and are more independent. They are also younger. They are not as willing to keep the family together if the spouse continues to drink. There are many more divorces, but fortunately, some of the divorcees continue to come to Al-Anon.*
>
> *I do think that Al-Anons today talk more freely and express their feelings more openly. Such openness was very hard for me and is sometimes difficult even today. Some of the things we discuss today are things we never could have been open about thirty years ago.*[15]

Lois's reply to this letter was simple and direct and came from her own personal experience. She wrote:

Alcoholism is an illness. It is like having diabetes or cancer or heart disease, not a moral problem or a weakness of the will. If we come to truly understand and believe this, why then shouldn't we be willing to help and encourage someone we say we love to find recovery from this terrible malady before giving up too quickly. We must also remember that the rewards for doing this, for bearing up under such a burden, can truly be great.[16]

Then, after suggesting that wives and families of alcoholics not only put their faith in Al-Anon but in AA as well, Lois went on to quote a Big Book passage written by Dr. William Silkworth at Bill's request. The doctor said:

The message which can interest and hold these alcoholic people must have depth and weight. In nearly all cases, their ideals must be grounded in a power greater than themselves, if they are to re-create their lives.

If any feel that as psychiatrists directing a hospital for alcoholics we appear somewhat sentimental, let them stand with us a while on the firing line, see the tragedies, the despairing wives, the little children; let the solving of these problems become a part of their daily work, and even of their sleeping moments, and the most cynical will not wonder that we have accepted and encouraged this movement. We feel, after many years of experience, that we have found nothing which has contributed more to the rehabilitation of these men than the altruistic movement now growing up among them.[17]

This reply by Lois, meant for all members of Al-Anon, once again underscored her belief that they should become avid readers of AA's Big Book since it spelled out the very program they themselves had supposedly come to live by.

Inevitably, the Clearing House outgrew the small space at the old clubhouse and moved to much larger quarters at 125 East Twenty-third Street, eventually taking over a second floor in that building as well. By this time, Margaret D., one of the young movement's earliest volunteers, had started working with Lois on the newsletter, choosing comments and news items from their mail to pass on to their rapidly growing list of member groups. Lois once described Margaret, who lived with her husband, Jack, in Yonkers, as the jolliest and most colorful of the original "pioneers," as she called those early workers.

"Margaret would bring in sandwiches for the small group of us for lunch," Lois recalled with a smile. "Then Anne or I would boil some water on a hot plate for tea or we'd make a small pot of coffee and sit around and have an informal Al-Anon meeting. Margaret would stick a cigarette into her long, gold cigarette holder and regale us with hilarious stories about her poor husband Jack. Then others would chime in with more funny stories about their husbands. As hard as we tried not to talk about our spouses, I think that finally being able to laugh at the past, at least some parts of it, helped us all get well again."[18]

While Lois and Anne's volunteer corps was growing, there was still much pressure on Lois to oversee their efforts, to discuss and plan the future needs of Al-Anon, from literature to conferences, and to guide its internal affairs, from organizational squabbles to enforcing the Traditions. All of this, together with her traveling and handling the chores at Stepping Stones when Harriet wasn't there, began to wear on Lois's health. She was now sixty-two, and even Bill was suggesting that she slow down just a bit.

It was January 23, 1954, and it had snowed quite heavily in Bedford Hills. Lois spent several hours that day shoveling their long driveway since Bill was in the city at Foundation meetings. She was to meet him there the following day to celebrate their thirty-sixth wedding anniversary. After all her shoveling she felt extremely tired, so she went to bed early that night.

The next morning she was still not feeling well, but nothing could keep her from their anniversary celebration. She left early for the city to do some shopping and to pick up the gift she had ordered for her husband, who was at the Bedford Hotel, where they planned to meet.

Lois was just leaving the store when it happened. She felt a sharp pain in her chest. She stopped for a moment and caught her breath, and the pain eased. She saw a movie theater down the street and thought seeing a good flick might relax her. However, only moments after she was seated, the pain started again. This time it was worse and it frightened her. She took a taxi to Bill's hotel. By the time she arrived, she could hardly walk through the lobby. Bill panicked when he saw Lois's condition. He immediately phoned Leonard Strong, and then rushed Lois to New York Hospital where a top heart specialist was waiting to treat her.[19]

In his wedding anniversary card to his wife, written before he knew of her heart attack, Bill's prophetic message was: "Come any peril, we know that we are safe in each other's arms because we are in God's."[20]

After some time in the hospital, Lois came home to Stepping Stones. Since the heart attack was a serious one, the doctors insisted she rest for several months and do no strenuous work for at least a year. For someone who had always been very active, this was difficult. But Bill took a long sabbatical from his AA affairs to make sure his wife did exactly what the doctors ordered.

And she did just that, spending time enjoying some books she had always wanted to read and watching many colorful birds that would pay brief visits to her windowsill.[21] Lois later said that most of all, the time off gave her a chance to be with Bill again, to be close to him and spend time talking about things they had just let drift by in their constant busyness.

One afternoon as they sat together looking through the window at the rolling hills surrounding their home, Lois remembered her husband squeezing her hand and pleading with her to do everything the doctors asked. Then he smiled and said: "After all I've put you through, I need you to stay around a while longer so I have time to make it all up to you."[22] That's when something became suddenly clear, Lois said, something she had finally come to realize after all these years. They had both taken such long journeys to find what they had both been looking for—a program, a way of life that had brought them back to each other in a way she had always hoped for, had always dreamed. For today they both loved each other unconditionally, and she knew in her heart—a heart that would soon be well again—that this love, this bond would last forever so long as Bill remained sober.

"I know it may sound kind of silly," Lois once shared with a close friend, "But I believe that a heart attack can sometimes be good for the soul. I know in my case it was. It helped me to realize again just how fragile life is, just how fleeting. There were no more days to be wasted. I had to focus on what was really important, like how dear Bill was to me and how much God had given us both through this terrible disease of alcoholism and this wonderful gift of recovery."[23]

Harriet was also there at Stepping Stones to help nurse Lois back to health. In fact, she stayed at the house for several weeks in order to be at Lois and Bill's beck and call.

"I had never stayed over at the house before that," Harriet said, remembering her shock at seeing her usually energetic friend so pale and weak upon her return from the hospital. "After I got her and Mr. Wilson off to bed that night, I found I couldn't go to sleep myself. As I lay there in the dark listening to that old house creak and whistle in the wind, I thought I'd be seeing ghosts. I had all I could do to make it through those two weeks."[24]

Lois laughed when Harriet told her the story and said she offered to move her bed in next to Harriet's to calm her down.

Lois wrote in her memoirs that Harriet was an absolute blessing. "Her loyalty, devotion and responsibility are outstanding, and it was a lucky day indeed when she came to us. She is my memory and checker-upper. I trust, need and love her."[25]

As soon as Lois had gained some strength, she began urging Bill to take her to Vermont. It was already May and the maple trees would be blooming and the wildflowers would be breaking through their green buds. While the Burnham cottage on Emerald Lake was no longer theirs, they could stay at the nostalgic Wilson House in East Dorset and visit with some old friends. Her doctors had recommended walking, and Lois promised to behave and not do anything too strenuous. So, Bill finally gave in and off they went.

Lois was never happier than the times she spent in Vermont and now that she was getting healthy again, her joy knew no bounds.

During the month she and Bill were there, walking through the woods and down the back roads, the sights and sounds brought back memories of their youth. They watched lizards slithering across fallen trees, frogs hopping into green ponds, and squirrels trying to transport large acorns across narrow tree limbs.[26] Lois's memoirs convey her happiness at this time. Perhaps just being there brought back her delightful "tomboy" days at the lake, those growing-up adventures, and her young womanhood when she met and fell desperately in love with the man of her dreams—who was now holding her hand once again as they traipsed through the countryside.

By the time they returned to Stepping Stones, she said, the flowers had blossomed, the lawns had turned green and the deer were once again nibbling on the small trees growing along the hillside. She said she felt refreshed and ready to go back to work even though Bill and the doctors told her it was still not the time.

Perhaps to celebrate her recovery, Lois decided to have a picnic upon her return home that June. Without hesitation, she invited every Al-Anon group in the country. She even suggested that Bill ask a large group of his AA friends. Lois would provide some refreshments, and her guests would bring picnic baskets. Harriet decided to cook up a large batch of Southern fried chicken specially for those who couldn't afford much more than a bus ticket or train fare to Bedford Hills. With bright sunshine and not a cloud in the sky, the picnic attracted a large crowd from the local area and a number of surrounding states. It turned into a beautiful day of sharing about the transformations in the lives of those gathered on the sprawling lawns of Stepping Stones. And it started a tradition that continues to this day—the Annual Stepping Stones Family Picnic for Al-Anons, AA's, and Alateens alike on the first Saturday of June.

The Al-Anon Clearing House was well ensconced in its new headquarters on Twenty-third Street by the time Lois arrived back. She was proud of the way Anne, Margaret D., and the others had kept things humming. But it wasn't long after her return that they all concluded there was much more to be done in terms of providing greater guidance and organization to the movement, which was now growing by leaps and bounds along with AA. Lois wrote in an Al-Anon newsletter:

*In the early days of Al-Anon we felt we should learn as much as possible about alcoholism, so we could help our mates. But again by degrees the emphasis began to shift toward detachment-*with-love *from the alcoholic. The idea was not only that the latter could not learn from mistakes if nursed and protected, but that the nonalcoholic should strive for spiritual development first and foremost. No one can directly change anyone but oneself.*

*However, detachment-*with-love *does not exclude knowledge about alcoholism, and such knowledge can be helpful as long as the spouse does detach with love. But the idea of "detachment" can be misunderstood and overemphasized. "With-love" is the important part of this idea. True love does what is believed to be best for the person loved, not what is easiest at the moment. Spoiling and pampering do not spring from love, but from lack of knowledge or from lack of discipline in the "spoiler." This is where many of us made our mistakes. For example, in protecting the one I loved from the consequences of his own actions, I was not helping Bill.*

Most people come to Al-Anon meetings to get the alcoholic in their lives sober and are shocked to learn they themselves need to change. It is sometimes harder for them to recognize that they are part of the problem than it is for drinkers to admit their own alcoholism.

The fundamentals of our program can be learned from our general literature. However, we soon realized that for people in certain relationships, such as male spouses, parents and children of alcoholics, specific literature would be helpful, and we started preparing it. The male spouse was often reluctant to join a group of females, so in addition to literature for men, stag groups evolved.[27]

At the Clearing House, Lois and Anne and their colleagues had been particularly concerned for some time about the special needs of the children of alcoholics, both early adolescents and teenagers. Many of these children had been coming to Family Group meetings from the very beginning, both at Annie Smith's home in Akron and in Lois's kitchen at Clinton Street. They came mainly because their mothers could not afford babysitters or did not want to leave their offspring home alone with a drunken father, especially an abusive one.

But as the Al-Anon program evolved and the sharing at meetings became more intimate, many women started to feel uncomfortable with children around, even their own. So they found another room for them to draw, play games, or simply talk among themselves. What these young people really needed was a program of their own, since many of them had also been severely affected by the disease and its consequences.

In 1958, Lois and her staff voted to appoint a devoted member and mother, Wanda R., to chair a committee to develop such a program. She and her volunteers wasted no time in gathering information from Family Groups across the country and meeting with many for their input. Soon her committee came up with the name Alateen, which was agreed upon. Then, with the approval of all the groups across the country, Al-Anon's basic program book, *Living with an Alcoholic*, was revised to include a chapter on the new Alateen program. It consisted of the same basic Twelve Steps and recommended that all Alateen groups have an Al-Anon sponsor to guide them, an individual who already was practicing the Twelve Step program of Al-Anon in his or her life.

In 1960, at the AA International Convention in Long Beach, California, workshops were held for the first time especially for these younger children of alcoholics, now members of Alateen, which had quickly grown to more than one hundred groups. AA and Al-Anon attendees were thrilled by these Alateen sessions and reported that the young people seemed to have grasped the program with more understanding and enthusiasm than they themselves had.

An article in the Sunday newspaper supplement *Parade* was the first publicity to appear about Alateen. It was followed by many pieces in other magazines and newspapers. These stories were so dramatic and moving that there was a surge of interest all over the country. An article in *Life* magazine, for example, brought in over five hundred inquiries within three weeks. Lois and Anne and their hardworking volunteers had to set up a special staff, headed by Wanda R., to serve the needs of this rapidly growing and much-needed offshoot of Al-Anon.

By now, the financial contributions from the expanding number of Family Groups in the United States, Canada, and overseas were able to fund the necessary growth of headquarters activities. Henrietta S., one of Lois's early "pioneers," was asked to serve as the first paid head of the Clearing House, which later became Al-Anon World Services, Inc.

Shortly afterward, Margaret D., another "pioneer," was hired to work full-time as editor of *The Forum* newsletter and to oversee the movement's other literature needs. In time, and as funds from donations and the sale of books and pamphlets grew, other paid staffers were brought on board to help plan, organize, and conduct national and international Al-Anon conventions and related functions. However, dedicated volunteers remained the backbone of the movement's service to its members, and Lois remained a chief recruiter until the day she passed away.

As Lois often pointed out, downplaying her role in Al-Anon's founding and development, she and Anne Bingham simply followed the path that AA had already laid out. However, she also recognized the great need and the great growth potential that lay ahead for Al-Anon since, as statistics show, every alcoholic affects at least four other people, from family members to co-workers.[28]

After holding several regional and one national Al-Anon Service Conference to elect delegates to serve as the movement's "group conscience," the Fellowship held its first World Service Conference in New York in April of 1961. Twelve delegates had been chosen from the twelve states and Canadian provinces with the largest Al-Anon populations: British Columbia, California, Florida, Illinois, Kansas, Michigan, Minnesota, New York, Ohio, Ontario, Pennsylvania, and Texas. By the following year there were twenty-four delegates, and by 1963, thirty-six. That year the number of Family Groups had reached fifteen hundred and had spread to distant lands.

Al-Anon was growing far faster than either Lois or Bill ever dreamed. And by now the groups themselves were running the Fellowship and the general public was becoming more aware of its existence.[29] When the Al-Anon Fellowship celebrated its fiftieth anniversary in 2001, there were thirty-five thousand Family Groups in one hundred and fifteen countries around the world, and its World Services headquarters moved into a large new complex in Virginia Beach, Virginia.

In 1985, Lois Wilson received the prestigious Humanitarian Award from the National Council on Alcoholism, now the National Council on Alcoholism and Drug Dependence, the organization founded by Marty Mann, the first woman to recover within Alcoholics Anonymous. (Mann died of a stroke on July 22, 1980, at the age of seventy-six.) In giving the award, the council's board of directors cited Lois for her "unique role in the history of alcoholism" and "her own living testimony of recovery."[30] The award also noted that Lois had demonstrated "that one dedicated individual seeking neither personal recognition nor financial gain can have a positive impact on the health of a society and on the lives of millions of people," and that she had "pioneered calling attention to alcoholism as a family disease and in bringing hope and health to the spouses and children of alcoholics." The citation concluded, "We salute Lois W. for her extraordinary contribution to the field of alcoholism."

In accepting the national honor, Lois, who was ninety-four at the time, said in a moving and gracious address:

> *I guess I am supposed to say something about how we never thought AA would ever amount to anything, but the truth is, as many of you know, my husband never had any small ideas.*
>
> *From the moment of his spiritual awakening in Towns Hospital, Bill always believed that if such a miracle could happen to him, it could happen to others, and if it could happen to others, it could happen to all the drunks in the world.*
>
> *The progress which has been made against alcoholism had other important beginnings of course, and among them is the day when Marty M. first heard of AA. At the time, Marty was a patient at Blythwood Sanitarium in Greenwich, Connecticut. Her psychiatrist had read the Big Book and was greatly impressed. But when he handed it to Marty, she threw it out of the window. Her doctor insisted*

that if she wanted his help, she would go after the book, read it and go to a meeting in Brooklyn.

I well remember the day she came to her first meeting. We were still holding the meetings in our home on Clinton Street at the time. Marty was afraid of what she would find down there in the parlor with all those men and she wanted to stay upstairs with me. But I finally persuaded her that the AA's both wanted and needed her, and we went downstairs together.

After that meeting, Marty sat around with a few others asking Bill questions. She had read the Big Book about twenty times by then and had loads of things to ask about. To her amazement, and everyone else's too, Bill answered them all to her satisfaction.

Another beginning was when Marty got the idea for the National Council on Alcoholism. Like Bill, she had a desire to help every suffering alcoholic she could and created an organization which for more than forty years has been dedicated to educating the public and removing their feelings of hopelessness, and ignorance, as well as the stigma, concerning this terrible disease.

I am deeply honored that the NCA has chosen me as the recipient of its Humanitarian Award for 1985. As many of you know, Bill always made it a policy never to accept awards or honors himself but rather to accept them on behalf of the Fellowship of Alcoholics Anonymous. I have followed a similar policy in regard to Al-Anon.

Therefore in closing, let me say that I accept this award gratefully on behalf of all the members of the Fellowship of Al-Anon, and I thank them and you from the bottom of my heart.[31]

In March of 2000, twelve years after her death, Lois was honored by the State of New York as one of the twentieth century's most important women, an acclamation that was part of the nation's celebration of

Women's History Month. The state's Office of Alcoholism and Substance Abuse Services lauded her for her "exceptional role and achievements in assuring service to individuals with alcohol and other drug-related problems," describing her as "a beloved symbol and inspiration to millions of AA and Al-Anon members." Throughout her life, the statement noted, "Lois was modest about her achievements, preferring instead to acknowledge the contributions of others."

It repeated her often-quoted expression that "It takes only one person to start something, but many others to carry it out" and concluded: "Throughout her life, Lois Wilson maintained a simple vision of the worldwide Al-Anon Fellowship. She talked easily about the spirituality of the program, always pointing towards Al-Anon's common purpose of recovery and service to others."[32]

As the prestigious honor from the Empire State highlighted, Lois always made light of her own accomplishments, trying to give the credit to others. This was certainly true in her relationship with Anne Bingham, with whom she remained close even after Anne's husband, Devoe, passed away and she eventually moved to California to reside near her daughter. The two cofounders were last together in Palm Springs in 1983, when Lois visited for a week and they reminisced about old times.

According to friends, Anne teased Lois about the occasion when they were invited to speak together at an Al-Anon meeting in western New Jersey and planned to spend the night. Anne left all of the details to her longtime cohort, even the driving, which Lois loved to do anyway. When they finally arrived at the church hall for the meeting, no one was there. They were a day early.

But Lois had a snappy comeback, reminding Anne of the time she had sent Lois all the way to Burlington, Vermont, supposedly to make a long talk to a large family group only to have a few people show up and limit Lois's remarks to five minutes. Concerning their visit in Palm Springs, Lois later shared with another close friend, "Anne and I just couldn't believe how far we had come and how fast the time had gone by."[33] Anne Bingham passed away the following year at the age of eighty-four. She died as she had lived in Al-Anon, quietly and peacefully. Her legacy in the Fellowship lives on.

Lois Wilson never lost her deepest belief that the principles upon which AA and Al-Anon were founded are fundamental and fitting for all people at all times. She knew, however, that unless individuals accept and apply these principles to their lives, the Fellowship will stagnate, retrogress, and perish. For, as she often said, "There is no standing still, in life or in Al-Anon."[34]

Lois spoke on behalf of Al-Anon many times and in many places, throughout the United States and in many foreign lands. And always in sharing her experiences, she talked about love, the pure, unconditional kind of love members find in the Fellowships of AA and Al-Anon—the kind of love that, if taken home, into the workplace, or out into the world, can bind people together against all strife, all illness, all hurt, and all disappointment. Late in her life, Lois Wilson penned in her memoirs:

> *AA and Al-Anon are great demonstrations of the love of one human being for another, of people for people. The joy and empathy felt at one of our gatherings are beyond description. Nowhere else have I seen folks so enjoy being together, and in no church or other assembly have I ever heard a prayer recited more movingly than at our Fellowships' meetings.*
>
> *What is love? What is it that passes between two people who love each other?*
>
> *Science has discovered that the emotions of fear and anger actually produce emanations in the human body that can be sensed by other men and women, children, animals and perhaps plants. But I have never heard that science has studied the great force of love.*
>
> *I suspect that love, too, is an actual physical emanation as well as a spiritual force—a telepathy of the heart and not just the absence of hurtful emotions.*
>
> *I deeply believe it is love that makes the world go 'round. God is love, and love is the creative force, the force that ties family and friends together. It inspires us to greater endeavor in all fields of activity, in love of God, love of man, love*

of ideas, love of self, love of things. The well of love refills itself. The more one gives of love, the more one has to give.

Children who are not loved grow up unhappy and rebellious. Even though they may be treated with kindness, that is not enough! They need the positive warmth and security of love. They may even need it physically as well as emotionally and spiritually.

This force, embodied as it is in God's love, kept Bill and me together and finally, through various channels, sobered him up. There are moments even now when the wonder and beauty of Bill's regeneration still fill me with awe.

I used to believe thinking *was the highest function of human beings. The AA experience changed me. I now realize* loving *is our supreme function. The heart precedes the mind.*

Gazing at the sky on a bright starlit night, we are overwhelmed with wonder at the seemingly limitless universe. Our finite minds cannot envision its extent and complexity, much less the possibility of other universes beyond. Likewise our finite minds sometimes question why a loving God seems to permit apparently God-loving and virtuous people to suffer the tragedies that occasionally befall them.

But our hearts do not need logic. They can love and forgive and accept that which our minds cannot comprehend. Hearts understand in a way minds cannot.[35]

16

Bill's Legacy:
Alcoholics Anonymous—
Love, Controversy, and Triumph

❧

*A*S AA AND AL-ANON GRADUALLY SPREAD THEIR HEALING
tentacles around the world, doctors, scientists, spiritual leaders, and social architects were eager to know more about the astonishing
results these two Fellowships were having on a segment of society once
almost forgotten and abandoned. Prominent politicians and celebrities
soon wanted to align themselves with the dramatic successes of these move-
ments. Newspapers, magazines, and motion picture producers sought out
stories of their "miraculous cures." Lois and Bill Wilson suddenly found
themselves, as one AA old-timer put it, "the royal couple of recovery."[1]

Lois winced when once told of that appellation although she couldn't
deny the growing demands on her and Bill's time and attention, and not
only from people in the Fellowships. Bill was now explaining the workings
of the program to the American Psychiatric Foundation, the American
Medical Association, the American Bar Association, church organizations,
and other groups around the country and around the globe.

"People mainly wanted to know more about Alcoholics Anonymous,"
Lois would say. "It took a while before a lot of them came to understand

the effects of alcoholism on families, that it's a family disease. But we finally broke through."[2] Still, the recovery of a poor, hopeless drunk—particularly one who had once been a movie star or sports celebrity—was apt to draw wider attention. So the spotlight was mostly on Bill and AA throughout the 1950s and 1960s.

Oftentimes in their travels, when out amid a throng of AA admirers, Lois sometimes watched in awe as people mobbed her husband as though he were some kind of mystic or messiah or recently canonized saint. As soon as they were alone, however, she would quietly nudge him and say, grinning: "Sweetheart, your halo's on crooked."[3]

But the truth was, alcoholics throughout the Fellowship, both here and abroad, literally believed Bill and Dr. Bob had saved their lives. And now with Dr. Bob gone, they couldn't get close enough to the remaining founder, both physically and emotionally.

John L. Norris, M.D., who served as one of AA's nonalcoholic trustees for twenty-seven years, often talked about this phenomenon. A very close friend of Bill's, "Dr. Jack," as he was fondly called by many AA members, once said, "One of the amazing things to me about Bill was the amount of devotion and real adoration he was getting almost everywhere he turned. How any human being could have been on the receiving end of the kind of devotion that he had from so many people, and keep any sort of personal humility was amazing."[4]

Lois was to face the same kind of devotion and adulation herself later on as the cofounder of Al-Anon, and it would only intensify right up to the day she died at the age of ninety-seven.

While Lois always remained her husband's biggest fan—perhaps becoming even more "addicted" to him than ever, in a more loving and less dependent way—she liked to tease him on occasion about his shortcomings, maybe to help keep his feet on the ground and his ego within bounds.

Still, it must be said that Bill Wilson was usually the first to admit he had many character defects and shortcomings, right up to the day he left this world and the great universal movement he and Dr. Robert Holbrook Smith had founded almost seventy years earlier. Lois usually smiled and nodded at such confessions, but not at the flaws she found exasperating at times.

One such shortcoming was Bill's penchant to monopolize the conversation when surrounded by guests in their living room at Stepping Stones after Harriet had served them all a home-cooked meal and a lip-smacking dessert. Lois recalled how he'd lean back in a straight chair, arms in motion, holding the floor as he expounded on whatever aspect of AA was occupying his mind at the moment. Once he got started, few had the audacity or temerity to interrupt. Even when Lois tried, as the clock ticked away, Bill would scowl in her direction and continue without missing a beat. He let everyone know when he was finished by plunking the legs of his chair noisily back down and folding his arms as if to say, "Now it's your turn."[5]

And then there was his tendency to exaggerate. One AA old-timer who knew Ruth Hock claimed she was constantly correcting Bill's "over-generous" estimates of membership figures or conference attendees. One example of this flaw was his often-quoted statement that there were more than five thousand members at AA's 1955 International Convention in St. Louis, when those handling the registration count said the number was actually closer to thirty-one hundred.

When Ruth teased her boss about such matters, the old-timer said, Bill would wink good-naturedly and reply: "You're spoiling all the fun."[6]

While Bill did handle the "hero worship" rather well, Lois often recalled with a twinkle in her eye just how disappointed her husband was if he were not recognized at all, even though he claimed he preferred anonymity. "He told me every time he went to a meeting in New York," she once shared with a friend, "he would try to sneak in unnoticed. But sooner or later someone would spot him and he would be asked to make a few remarks. Then he would come home and complain how he just wanted to be another AA member attending a meeting anonymously."

"Then on our first trip across the country by car," she continued, "we stopped off in Barstow, California, a little town out in the desert. We learned there was an AA meeting that night at a local church. When we arrived, no one had any idea who Bill was. Since we were from back East, however, they wanted to know if we had met any of the old-timers who started the program. I could tell Bill was just busting to tell them he not only met the founders but he was one of them. But I kept pinching his arm and we left the meeting without anyone being the wiser. Later in the car Bill laughed and said it was good for his humility. I said, 'What humility?' and we laughed some more."[7]

The truth was, Bill Wilson loved to be recognized. In fact, when *Time* magazine was doing a major story about Alcoholics Anonymous in the 1960s and wanted to put his picture on the cover, calling him, as Aldous Huxley once said, "the greatest social architect of the century,"[8] Lois remembered how he struggled with his decision: it would be against the very tradition of anonymity he himself wrote. He grudgingly turned down the request.

Some years later, after Bill had passed away, one of his closest friends, a great philanthropist named Brinkley Smithers, was asked how the AA cofounder was able to muster enough humility to pass up such an immense honor. Smithers laughed and replied, "You just didn't know Bill Wilson. How many guys do you know who could go around for years bragging about turning down the cover of *Time* magazine?"[9]

When Lois later heard about Brinkley's comment, she also laughed and said, "That was my Bill and I loved him for exactly who he was."[10]

Lois enjoyed sharing another incident involving her beloved husband's lifelong struggle to simply be, as his cofounder Dr. Bob used to put it, "just another anonymous drunk." She was with her husband hurrying through LaGuardia Airport to catch a plane to an AA conference in Atlanta when Bill literally bumped into Joe Hirshhorn, the well-known financier whom he hadn't seen in over thirty years—and whose wine cellar he once ransacked. They were both so excited about meeting that they kept shaking hands and patting each other on the back.

Finally, Joe wanted to know what had happened to Bill, why he disappeared from sight, why he hadn't heard anything from him or about him all these years.

Lois looked on as her husband stammered, "Haven't you heard, Joe? I . . . I mean, about this AA thing?"

"I could tell from the blank look on Joe Hirshhorn's face that he had no idea at first what Bill was talking about," Lois remembered. "Then suddenly his face lit up and he smiled at Bill and said, 'Hey, that's great! You really needed AA, that's for sure.' Then Joe rushed away. I could see how disappointed Bill was over Joe's reaction."[11]

Lois knew that the wealthy art collector was one man her husband would have wanted to acknowledge his enormous contribution to society, a prominent figure who knew him only as a drunk and now failed to recognize his great achievement. She said she squeezed his hand, kissed him on the cheek, and led him off to catch their flight.

While Bill would have liked Joe Hirshhorn's recognition, he already had it from an even greater financial tycoon—John D. Rockefeller, Jr. For some years now a Christmas card sat atop the fireplace mantel at Stepping Stones containing the following message:

"How gratifying it must be to know how many people your organization has helped! Your leadership throughout has been an inspiration. Sincerely, John D. Rockefeller, Jr."[12]

As for Bill's flaws, his ego, his outspokenness, his tendency to exaggerate, they were all part of his biggest character defect—one he often spoke of himself—his drive for power and success. But Lois said she came to understand that without these tendencies, these innermost desires to always want "doubles of everything," AA would never have gotten off the ground, much less grown into the worldwide organization it is today.

A former Chicago bartender, sober in AA for more than twenty years, astutely said, "God put a bright, ego-driven Wall Street promoter together with a laid-back practical country doctor, mixed well, shook and stirred, and out poured the miraculous cocktail of Alcoholics Anonymous."[13] And over the years it has become a proven potion that saves lives and restores families, but only when those in need reach out for it. According to national statistics, there are more than forty million people in the United States alone who drink alcoholically. Yet, the sad truth is, even today only a small percentage of them are willing to try this "miraculous cocktail." And among those willing to give it a sip, many soon reach back for their tried-and-true "magic elixir" called booze because it works faster to ease their fears and frustrations, to take the edge off their anger and despair. AA admittedly takes more time, and too many impatient alcoholics refuse to wait. So they drink again even though deep down they know it is taking them down. That's the insidious, inexplicable disease of alcoholism.

As Bill often said, alcoholic behavior is "self-will run riot," and "self-centeredness is the root of our problem." And the answer? "Only through utter defeat," he wrote, "are we able to take our first steps toward liberation and strength. Our admissions of personal powerlessness finally turn out to be firm bedrock upon which happy and purposeful lives may be built."

While AA does take time to work its own magic, its history from the beginning shows that about 50 percent of alcoholics who come and give the program a serious try stay sober. Another 25 percent who come with reservations as to whether they are "real alcoholics" do find sobriety after some relapses. The remainder who come to the Fellowship under pressure or in serious denial soon leave, and their disease continues to progress until they hit a much lower "bottom." But many of these people in whom the seed is planted return over time.[14]

"It is frequently the denial of their disease that keeps them from coming to AA in the first place," Lois noted. "It is a pity that so many alcoholics still have to suffer the same pain and loss that Bill did before trying Alcoholics Anonymous. Although I am happy to see both men and women coming to the program today at a much younger age. They can have such a wonderful life."[15] And that's exactly what Bill Wilson found—a wonderful life. For after his spiritual experience and his meeting with Dr. Bob, he came to truly love and care for his fellow drunks. This ability to love again helped reunite him with his long-suffering wife, opened the door to her own discoveries, and enabled him to be mindful and considerate of others as well.

Lois also observed how her husband's dramatic change from almost total self-centeredness to sincere concern for others also affected his relationship with his mother and father, whom he had seldom seen or communicated with during those terrible years of drinking.

Bill's father, Gilman, and his second wife, Christine, had moved from Florida shortly after the highway project he had been working on was completed. He returned to the quarries in British Columbia, where his health began to deteriorate. He suffered from hardening of the arteries. During the late 1940s and early 1950s, Bill scraped together at least a hundred dollars each month to send to his father to help with his medical expenses. Bill also brought Gilman and Christine to Bedford Hills for extended visits. After so many lost years, they finally built a loving father-and-son relationship.

Soon, however, Gilman's health worsened. Through some AA friends in Vancouver, Bill had his father admitted to a nursing home. Gilman Wilson died on February 14, 1954, just three weeks after Lois had her heart attack. He was eighty-four. Bill had his ashes returned to East Dorset, where he buried them in the small country cemetery amid the Wilson clan. Then it was left to Bill to inform his mother, the woman who long ago had been his father's wife.

By now, Bill and Dr. Emily Griffith had grown very close even though she still lived on the West Coast. He visited his mother on his travels, and she often wrote or phoned simply to say how proud she was of his work. She said she knew so many people in California who were benefiting from AA.

Lois and her mother-in-law had long since buried the hatchet. Once Bill sobered up and Lois came to realize that she herself needed to change, she and Dr. Emily became very good friends. In fact, now a widow, Bill's mother was a frequent guest at Stepping Stones. While there, she fell in love with Al-Anon, which made Lois immensely proud. They often went to meetings together. After Lois invited her to volunteer at the Al-Anon Clearing House, Dr. Emily was soon "bossing" the other volunteers around. Lois would simply smile and shrug as if to say, "Some things never change."

In 1956, Bill persuaded his mother to move East. She agreed, but although she was now eighty-five, she insisted on having her own place in Westchester. Lois and Bill took Emily for rides in the countryside and for brief visits to East Dorset. They were brief because Emily was always in a hurry to leave Vermont. Perhaps it held too many upsetting memories for her.

It was in the winter of 1960 when Bill was forced to put his mother into a nursing home in Dobbs Ferry, New York, where he could visit with her often. Her physical and mental condition was such that she required constant care. Emily Griffith died there on May 15, 1961, at the age of ninety-one. Despite whatever upsetting memories there might have been, Bill and Lois buried her in East Dorset.

Lois said she came to admire the way her husband was able to handle the many ups and downs in his life, the adversities that in the past would have made marvelous excuses for him to drink again. But each new difficulty, every new challenge only seemed to strengthen his sobriety and his ability to lead his now vast army of recovered alcoholics.

Lois often recalled one of the most pivotal times in her husband's life. It was at AA's International Convention in St. Louis in 1955. Until then, Bill still held tightly to the reins of the Fellowship, listening but also guiding the voice of the "group conscience," especially in matters that could, in his judgment, prove controversial or harmful to the movement.

But at that four-day event, Bill finally dismounted the tiger he had been riding for more than twenty years. He sat on stage as the membership unanimously approved merging the Alcoholic Foundation and AA's General Service Office into one organization called Alcoholics Anonymous World Services, Inc. He forced himself to let go and let the elected board of alcoholic and nonalcoholic trustees run the Fellowship with as little interference from him as his "humility" would allow. He would now become its "roving Ambassador."

AA's cofounder was fifty-nine. He now had a good income from the sale of the Big Book and was finally free to pursue many of the interests and subjects that had been whirling around in his brain for some years. He wanted to write more books and more articles for AA's *Grapevine* magazine. He wanted to travel more and share experiences with AA members around the globe. He wanted to seek out and investigate some of the lesser-known and more intriguing paths to spiritual and mental health, both to find help for his own recurring depressions and to assist others with similar problems.

As Lois once said, Bill suddenly possessed the rabid curiosity of that schoolboy back in East Dorset who wanted to know what made a boomerang return and a tiny crystal radio crackle with voices hundreds of miles away. At the same time, like a father who never ceases worrying about his children no matter how old they are, Bill could not break completely with his own "offspring."

"He kept an office at AA headquarters," Lois remarked with a smile, "just to make sure he knew what was going on. I think it was to be sure everyone was doing things right—his way. He also loved to walk down the hall to the conference room to check the world map on the wall that had pins indicating the number of groups now officially registered with World Services. In fact, he loved to put the new pins in himself."[16] By the late 1950s, after Bill had resigned his stewardship, there were more than 12,000 AA groups in some 75 countries including the United States, with an estimated membership of more than 200,000. By 2002, there were more than 100,000 groups in over 150 countries and an estimated membership of three million recovering alcoholics still attending meetings. No one knows how many thousands more left AA but remained sober by continuing to practice the Twelve Steps in their lives.

As for his writings, Bill turned out numerous articles for the *Grapevine* concerning the principles of the program and the importance of "walking the walk, not just talking the talk." A series of his essays became a book published by AA World Services, *The Twelve Steps and Twelve Traditions*. In 1957, he wrote about the early history of the movement, its first twenty-one years, and the people and concepts behind its growth and success in another book, *Alcoholics Anonymous Comes of Age*.

Lois used to remark that her husband seemed to become a more prolific writer with age, perhaps because he had more time or became more productive or simply because he came to see things much more clearly through sober eyes.

Lois said Bill loved the studio he and his friends built on a hill near their house. "He would spend hours there meditating and writing whenever we were home. He called the studio 'Wits End' because that's where he found so much peace and contentment, writing about what he loved and dreaming about the things he still wanted to do."[17]

And then there were the traveling years. Lois and Bill first toured the Northwest together, then the West Coast, and then all sections of America where new AA and Al-Anon groups were being established. They would speak at these groups and attend various regional conferences, explaining in detail the concepts and Traditions that made both Fellowships so meaningful and so beneficial.

Bill also visited drunks in the alcoholic wards of local hospitals and at halfway houses while Lois met with families and shared with them the inspiring program of Al-Anon. Soon they were traveling overseas, accepting invitations from AA and Al-Anon groups in England, Scotland, Ireland, France, Germany, Norway, Sweden, and Denmark.

"We were like motorcycle hobos all over again," Lois would laugh, "only this time we were traveling all around the world, but without our bike and sidecar. And wherever we went, everyone greeted us so warmly, like they were close friends we simply hadn't met yet."[18]

Lois loved to tell the story of their first visit to Oslo, Norway, and how AA and Al-Anon had reached the shores of that distant land. "It wasn't until we arrived," she recounted, "that we discovered the Oslo group had actually been founded by a coffee shop owner from Greenwich, Connecticut. He had come to America from Norway and after twenty years of drinking he wound up as a derelict. But in 1947, he found AA and a brand new life."

After getting back on his feet, Lois explained, the man opened a coffee shop and began to make a good living. As his shame and guilt left, he finally wrote to his family back in Oslo telling them his story. Within a matter of weeks he received a letter back pleading for his help. His only brother had also become a hopeless drunk and was about to lose his job on an Oslo newspaper. The family also feared he was about to lose his life.

The coffee shop owner quickly sold his business and bought a ticket to Norway. But upon arriving home, his brother expressed no interest in hearing about AA or listening to a translation of the Steps or any stories of sober members. He only wanted to keep drinking. Thoroughly discouraged, the coffee shop owner began talking with local doctors and ministers, but found a shocking lack of interest wherever he went. So he started making plans to return to Connecticut.

On his last night in Oslo, his brother called, sick and fearful of dying. He asked how these anonymous American friends found a way to stop drinking. So the two sat down and his brother explained the program of Alcoholics Anonymous. This time it worked. Sober and back at his job, the brother ran a small ad in his newspaper, asking that anyone with a drinking problem call him. The wife of a florist answered his ad and the two brothers made their first Twelfth Step call. Soon there was another call, then a third and a fourth, and AA was established in Norway. Al-Anon was soon to follow.

When the Wilsons arrived at the airport in Oslo, Lois recalled, a large number of sober AA's were waiting to welcome them. They learned that there were hundreds of members and that new groups were popping up all the time.

While Lois would tease about Bill's "flaws," she was always willing to expound on her husband's positive attributes and accomplishments. However, she was reticent when it came to discussing those events that created controversy in AA or Al-Anon. She was deeply concerned, particularly after Bill's passing, about protecting his reputation and preserving his legacy. But the truth was, being a seeker unafraid to investigate and test ideas and potential remedies that might benefit himself and his fellow alcoholics, Bill was bound to stir up a hornet's nest now and then. And he did just that on several occasions, sometimes dragging his unsuspecting wife into it with him.

Two major controversies actually began with a chance meeting with famed physicist Dr. J. Robert Oppenheimer, known as the "father of the atomic bomb." Lois and Bill had finally saved enough money to take a two-week vacation at Trunk Bay in the Caribbean. They found themselves staying at the same resort as the Oppenheimers. The couples hit it right off. During long walks on the beach, Dr. Oppenheimer, after hearing about his friend's alcoholism and lifelong bouts with depression, revealed his efforts to discover the possible chemical composition of neuroses—especially in the form of depression. He invited Bill to visit his Institute for Advanced Study at Princeton University to evaluate his work on the chemistry of the brain.

Perhaps another factor that sparked Dr. Oppenheimer's interest was Bill's fascination and involvement with psychic phenomena. In fact, soon after Bill sobered up, he came to think of himself as having some psychic ability and believed he was capable of picking up energy from others, even those who had passed from this life.

His belief in clairvoyance and other extrasensory manifestations came from his deeply held conviction following his spiritual experience that life after life is a matter of fact as well as faith. This led to his attempts to get in touch with other lives in other times. Both he and Lois had discovered early on that Dr. Bob and Annie Smith also had great interest in the field of extrasensory phenomena.

Bill and Lois came to hold frequent Saturday evening "spook sessions" at Stepping Stones, joined by such friends as Anne and Devoe, Ruth and Wilbur, Tom P. and Adelaide, and Dr. Bob and Annie when they were in town. They would conduct various psychic experiments, often involving a Ouija board, in a downstairs bedroom that was quickly dubbed by Anne Bingham as the "Spook Room."

While reluctant to discuss all that went on because of its somewhat controversial nature, Lois did describe once how some of the dramatic sessions were conducted.

She said Bill would lie down on the couch. People would come in and they'd carry on some story. There would be long sentences Bill would utter, sometimes in different languages, and Anne would try to write them down. Lois said sometimes it made sense and sometimes it didn't. And sometimes even stranger things would happen.[19]

Lois said her husband's motives in almost everything he did were always somehow connected to AA—in this case they were to deepen his spirituality by trying to discover more about God's workings, wonder, and wisdom.

Lois revealed that Dr. Oppenheimer actually invited her husband to work with him at Princeton, mainly to oversee the research being done on the possible physiological and chemical aspects of depression, a problem Bill had always approached in terms of its psychological and spiritual ramifications. She said Bill had to politely turn down the scientist's invitation because, as the "symbolic" leader and the cofounder of Alcoholics Anonymous, he was concerned that its members might feel he would be violating the Sixth Tradition: "An A.A. group ought never endorse, finance, or lend the A.A. name to any related facility or outside enterprise, lest problems of money, property, and prestige divert us from our primary purpose."[20]

Nevertheless, Lois said, Bill's frequent visits to Dr. Oppenheimer's institute and their numerous conversations opened his mind to many new discoveries that might help those in the Fellowship suffering as he did from other maladies related to or beyond the disease of alcoholism. He soon learned that while he had been concentrating his energies on arresting alcoholism through what he called spiritual means, many scientists had begun looking into the interrelated social, psychological, and biochemical aspects of the illness.

Two such men were Drs. Humphrey Osmond and Abram Hoffer, both psychiatrists who were working with alcoholics and schizophrenics at a mental hospital in Saskatoon, Saskatchewan. Through some mutual friends, Bill was introduced to the doctors and quickly became excited by their experiments since he believed he and they were working on "parallel tracks."

Bill had already discovered that many "hopeless cases" such as himself could be reached through what he called "ego deflation at depth"— hitting a bottom that finally breaks through the wall of the ego. Drs. Osmond and Hoffer were trying to reach the same end with their alcoholic patients through chemical means. The psychiatrists were using an experimental synthetic chemical called lysergic acid diethylamide, which would later become notoriously known as LSD.

Lois always disliked discussing this particular chapter in her husband's life because of its "complete misunderstanding" and the "terrible rumors that were spread" when all Bill did, she said, was simply involve himself in an investigation he believed might possibly help his fellow drunks. Encouraged by the two psychiatrists to be a "comparison case," Bill participated briefly in their controlled experiments, taking small doses of LSD in August of 1956. But this quickly came to an end when word somehow began spreading through the AA community that "Bill Wilson is taking drugs."[21]

Upon returning to New York, members and trustees alike, including Dr. Jack Norris, expressed outrage that the cofounder of Alcoholics Anonymous would even consider experimenting with a then totally unfamiliar, poorly researched, and possibly mind-altering substance—even though no one at the time knew anything about "acid trips" or whether it was an addictive chemical. Bill assured everyone his involvement in the research was over and then had both scientists confirm to his colleagues that the chemical contained "no addictive properties."[22] "Bill tried to explain the reasons he did it," Lois once remarked, "but nobody would listen. Bill actually had the doctors give me some when I was with him one day in Saskatoon and it had no effect on me at all. It wasn't until much later that we all learned what effect much larger doses could have on the mind."[23]

Nell Wing was willing to elaborate a bit more on the controversy.

"Bill wanted to see what it was like," she said. "He was intrigued with the work that [the doctors] were doing in Saskatoon with alcoholics. And he thought: anything that helps the alcoholics is good and shouldn't be dismissed out of hand. Techniques should be explored that would help some guy or gal recover who could not do it through A.A. or any other way."[24]

The truth of the matter was, Bill Wilson had always been on record against giving alcoholics drugs, at least those narcotics whose severe addictive effects were already well known. But LSD was then an "experimental chemical." Even the psychiatrists themselves abandoned their project once they saw there were few, if any, beneficial effects. Bill closed that particular chapter in his life when he told a close friend one day that he considered the chemical to be of some value to some people and practically no damage to anyone. He added that it will never take the place of any of the existing means by which we can reduce the ego and keep it reduced.[25]

Just when Lois felt relieved that the controversy was finally behind them, Bill jumped from the frying pan into the fire. And to her dying day, Lois could never really understand what all the fuss was about.

It concerned her husband's sudden, outright, and unabashed endorsement of one of the lesser-known vitamins at the time—vitamin B-3, better known as niacin. He began proclaiming its beneficial effects for alcoholics after becoming engrossed himself in the many studies that had been done on its properties and alleged curative powers. Bill became absolutely convinced of three things. First, giving niacin as part of the alcoholic's detoxification process could lessen the effects of alcohol withdrawal. Second, studies showed that it stimulated the blood vessels, particularly in the brain, which helped alleviate depressive mood swings. And third, it prevented to some extent a drop in blood sugar, which researchers said improved the feelings of both physical and psychological well-being.

"I think the problem was," Lois once hinted to a close friend, "that with most things Bill got interested in, he became overenthusiastic. Wherever we went, he was telling everyone to take niacin. He even had me taking it and I must admit it seemed to help. In fact, I still take it. Maybe some people didn't realize that niacin is only a vitamin, not a mood changer. It helps without hurting."[26]

Lois was absolutely right about Bill's excessive enthusiasm getting him into hot water again. He was spreading his niacin gospel wherever he went. He even wrote several papers on the subject, which he distributed far and wide. Soon the pros and cons of vitamin B-3 were being argued in AA meetings, which ran head-on into another of the Fellowship's Traditions, the Tenth: "Alcoholics Anonymous has no opinion on outside issues; hence the A.A. name ought never be drawn into public controversy."[27]

Once again a group of AA trustees sat down with their cofounder to express their concern about the latest hornet's nest he was stirring up. They had no argument over his promoting the values of niacin; they asked only that he not mix it up with the AA name or in AA activities. Despite his absolute conviction about niacin's beneficial effects for all alcoholics, Bill agreed to separate his personal interest in it from the Fellowship. This solution quickly ended the controversy.

Lois said that her husband's interest in vitamin therapy did not end with niacin. She said they both came to believe that other vitamins offered their own specific benefits as well. While she approached the subject in her usual low-key style, Lois said Bill could talk for hours about how various vitamin regimens could help alcoholics in their early stages of physical recovery and later with their mental and emotional recovery.

"I think at one time we had almost every vitamin there was here at Stepping Stones," Lois would smile. "I must admit it became a bit confusing after a while so I just stuck to the few I knew the most about, like B-12, C, and E, and of course, niacin."[28] Over the years of Bill's investigation into vitamins and related natural health therapies, he was introduced to a woman in Mount Kisco, New York, who had spent many years following a similar avocation—improving mental and physical well-being through natural remedies. Her name was Helen Wynn, a woman of pleasant looks and a stoic disposition, said several people who knew her.

According to mutual acquaintances, Helen and Bill became good friends and were seen together now and then shopping at pharmacies and health food outlets or having lunch on occasion to discuss their latest finds—a new Chinese herb, an Indian root, or a newly discovered bene-fit of an A-vitamin. Then the rumors began.

It should be mentioned that AA's cofounder had always been open and friendly with the women at the Central Office—too friendly, some of his detractors might whisper. He even had an open ear for women alcoholics in the Fellowship who wanted his advice or some encourage-ment now and then. So the rumors were not just about Helen Wynn but about Bill's "womanizing" in general.

The gossip was whispered at first, then it grew less subtle and finally became downright mean. Nell Wing, for example, became a target. She once heard a third- or fourth-hand story about herself and Bill—a man she always looked up to as a father figure. She was mortified and thought about leaving her job as AA's archives director. Then one day while at Stepping Stones, she decided to tell Lois what had happened. Nell said she was astonished by her dear friend's response. "Lois told me," Nell said, "that the founder of any great movement or organization, especial-ly one like Alcoholics Anonymous, can develop enemies, men who fall away, get drunk and then angry and jealous. And when they find people putting someone like Bill up on a pedestal, they know that even the rumor of such frailties or indiscretions can bring him down and make them feel bigger in their own eyes. But the real problem is that such rumors can disillusion members and cause great harm to AA. So Lois told me not to pay any attention to such hurtful stories but simply to trust in my own feelings and in what I really knew."[29]

How did Lois react to these rumors? She followed the same advice she gave to Nell. She decided the best way to respond to such "hideous gossip" was not to respond at all. She simply showed her great love and support for her husband at every opportunity despite the pain such stories must have wrought and the deep resentments she must have had as the sick rumormongering continued. Even today, more than thirty years after Bill's death, there are those who for some reason still seem to enjoy digging up and passing along such ugly gossip.

As for Helen Wynn, who has since passed away, there is a gentlemen who knew her quite well back then—her dentist for many years in Mount Kisco. Preferring to remain anonymous, the dentist also remembered meeting Bill on two separate brief occasions.

"If ever there was a platonic relationship," he volunteered, "this surely was one. I mean, I knew Helen quite well and I must say she wasn't what you would ordinarily call a 'loose woman,' if you know what I mean. In fact, she appeared to be just the opposite, rather uptight and very businesslike if not downright bossy. I really couldn't see them together except maybe as friends or business associates."[30] Lois once said she never knew anything about Helen Wynn until after Bill's death, when she discovered her husband had left the woman some money in his will. When asked about it, Lois simply shrugged and said her husband left money to several other people as well—and that was to be her final comment on the matter.[31]

Most old-timers in the AA program have little or nothing to say about their cofounder's so-called womanizing. But there were two who knew Bill back then, Jim G. and Jack O., who claim his relationship with the Mount Kisco woman was really no different from those with his other female friends and colleagues, whom he admittedly loved being around.

"But if you're talking sex," Jim G. said quite frankly, "I honestly don't know, although I'm inclined to doubt it. Why? Look, everyone has their temptations, their appetites you might say. And if you're looked upon as kind of a savior like Bill was, I guess there's more opportunity to be tempted.

"However, let's not forget this is the same guy who had a spiritual experience, the same guy I believe was divinely inspired to write the Big Book, and the same guy who wrote in that Big Book that our sobriety depends upon our spiritual condition. Where I come from, if you're a married guy screwing around with babes, you're not in a good spiritual condition. And if you're not in a good spiritual condition, you're not going to stay sober for very long. And Bill Wilson was sober—and for a very long time."[32] How often Lois heard these rumors, or whether they even permeated their circle of AA and Al-Anon friends, no one really knows. The only thing that does appear certain is that despite the LSD and niacin controversies, and unseemly gossip at times, none of this apparently interfered with Lois and Bill's life together at Stepping Stones. Harriet Sevarino, their longtime housekeeper, was among many who testified to that.

"When they would walk together in the gardens or along the dirt paths," Harriet said, "they would always be holding hands. And I would see them kiss each other hello and good-bye whenever I was around. You could tell they really loved and cared for each other. And don't forget, I was with them over thirty-five years."[33]

Nell Wing also fondly recalled the strong bond between "two of the most important people in my life." As she put it: "Certainly they had their little spats and misunderstandings, but they were usually brief and never dragged on. Lois and Bill not only adored each other but they respected each other. To me, I think that's what really keeps people together for such a long, long time—love and respect."[34]

Nell and Harriet said it was evident again on the evening of January 24, 1968, when they were both at Stepping Stones for the surprise celebration of Lois and Bill's fiftieth wedding anniversary. Nell had been staying at the house, working with Bill on some correspondence he needed to get out. She sensed that both he and Lois were expecting some kind of surprise party for their anniversary and appeared quite disappointed that nothing was happening. To keep them even more in the dark, Nell said she was taking them to lunch to celebrate the occasion. That's when Lois and Bill's spirit seem to rise, thinking the party would probably be at the restaurant.

Their faces fell again when they walked into the nearby bistro and saw only a few unfamiliar faces in the place. Nell could hardly contain herself although she did say they had a very pleasant, drawn-out lunch.

During the ride back to the house, no one said a word. But as they reached the top of the long driveway, Lois almost had another heart attack. The yard was filled with cars and a throng of relatives and close friends were standing there to greet them—sisters and brothers, nieces and nephews, and AA and Al-Anon friends from as far away as Arizona and California. Harriet had prepared a marvelous buffet that not only satisfied all of the guests, but also soothed the slightly jarred egos of the fiftieth wedding anniversary celebrants.[35]

Lois recalled that after everyone had gone that evening, she and Bill sat together in front of the large stone fireplace. They watched the sparks crackle off the flaming pine logs and shared their memories of the years that had flown by—their youthful hopes and dreams, their struggles with a disease they once knew nothing about, and the awesome opportunity God had given them to share their recovery and experiences—the pain and the joy, the sorrow and the elation—with their fellow sufferers throughout the world. They sat together long after midnight wondering what the future might hold, hoping they would have many more nights like this, many more years of sharing their love with each other and all those still in need of what they had found.

But that dream wouldn't come true. For while their fiftieth wedding anniversary was a milestone in their lives, the celebration was tempered somewhat by Bill's growing health problems. He was seventy-two now, and his deteriorating health had become quite obvious to all who were close to him—especially Lois.

"He was trying so hard to stop smoking," Lois said. "He would often get angry with himself whenever he would light up another cigarette. I knew there was nothing I could say that would help. I had already said it all."[36]

So had Dr. Leonard Strong, who had been warning his brother-in-law for years to stop smoking: his coughing and wheezing could lead to serious heart and lung problems. Bill would merely smile and nod and promise to try harder. In 1965, pulmonary specialists diagnosed Bill with emphysema and told him that unless he gave up tobacco completely, he could be dead in a very few years. Bill no longer smiled and nodded, but neither did he say anything to Lois. He simply continued struggling to break what he always called his "nasty old habit."

Lois soon learned the truth and did everything she could to keep her husband healthy, encouraging him to walk every day to help his breathing and strengthen his lungs. "Sometimes when we were out walking together," Lois recalled, "Bill would begin coughing and gasping for breath. So he began carrying a pocket inhalator with him, a small device that would pump medication into his mouth and down into his lungs. It would help him to stop coughing and wheezing. It could be very frightening at times."[37]

Bill had loved to walk for miles, Lois said, but now her husband had to stop and rest more frequently, often perching on a tree stump until he caught his breath. Their neighbors, who for years would wave as they passed by, began to notice that Bill was slowing down, not walking as often, and soon not walking at all.

Lois would sadly reminisce about the year everything took a turn for the worse. It was 1969 and it actually began on an upbeat note. Bill had clung to his latest New Year's resolution and had actually stopped smoking. In fact, even those sullen moods that always accompanied his many stabs at quitting were gone. He was smiling and boastful that cigarettes were finally out of his life, once and for all. He felt so good that one day after an ice storm in late February, he climbed up on the roof of his studio to survey the damage it had caused. He slipped and fell into the snow, ice, and slush and wound up in the hospital several days later with his first bout of pneumonia. It would reoccur several times over the coming year, due to his worsening emphysema.

"Bill stopped going into his office in New York," Lois explained, "because by the end of the day he was so tired he could hardly walk the few blocks to Grand Central Station for the train ride home. So Nell began spending more time with us at Stepping Stones, helping Bill answer his mail. I think many times she would write the letters for him, she knew so well what he wanted to say. And she was such a big help to me. I don't know what I would have done without her during those last few years when Bill was so sick."[38] Lois said her husband's last public appearance was at AA's huge International Convention in Miami Beach over the July Fourth weekend of 1970. Despite his failing health and frequent need for oxygen, Bill insisted on attending the worldwide gathering of AA's held every five years. He and Lois arrived a few days early so that he could rest up for the five major talks he always gave at these

Conventions. But the evening before the usual opening day press conference, Bill's breathing took a turn for the worse. He was also having chest pains. He was rushed by ambulance to the Miami Heart Institute, where his fellow AA member and devoted friend Dr. Ed Bradley was the director. He was given oxygen and was soon resting comfortably.

"Bill had his heart set on being with his fellow AA's," Lois shared. "So, on top of his physical problems he also became very depressed. He made Dr. Ed promise to get him well enough to attend at least one of the major meetings at the Convention. I didn't think it was possible, but it happened."[39]

In the meantime, other AA's had to fill in for their cofounder. Dr. Norris substituted at the press conference. Bernard Smith, the past chairman of the General Service Board and another close friend, delivered the main Saturday night talk Bill was scheduled to make. He assured everyone that their beloved Bill W. was on the road to recovery.

Lois managed to sneak away from the hospital to fulfill her Al-Anon commitments and also to attend a number of AA gatherings on her husband's behalf. Lois had often said that she, like Annie Smith, felt as much at home in AA as she did in Al-Anon. She never had a problem talking about the AA Fellowship's miraculous beginnings, its colorful growing-up years, and where it stood today. And she continued to accept invitations to speak at AA gatherings throughout the rest of her life.

Lois said that by Sunday morning, her husband insisted he was feeling well enough to leave the hospital and attend the convention's closing session. Dr. Ed, despite his concerns, accompanied Bill and Lois in an ambulance that took them directly to the convention center's stage entrance. Wearing a nasal tube and taking oxygen, Bill was helped into a wheelchair and pushed onto the stage to the surprise and rousing cheers of more than twenty thousand people.

"I still choke up when I think about it," Lois once told a close friend. "Everyone stood and shouted and applauded for almost five minutes. Bill kept raising his hand for them to be seated but they just had to let him know how much they loved him. His eyes filled up and he kept wiping away the tears."[40] Then everyone seemed to gasp in unison as his lanky frame rose slowly from the wheelchair and his ashen face moved close to the microphone. He began to speak, and for a few minutes he was his old self, the man who could mesmerize thousands, the leader every drunk in the world who wanted sobriety was willing to follow. That Sunday morning Bill Wilson knew more than ever why he was still sober and the debt he owed not only to his pal Dr. Bob but also to every recovered alcoholic who had followed them. Perhaps that's why, as his lungs tightened and his breathing came again in gasps, he closed his last brief AA talk to his fellow drunks with an ancient Arabian greeting, "I salute you, and I thank you for your lives."[41]

Lois said her husband was rushed from the stage back into the ambulance and returned to the Miami Heart Institute, where he stayed until the end of the month. Upon his arrival back at Stepping Stones, Bill promptly caught pneumonia once again. He was taken to Northern Westchester Hospital for a few weeks, then brought home. Then, two more times, just as soon as he was able to walk again, the pneumonia returned and he was back in the hospital. Even at home, Bill was now on oxygen twenty-four hours a day. Soon he was totally bedridden and had nurses caring for him around the clock. Despite all this help, it was still exhausting for Lois, who was now seventy-nine.

"When Bill would be awake," she once told a friend, "he would want me to read to him or pray with him. No matter what the hour he would call for me and I would come. If I had the strength, I would never have left his side. He was still the most important thing in my life."[42] Dr. Ed remained in constant touch from Miami. In early January of 1971, he called to say the Heart Institute had developed a new type of breathing apparatus he thought might help Bill. It was similar to the decompression chambers used by deep-sea divers. Lois sensed it was a last-resort measure, but her husband still had great confidence in his cardiologist. So she made plans to fly down to Miami with Bill and Nell in a Learjet chartered by their philanthropist friend Brinkley Smithers. They left from Westchester County Airport on the cold and windy Sunday morning of January 24, 1971—Lois and Bill's fifty-third wedding anniversary.

Lois's recollections of that day were blurred by her deep distress over Bill's fragile condition and fears that he might never reach Miami alive. But Nell vividly recalled that "mercy flight." "Dr. Ed had flown up on the jet to be with us and watch over Bill as best he could on the return flight," Nell explained. "He had Bill placed on a stretcher across the backs of several seats, wearing his oxygen mask. He put Lois at his side where her physical presence and her own special love would aid him most. I sat at the foot of the stretcher.

"As we flew, Bill slipped in and out of hallucinations, seeing dead or absent relatives at his feet, whom he would describe in detail for us. His left arm would occasionally slip off the narrow stretcher and hang down. I would lift it back onto his lap and give him a pat. He would try to smile and give my hand a grateful squeeze. I simply said, 'Hold fast, Bill—one of his favorite expressions—Hold fast, Bill.' "[43]

Arriving in Miami around noon, AA's had arranged for an ambulance to rush Bill to the Heart Institute. Lois spent the rest of the day at her husband's side. When he was placed in the breathing apparatus, she sat next to him hoping and praying this latest technology would perform some kind of a miracle. It was after eight o'clock that evening when Bill finally dozed off and she left his side. Lois and Nell checked into adjoining rooms at a nearby Holiday Inn, had a bite to eat, and then, thoroughly exhausted, fell into a deep sleep. What happened next was something Lois never forgot.

There was a knock on her motel door around six that morning. When she opened it, there stood Dr. Ed, his eyes filled with tears. He said they had twice tried to revive Bill from a coma. They worked on him throughout the night. They couldn't save him. He reached out and held Lois in his arms as she sobbed uncontrollably.[44]

William G. Wilson died at 11:30 p.m. on January 24, 1971, the fifty-third anniversary of his marriage to Lois Burnham Wilson. He was seventy-five. The death certificate said he had advanced emphysema for three years and pneumonia for two weeks. It also read that congestive heart failure was a major contributing cause of his death.

Nell remembers flying back from Miami with Lois that Monday afternoon. They barely talked. At one point through her grief and tears, Nell recalled her dear friend murmuring to herself, "Maybe I was too possessive. I wanted so much of his time, to be with him. Because I loved him. I loved him so much."[45]

Nell also knew how deeply hurt Lois was over not being called by the hospital when her husband was close to death. Lois wrote about that pain in her memoirs:

"Bill's death had been expected by the doctors at several periods during his illness, and I had known it was a probability; but we had both been so hopeful about this new treatment of Ed's.

"The missing him would come later. But the hurt of not being at his side at this supreme moment was immediate. Why was I not called? Bill and I had shared so many of life's adventures; now, when the door opened for him into the greatest of mystical experiences, I was not there.

"I try to be practical about it. It was to save me that the doctors hadn't called me. Perhaps they were being kind to me. The pain might have been worse if I had been there. Bill might have been in a coma and not known me. But even so I wanted to be there, and the hurt of not being at his side is still with me."[46]

Since the Twelve Traditions of Alcoholics Anonymous state nothing about a member's anonymity after passing away, the whole world came to know the full name of the Fellowship's cofounder on Tuesday, January 26, 1971, when Bill's biography and picture were displayed on the front page of the *New York Times*.

Memorial services were held in cities across the country and in capitals around the world. Tributes were paid to Bill and the founding of AA by U.S. and foreign dignitaries alike, from religious leaders to movie stars and from well-known social leaders to the lowliest of drunks recently arrived at the doorstep of the Fellowship.

But perhaps the most moving memorial service was the one Lois held at Stepping Stones on the afternoon of January 27. While the old country house high on a hill overlooking the Hudson River valley found itself jammed with friends, relatives, and AA and Al-Anon members, Lois and Bill's favorite prayer, the Prayer of St. Francis of Assisi, could be heard quietly echoing through the rooms and drifting softly out across the snow-covered grounds and bare-limbed trees and shrubs. Lois often said it filled everyone there that day with a sense that Bill was still among them and that his spirit would always be wherever an alcoholic was in need. They prayed:

> *Lord, make me a channel of thy peace; that where there is hatred I may bring love; that where there is wrong, I may bring the spirit of forgiveness; that where there is discord, I may bring harmony; that where there is error, I may bring truth; that where there is doubt, I may bring faith; that where there is despair, I may bring hope; that where there are shadows, I may bring light; that where there is sadness, I may bring joy.*
>
> *Lord, grant that I may seek to comfort rather than to be comforted; to understand, than to be understood; to love, than to be loved. For it is by giving that one receives. It is by forgiving that one is forgiven. It is by dying that one awakens to Eternal Life. Amen.*

• • •

Bill Wilson was buried without fanfare in the small family cemetery in East Dorset, Vermont, near his parents who bore him and his grandparents who raised him. The simple gravestone that contains his name and military rank is made of the same white marble his father once quarried in the nearby Green Mountains. There is no mention of Alcoholics Anonymous.

17

Lois's Legacy: Al-Anon, Alateen, and the Stepping Stones Foundation

❧

LOIS SAT BY HERSELF IN THE SPOOK ROOM FOR DAYS ON END, HER Bible in her lap, listening to the March winds whistling through the eaves of the old house and wondering, perhaps hoping, that somewhere in those strong, breathlike gusts she might hear Bill's voice whispering to her or feel his presence beside her.

If Bill was able to contact those on the other side during the many evenings they spent at "spook sessions" with their friends in this room, then why couldn't he contact her? she would ask herself. Or why couldn't she contact him, just to know that he was waiting for her and to let him know she would be along very soon? So she sat and listened and softly murmured how much she missed him and still loved him.

Harriet would bring in a breakfast tray filled with tea, toast, and cereal and place it next to her chair. It wouldn't be touched. Later she brought a small sandwich and a cup of hot cocoa for lunch. She even tried to entice her grieving friend with a small portion of Southern fried chicken and creamy mashed potatoes for dinner. It would all simply sit on the tray and get cold.

"She wasn't eating enough to keep a bird alive," her housekeeper recalled. "She was already skin and bone so I called the doctor. She got angry with me but I wasn't going to sit there and watch her die. I kept telling her that Mr. Wilson wouldn't want that either."[1]

Lois didn't even answer the many telephone calls or see the friends who wanted to visit. She simply wanted to be by herself. She wanted to be left alone. In truth, she wanted to be with Bill.

Nell joined her on weekends. In her own loving way she began to force Lois to eat something, patiently spoon-feeding her at times while sharing the latest tidbits about AA and Al-Anon she had picked up at her job as chief archivist at AA World Services.

Soon spring arrived and Nell had Lois out in the gardens, quietly admiring the first crocus emerging from its long winter sleep and watching a family of deer drink from the rippling brook that ran down the hillside.

But while the hurt of not being at her husband's side the night he passed away had now eased a bit, the pain of missing him was even more intense. She felt it each time she walked along a path near the house, each time she gazed toward his studio on the hill, each time she opened a dresser drawer or sat before the fireplace. He was all around her, yet he wasn't. What reason did she have to go on? she asked herself. Why couldn't it all simply end so she could be with her Bill once again?[2]

It wasn't until one weekend in early May that she found the answer. She and Nell were seated on the screened-in back porch drinking tea. That's when Nell broached the subject of the annual Al-Anon Family Picnic. Lois almost dropped her teacup. She had completely forgotten that the first Saturday of June was right around the corner, and if there was to be a picnic this year, preparations had to be made. And, as Nell reminded her, hundreds of Al-Anon and AA members and their families were anxiously waiting to hear from her. To see her. To be with her one more time.

That's when Lois suddenly realized how selfish she had been in her grief. Certainly she missed Bill. She always would, no matter how much longer she lived. And the pain of missing him would always be there. But her sorrow had turned into self-pity, and her self-pity had isolated her from all those who needed to share her life, her love, her experience—and all those she also needed in order to feel well again, to feel whole and useful and to carry on the work both she and Bill had been chosen to do.

A few phone calls to Al-Anon friends turned out a horde of volunteers. They rented camp chairs for the front lawn, bought cases of soft drinks, hung signs, set up the loudspeakers and microphone, and selected the guides to show visitors around the house and grounds. Word soon spread far and wide, and even the weather forecast of severe thunderstorms and heavy rains dimmed no one's enthusiasm. It rained before sunrise, but by noon the clouds had parted and the lawns had dried. Hundreds of Al-Anon, AA, and Alateen members gathered that day to bolster Lois, to salute their founders, and to share the blessings of sobriety with one and all. That was also the day when everyone became true believers that: "It never rains on Lois's picnic. It wouldn't dare." And the truth is, it rarely has.[3]

This was to be the first time Lois would greet everyone all by herself. Tears ran down her cheeks when she spoke to the crowd about Bill's passing, but she went on to assure those in all three Fellowships that her husband's spirit was there among them and always would be. Anne Bingham then said a few words, as did several other Al-Anon, AA, and Alateen members. No one left Stepping Stones that day with a dry eye, but everyone left with a full heart, a renewed spirit, and an even greater love and respect for the lady who always opened her home to them and always would—even long after she had finally joined Bill.

The love and support Lois received that beautiful spring afternoon totally invigorated her, together with the several thousand cards and letters piled up on her desk, which she now began to read. Before long she was back out on the road, accepting invitations to speak at Al-Anon and AA conferences and conventions, both on Bill's behalf and on her own.

One day the thought occurred to her that she and Bill had planned to visit AA and Al-Anon groups all around the world, especially those in far-flung places where the Fellowship had taken hold during the last few decades. So why not do it now? She almost sensed that Bill was urging her on.

The growing royalties from Bill's book, which was their only income, could certainly underwrite such a venture. So, after speaking with Nell and a few other friends, Lois decided to pack up and take off.[4] Lois had wanted Anne Bingham to join her, but Anne had recently moved to California to be near her daughter and also hadn't been feeling well. So she invited her friend Evelyn Canavan, one of the early volunteers at the Al-Anon Clearing House and at the time a staff worker at Al-Anon World Services, Inc., which was then in New York.

Together, and with the help of other staffers, they contacted various groups around the globe. The response was immediate and enthusiastic. Every group wanted Lois to visit and speak about her own experiences, the founding of Al-Anon, and also about her and Bill's life together and the start of AA. Regional meetings were arranged. There were many offers to help with travel plans, sightseeing tours, and a host of events that spelled the warmest of hospitality.

Although she had just turned eighty-three, Lois embarked on her journey with the zest and excitement of a teenager. Even Evelyn, who was fifteen years younger, was amazed. Their first stop was Africa and a tour of the wild animal reserves near Nairobi and Victoria Falls, between Zambia and then-Rhodesia. Lois's "youthful exuberance" was evident every time she told the story about staying at a tourist inn called The Ark where buzzers and spotlights would wake you in the middle of the night when elephants and rhinos came to visit a waterhole within eyeshot of the facility. She would always add that the experience was only dimmed by not having Bill along with her.[5]

They were greeted in Johannesburg by a large and excited AA and Al-Anon delegation. When both Lois and Evelyn spoke later at a private hall, it was so crowded that people were standing in the street and sitting in the windows. Lois was delighted to learn that despite South Africa's segregation policy at the time, AA and Al-Anon meetings were places where all the races could assemble together.

After a few days' rest, Lois and Evelyn embarked on a six-day trek to Durban, a seaport on South Africa's east coast. Once again, as they rode across the mostly barren land in a zebra-striped bus, they were awed by the thousands of wild animals—lions, tigers, zebra, apes, monkeys, ostriches, and antelope.

One of their saddest, yet most memorable experiences occurred in

Durban where they were both invited again to speak before several large gatherings of AA's and Al-Anons. These meetings were held in a small private hall since larger government-run facilities at that time did not allow blacks and "coloreds" to gather there. However, AA's and Al-Anons of all races were permitted to meet as a group in private places. Since most of these facilities were rather small, members of the Fellowships eager to see and hear Lois were jammed into every nook and cranny and even crowded the streets outside the windows. Lois always spoke of the people's warmth and hospitality and how they all held hands to close the meetings with a prayer.

Lois and Evelyn were also warmly welcomed when they arrived in Capetown, South Africa. From their hotel room they could look out toward the Cape of Good Hope and see both the Indian and the Atlantic Oceans. And the meetings in the city where they spoke were also filled to capacity.[6]

The Al-Anon globetrotters then flew off to Perth, Australia, where Lois shared at a large gathering of Fellowship members at a Franciscan monastery. She later told friends she felt the spirit of St. Francis was at her side. Flying into Melbourne, she arrived in time to speak at Al-Anon's first conference of delegates in that city. The following day, however, she came down with a very bad cold and had to postpone their trip to Christchurch in New Zealand for almost a week. But when they did arrive they received a warm welcome.

Then it was back to Australia for a gathering of more than a thousand Fellowship members at the Town Hall in Sidney and a sumptuous dinner the following night with another throng at a rotating restaurant atop Sidney's tallest building.

Hong Kong was next on the agenda, a crowded, bustling place where Lois and Evelyn gawked at people of every nationality walking the streets and merchandise of every variety lining the shop windows. Many of the members attending Fellowship gatherings where they spoke were American businessmen and -women working for the numerous U.S.-based companies on the island. Lois recalled that during one sightseeing tour she and Evelyn were able to see across to Communist China.

The next leg of their journey took them to a country Lois was eager to visit—Japan. However, one thing about the country greatly disappointed her at the time. She felt that in the nation's rush to industrialize and modernize, the beauty she had seen in historic Japanese paintings and artwork had been somewhat distorted. In Tokyo, for example, she said all of the trees and shrubbery bordering the roadways looked alike. There was nothing unique or distinctive about them. She said they almost looked artificial. Nevertheless, Lois did find many spots of beauty, which she photographed and talked about on her return home.[7]

Since alcoholism was and still is a big problem in Japan, Lois and Evelyn found both the AA and Al-Anon meetings packed, although the turnout surely had to do with these two special guests. Lois said she would never forget the love and warmth showered on them by both the Japanese and American members who filled the rooms.

The two traveling ladies felt exactly the same way in Honolulu, the final stop and most fitting climax to their world tour. Lois said it seemed like every beautiful flower grown in Hawaii was hung around their necks by their grateful AA and Al-Anon hosts. The outpouring of their love was the balm Lois needed to fill her once again with deep gratitude and to further ease the pain of losing Bill. The memories of all the people they met and the places they visited on their global tour stayed with Lois for the remainder of her years.[8]

Lois's suitcases were barely unpacked when she was back at the Al-Anon World Services office in New York catching up on things. She was particularly curious about the progress being made on gathering material for the Fellowship's archives to maintain the history of the movement. This was a job she placed in the hands of her very good friend and long-time volunteer Ruth L., who then lived in nearby Chappaqua. She later became a member of Al-Anon's board of trustees.

"Lois was twenty-five years my senior," recalled the former trustee, "yet at times she had more energy and more excitement about her than anyone in the office. She was into everything, not just the archives. Lois was mainly interested in the development of Alateen. Until the day she passed away, she was focused on the welfare of the children of alcoholics, perhaps because she felt they were all her children too."[9] Ruth said Lois often talked about the very first youngster she heard speak at a meeting shortly after Alateen was formed. Something the shy, nervous teenage girl said struck Lois so deeply she quoted some of her words in a pamphlet she later wrote for Al-Anon.

"When Daddy stumbled up the steps late at night," the young girl said, "my little dog Trixie would crawl under the covers at the foot of my bed and shake. I'd cover my own head and pray that Dad would make it up to bed . . . This stopped after Dad's first AA meeting. I went with him to his second. So did Mother."[10]

One of the projects Lois worked on the hardest was finding and encouraging Al-Anon members to serve as sponsors for Alateen groups, to explain the Twelve Steps and how to apply them to one's own life. She was always disappointed when parents seemed unwilling to accept this responsibility. She once commented that AA's are happy to sponsor fellow members and to serve at various functions and activities in their groups, but that many Al-Anons are unwilling to guide young Alateen members. In fact, some parents didn't want their own children attending Alateen meetings.

Lois always felt this had something to do with some AA members fearing they would be "exposed" or talked about in Al-Anon and Alateen meetings. They didn't understand that Al-Anon and Alateen members talk about themselves, their own problems, and their own concerns and are always advised to say little or nothing about the alcoholics in their families.[11] In many families where there is the problem of alcoholism, children lose their respect for both parents—one for drinking and the other for enabling. Through the practice of the Alateen principles, she would explain, young members acquire a better understanding of the disease and its effects on them and their parents, which often leads to a rekindling of parental respect and a growing respect for themselves.

Recognizing that some children of alcoholics rebel against authority, get caught up in drugs and alcohol themselves, and can sometimes fall into criminal activities, Lois devoted much of her time and energy to helping them. She loved all children but especially those whose parents were trying to put the programs of AA and Al-Anon into their lives. And though many of the youngsters often felt lost and insecure, she believed that all could recover and find a good life. That's why she was hell bent on making Alateen a strong and successful program.[12]

Ruth L. said it was about ten months after the world tour when Lois started to feel run down. So she went for a physical examination. Tests uncovered a small lump in her breast. The doctor said it was cancerous and that her breast had to be removed. "It didn't seem to faze her at all," Ruth remembered. "And it was amazing how she went through that operation so calmly and with such a positive attitude. You could tell she really had the Twelve Steps in her life. Maybe that's why she recovered so well."[13]

Four months later, Lois was making her excursions again to the Al-Anon office at least twice a week and was back on the phone trying to drum up Alateen sponsors. She soon had a full calendar, attending local Al-Anon meetings, speaking at conventions, lunching with friends, and entertaining visitors to Stepping Stones. Newly elected delegates from all over the country came and spent the day at Stepping Stones, as did the crowds of foreign visitors attending AA's International Conventions. Lois permitted "anonymous" interviews with newspapers and magazines, but never television interviews or photography. She took great care to abide by Al-Anon's principle of anonymity. It was always "Lois W." at the level of press, radio, and television.

The sprightly senior citizen continued to travel widely. One of her favorite trips was to Palms Springs, California, in 1983, where she was invited to address the Chapter Five AA Group, which was made up of recovered motorcyclists, including many former Hell's Angels members. One huge, grinning biker gave Lois his Chapter Five jacket and patch along with a note that read, "Since I gave you my patch, you are 'my old lady.'" Lois was ninety-two at the time and proudly displayed the jacket, patch, letter, and a photo of the gathering in the upstairs room at Stepping Stones. They are still there.

Shortly after her return, Lois developed ileitis and colitis, an inflammation of the lower intestines and colon, which can be painful and debilitating. As a result, she was going to meetings less frequently and canceling luncheons with Ruth, Henrietta Sutphin, her dear friend who was then the executive director of Al-Anon World Services, and also Margaret D., editor of Al-Anon's *The Forum*, now a magazine.

"She would have these terribly painful attacks," Ruth recalled, "and just wasn't up to going out as much. So I began to visit her more frequently at Stepping Stones, as did Henrietta and Margaret and many of her other friends like Bernadette B. and Penny B."[14] Lois never feared growing old, only incapacitated. In fact, she used to tell everyone how much she looked forward to her hundredth birthday. But as she began to suffer the usual ailments of aging on top of her cancer and colitis, she became more and more concerned about the future of Stepping Stones after she died: the house, the property, and the priceless historical memorabilia related to the Fellowships. She had expected her husband to resolve the matter.

But when Bill had finally recognized the seriousness of his own illness and began preparing his last will and testament, he wanted to leave Stepping Stones and most of his income to Alcoholics Anonymous once Lois had also passed away. He had hoped that members could visit and gather there as they always had during his lifetime and continue to enjoy the beautiful house and grounds that God in His generosity had given him and his wife. And he expected that most of his royalties, after he left a few gifts for others, would be enough to maintain the estate. Lois was in complete agreement with his wishes, adding only that some of their funds go to Al-Anon.

Ironically, however, AA had to remind its cofounder that he and Dr. Bob had written a Tradition years before that precluded the Fellowship from owning property or accepting gifts of more than three hundred dollars from any single contributor. And the Wilson estate was now valued at more than half a million dollars, not including the continuing stream of royalty income from Bill's writings. The Seventh Tradition covering the matter read, "Every AA group ought to be fully self-supporting, declining outside contributions."[15] Perhaps Bill thought AA World Services would make an exception in his case. After all, he and Dr. Bob had created, nurtured, guided, and built AA into a worldwide organization. But they had also written and adopted the Twelve Traditions in order to protect the future of their creation. Thus, in its collective wisdom, AA decided it could not make an exception—and didn't. So, as one AA old-timer put it, Bill did "exactly what any alcoholic would do. He left the problem for his wife to figure out."[16]

By now the old country house in Bedford Hills was practically a museum. In the large upstairs library room, for example, Lois had framed and hung pictures of Dr. Bob, Annie Smith, Ebby Thacher, Dr. William Silkworth, Dr. Leonard Strong, Dr. Sam Shoemaker, Anne Bingham, the early Al-Anon "pioneers," and many, many others who were instrumental in helping to start and foster the growth of the Fellowships.

There were also, of course, photographs of Bill in his army uniform, Lois and Bill and family members at Emerald Lake, their exciting motorcycle trip, gatherings of friends at Stepping Stones, and their travels together around the world. Lois had spent many months carefully writing descriptive captions for them. On tables around the room were albums filled with cards and letters from AA and Al-Anon groups worldwide, and even more photos of her and Bill's visits with their fellow members across America and around the globe. All of this was on display not simply for Lois's enjoyment, but to show visitors how it all began, who was responsible, and the breathtaking power of it all as it grew.

It was the summer of 1979, and the value of Lois's estate had grown considerably since her husband's death. She was now eighty-seven, and her thoughts were frequently concentrated on trying to find some way of leaving everything to Al-Anon. But, like Bill, she faced the same roadblock. She had written the very same Tradition for the family groups that prevented her own beloved Fellowship from accepting the estate. While disappointed at first, she soon came to realize that some of her other goals in the field of alcoholism might contradict other Traditions as well.

For example, Lois used some of her own income at times to finance new approaches to alcoholism research and various educational programs related to the disease. Al-Anon could not support such ongoing activities since the Traditions precluded it from being involved in "outside issues" that might possibly draw it into "public controversy." And Lois's desire to foster and finance even more educational and promotional projects aimed at reducing the stigma of alcoholism and raising public awareness of its effects on the family and society—this certainly contradicted the Tradition that states Al-Anon is a program "of attraction, not promotion."

So she began discussing her dilemma with some very close friends whose opinions she valued, such as Brinkley Smithers; Marty Mann; her accountant, Owen Flanagan; her younger brother, Dr. Lyman Burnham; Henrietta Sutphin; and her attorney, Bernard Smith, who was also the lawyer for Alcoholics Anonymous and had crafted her husband's will. They all concluded that, in order to achieve her desired goals, a nonprofit foundation should be created through which Lois could carry on her work now and long after she went to her final reward. And they suggested such a foundation could be charged with employing her funds to maintain the house and grounds in perpetuity, as she and Bill wished, so that it would always be there and open to every member of AA, Al-Anon, and Alateen. Lois agreed with the recommendation. In fact, she was very excited about the idea that she and Bill would continue to inform the world about the disease and its consequences "forever and forever and forever."[17]

On December 24, 1979, the Stepping Stones Foundation was born and certified as a nonprofit corporation by the state of New York. Lois obviously chose to name the Foundation after her home so that it would always reflect the work she, Bill, and others had carried on there. The Foundation's first meeting was held on December 27 to officially elect its officers and board of trustees. Lois was named president; Lyman, vice president; Henrietta, treasurer; and Nell Wing, secretary.

As Lois had directed, the purpose of the Stepping Stones Foundation is to share the story of hope for recovery from alcoholism in the individual and the family that is embodied in the lives and home of Lois and Bill Wilson.[18] Lois had arranged that it be funded by the major portion of the royalties she inherited from Bill for a period of ten years following her death. She wanted to give it enough time to become well established so that it could eventually support itself, should there not be enough income to underwrite her desired goals. In truth, while the stream of royalty income for the Foundation ended in 1998, the interest income generated from Lois's estate is ample to maintain the house and grounds for some years to come, although additional funds need to be generated today to achieve the broader purposes of the Foundation.

While Lois was eager to have the entire world understand more about the terrible disease that had afflicted her husband and millions of others, she was also pleased that the Foundation would assure that their home and gardens would always be there for members of the Fellowships. She knew that Stepping Stones would continue to be of historical importance. In fact, it is not an exaggeration to say that almost everyone in AA, Al-Anon, and Alateen can trace their sponsorship to the two people who lived in that cozy brown-shingled country house. Coming to Stepping Stones for many is just like coming home.

Stepping Stones today is a historic museum of sorts, which makes available a secure and accessible display of the Foundation's physical assets. It is also a center at which those for whom the Foundation was established may enjoy social and educational experiences. These include showings of a film biography of Bill and Lois and other films on the problems of alcoholism for the individual and the family, a lecture series and seminars offered in collaboration with nearby colleges, and, of course, Lois's annual Al-Anon Family Picnic, which the Foundation continues to host.

Other special programs, with media involvement, are available for researchers and opinion leaders seeking access to the archives or wishing to promote public policy for increased understanding of the treatment for alcoholism.

From its earliest beginnings, Lois and her Foundation trustees began undertaking important projects related to alcoholism, often in partnership with prominent organizations in the field. The Foundation sought to discover the best ways to stir public interest in a problem that continues to invade every aspect of society. On October 18, 1984, Lois convened a large group of leading professionals in the field at Stepping Stones to help her pinpoint those publics most in need of understanding more about the disease and the most effective ways of reaching them.

The group, including physicians, psychologists, educators, and social workers representing many important organizations, probed into why, after all that had been written about alcoholism over the years, there was still so much ignorance and misunderstanding about the disease in schools, medical institutions, the business world, military services, and religious organizations of every denomination. After welcoming everyone on behalf of the Foundation, Lois commented:

"Since my husband was the cofounder of Alcoholics Anonymous, the subject of alcoholism has been very close to our hearts. And we've been a little tied down in one respect because AA and Al-Anon are very restrictive about their outside interests and, in fact, they have no connection with anything else that has an interest in alcoholism.

"So, this is really quite something for me to be into and I'm sure it's something that Bill would be very much interested in because we're now able to do things that AA cannot do—to find some way to help the public understand alcoholism better than it does. So we're ready today to see how we as a Foundation can help the most with the dire and serious problems that still face us."[19]

As a result of this seminar, the National Council on Alcoholism joined with Stepping Stones to produce two important public service announcements: one focusing on fetal alcohol syndrome, titled "What You Drink, Your Baby Drinks," and another on the number one drug problem among youth—alcohol—titled "Alcohol Is a Dangerous Drug." Lois was particularly interested in this second project because of her dedication to helping the children of alcoholics through Alateen.

The Stepping Stones Foundation and the National Council attracted a number of leading stars from the world of movies, television, and music to volunteer their time and tape thirty- and sixty-second radio and TV spots. They included Elliott Gould, Robert Urich, Ali MacGraw, Brooke Shields, Margot Kidder, Stacy Keach, David Hasselhoff, Reggie Jackson, Melissa Manchester, Reba McEntire, Loretta Swit, Brenda Vaccaro, Meredith Baxter-Birney, Susan Sullivan, Tyne Daly, Judy Collins, Michelle Lee, Rita Moreno, and Casey Kasem. Both campaigns were very successful, reaching millions.

As Lois had hoped, the Foundation continued its effective work after her passing to create greater awareness of alcohol addiction. In October of 1993, for example, with some new trustees elected to the board, Stepping Stones sponsored a major three-day seminar at the Edith Macy Conference Center in Briarcliff Manor, New York. The goal was to bring together leaders in treatment, government policy, medicine, research, and education in order to create a coalition with a stronger voice in the field of alcoholism to inform and better educate the public on the perils of this disease and provide more resources for recovery.

The group wrote the following accords:

To fight for a comprehensive range of quality treatment services for alcoholism and related addictions as primary diseases in the nation's health-care system.

To acknowledge that family members have a right to specific and appropriate care whether or not the addicted person is in treatment.

To develop immediately plans that bring the weight of our organizations to bear in the ongoing health-care debate.

To submit a list of resources and special skills that our organizations will commit to these accords.

To acknowledge that the research technology is now available to find the precise causes of addiction and the capability to develop more effective approaches to treatments, prevention and public policy.

To update our message to the public so we state pride in our accomplishments, acknowledge our limitations, and offer hope for medical answers to addictive diseases in the future.[20]

The seminar led to the formation of the National Leadership Forum, a coalition of more than fifty private organizations and government agencies that today continues to focus on advocacy, education, research, and policy.

As the computer generation exploded on the scene, the Stepping Stones Foundation continued to keep pace after Lois's passing by creating its own Web site, www.steppingstones.org. Visitors to the site can take a virtual tour of the house and grounds, read biographies of Lois and Bill, learn about the Foundation and its mission, view some of the treasures in its archives, subscribe to the Foundation's newsletter, and exchange e-mail.

With her Foundation now in place and her final affairs now in order, Lois found herself much more at ease despite her ailments and physical discomforts. She managed to attend various AA and Al-Anon functions, never missing two in particular: Akron's Founders Day celebration, still held each June to honor Bill and Dr. Bob and the start of AA, and the AA Intergroup Dinner at New York's Hilton Hotel, which was established to mark her husband's birthday every year. It remains a major annual fund-raising event to support the city's Intergroup activities—receiving phone calls from active alcoholics, assigning members to make Twelfth Step calls, publishing meetings lists, and so on.

Lois also never missed one of AA's International Conventions. As she once said, "We get something at these huge, unique gatherings that cannot be gained in any other way. The combined emotional impact of so many people behaving and striving for the same ideals is felt by everyone and brings a rich kind of joy."[21] In fact, the last major gatherings Lois attended were AA's International Convention and Al-Anon's first International Convention, both held in Montreal in 1985. She was ninety-four at the time, and despite her frailties, she spoke to a standing ovation at an Al-Anon breakfast and was the featured speaker at AA's closing ceremonies.

"She made such a wonderful talk," recalled Ruth L., who was at her side over those four days. "There must have been at least forty thousand people there and you could hear a pin drop as she spoke. They hung on her every word."

Ruth remembered her dear friend's closing remarks: "People keep asking me," Lois said, "how you get the spiritual part of the program. I keep telling them, there is no spiritual part. The whole program is spiritual because what we have is basically a spiritual illness and the Twelve Steps contain the medicine we take to recover."[22]

After returning home, Lois tripped and fell in the house one day and fractured her hip. The long, painful healing process sapped much of her strength. She was in and out of the hospital several times, and her recovery was complicated by a bout with pneumonia. Nell was there at Stepping Stones most of the time now, along with many of Lois's close Al-Anon and AA friends.

"She had her good days and her bad days," Nell said. "But while her body was getting weaker, her mind was still strong and alert. When one of us would tease her, she would always tease us right back."[23]

It was in late September of 1988 when Lois came down with another bad cold, and around October 3, she took a turn for the worse. She now had chest pains and was on the verge of pneumonia once again. She was rushed by ambulance to Northern Westchester Hospital in Mount Kisco, where her husband had often gone. She had a breathing tube placed down her throat and was sedated to ease her pain.

A close friend who spent much of the next two days with her said Lois would point to the breathing tube as though begging to have it removed. At one point she moved her fingers to signal she wanted to write a message. Handed a pad and pencil, the frail, now totally incapacitated lady scribbled the words: "Tell them . . . I want to see my Bill."[24] Her cousin, Anne Burnham Smith, finally consented to have the tube removed. Lois smiled and was able, in a deep hoarse voice, to say farewell to all her friends and loved ones gathered around her bedside.

Lois Burnham Wilson joined her beloved Bill later that evening. It was October 5, 1988. She was ninety-seven years old.

Even though her death was not unexpected, everyone close to Lois was devastated. As Nell Wing put it: "I anticipated the emotional loss but not the physical part, the exhaustion and depression that lasted several months. Not a day passes that I do not silently express my gratitude and love for her friendship and to Bill for his friendship too."[25]

Newspapers across the country unveiled the last name of Al-Anon's cofounder, confirming what many already knew. And thousands attended a memorial service at the Marble Collegiate Church in New York City arranged by Al-Anon World Services. Many more thousands attended similar services all over the world. So many people in so many lands had come to understand by then the far-reaching universal contribution Lois and Bill Wilson had given to society. It all began with Bill's recognition that alcoholics needed their own Twelve Step program to get sober and Lois's insight that families of alcoholics needed a similar yet separate Fellowship to recover from the same disease. By now, the AA and Al-Anon experiences had spread far and wide to help solve almost any human problem imaginable—emotional illness, gambling, overeating, narcotics addition, sexual obsession, smoking, and many more. There are self-help groups based on the Twelve Steps today for widows and widowers, parents who have lost a child, women with mastectomies, other cancer patients, and victims of most chronic illnesses. The total membership in such self-help groups is estimated in the tens of millions. And it all started with Lois and Bill's willingness to share their respective programs and experience with anyone who could be helped by them. As Lois once said in one of her talks, "I believe the Twelve Steps can save the world. Bill was out to save the world, and I don't think that was an exaggeration. It could really happen with people living by these principles."[26]

Lois Wilson was indeed one of the twentieth century's most important women. Her life had been somewhat overshadowed by that of her husband, but in recent years she has emerged more visible than before for her unique contributions to humanity. It was through her tireless efforts that Al-Anon became the strong organization it is today, still attracting members through its message of hope and renewal.

It is almost mystifying that all the praise, accolades, and adulation heaped upon this remarkable lady, both from the public and from within AA, Al-Anon, and Alateen, never seemed to change her steadfast character and loving demeanor in any way. Perhaps what she wrote in her memoirs only a few years before her death explains it to some degree.

"I hope I understand correctly AA and Al-Anon members' special devotion to me. As the only living survivor of the AA founders and their wives and as Bill's widow, I am a symbol to AAs of their beloved Fellowship. I shall always be grateful for the warmth and acceptance they show me."[27]

She said that Al-Anon will always be the most essential part of her life. After all, its principles and people like Annie Smith and Anne Bingham helped save her sanity and lead her to a way of life she never dreamed possible.

Lois loved to recall what Bill used to share when he would close the meeting each year at the Stepping Stones picnic. "We AAs don't stay away from drinking," he would say, "we grow away from drinking. And if our spouses don't grow along with us, we grow away from them."[28]

Lois always thanked God that through their respective programs, she and Bill continued to grow closer together and she was always grateful for that.

· · ·

Lois Wilson is buried next to her husband in the small family cemetery in East Dorset, Vermont. Her name is chiseled on the simple white marble gravestone. There is no mention of Al-Anon.

Notes

CHAPTER 1: WHEN WILL IT END?

1. Lois Wilson, personal conversations with author, 1986–87.
2. Ibid; Lois Wilson, taped interviews by author, 1976.
3. Wilson, taped interviews. This same information was also contained in thoughts Lois often shared with her Al-Anon friends.
4. *Lois Remembers: Memoirs of the Co-founder of Al-Anon and Wife of the Co-founder of Alcoholics Anonymous* (New York: Al-Anon Family Group Headquarters, 1979), 83–84; Wilson, personal conversations.
5. Ibid.
6. Wilson, taped interviews; Wilson, personal conversations.

CHAPTER 2: HOW IT ALL BEGAN

1. *Lois Remembers: Memoirs of the Co-founder of Al-Anon and Wife of the Co-founder of Alcoholics Anonymous* (New York: Al-Anon Family Group Headquarters, 1979), 4.
2. Ibid., 5; Lois Wilson, personal conversations with author, 1986–87.
3. Robert Thomsen, *Bill W.: The Absorbing and Deeply Moving Life Story of Bill Wilson, Co-founder of Alcoholics Anonymous* (New York: Harper & Row, 1975), 80; Wilson, personal conversations.
4. Anonymous Al-Anon friends of Lois Wilson, taped interviews by author, 2002.
5. *Lois Remembers*, 10–11, 35; Wilson, personal conversations.
6. Thomsen, *Bill W.,* 80; Wilson, personal conversations.
7. *Lois Remembers,* 10; Wilson, personal conversations.
8. Anonymous Al-Anon friends, taped interviews; Wilson, personal conversations.

CHAPTER 3: LOVE ALMOST AT FIRST SIGHT

1. Lois Wilson, personal conversations with author, 1986–87; *Lois Remembers: Memoirs of the Co-founder of Al-Anon and Wife of the Co-founder of Alcoholics Anonymous* (New York: Al-Anon Family Group Headquarters, 1979), 12.

2. *Lois Remembers,* 15; Wilson, personal conversations.
3. Robert Thomsen, *Bill W.: The Absorbing and Deeply Moving Life Story of Bill Wilson, Co-founder of Alcoholics Anonymous* (New York: Harper & Row, 1975), 16.
4. Ibid., 44.
5. Ibid., 61; *Pass It On: The Story of Bill Wilson and How the A.A. Message Reached the World* (New York: Alcoholics Anonymous World Services, 1984), 35.
6. Wilson, personal conversations.
7. Ibid.
8. Ibid.
9. Lois Wilson, taped interviews by author, 1976.
10. Wilson, personal conversations; *Lois Remembers,* 14.
11. Wilson, taped interviews.
12. Ibid.; Wilson, personal conversations; *Lois Remembers,* 16; *Pass It On,* 48.

CHAPTER 4: WAR CHANGES MANY THINGS

1. *Lois Remembers: Memoirs of the Co-founder of Al-Anon and Wife of the Co-founder of Alcoholics Anonymous* (New York: Al-Anon Family Group Headquarters, 1979), 16–17.
2. Ibid., 16; Lois Wilson, personal conversations with author, 1986–87.
3. Lois Wilson, taped interviews by author, 1976; Wilson, personal conversations; *Lois Remembers,* 19.
4. Ibid.
5. Ibid.
6. *Lois Remembers,* 18; Wilson, personal conversations.
7. Robert Thomsen, *Bill W.: The Absorbing and Deeply Moving Life Story of Bill Wilson, Co-founder of Alcoholics Anonymous* (New York: Harper & Row, 1975), 90.
8. Ibid., 92; Wilson, taped interviews; Wilson, personal conversations.
9. Thomsen, *Bill W.,* 91.
10. Ibid., 99.
11. *Pass It On: The Story of Bill Wilson and How the A.A. Message Reached the World* (New York: Alcoholics Anonymous World Services, 1984), 54.
12. Wilson, taped interviews; Wilson, personal conversations.
13. Wilson, personal conversations.

14. Wilson, taped interviews; *Lois Remembers,* 75.
15. Wilson, personal conversations; *Lois Remembers,* 22.
16. Wilson, taped interviews; Wilson, personal conversations; Thomsen, *Bill W.,* 111.
17. Wilson, taped interviews; Wilson, personal conversations.
18. Wilson, personal conversations; Thomsen, *Bill W.,* 113; *Lois Remembers,* 23–24.
19. *Lois Remembers,* 26. It should be noted that the organization's viewpoint on the subject has long since changed.
20. *Lois Remembers,* 26; Thomsen, *Bill W.,* 119–20; Wilson, personal conversations.
21. Wilson, taped interviews; Wilson, personal conversations.
22. Ibid.; *Lois Remembers,* 27.
23. Wilson, taped interviews; Wilson, personal conversations; Thomsen, *Bill W.,* 133.
24. Wilson, taped interviews; Wilson, personal conversations.
25. *Pass It On,* 65–66; Thomsen, *Bill W.,* 135.
26. Wilson, personal conversations.
27. Ibid.; Wilson, taped interviews.

CHAPTER 5: THE OPEN ROAD TO SUCCESS

1. *Lois Remembers: Memoirs of the Co-founder of Al-Anon and Wife of the Co-founder of Alcoholics Anonymous* (New York: Al-Anon Family Group Headquarters, 1979), 34; Lois Wilson, personal conversations with author, 1986–87.
2. *Lois Remembers,* 36; Wilson, personal conversations.
3. Lois Wilson, taped interviews by author, 1976; Wilson, personal conversations; Robert Thomsen, *Bill W.: The Absorbing and Deeply Moving Life Story of Bill Wilson, Co-founder of Alcoholics Anonymous* (New York: Harper & Row, 1975), 141; *Lois Remembers,* 35.
4. Thomsen, *Bill W.,* 141; Wilson, personal conversations.
5. Wilson, personal conversations; *Lois Remembers,* 35.
6. Wilson, taped interviews; Wilson, personal conversations.
7. Wilson, personal conversations; *Pass It On: The Story of Bill Wilson and How the A.A. Message Reached the World* (New York: Alcoholics Anonymous World Services, 1984), 69; Thomsen, *Bill W.,* 146–47.

8. *Lois Remembers,* 38; Wilson, personal conversations.
9. Wilson, personal conversations.
10. *Lois Remembers,* 39.
11. Wilson, personal conversations; Lois Wilson, *Diary of Two Motorcycle Hobos* (Privately printed, 1973), 13, 31; *Pass It On,* 70; Thomsen, *Bill W.,* 151–52.
12. *Lois Remembers,* 40–41.
13. Wilson, *Diary of Two Motorcycle Hobos,* 39.
14. Ibid., 47–49.
15. Wilson, personal conversations.
16. *Lois Remembers,* 57.
17. Ibid., 60.
18. Ibid.; *Pass It On,* 75.
19. *Lois Remembers,* 60.
20. Wilson, *Diary of Two Motorcycle Hobos,* 107.

CHAPTER 6: SOCIAL DRINKING—UNSOCIAL BEHAVIOR

1. Lois Wilson, taped interviews by author, 1976; Lois Wilson, personal conversations with author, 1986–87.
2. Wilson, taped interviews.
3. *Lois Remembers: Memoirs of the Co-founder of Al-Anon and Wife of the Co-founder of Alcoholics Anonymous* (New York: Al-Anon Family Group Headquarters, 1979), 65.
4. Lois Wilson, *Diary of Two Motorcycle Hobos* (Privately published, 1973), 114.
5. Wilson, personal conversations.
6. *Pass It On: The Story of Bill Wilson and How the A.A. Message Reached the World* (New York: Alcoholics Anonymous World Services, 1984), 79.
7. Wilson, personal conversations.
8. *Pass It On,* 79–80.
9. Ibid., 80.
10. Wilson, taped interviews; Wilson, personal conversations.
11. Wilson, personal conversations.
12. Ibid.; *Lois Remembers,* 73–74; Wilson, taped interviews.
13. Wilson, taped interviews; Wilson, personal conversations.

14. Other versions of this story came from Bill Wilson, who went into a blackout, and from Lois Wilson, who was always reluctant to discuss it fully.
15. *Pass It On*, 95.
16. Wilson, personal conversations.
17. Ibid.
18. *Lois Remembers*, 79.
19. Ibid., 35.
20. Wilson, taped interviews; Wilson, personal conversations.
21. Ibid.
22. Ibid.
23. Lois had put this incident completely out of her mind. She wrote in *Lois Remembers* that she didn't learn of the letter to the adoption agency until 1974. She later recalled in interviews, as she put all the pieces together, that Elise actually told her in 1929 shortly before the stock market crash. It only came back to mind in 1954, a few years after she and Anne Bingham founded Al-Anon. See chapter 14, pages 278–81.
24. *Lois Remembers*, 72.

CHAPTER 7: THE CRASH

1. Lois Wilson, personal conversations with author, 1986–87.
2. Ibid.; *Lois Remembers: Memoirs of the Co-founder of Al-Anon and Wife of the Co-founder of Alcoholics Anonymous* (New York: Al-Anon Family Group Headquarters, 1979), 74.
3. *Lois Remembers*, 75.
4. Wilson, personal conversations.
5. *Pass It On: The Story of Bill Wilson and How the A.A. Message Reached the World* (New York: Alcoholics Anonymous World Services, 1984), 81; *Lois Remembers*, 79; Also from the Bible on display at Stepping Stones in Bedford Hills, New York.
6. *Lois Remembers*, 72; *Pass It On*, 81–82.
7. Wilson, personal conversations.
8. Ibid.; Lois Wilson, taped interviews by author, 1976.
9. Wilson, personal conversations.
10. *Pass It On*, 84.
11. Wilson, taped interviews; Wilson, personal conversations.

12. Ibid.
13. Ibid.
14. Ibid.
15. Ibid.
16. *Pass It On,* 81; *Lois Remembers,* 71.
17. Wilson, taped interviews; Wilson, personal conversations.
18. Ibid.
19. *Lois Remembers,* 72.

CHAPTER 8: WHEN LOVE IS NOT ENOUGH

1. Lois Wilson, personal conversations with author, 1986–87.
2. Ibid.
3. *Lois Remembers: Memoirs of the Co-founder of Al-Anon and the Wife of the Co-founder of Alcoholics Anonymous* (New York: Al-Anon Family Group Headquarters, 1979), 77–78.
4. Lois Wilson, taped interviews by author, 1976; Wilson, personal conversations. These interviews and conversations contained thoughts Lois often shared with Al-Anon friends and in her Al-Anon talks.
5. Wilson, taped interviews; Wilson, personal conversations.
6. Ibid.
7. Ibid.
8. Ibid.
9. Robert Thomsen, *Bill W.: The Absorbing and Deeply Moving Life Story of Bill Wilson, Co-founder of Alcoholics Anonymous* (New York: Harper & Row, 1975), 172–73; Wilson, personal conversations.
10. *Lois Remembers,* 82, 86.
11. Thomsen, *Bill W.,* 173–74.
12. Wilson, taped interviews.
13. *Lois Remembers,* 82; Wilson, personal conversations.
14. Wilson, personal conversations.
15. Ibid.; Wilson, taped interviews.
16. *Lois Remembers,* 84–85.
17. Wilson, personal conversations; Wilson, taped interviews.
18. Thomsen, *Bill W.,* 180, 182–83; *Pass It On: The Story of Bill Wilson and How the A.A. Message Reached the World* (New York: Alcoholics Anonymous World Services, 1984), 90–92.

19. *Pass It On,* 106.
20. *Lois Remembers,* 83.
21. Wilson, taped interviews; Wilson, personal conversations.
22. Wilson, taped interviews; *Pass It On,* 106.
23. Wilson, taped interviews; Wilson, personal conversations.
24. Ibid.
25. Ibid.
26. *Pass It On,* 102.
27. Wilson, taped interviews.
28. *Pass It On,* 108.
29. Ibid.
30. Ibid.

CHAPTER 9: RECOVERY FOR WHOM?

1. Lois Wilson, taped interviews by author, 1976; Lois Wilson, personal conversations with author, 1986–87.
2. Robert Thomsen, *Bill W.: The Absorbing and Deeply Moving Life Story of Bill Wilson, Co-founder of Alcoholics Anonymous* (New York: Harper & Row, 1975), 195. Bill Wilson frequently shared this story in his AA talks.
3. Wilson, taped interviews; Wilson, personal conversations; Thomsen, *Bill W.,* 186.
4. Wilson, personal conversations.
5. *Pass It On: The Story of Bill Wilson and How the A.A. Message Reached the World* (New York: Alcoholics Anonymous World Services, 1984), 110.
6. Thomsen, *Bill W.,* 199.
7. *Pass It On,* 110–11.
8. Wilson, taped interviews; Wilson, personal conversations.
9. Ibid.; *Lois Remembers: Memoirs of the Co-founder of Al-Anon and Wife of the Co-founder of Alcoholics Anonymous* (New York: Al-Anon Family Group Headquarters, 1979), 87–88.
10. Wilson, personal conversations.
11. *Pass It On,* 111.
12. Wilson, taped interviews; Wilson, personal conversations.
13. *Pass It On,* 113; Thomsen, *Bill W.,* 207.
14. Wilson, personal conversations.
15. Ibid.; Wilson, taped interviews; *Lois Remembers,* 88.

354 Notes to Pages 162–179

Notes to Pages 162–179

16. Thomsen, *Bill W.,* 210–11; *Pass It On,* 116.

17. *Lois Remembers,* 72.

18. Thomsen, *Bill W.,* 214.

19. Wilson, personal conversations.

20. Ibid.; *Pass It On,* 119.

21. Wilson, taped interviews; Wilson, personal conversations.

22. Ibid.

23. Ibid.

24. Wilson, personal conversations; *Pass It On,* 93.

25. *Pass It On,* 119–20.

26. Wilson, taped interviews; Wilson, personal conversations.

27. *Pass It On,* 121; *Lois Remembers,* 89.

28. *Pass It On,* 121.

29. Ibid., 125.

30. Wilson, taped interviews; Wilson, personal conversations.

31. *Lois Remembers,* 91.

32. Wilson, taped interviews; Wilson, personal conversations.

33. Wilson, personal conversations.

34. Wilson, taped interviews; Thomsen, *Bill W.,* 233.

35. Wilson, taped interviews.

36. Wilson, personal conversations.

37. Ibid.; Wilson, taped interviews.

CHAPTER 10: GREAT DREAMS IN AKRON

1. Lois Wilson, taped interviews by author, 1976; Lois Wilson, personal conversations with author, 1986–87.

2. Bill Wilson to Lois Wilson, May 1935, Stepping Stones Foundation Archives; *Pass It On: The Story of Bill Wilson and How the A.A. Message Reached the World* (New York: Alcoholics Anonymous World Services, 1984), 146.

3. Wilson, personal conversations; *Lois Remembers: Memoirs of the Co-founder of Al-Anon and Wife of the Co-founder of Alcoholics Anonymous* (New York: Al-Anon Family Group Headquarters, 1979), 97.

4. Bill Wilson to Lois Wilson, May 1935, Stepping Stones Foundation Archives; *Pass It On,* 146.

5. *Pass It On,* 137, 142.

6. Wilson, taped interviews; Wilson, personal conversations.

7. Robert Smith, Jr., taped interview by author, 2001; Robert Smith, Jr., personal conversations with author, 1999–2000.

8. *Pass It On,* 143.

9. Wilson, taped interviews; Wilson, personal conversations.

10. *Pass It On,* 144.

11. Wilson, taped interviews.

12. Ibid.; Wilson, personal conversations.

13. Wilson, personal conversations; *Lois Remembers,* 97.

14. *Dr. Bob and the Good Oldtimers: A Biography, with Recollections of Early A.A. in the Midwest* (New York: Alcoholics Anonymous World Services, 1980), 90.

15. Wilson, taped interviews; Wilson, personal conversations.

16. *Lois Remembers,* 96.

17. *Dr. Bob and the Good Oldtimers,* 91.

18. Wilson, personal conversations.

19. Smith, taped interviews; Smith, personal conversations.

20. Wilson, taped interviews; Wilson, personal conversations.

21. Ibid.

22. Ibid.

CHAPTER 11: NIGHTMARE ON CLINTON STREET

1. *Lois Remembers: Memoirs of the Co-founder of Al-Anon and Wife of the Co-founder of Alcoholics Anonymous* (New York: Al-Anon Family Group Headquarters, 1979), 106.

2. Lois Wilson, personal conversations with author, 1986–87.

3. Ibid.; Lois Wilson, taped interviews by author, 1976.

4. Ibid.

5. *Pass It On: The Story of Bill Wilson and How the A.A. Message Reached the World* (New York: Alcoholics Anonymous World Services, 1984), 176.

6. Ibid., 161.

7. *Lois Remembers,* 118–20.

8. Ibid., 98; Wilson, personal conversations.

9. Wilson, personal conversations.

10. *Pass It On,* 164.

11. Wilson, taped interviews.

12. Ibid.; Wilson, personal conversations; *Lois Remembers,* 120.

13. *Pass It On,* 162.

14. Wilson, taped interviews; Wilson, personal conversations; *Lois Remembers,* 103.

15. Robert Thomsen, *Bill W.: The Absorbing and Deeply Moving Life Story of Bill Wilson, Co-founder of Alcoholics Anonymous* (New York: Harper & Row, 1975), 256; *Pass It On,* 169, 171.

16. Wilson, taped interviews; Wilson, personal conversations; *Lois Remembers,* 119.

17. Wilson, taped interviews; Wilson, personal conversations; *Lois Remembers,* 119–20.

18. *Lois Remembers,* 105–6.

19. Ibid., 105; Wilson, personal conversations.

20. Ibid.

21. *Lois Remembers,* 120; Wilson, personal conversations.

22. Wilson, taped interviews; Wilson, personal conversations.

23. *Dr. Bob and the Good Oldtimers: A Biography, with Recollections of Early A.A. in the Midwest* (New York: Alcoholics Anonymous World Services, 1980), 91.

24. Wilson, personal conversations; *Lois Remembers,* 96.

25. Wilson, taped interviews.

26. *Lois Remembers,* 117–18; Wilson, personal conversations.

27. Wilson, personal conversations.

28. Ibid.; Wilson, taped interviews; *Lois Remembers,* 135.

Chapter 12: Facing Her Own Addiction

1. *Pass It On: The Story of Bill Wilson and How the A.A. Message Reached the World* (New York: Alcoholics Anonymous World Services, 1984), 175–76; Robert Thomsen, *Bill W.: The Absorbing and Deeply Moving Life Story of Bill Wilson, Co-founder of Alcoholics Anonymous* (New York: Harper & Row, 1975), 258.

2. Thomsen, *Bill W.,* 258.

3. Lois Wilson, personal conversations with author, 1986–87.

4. *Pass It On,* 176–77.

5. Thomsen, *Bill W.,* 259.

6. Wilson, personal conversations.

7. Lois Wilson, taped interviews by author, 1976.
8. Ibid.
9. Ibid.; Wilson, personal conversations; *Lois Remembers: Memoirs of the Co-founder of Al-Anon and Wife of the Co-founder of Alcoholics Anonymous* (New York: Al-Anon Family Group Headquarters, 1979), 135; Wilson, personal conversations.
10. Ibid.
11. Wilson, taped interviews; Wilson, personal conversations.
12. Ibid.
13. Ibid.
14. *Lois Remembers,* 117.
15. Wilson, personal conversations.
16. Ibid.
17. *Lois Remembers,* 104.
18. Ibid.
19. Wilson, personal conversations.
20. *Pass It On,* 181.
21. Ibid., 184.
22. Ibid., 184–85.
23. *Lois Remembers,* 109–110.
24. Wilson, taped interviews.
25. *Lois Remembers,* 98.
26. Ibid.
27. Ibid., 99; Wilson, personal conversations.
28. Wilson, personal conversations.
29. Ibid.
30. Ibid.; Wilson, taped interviews; *Lois Remembers,* 99.
31. Wilson, personal conversations.
32. Ibid.
33. Ibid.
34. *Lois Remembers,* 99.

CHAPTER 13: AN UNSETTLED WORLD—AN UNSETTLED LIFE

1. Lois Wilson, taped interviews by author, 1976; *Pass It On: The Story of Bill Wilson and How the A.A. Message Reached the World* (New York: Alcoholics Anonymous World Services, 1984), 188.

2. Lois Wilson, personal conversations with author, 1986–87.
3. *Pass It On,* 189.
4. Robert Smith, Jr., taped interviews by author, 2001.
5. Ibid.
6. Wilson, personal conversations.
7. *Lois Remembers: Memoirs of the Co-founder of Al-Anon and Wife of the Co-founder of Alcoholics Anonymous* (New York: Al-Anon Family Group Headquarters, 1979), 102.
8. Wilson, taped interviews.
9. Ibid.; Wilson, personal conversations; *Lois Remembers,* 111.
10. *Alcoholics Anonymous,* 3rd ed. (New York: Alcoholics Anonymous World Services, 1976), 58.
11. *Pass It On,* 198–99.
12. Robert Thomsen, *Bill W.: The Absorbing and Deeply Moving Life Story of Bill Wilson, Co-founder of Alcoholics Anonymous* (New York: Harper & Row, 1975), 283.
13. Wilson, taped interviews; Wilson, personal conversations.
14. Thomsen, *Bill W.,* 284; *Pass It On,* 196.
15. Wilson, personal conversations.
16. *Pass It On,* 199.
17. *Lois Remembers,* 113–14.
18. Wilson, personal conversations.
19. Thomsen, *Bill W.,* 285–86; *Pass It On,* 203–4.
20. Wilson, personal conversations.
21. Ibid.
22. Ibid.
23. *Lois Remembers,* 125.
24. Wilson, taped interviews.
25. Ibid.
26. *Lois Remembers,* 126.
27. Ibid.
28. Wilson, taped interviews; Wilson, personal conversations.
29. *Pass It On,* 232.
30. Ibid., 233.
31. Wilson, personal conversations.
32. *Lois Remembers,* 130.

33. *Pass It On,* 238.
34. *Lois Remembers,* 131.
35. *Pass It On,* 239.
36. Wilson, personal conversations.
37. Ibid.; Wilson, taped interviews.
38. *Pass It On,* 245.
39. Ibid., 247.
40. *Lois Remembers,* 132.
41. Wilson, personal conversations.

CHAPTER 14: THE EVOLUTION OF AL-ANON

1. *Lois Remembers: Memoirs of the Co-founder of Al-Anon and Wife of the Co-founder of Alcoholics Anonymous* (New York: Al-Anon Family Group Headquarters, 1979), 133.
2. Ibid., 133.
3. Lois Wilson, personal conversations with author, 1986–87.
4. Ibid.
5. *Lois Remembers,* 136.
6. Ibid.
7. Ibid., 137.
8. Ibid., 138.
9. Ibid., 137.
10. William Silkworth, interview, 1940s, text from Stepping Stones Foundation Archives.
11. *Dr. Bob and the Good Oldtimers: A Biography, with Recollections of Early A.A. in the Midwest* (New York: Alcoholics Anonymous World Services, 1980), 328–29.
12. Robert Smith, Jr., taped interviews by author, 2001.
13. *Lois Remembers,* 173.
14. Wilson, personal conversations.
15. *Lois Remembers,* 173–74.
16. Ibid.
17. *First Steps: Al-Anon . . . Thirty-Five Years of Beginnings* (New York: Al-Anon Family Group Headquarters, 1986), 48.
18. *Lois Remembers,* 175.
19. Wilson, personal conversations.

20. Ibid.

21. Ibid.

22. *Alcoholics Anonymous,* 3rd ed. (New York: Alcoholics Anonymous World Services, 1976), 108–10.

23. *Al-Anon's Twelve Traditions,* © Al-Anon Family Group Headquarters, Inc. Reprinted with permission.

24. *Alcoholics Anonymous,* 59.

25. Wilson, personal conversations; Lois Wilson, taped interviews by author, 1976; *Lois Remembers,* 74.

26. Ibid.

Chapter 15: A Heart Attack Can Be Good for the Soul

1. Harriet Sevarino, taped interviews by author, 2001–2002.

2. Ibid.

3. *Alcoholics Anonymous,* 3rd ed. (New York: Alcoholics Anonymous World Services, 1976), 59.

4. Sevarino, taped interviews.

5. *Lois Remembers: Memoirs of the Co-founder of Al-Anon and Wife of the Co-founder of Alcoholics Anonymous* (New York: Al-Anon Family Group Headquarters, 1979), 169.

6. Lois Wilson, personal conversations, 1986–87.

7. Nell Wing, *Grateful to Have Been There: My Forty-Two Years with Bill and Lois, and the Evolution of Alcoholics Anonymous,* 2nd ed. (Center City, MN: Hazelden, 1998), 143.

8. Ibid., 65–68.

9. Ibid., 66.

10. Ibid., 68–69.

11. Ibid., 69–70.

12. Mary C. Darrah, *Sister Ignatia: Angel of Alcoholics Anonymous* (Chicago: Loyola University Press, 1992), 226.

13. *First Steps: Al-Anon . . . Thirty-Five Years of Beginnings* (New York: Al-Anon Family Group Headquarters, 1986), 65–66.

14. Ibid.

15. *First Steps,* 66.

16. Lois Wilson to Cleveland Al-Anon member, Stepping Stones Foundation Archives.

17. *Alcoholics Anonymous,* xxvi.
18. Wilson, personal conversations.
19. *Lois Remembers,* 156.
20. Bill Wilson to Lois Wilson, Stepping Stones Foundation Archives.
21. *Lois Remembers,* 156.
22. Wilson, personal conversations.
23. Lois Wilson, taped interviews by author, 1976.
24. Sevarino, taped interviews.
25. *Lois Remembers,* 157.
26. Ibid., 156.
27. Ibid., 189–90.
28. *Lois Remembers,* 181–82.
29. Ibid.
30. National Council on Alcoholism, award presentation, Humanitarian Award, 1985. Cited text provided by Stepping Stones Foundation Archives.
31. Lois Wilson, acceptance speech, Humanitarian Award, National Council on Alcoholism, 1985. Cited text provided by Stepping Stones Foundation Archives.
32. State of New York, Office of Alcoholism and Substance Abuse Services, Woman of the Year honors, March 2002. Cited text provided by Stepping Stones Foundation Archives.
33. Anonymous Al-Anon friends of Lois Wilson, taped interviews by author, 2002; Wilson, personal conversations.
34. Wilson, personal conversations.
35. *Lois Remembers,* 195.

CHAPTER 16: BILL'S LEGACY: ALCOHOLICS ANONYMOUS—LOVE, CONTROVERSY, AND TRIUMPH

1. Anonymous Al-Anon friends of Lois Wilson, taped interviews by author, 2002.
2. Lois Wilson, taped interviews by author, 1976.
3. Lois Wilson, personal conversations with author, 1986–87.
4. *Pass It On: The Story of Bill Wilson and How the A.A. Message Reached the World* (New York: Alcoholics Anonymous World Services, 1984), 268.
5. Wilson, taped interviews.

6. Brinkley Smithers, taped interviews by author, 1976.

7. Wilson, personal conversations.

8. Robert Thomsen, *Bill W.: The Absorbing and Deeply Moving Life Story of Bill Wilson, Co-founder of Alcoholics Anonymous* (New York: Harper & Row, 1975), 365.

9. Smithers, taped interviews.

10. Wilson, personal conversations.

11. Ibid.; *Lois Remembers: Memoirs of the Co-founder of Al-Anon and Wife of the Co-founder of Alcoholics Anonymous* (New York: Al-Anon Family Group Headquarters, 1979), 75–76.

12. John D. Rockefeller, Jr., to Bill Wilson, Stepping Stones Foundation Archives.

13. Anonymous Al-Anon friends, taped interviews.

14. Nell Wing, *Grateful to Have Been There: My Forty-Two Years with Bill and Lois, and the Evolution of Alcoholics Anonymous,* 2nd ed. (Center City, MN: Hazelden, 1998), 56.

15. Wilson, personal conversations.

16. Ibid.

17. Ibid.; *Pass It On,* 304; *Lois Remembers,* 137.

18. Wilson, personal conversations.

19. *Pass It On,* 278–79; *Lois Remembers,* 139.

20. Bill W., *Alcoholics Anonymous Comes of Age: A Brief History of A.A.* (New York: Alcoholics Anonymous World Services, 1957), 107.

21. Wilson, personal conversations.

22. *Pass It On,* 372.

23. Wilson, taped interviews.

24. *Pass It On,* 370.

25. Ibid., 375.

26. Wilson, personal conversations.

27. Bill W., *Alcoholics Anonymous Comes of Age,* 123.

28. Wilson, personal conversations.

29. Nell Wing, interview by author, 1986.

30. Mount Kisco dentist, phone interview by author, 2002.

31. Wilson, personal conversations.

32. Anonymous Al-Anon friends, taped interviews.

33. Harriet Sevarino, taped interviews by author, 2001–2002.

34. Wing, interview.
35. *Lois Remembers,* 159.
36. Wilson, personal conversations.
37. Ibid.
38. Wilson, taped interviews; Wilson, personal conversations.
39. Ibid.
40. Ibid.
41. *Pass It On,* 402.
42. Wilson, personal conversations.
43. Wing, *Grateful to Have Been There,* 3.
44. *Lois Remembers,* 160.
45. Wing, interview.
46. *Lois Remembers,* 161.

CHAPTER 17: LOIS'S LEGACY: AL-ANON, ALATEEN, AND THE STEPPING STONES FOUNDATION

1. Harriet Sevarino, taped interviews by author, 2001–2002.
2. Lois Wilson, personal conversations with author, 1986–87.
3. Nell Wing, interview by author, 1986.
4. *Lois Remembers: Memoirs of the Co-founder of Al-Anon and Wife of the Co-founder of Alcoholics Anonymous* (New York: Al-Anon Family Group Headquarters, 1979), 162.
5. Ibid.
6. Ibid., 163–64.
7. Ibid., 165–66.
8. Ibid.
9. Anonymous Al-Anon friend of Lois Wilson, taped interviews by author, 2002.
10. *Lois Remembers,* 183–84.
11. Ibid., 184–85.
12. Ibid., 183.
13. Anonymous Al-Anon friend, taped interviews.
14. Ibid.
15. Bill W., *Alcoholics Anonymous Comes of Age: A Brief History of A.A.* (New York: Alcoholics Anonymous World Services, 1957), 114.
16. Anonymous Al-Anon friend, taped interviews.

17. Lois Wilson, taped interviews by author, 1976.
18. Mission statement, Stepping Stones Foundation, 1979, Stepping Stones Foundation Archives.
19. Lois Wilson, address to professionals, Stepping Stones Foundation, 18 October 1984. Cited text provided by Stepping Stones Foundation Archives.
20. Cited text provided by Stepping Stones Foundation Archives.
21. Wilson, personal conversations.
22. Anonymous Al-Anon friend, taped interviews.
23. Wing, interview.
24. Anonymous Al-Anon friend, taped interviews.
25. Wing, interview.
26. These are comments that Lois Wilson frequently shared in her Al-Anon talks.
27. *Lois Remembers,* 168.
28. Ibid.

Index

About the Author

❧

WILLIAM BORCHERT WAS NOMINATED FOR AN EMMY IN 1989 for writing the highly acclaimed Warner Brothers/Hallmark Hall of Fame movie *My Name Is Bill W.*, which starred James Garner, James Woods, and JoBeth Williams. The film was based on material gathered from personal interviews and in-depth research.

Borchert began his career as a journalist, working first as a reporter for one of New York City's largest daily newspapers and also for a major media wire service. Later, as a byline feature writer, he covered many of the nation's most important news stories—from Governor George Wallace barring the doors of the University of Alabama against black students to the U.S.-Russian space race to the last victim of Sing Sing prison's electric chair.

After writing for a national magazine and creating syndicated shows for radio, Borchert became a partner at Artists Entertainment Complex, a new independent film and talent management company that went on to produce a number of box office hits. These included *Kansas City Bomber* starring Raquel Welch, *Serpico* starring Al Pacino, and *Dog Day Afternoon* also starring Al Pacino.

A member of the Writers Guild of America and a director of the Stepping Stones Foundation, Borchert continues his active writing career with several other important film and book projects currently in development. While he and his wife, Bernadette, have an apartment in New York, they reside much of the year in their lovely home in Little River, South Carolina, where they are frequently visited by their nine children and twenty-three grandchildren.